THE BOOK OF VB .NET

THE
BOOK
OF VB .NET

.NET INSIGHT FOR VB DEVELOPERS

Matthew MacDonald

**NO STARCH
PRESS**

San Francisco

THE BOOK OF VB .NET. Copyright ©2002 by Matthew MacDonald.

Printed in the United States of America

1 2 3 4 5 6 7 8 9 10–05 04 03 02

Publisher: William Pollock
Editorial Director: Karol Jurado
Cover and Interior Design: Octopod Studios
Composition: 1106 Design, LLC
Copyeditor: Nancy McLaughlin
Proofreader: Ruth Stevens

Distributed to the book trade in the United States by Publishers Group West, 1700 Fourth Street, Berkeley, CA 94710; phone: 800-788-3123; fax: 510-658-1834.

Distributed to the book trade in Canada by Jacqueline Gross & Associates, Inc., One Atlantic Avenue, Suite 105, Toronto, Ontario M6K 3E7 Canada; phone: 416-531-6737; fax 416-531-4259.

For information on translations or book distributors outside the United States and Canada, please contact No Starch Press, Inc. directly:

No Starch Press, Inc.
555 De Haro Street, Suite 250, San Francisco, CA 94107
phone: 415-863-9900; fax: 415-863-9950; info@nostarch.com; http://www.nostarch.com

Library of Congress Cataloguing-in-Publication Data

MacDonald, Matthew.
The book of VB. NET : .NET insight for VB developers / Matthew MacDonald.
       p. cm.
  ISBN 1-886411-82-4
1. Microsoft Visual BASIC. 2. BASIC (Computer program language) I. Title.
QA76.73.B3 M28 2002
005.2'768--dc21

2002000729

DEDICATION

For Faria

ACKNOWLEDGMENTS

The collection of .NET titles on the bookstore shelves is embarrassingly large. When writing a book about a language as popular as VB .NET, the challenge isn't finishing it, but making sure that it's *really* insightful, friendly, and useful beyond the standard MSDN documentation. To that end, I have to thank countless other developers and .NET aficionados whose words—in books, articles, web sites, discussions groups, and emails—have provided the seeds of insight that have enhanced the pages of this book. I hope the readers of this book will also learn from and become a part of the broader .NET community.

Closer to home, I should thank all the pleasant people at No Starch who have worked with me throughout this project, including Bill Pollock, Amanda Staab, and especially Karol Jurado. I also owe a heartfelt thanks to my copyeditor Nancy McLaughlin, whose light touch and unerring consistency kept everything together as the book entered its final stages.

Lastly, I need to thank my parents (all four of them) for all the things that parents do, and my wife, who is endlessly supportive and as dedicated to my dreams as I am.

Matthew MacDonald
Toronto, Ontario

BRIEF CONTENTS

CONTENTS IN DETAIL

INTRODUCTION

1

THE .NET REVOLUTION

2

THE DESIGN ENVIRONMENT

3

VB .NET BASICS

4

WINDOWS FORMS

5

OBJECT-ORIENTED PROGRAMMING

6

MASTERING OBJECTS

7

BUGPROOFING

8

DEALING WITH DATA: FILES, PRINTING, AND XML

9

DATABASES AND ADO.NET

10

THREADING

11

SETUP AND DEPLOYMENT

12

WEB FORMS AND ASP.NET

13

WEB SERVICES

14

MIGRATING TO VISUAL BASIC .NET

INTRODUCTION

Since its creation, Visual Basic has steadily grown into the world's most popular programming language. But popularity doesn't always mean respect, and for years the development community has been split between those who think Visual Basic is a revolutionary way to solve just about any programming problem, and those who think VB should be sent to the bargain bin to make room for a return to "serious" C++ or Java coding. As a result, Visual Basic programmers have a reputation for being a slightly paranoid bunch.

Now Microsoft is introducing Visual Basic .NET, and the developer community is split once again—but with a different dilemma. This time the battle is between longtime Visual Basic developers who don't want the aggravation of another change, and those who've realized that VB .NET is nearly a new language—one that cleans out old cobwebs, levels the playing field between VB and other programming languages, and introduces an avalanche of elegant, flexible, and easy-to-use new features. In fact, Visual Basic .NET is the Visual Basic makeover many programmers have spent years waiting for.

Two things are certain. VB .NET is the most hotly anticipated new language release in a decade. And writing VB .NET programs doesn't have to be difficult. With this book, you'll learn how you can use your existing Visual Basic skills and master the new .NET way of thinking.

Who Should Read This Book

This book is a comprehensive tour through the world of VB .NET. It's aimed at Visual Basic developers who want to shed some of their current habits and start learning about the way the .NET platform works and thinks. We won't spend any time rehashing basic syntax, but we will spend a *lot* of time exploring new .NET concepts.

To get the most out of this book, you should have some experience developing with Visual Basic. It doesn't matter if you've tackled advanced subjects, such as Internet applications and object-oriented programming—these are well explained in the book—but you should be familiar with all the "Visual Basic basics," such as variables, controls, loops, conditions, and functions. If you've never programmed with Visual Basic or another programming language like Java, this isn't the best book for you.

If you're a seasoned developer, welcome aboard! You'll soon get a handle on Visual Basic .NET's most exciting new innovations, and pick up some invaluable tricks on the way. But do expect to find that things have changed.

What You Will Learn

Many of the chapters in this book could be expanded into complete books of their own. It's impossible to cover all the details of VB .NET, so this book strives to give you the essential facts and insights. The emphasis isn't on becoming a "language nerd" (learning every syntax trick in the book), but on gaining the insights you'll need in order to understand .NET development and be able to continue learning on your own. We'll go about our journey in a lively, no-nonsense way.

Each chapter begins with a "New in .NET" section that gives experienced developers a quick introduction to what has changed since Visual Basic 6. The rest of the chapter takes a lightning tour through a single aspect of VB .NET programming. The code examples are tightly focused on specific concepts—you won't find toy applications that are written just for the book. (Those sort of examples tend to look great while flipping through the book in the bookstore, but end up being much less helpful once you get started.)

At the end of every chapter is a "What Comes Next?" section that provides some ideas about where you can find more information on the current topic, and maybe even become a VB .NET guru.

NOTE *No single book can teach you the entire .NET platform, and this book doesn't attempt to hide that fact. Instead, the emphasis is on introducing fundamental techniques and concepts, and giving you the resources you'll need in order to continue learning and exploring the areas that interest you most. To accomplish all this, the book is complemented by code examples, references to additional online material, and helpful tips about planning, design, and architecture. For best results, try to read the chapters in order, because later examples will use some of the features introduced in earlier chapters.*

Code Samples

Practical examples often provide the best way to learn new concepts and see programming ideas in action. With that in mind, this book includes a wealth of code samples and fragments to help stimulate your mind and keep you awake. The design philosophy for these samples is straightforward: demonstrate, as concisely as possible, how a .NET developer thinks. This means that all examples are broken down to their simplest elements. It also means that code is sometimes arranged in a slightly more sophisticated way than the typical "hello world" program. The hope is that these code samples represent a kernel of coding insight, and show not only how to use Visual Basic .NET commands, but also how to structure a program so that it can be enhanced, and can eventually grow into a full-blow application. In these cases, the text will explain why the code is organized the way it is, and give a couple of tips about what a developer's next step might be to improve and extend it.

The code samples in this book are provided online, grouped by chapter, at http://www.prosetech.com/nostarch. These examples aren't exactly the same as the code fragments in the book. For example, they might have a little extra code or user interface designed to make it easier to test a given feature, which would just be a distraction in a printed example. These samples provide an excellent starting point for your own .NET experimentation.

Complaints, Adulation, and Everything in Between

While I'm on the subject of website support, I should probably add that you can reach me via email at nostarch@prosetech.com. I can't solve your Visual Basic .NET problems or critique your own code creations, but I *would* benefit from information about what this book does right and wrong (and what it may do in an utterly confusing way). You can also send comments about the website support for this book.

Chapter Overview

Here's a quick guide that describes what each chapter has to offer. Some of the later chapters build on concepts in earlier chapters, so it will probably be easiest to read the book in order, to make sure you learn the basics about Windows Forms, object-oriented programming, and Visual Basic .NET syntax changes before moving to the more advanced, specialized topics like web applications and database programming.

Chapter 1. The .NET Revolution
What is this thing called .NET anyway? Learn why Microsoft decided to create a whole new framework for programming, and what they threw in.

Chapter 2. The Design Environment
Visual Basic's integrated design environment (IDE) is every programmer's home away from home. In VB .NET, it's been given a slick makeover and new features such as integrated help, macros, and a collapsible code display.

Chapter 3. VB .NET Basics

I warned you that things had changed. Here you'll get your first real look at the .NET world, with an overview of language changes, an exploration of the class library, and an introduction to namespaces.

Chapter 4. Windows Forms

Windows Forms are an example of the good getting better. Visual Basic has always made it easy to drag-and-drop your way to an attractive user interface, and with the revamped Windows Forms model you'll get some long-awaited extras, such as automatic support for resizable forms, a variety of new controls, and the ability to finally forget all about the Windows API.

Chapter 5. Object-Oriented Programming

This chapter teaches you the basics of object-oriented development, the most modern and elegant way to solve almost any programming problem. VB .NET is built almost entirely out of objects, and understanding them is the key to becoming a .NET expert.

Chapter 6. Mastering Objects

At last, Visual Basic .NET is a full object-oriented programming language. In this chapter, we'll continue to explore VB .NET's new OO features and advanced class construction techniques including interfaces and inheritance, the most anticipated Visual Basic enhancement ever.

Chapter 7. Bugproofing

Visual Basic .NET retains most of VB's legendary debugging tools, with a few refinements. This chapter describes debugging in the IDE, outlines some tips for making bug-resistant code, and introduces the new model of structured exception handling.

Chapter 8. Dealing with Data: Files, Printing, and XML

Traditional Visual Basic functions have been replaced with objects that let you manage files, serialize objects, print data, and manipulate XML. But the greatest enhancement may be VB .NET's new print preview control.

Chapter 9. Databases and ADO.NET

Visual Basic .NET includes ADO.NET, a revamped version of ADO that works natively with XML and disconnected DataSets. Again, the .NET team has been up late at night tweaking things, and the changes are bound to surprise you.

Chapter 10. Threading

Visual Basic .NET now goes where only C++ and other heavyweights could venture before: multithreading. But just because you can thread doesn't mean you should. In fact, threading is still the best way to shoot yourself squarely in the foot. Read this chapter for some advice about when to create threads (and when not to), and how to use them.

Chapter 11. Setup and Deployment

What if setting up an application were as easy as copying files? With .NET, major changes to the way we think about applications just might help you stay out of the registry and completely avoid DLL Hell.

Chapter 12. Web Forms and ASP.NET

This chapter describes the basics of ASP.NET, Microsoft's all-in-one solution for creating web-based applications. Finally, after years of promises, creating scalable web applications with rich user interfaces is just as easy as creating a desktop application.

Chapter 13. Web Services

Central to the .NET platform is the vision of software as a service, with web servers around the globe providing features and functions that you can seamlessly integrate into your own products. Read this chapter to start creating web services and—best of all—let Visual Basic .NET take care of all the plumbing.

Chapter 14. Migrating to Visual Basic .NET

Now that you know the details of .NET development, it's time to evaluate whether you should upgrade your existing projects. Migration can be a daunting process, and this chapter offers some advice to help you deal with conversion anxiety.

What Comes Next?

If you've made it this far, I'll assume you're continuing for the rest of the journey. For best results, you should already have a copy of Visual Studio .NET, which we'll explore in Chapter 2. But first, we'll start with Chapter 1—and clear up the cloud of jargon and hype that surrounds .NET. Along the way, you'll discover why so many people find Microsoft's new platform so exciting.

1

THE .NET REVOLUTION

This chapter presents the "big picture" of Visual Basic and the .NET framework. You'll get an overview of what has changed, why it's different, and just what life will be like in the .NET world. Along the way, we'll sort through Microsoft's newest jargon, demystifying the CLR (Common Language Runtime), "managed" code, and the .NET class library. This chapter is perfect for anyone wondering, "What the heck is .NET?" or "Why do we need a new programming philosophy?" or "What has Microsoft promised us this time?"

NOTE *This is the only chapter in the book that doesn't start with a "New in .NET" section. Think of this chapter as an at-a-glance preview of all the changes you'll see for the next few hundred pages, with a little bit of history to explain why the revolution was needed.*

A Brief History of Visual Basic

Visual Basic has its roots in BASIC, a simple teaching language that programmers once learned before graduating to more serious venues like C. Visual Basic inherited at least part of the BASIC legacy, beginning its life with the goal of being the easiest way for anybody to program . . . anything.

It's probably because of this history that Visual Basic developers have always had their hands full demonstrating that their favorite language is more than just a toy. Time and time again, as programming methodologies and application demands have changed, it has seemed that Visual Basic's time in the spotlight was about to end. Instead, VB has not only kept stride, it has made the world rethink computer programming—first with version 1.0, which introduced the easiest way to create a graphical user interface; then with version 4.0, which provided the easiest way to talk to a database; and finally with version 5.0, which gave us the easiest way to go "object-oriented."

Now, with Visual Basic .NET, we have the easiest way to create scalable web applications. But for faithful VB coders, this isn't the whole story. VB .NET also represents a major redesign and refinement of the Visual Basic language. Commands that you could use all the way back in Visual Basic 1.0 will earn you a blank stare from the VB .NET compiler, and traditional programming tricks and hacks are guaranteed to get you into trouble again and again. You won't be able to drop projects from earlier versions of Visual Basic into the new VB .NET, but if you're starting a new project, you're likely to have more programming fun than you've ever had before.

Modern-Day Problems

Have you heard the argument, "Before you can understand the solution, you have to understand the problem"? In this case it's true, so before we go any further, let's take a look at some of Visual Basic's most infamous shortcomings.

Visual Basic's Quirky Mix

Visual Basic's evolution has been so quick that the last version (6.0) was a mixture of cutting-edge features and Paleolithic throwbacks. For example, Visual Basic 6 provides a great framework for creating a graphical user interface, allowing you to configure controls and windows just by setting convenient properties. But if you go one step farther into an unsupported area, you'll quickly feel abandoned. Want to stop a window from resizing to specific minimum dimensions? Want to add your program's icon to the system tray? How about disabling a window's Maximize button without hiding its Minimize button? To perform any of these common tasks, you have to plunge into the Windows API, a library of perplexing C routines. And watch out: If you misuse an API function, you can easily crash your program—and even the entire development environment!

I could go on to talk about a number of other hangovers from the past, like Visual Basic's "evil" type conversion mechanism, which tries to make your life easier by letting you convert data types without following the proper rules—thus making it possible for you to overlook serious errors. Then there is the archaic practice of referring to open files with numbers. And who can explain why a world-class object-oriented programming language still has the Goto command?

Isolated Languages

If you've dabbled in more than one programming language, you've probably realized that everyone does things a little bit differently. This is certainly true for Windows programming, where C++ uses the MFC library, J++ uses WFC, and Visual Basic uses its own framework (with sprinkles of the Windows API thrown in for good measure). Basically, programmers suffer endless headaches trying to understand each other, and must consider the quirks and idiosyncrasies of every language before they can choose one to use for development. And if a problem is solved in C++, Visual Basic developers usually need to solve it all over again.

Enterprise Development Headaches

Three-tier design. Distributed objects. Load balancing. It all sounds good on paper. Data objects reading and writing to the database, business objects processing the results, and a Windows application displaying the results, with everyone talking together using COM. But if you've ever tried to create a distributed program, you've probably discovered that setting it up, registering your components, and maintaining version compatibility add a whole new set of agonizing problems that have nothing to do with programming.

DLL Hell

DLL Hell is a particularly ugly example of the problem with component-based programs. Most Visual Basic programs rely heavily on specialized components and controls, sometimes without the programmer even realizing it. These programs work fine when the correct version of every dependent file is present on the system, but if the user installs an application that mistakenly overwrites one of these files with an older version, or updates some but not all of a set of dependent files, then strange problems start to come out of the woodwork. Such problems are a nightmare to try and identify, and the worst part is, they usually appear long after a fully functional application has been installed. The end result? Fragile programs that can easily be disrupted when other applications are updated or uninstalled.

Incomplete Support for Object-Oriented Programming

Before I even knew what polymorphism and inheritance were, I knew that Visual Basic didn't have them. Never mind that VB had all the other tools needed to write elegant programs based on objects; there was no escaping the talk about its limitations. No other limitation did more to crush the personal self-esteem of the dedicated VB programmer.

The .NET Vision

Most people were expecting Microsoft to deal with some of these complaints by bolting on a few new features, as it has for the last few versions of Visual Basic. But as advanced developers started to expand the types of programs that Visual Basic was used for, cracks in the VB picture started to appear—everywhere. Applications became more complicated, and language enhancements only brought more inconsistencies and deficiencies to light. At some point, the people at Microsoft decided to start over and build a new set of languages from the ground up. The .NET framework is the result of that new start.

The Ingredients of .NET

Like COM and ActiveX, the .NET framework means a lot of different things, depending on whom you talk to in Microsoft's marketing department. On the programming side, .NET is made up of the *Common Language Runtime (CLR)* and a set of *unified classes*. The .NET framework (as shown in Figure 1-1) sits on top of the Windows platform, which provides its own set of services (for example, the IIS server built into Windows lets your computer be a web server).

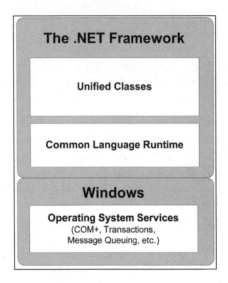

Figure 1-1: The .NET Framework

The Common Language Runtime (CLR)

The CLR (see Figure 1-2) is a runtime environment that processes, executes, and manages Visual Basic code. It's a little like the traditional Visual Basic runtimes (for example, VBRUN300.DLL or MSVBVM60.DLL), but with increased responsibility. CLR tasks include memory management, thread management, and security checking. Many of these features have been available in the Visual Basic world for years, albeit in a somewhat less ambitious form. In fact, much of the excitement about C# (another recently released .NET language) is coming from C++ programmers who have never experienced some of the advantages that VB programmers take for granted, like automatic memory management.

Code that executes inside the CLR is called *managed code*. Visual Basic .NET code is always managed code, which means that it works with CLR services, and operates under the CLR's careful supervision.

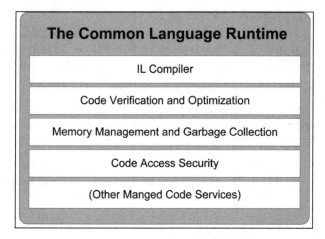

Figure 1-2: The Common Language Runtime (CLR) Environment

The .NET Classes

The .NET classes contain the tools that let you perform all kinds of tasks, from writing to a database to reading from a web page (see Figure 1-3). In the past, these capabilities were either hard-coded into the language with special functions, or provided through ActiveX add-ins. Think of the integrated class library as a supremely well-organized programming toolbox.

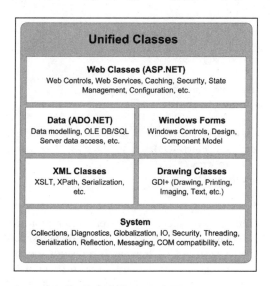

Figure 1-3: The Unified Classes in .NET

Speaking the Same Language

Within .NET, each programming language still has its own syntax. For example, every line in C# ends with a semicolon (;). But these differences are really just superficial.

- Every .NET language is built on the CLR.
- All .NET languages share a common set of class libraries, which they use to do everything from displaying a Windows message box to retrieving a file from the Internet.

Not convinced? Look at the similarity of these two .NET-based programs, which accomplish the same thing—first in Visual Basic, and then in C#:

The VB .NET Version

```
Private Sub CreateTextBox()
    ' This function makes a new textbox,
    ' and puts some text in it.
    Dim MyText As New Textbox()
    MyText.Location = New Point(25,25)
    MyText.Size = New Size(25,125)
    MyText.Text = "This was made in VB!"
    Me.Controls.Add(MyText)
End Sub
```

The C# Version

```
private void CreateTextBox()
{
    // This function makes a new textbox,
    // and puts some text in it.
    Textbox MyText = new Textbox();
    myText.Size = new Size(25,125);
    myText.Location = new Point(25,25);
    myText.Text = "I come from C# ...";
    this.Controls.Add(myText);
}
```

There are some obvious superficial differences here; for instance, you're probably wondering what's going on with all the curly brackets, slashes, lowercase names, and semicolons in C#. However, if you study the two programs carefully, you'll realize that their differences are simply matters of syntax. Every line in the VB program has a direct "translation" into a line in the C# program. The code is written a little differently, but it uses the same concepts. Or to be more picturesque, the two languages use different words, but have the same grammar.

The full effects of these changes are amazing, and they might not be felt for a year or more. At last, Visual Basic programmers can interact with the full Windows developer community! If someone has solved your problem in C#, you can now benefit from their experience and translate their solution into VB .NET without a lot of trouble.

Deep Language Integration

The power of CLR integration extends beyond the way you code. Behind the scenes, the same engine is processing code from different .NET languages. This deep integration means, for instance, that code written in Visual Basic can inherit procedures and properties from classes written in C#, and that exceptions thrown from code written in C# can be caught by code written in Visual Basic.

In fact, when you create an EXE file, every CLR language compiles into the same CPU-independent bytecode: *Microsoft Intermediate Language,* or *MSIL.* This means that ultimately, different .NET languages have essentially the same performance—so programming in VB .NET instead of C# is nothing more than a lifestyle choice.

Pre-built Infrastructure

If you're an experienced developer, it has probably dawned on you that developers are paid to solve the same problems over and over again. Most internal business applications boil down to databases, web development always involves tackling site-management issues, and even first-person games require the traditional 3D-rendering engine. In the past, Microsoft has been tremendously successful designing some of the basic infrastructure that we all need, creating such tools as ADO for universal database access and MTS for managing transactions. Microsoft's philosophy has been that they should supply the infrastructure, while the programmer writes the specific "business logic" that distinguishes one project from the next. And it's likely (unless you want to spend your time wrestling with low-level details such as multi-user state management, database-specific APIs, and messaging) that you heartily agree.

The .NET framework extends this philosophy with its common class library. Here you can find cutting-edge tools for creating everything from a Windows service to an ASP.NET Internet application ready to serve thousands of eager e-shoppers.

Web Services and the Next-Generation Internet

Microsoft is also using .NET to expound their vision of "software as a service." The story goes a little bit like this: Many years ago, Windows applications were isolated. Integrating parts of different applications was difficult unless they resided together in a rigorously thought-out DLL. Code sharing really only occurred inside the walls of individual companies. Then, along came COM and ActiveX technology. All of a sudden, programmers had exciting new ways to communicate. Dozens of vendors offered custom controls that you could easily and painlessly drop into your applications. Other developers discovered how easy it was to use automation features to drive COM programs by "remote control." For example, you could create a spreadsheet in Excel from within VB, or even perform a search operation in Word from within C++, using an easy-to-understand object model.

Where am I going with this? The idea is that the Internet is now at roughly the same stage in its evolution. We finally have interactive web applications for tracking stock portfolios and ordering books, and yet we don't have an easy way to integrate parts of web applications without resorting to awkward tricks such as frames and "screen scraping," where information is read from a predefined line in a web page. These techniques are difficult to maintain, and to extend. What happens if a website changes its content or goes out of business? In short, a better solution is needed.

That's where Web Services come in. A *Web Service* is an application that exposes its functionality over the Internet using standard Internet protocols, such as HTTP and XML. A developer can use a Web Service just as easily as a local component, without worrying about the technology involved.

Open Standards: XML, SOAP, WSDL, and Other Letters from the Alphabet

Open standards? *Microsoft*? That's what flashed through my mind when I heard that the .NET framework was going to have key technologies based on open standards such as XML. Finally, Microsoft has recognized that the world of the Internet is a diverse one, and that in order for developers to adopt Microsoft tools, they need innovations based on a solid foundation of platform-independent, widely accepted open standards. That means that .NET can transfer a database table using XML markup, and provide Web Services that can be used by applications on Unix or Macintosh computers.

But how open are their "open standards"? Or, to put it another way, is the Microsoft implementation of these open standards really able to interact with other operating systems and programming languages? Only time will tell. There are encouraging signs that Microsoft has accepted the fact that programmers refuse to be cut off from innovations in the rest of the world. However, with the accommodating .NET framework and its elegant class libraries, developers may find that using a Web Service in another language just can't match the effortless plug-in design of .NET.

Metadata: The End of DLL Hell?

Programs in .NET are *self-describing*. In other words, when you create a .NET EXE file, it doesn't just contain your compiled program; it also has information that describes the other components it needs in order to work, and which version of each component is supported. Previously, this information was buried in the Windows registry, which meant that every application had to go through a registration process, and that its registry information had to be rigorously updated to keep from becoming out-of-date and conflicting with the application itself.

So is DLL Hell really over? The answer is Yes. And No. Well, as you'll find out in Chapter 11, there *is* a Global Assembly Cache (GAC) where applications can share components, just as they always have. No one wants to distribute a separate version of the .NET framework with every application they make. Fortunately, the amazing version control and management features provided by the Global Assembly Cache should guarantee that DLL Hell will never appear again. Probably.

Still Want More Details?

For more information about the technical details of the .NET framework and its underlying architecture, you can refer to the MSDN help included with Visual Basic .NET, or *The Visual Studio .NET Developer's Guide* (No Starch Press). Of course, in later chapters of this book we'll get more in-depth, addressing such key technologies as object-oriented programming, Web Services, and assemblies.

Is VB .NET Still VB?

Microsoft has played it a little risky and completely tossed out some of the old Visual Basic nightmares. As a result, VB .NET looks quite a bit different than previous releases of Visual Basic programs. In fact, many time-honored commands are no longer available in .NET. Below are some of the advances that you should cheer about . . . and some other changes that you won't be celebrating.

Ten Enhancements You Can't Live Without

- Visual Basic is truly object-oriented—at last.
- The new Windows Forms model for programming a user interface is more powerful than ever, and bundles convenient controls for everything from system tray icons to print previewing.
- No automatic type conversion: Option Strict lets you turn off this dangerous "convenience."
- Structured error handling makes it as easy to trap an error in Visual Basic as in any other modern programming language.
- ASP.NET provides the easiest and most powerful system to date for programming web applications.
- Function overloading now allows you to create different versions of functions with the same name, but with different arguments. Visual Basic .NET will use the correct one automatically.
- Even critics can't deny that the new development environment is heart-stoppingly beautiful. Does any other language offer a collapsible code, intelligent dynamic help, and an entire programming language for creating macros?
- A new event model lets you connect multiple event handlers to a single control and store function references in special procedure variables, called *delegates.*
- Initializers let you set the value of a variable on the same line where you declare it.

- Metadata means that DLL Hell may finally be a thing of the past. You can now set up a program just by copying its directory—a capability that hasn't existed in the Windows world for years.

Ten Changes That May Frustrate You

- You can't fix problems while debugging. Every time you make a change, the project will need to be recompiled.
- Arrays must always have a lower boundary of 0.
- Existing Internet projects using Web Classes or DHTML aren't supported, and will need to be rewritten from scratch into ASP.NET applications.
- There are no more default properties, so you can't abbreviate Text1.Text as just Text1.
- The techniques you used in the past to print documents, draw graphics, read text files, and provide context-sensitive help have changed—get ready to learn these basics all over again.
- There is no deterministic finalization. When you're finished with an object, it may still hang around in memory for some time until it's cleaned out. This means that you can't rely on events that take place when an object is unloaded.
- Older database access methods, such as RDO and DAO, are not fully supported. (For example, they can't be used for data binding.)
- Even if you use the upgrade wizard, a great deal of code may need to be rewritten, including routines for reading from and writing to files, and for creating printouts. In fact, for complex applications, you may have to abandon the whole idea of migration.
- There is no way of accessing pointers. (In earlier releases of Visual Basic, pointer access was dangerous and unsupported, but was still possible by those who knew the "secret" functions, such as StrPtr and ObjPtr.) You can, however, still easily get a window or control handle.
- Goto, Gosub, and line numbers are no longer supported.

The Dark Side of .NET

Not every Visual Basic programmer is happy with the radical changes Microsoft has made. To some critics, .NET's drive to modernize programming has left Visual Basic .NET looking more like Java than .NET. They argue that years of Visual Basic legacy are being left behind, and that compatibility with old code is being rudely broken. There's more than a grain of truth to these complaints.

So is .NET worth it? The only answer I can give is a resounding "Yes." Visual Basic .NET has changed enough to make life a little painful for developers, but once you understand the new changes, your coding days will be easier and more productive. In a sense, Microsoft is gambling that developers will be so eager to program with an elegant, revitalized version of Visual Basic that they'll sacrifice backward compatibility. Sometimes change hurts.

What About COM?

COM is the *Component Object Model*, the fundamental technology that allows programs to communicate together, and allows parts of programs (their *components*) to interact as well. Until now, COM was supposedly the basis of Windows programming—so where has it gone?

This is a question that's bound to be asked again and again. In fact, you might want to get clear on the answer, just so you can impress curious colleagues when they ask you. (And ask you they will.) As Microsoft points out, there are hundreds of millions of COM applications, including such heavyweights as Microsoft Office. COM will be around as long as Windows is around; in fact, Windows won't boot without COM.

That said, .NET is not built on top of COM. Programs written in .NET communicate natively; because their languages are all based on the CLR, they don't need to work through obscure COM interfaces. In fact, .NET is really a next-generation version of COM. (At one point, parts of it were even called COM+ 2.0.) But don't panic. Microsoft has worked long and hard to make sure that COM applications can communicate seamlessly with .NET, as you'll see in Chapter 14 when we explore migration. One day you may wake up to a world without COM . . . but it won't be anytime soon.

What Comes Next?

Throughout the rest of the book, the .NET framework will never be far from our discussion. Even though this is a book about writing software using the VB .NET programming language, our time will be evenly divided between VB syntax and the common classes that are part of .NET. You just can't master VB .NET development without spending a good amount of time becoming familiar with the class library. Conversely, many VB concepts, like objects, exceptions, and threading are built into the CLR, and shared by all .NET languages.

There is an advantage to this organization: once you've mastered VB .NET, you aren't all that far from becoming an accomplished C# coder—if it interests you. Perhaps the most exciting fact about life in the .NET world is that language wars are (mostly) dead, and the broad community of .NET developers can share tips, tricks, and insights across language boundaries.

2

THE DESIGN ENVIRONMENT

The changes in the Visual Studio design environment haven't generated the same amount of attention as other new features like language enhancements and Web Services. That's because the *integrated design environment* (IDE) doesn't determine what you can and can't do with a well-written program. In fact, you can create a Visual Basic .NET project using nothing more than Notepad, and compile it at the command line using the vbc.exe utility included with the .NET framework, even if you don't have the complete Visual Studio package installed. The IDE is really nothing more than a helpful work area for designing programs.

On the other hand, there are several good reasons to explore the IDE in detail, as you'll see in this chapter. For one thing, it's changed so much since Visual Basic 6 that even experienced programmers may find themselves somewhat lost. But most importantly, if you master the IDE you'll become a more productive developer, with tools like integrated help, flexible macros, and a customizable code display ready at your fingertips. Look at the new IDE features in Visual Studio. NET as your reward for upgrading to the new .NET platform. Stepping up to Visual Basic .NET requires some relearning and a little hard work, but in the end you'll get to spend your programming hours in a state-of-the-art environment equipped with conveniences that no other programming tool can boast.

This chapter describes each part of the Visual Studio .NET interface, along with additional tips for configuring the IDE and working with macros and other time-savers. You won't start creating a real application yet, but you will learn how to master Visual Studio .NET's rich design environment.

New in .NET

The IDE in Visual Studio .NET has evolved from a mix of different ancestors. It combines the best of Visual InterDev, Visual Basic, and Visual C++. It also throws in some of the attractive new interface elements turning up in products like Office XP and Windows XP. Some of the most obvious changes are summarized below.

True Integration

It's always been called the "integrated" design environment, but up until .NET, it's been anything but. While different Visual Studio products like Visual Basic, Visual C++, and Visual InterDev have had similar interfaces, they've also had a whole host of subtle differences. As you discovered in the first chapter, one of the core goals of the .NET framework is to integrate different languages, and this strategy extends to the development environment. With Visual Studio .NET, programmers of all stripes share the same IDE, and can use identical components like debugging tools and menu designers.

The New "Look"

Could Microsoft release a groundbreaking new product without revamping the interface? Probably not. As we've seen with Windows 95, 98, and 2000, Microsoft tries to combine technological advances that are buried under the hood with painstaking design enhancements. Visual Studio .NET follows this trend. Depending on your outlook, it's a welcome improvement, an inconsequential change, or a distracting nuisance. In any case, get ready to look at a new set of hand-detailed icons and learn to use windows that dock, tab, collapse, and hide automatically.

Enhanced IntelliSense

Visual Basic programmers have always been able to count on catching typos and minor mistakes thanks to the built-in syntax checker. IntelliSense remains in Visual Basic .NET, with a few refinements. Now errors are underlined (as they are in Microsoft Word, for example), and a ToolTip explains the problem when you hover your mouse over the offending code. When you start a conditional or loop structure, Visual Basic .NET automatically adds the last End If, End Case, or Loop line. And if you let it, the editor will automatically format your code with the appropriate indenting.

Dynamic Help

You can get help before you ask with Visual Basic .NET's dynamic help feature. And even if you choose to work with the traditional "external" help, you'll notice that Microsoft has updated the MSDN help to the MSHelp 2.0 standard, which sports a nicely redesigned interface of its own.

Macros

Visual Basic .NET allows you to record simple macros, or make more complex ones using a built-in macro editor. It's the first indication of Visual Studio .NET's new Automation model, which allows developers to interact with the development environment to create enhanced add-ins and customized programming tools.

Starting Out in the IDE

You know the drill. It's time to load up the design environment by clicking on a desktop icon or browsing to the Visual Studio .NET shortcut in your Start menu.

Although well organized, the Visual Studio .NET interface is somewhat complicated, with a wealth of features packed into every corner of the IDE. In the following sections, we'll look at different aspects of the Visual Studio .NET interface one-by-one, and explain the concepts you need to know to become completely comfortable in your new programming home.

NOTE *To be technically correct, Visual Basic .NET is the programming language that you use, while Visual Studio .NET is the integrated editing tool (also known as the IDE) that provides all the conveniences from automatic syntax checking to a built-in forms designer. For familiarity, though, this book sometimes refers to the editor as though it is a part of Visual Basic .NET.*

The Start Page

When you first open Visual Studio .NET you will begin at your personal Start Page (as shown in Figure 2-1). Each developer has a personal Start Page, much as every user has a separate Windows desktop.

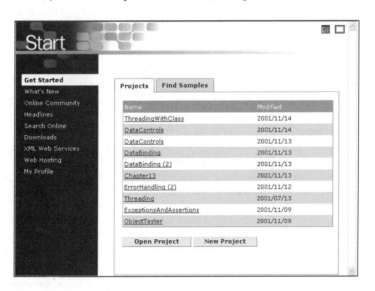

Figure 2-1: The Start Page

At first glance, the Start Page seems to be little more than a bit of HTML that allows you to see recent projects, set some options, and review some information. Under the hood, however, the Start Page serves a valuable function, providing you with a convenient link to the MSDN (Microsoft Developer Network) information drawn from Microsoft's own web site (http://msdn.microsoft.com). You could browse to this information on your own using a web browser (and currently, most developers do), but Visual Studio .NET incorporates it into the interface to spare you the trouble of having to search around on the web. It's a simple idea, but it's an idea that can help you stay up-to-date with the latest developments, trends, and bug fixes.

What's New

Use the What's New link to get information about Visual Studio .NET. This information is drawn from the included help files, which are copied to your computer when you perform the Visual Basic .NET installation.

Online Community

Use the Online Community link to see a list of .NET newsgroups: electronic bulletin boards on the Internet where you can post questions, answers, and comments to a community of subscribed users. Newsgroups are a holdover from the early days of the Internet, and are mostly used by academics and professionals today. If you don't already use newsgroups, you may want to try them out, as they are often the best way to have a programming question answered quickly. They also give you a chance to stay connected with the larger community of Visual Basic developers.

Newsgroups can't be opened directly in the IDE. When you click on one of the newsgroups in the Online Community list, your default newsreader program will open, and it may prompt you to subscribe to the newsgroup (which just means it will store a link to it and keep track of what messages you have and haven't read). Typically, you'll use an Internet mail program like Outlook or Outlook Express to read newsgroup postings.

The only problem with the Online Community feature is that the list is limited to the newsgroups that Microsoft hosts. While these are probably destined to become some of the most popular programming groups, other excellent newsgroups are available elsewhere. For example, DevX provides some excellent newsgroups that can also be accessed through a web browser interface. Go to http://news.devx.com, search or browse your way to groups like vb.dotnet.technical and vb.dotnet.discussion, and rub shoulders with programming greats and novices alike.

Headlines

Use Headlines to browse the wealth of information available on Microsoft's MSDN developer resource site. By choosing the appropriate tab across the top, you can quickly jump to a list of recent articles from the knowledge base (answers to technical problems or fixes for known bugs), technical articles, and news releases.

Here's where Visual Studio .NET gets interesting. If you click directly on a link, the related web page will open inside the Visual Studio .NET interface. This is usually not the most convenient behavior. Instead, you can right-click on a link and choose to open the link in a new Visual Studio .NET window (see Figure 2-2). Or, if your screen area is becoming limited and you're feeling a little claustrophobic, right-click and select the external window option. The page will then open in a separate window using your default Internet browser. This is a nice solution if you want to open an article you plan to read later.

Figure 2-2: Options for opening a new window

Search Online

Use Search Online to search the MSDN library. This allows you to find information about specific issues or topics without needing to bookmark a lot of extra pages. As an interesting side note, Microsoft is following its own advice with Visual Studio .NET's seamless Internet integration. As you'll find out in the Web Services chapter of this book, Microsoft (and many other leading technology companies) see the computer industry evolving into a model where numerous discrete components provide services to other applications over the Internet. Features like the MSDN Search Online option resemble Web Services because they seamlessly incorporate a piece of Internet functionality into a Windows application (in this case, Visual Studio .NET).

Downloads

Use Downloads for source code, service packs, and other updates. It's similar to the Windows Update feature found in current versions of the Windows operating system, except you'll find other useful utilities and Visual Studio .NET add-ons beyond just program updates. For example, you might find tools for programming with Office applications or mobile browsers.

XML Web Services

You can use this link to browse the Web Services other developers have created and are hosting on the Internet. We'll talk about Web Services in detail in Chapter 13.

Web Hosting

The Web Hosting section is a shameless example of promotional cross-selling, and a useful resource for the budding Internet developer. The services listed in this section are early adopters of Microsoft's new ASP.NET technology for Internet application development, which we will examine later in Chapters 12 and 13. If you sign up with one of these companies, you can create ASP.NET applications and upload them directly to the web server you're using without leaving the development environment.

My Profile

This page allows you to customize the Visual Studio .NET environment according to your preferences (as shown in Figure 2-3). For example, specifying the language you like to program with (VB, of course) will determine the default program types Visual Studio displays when you start a new project, although it won't prevent you from creating projects in other languages. The other features are summarized below.

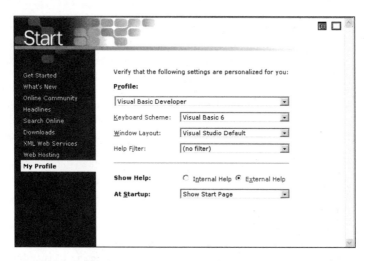

Figure 2-3: Profile settings

- **Keyboard Scheme** determines the hotkeys Visual Studio .NET will use. For example, if you select Visual Basic 6, the IDE will use most of the shortcuts used in the last version.

- **Window Layout** is a little trickier. I recommend that you stick with Visual Studio Default, and get used to the changes. Choosing Visual Basic will result in some changes, but the interface still won't match the older IDE.

- **Help Filter** sets the default MSDN topics that the integrated help will search when you press F1 or browse through the topics. Many programmers leave the filter off to prevent .NET from accidentally filtering out some content that might be important.

- **Show Help** allows you to choose between integrated help (Internal Help) or external help. Integrated help shows help information in a Visual Studio window while you work with your code. External help uses the traditional help system, which launches a new HTML Help window when you press F1. This selection is a matter of personal choice.

- The **At Startup** option allows you to configure what Visual Studio does when you first load it. For example, you can configure it to automatically open the most recent project. Of course, as you've discovered in this section, the Start Up page is really the most powerful option, so why change anything?

Get Started

I've left the first section for last. Get Started provides a list of recent projects, as well as links for reporting a Visual Studio bug or creating a new project.

You can also search (by keyword) for specific code examples (see Figure 2-4). The search will first examine all the examples that are installed with Visual Basic .NET, and then continue its hunt online at Microsoft's MSDN knowledge base. Be warned: the search rarely finds what you intend.

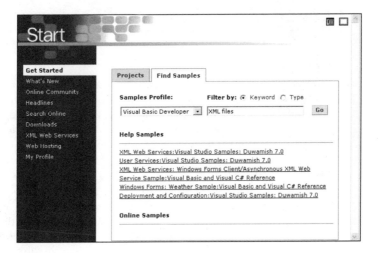

Figure 2-4: Hunting for samples

The examples aren't perfect (or always that interesting) but they do provide an impressive range of different demonstrations. To use a sample, you may need to install it first. Just click on its name in the search results, and a special page in the MSDN help will automatically appear with all the necessary instructions.

Manipulating IDE Windows

Before you go any further, you may want to create a project so that you can see the interface components this chapter describes. You won't actually do much with this first program—not even make it display a "hello world" message—but you will get your first look at the full design-time environment.

To create a new project, click the New Project button in the Get Started section of the Start Page. A window will appear (see Figure 2-5) listing the different project types you can create.

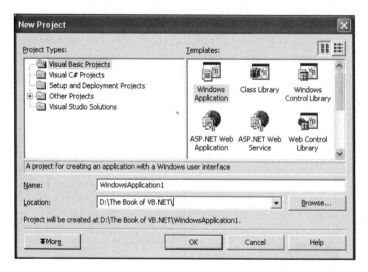

Figure 2-5: Creating a project

For now, keep the default (Windows Application), and click OK to continue. A new Windows Form will appear, along with some additional docked windows.

As with Visual Basic 6, when you double-click the form you open a new code display window. You can switch back and forth between code and design views with the buttons at the top of the Solution Explorer window.

Window Navigation

You might notice that you haven't really left the Start Page behind. Instead, you've just opened a new window. To find out what windows are open at any time, check the row of tabs at the top of the window, just under the menu (see Figure 2-6). You can also use these tabs to jump from one window to another.

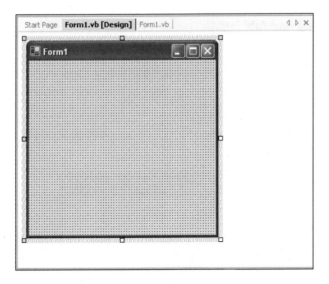

Figure 2-6: The tabbed window display

Code display windows reflect the name of the appropriate file (for example, Form1.vb), while form design windows add the word "design" (for example, Form1.vb [Design]).

Basic Facts About the IDE

The IDE uses tabbed windows to organize a great deal of information without creating excessive clutter. One of the most remarkable features of the IDE is that just about everything you need is only a few clicks away . . . once you understand how to get there.

The IDE does demand some minimum requirements, however. First of all, you can't realistically use the IDE with a small monitor (or with a large monitor using a low resolution). If your current screen resolution is less than 1024 x 768, be ready to endure some clutter and suffer a severe reduction in quality of life while using the IDE. With Visual Studio .NET, the greater your resolution is, the more convenient the IDE will be. Generally, a 19" monitor is best, and the greatest treats may be reserved for those who are experimenting with dual monitor support.

Just as with Visual Basic 6, the IDE is built out of a collection of different windows. Some windows are used for writing code, some for designing interfaces, and others for getting a general overview of files or classes in your application. But before we study the purpose of each window type, it helps to have an understanding of how you can manipulate and configure windows in the IDE.

Docking and Tabbing

All the secondary IDE windows support docking, which allows them to latch on to a side of the main IDE window, rather than floating together in a jumbled mess. In addition, some related windows use tabbing. For example, the Solution Explorer and Class View windows both serve a similar purpose: they provide a high-level view of your project. When both these windows are open, they will be located at the same spot in the window (usually the top left), and only one will be visible at a time (see Figure 2-7). You can switch back and forth by clicking on a tab.

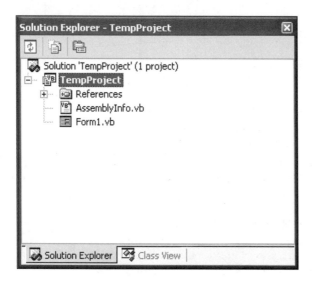

Figure 2-7: The grouped Solution and Class windows

Other linked windows include the Autos, Locals, and Watch debug windows (which only appear while an application is running), and the Output and Task List windows at the bottom of the IDE. Some linked windows really don't have a lot to do with one another, and are grouped in the interest of saving space. For example, the Properties window and the Dynamic Help window both reside in the lower right corner of the IDE. Similarly, the Toolbox and the Server Explorer window are linked on the left of the IDE.

You can drag windows to different areas of the screen to change the way they are docked and grouped. For example, in Figure 2-8, several windows are grouped along with the Server Explorer and Class View windows.

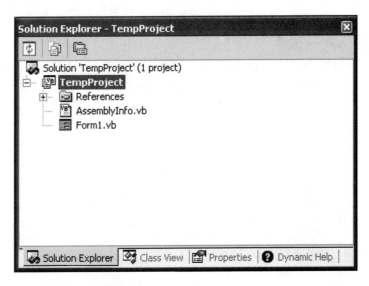

Figure 2-8: A custom grouping

As with the Visual Basic 6 IDE, rearranging windows on your own isn't easy. After a prolonged bout of experimentation, you're likely to wind up with windows in the wrong places or grouped with the wrong windows. Correcting these problems can be awkward, and you may find it easiest to reset the display to its default layout. To do this, select Tools • Options from the menu. Select Environment, and click the Reset Window Layout button in the General area. Everything will be restored to its original layout.

Automatic Hiding and Pushpins

The IDE windows also support automatic hiding. You've probably encountered this feature with the Windows taskbar. When you enable the taskbar's auto-hide feature you conserve screen space. The taskbar remains hidden while you work in an application, and slides into view when your mouse moves close to it.

By default, the Toolbox and All: Server Explorer (Figure 2-9) are set to hide automatically. An icon is displayed at the left edge of the screen, and if you hover over it, the appropriate window will slide out. Note that the Toolbox and All: Server Explorer windows are tabbed. The bigger tab (the one with the text) is the one that was last selected.

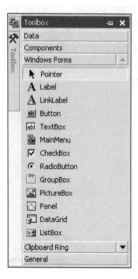

Figure 2-9: The Toolbox (and All: Server Explorer)

When you move your mouse to the left of the screen, the window will slide out. However, this behavior is frustrating when you are designing a form's interface, both because the window constantly slides in and out of view, and because it obscures part of the form you're editing when it appears. When you need to work with the toolbox, click the pushpin in the top right corner of the window when it slides into view. This disables the automatic hiding feature (until you click the pushpin to "unpin" the window). Similarly, you can free up real estate by unpinning other .NET windows. In practice, you'll probably prefer to have everything you need on the screen waiting for you, rather than interactively bouncing on and off of it, but the auto-hide feature does give you some ability to free up space when needed.

Splitting Windows

If, on the other hand, you've decided that you have too much free space in your IDE, you can create multiple views. For example, you can create a new list of tabbed windows in a different portion of your window (Figure 2-10). Just right-click on the list of tabs and choose either New Horizontal Group or New Vertical Group. The window will be split with two tab groups. You can now right-click and choose options to move different windows from one tab group to another. This trick allows you to organize your environment when editing a large project.

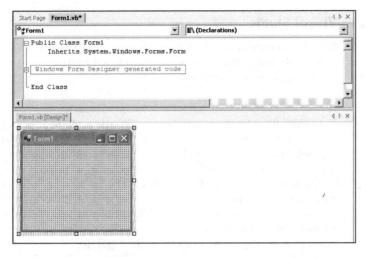

Figure 2-10: Organizing windows with multiple tab groups

You can also split each one of your code display tabs by selecting Window • Split from the menu (Window • Remove Split takes it away). This allows you to see more than one portion of the code in a single file (as shown in Figure 2-11). This is useful when you want to update one section of code to correspond with another.

All views are updated automatically when you make a change in any pane.

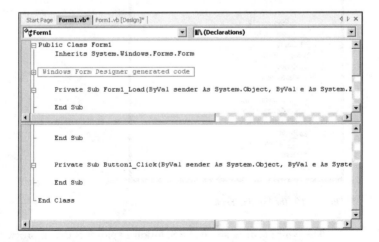

Figure 2-11: Using split windows

Windows in Visual Studio .NET

Now that you understand how windows work in Visual Studio .NET, it's time to take a look around the design environment, and find out how project information is organized and displayed.

The Solution Explorer

The Solution Explorer window (Figure 2-12) shows all the files and references that are part of the current project. The Solution Explorer replaces the Project Explorer in Visual Basic 6, and it works similarly, with a couple of important differences. The Solution Explorer can contain multiple projects, much like a project group in earlier Visual Basic versions. The Solution Explorer can also contain other files that are used in your solution but contain data rather than code. For example, you can include pictures, XML documents, and other files. Having the Solution Explorer track these dependencies for you is a substantial improvement. In the past, an obscure part of a program might use a LoadPicture method to change the display based on an external bitmap file. If you don't know about this requirement, you might not make sure the picture is in the application directory, which is sure to cause a problem when you run the program.

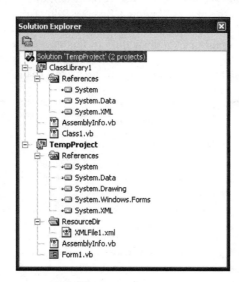

Figure 2-12: The Solution Explorer

Once nice feature about the Solution Explorer is that it provides significant file management features, allowing you to create folders to organize dependent files, and easily rearrange and rename files without breaking other portions of your code.

The Class View

The Class View (Figure 2-13) shows you all the classes that you have defined. By default, when you start a Windows application you will only have one class, which represents the definition for your first form.

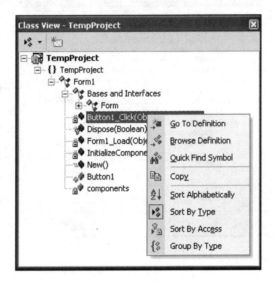

Figure 2-13: The Class View

The Class View is a much more flexible way to look at forms than the file view. It allows you to expand a specific form class and see its properties (including the controls that it contains), its methods and event handlers, and any custom properties and functions you have added. By right-clicking on a class member and choosing Go To Definition, you can jump to the place in the code where it is declared.

TIP *Much more information about classes, including how to create them and why you should, is provided later in Chapter 5.*

The Toolbox

The toolbox window is similar to the toolbox in Visual Basic 6, but more carefully organized. It provides controls you can use when designing a graphical interface, and a convenient method for copying scraps of code from one module to another.

When you have a design view of a form open, the toolbox displays a tab called Windows Forms that is filled with the controls you can use. By default, these controls are displayed in a list view that displays the name of each item, but you can also change it to the more compact icon display used in Visual Basic 6 by right-clicking and clearing the checkbox next to the List View option. Other tabs, like Data and Components, provide more options.

You can add items to the toolbox by right-clicking on it and choosing Customize Toolbox (see Figure 2-14).

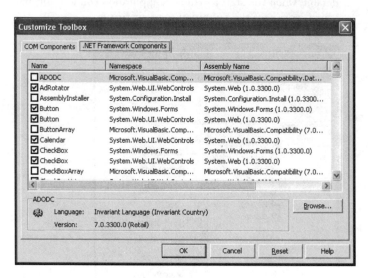

Figure 2-14: Customizing the Toolbox

The window that appears will have two tabs, one for COM components (like your favorite ActiveX controls), and one for .NET assemblies (which will generally provide better performance in your application). Most of the .NET elements you need will already be there. After all, what's the point of having a component if you can't find it to use it? Controls that don't apply (like those reserved for web pages in ASP.NET forms), and controls provided solely for compatibility (like replacements for control arrays, which are no longer directly supported or recommended in VB .NET) won't be selected.

The Toolbox in Code View

If your toolbox is empty, it's probably because you aren't currently designing a Windows form. If you haven't started a project, or if you are in code view, no controls will be shown.

However, the toolbox does provide an interesting service while you are editing code. Every time you copy a portion of text, an icon for it automatically appears at the Clipboard Ring tab of the toolbox (as shown in Figure 2-15). To paste a specific selection, you can double-click the icon, or drag and drop it to the appropriate position in your code. If you can't tell what text a given icon corresponds to, hover your mouse over it for a second to display the first full line.

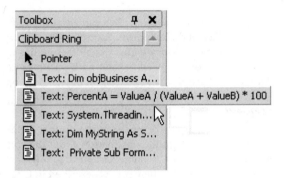

Figure 2-15: The Clipboard Ring

You can remove items using the right-click context menu, or by clicking on an item and pressing the delete key.

The Properties Window

The Properties window is the least changed window in the IDE. It still occupies the same place in the IDE, and is used for the same purpose: setting the properties for the controls in your application.

One enhancement is the new collapsible interface that allows you to either show or hide categories by clicking on the plus (+) and minus (-) boxes next to the category heading (see Figure 2-16). Category headings are indicated with a gray background. The collapsible interface also applies to some properties that use special data types. For example, forms have a Font property that references a Font object. You can set the information for this font object by clicking the ellipsis (. . .) next to the word "Font," or you can expand the Font property to show all the sub-properties. These are the properties of the related font object, such as Name, Size, and Unit.

Figure 2-16: The collapsible Properties window

Properties don't just apply to controls. You can also use the Properties window to set solution, project, and file options. Just select the corresponding item in the Solution Explorer. Note, however, that not all the options will be displayed in the Properties window. You still need to right-click on a project or solution, and select Preferences to have access to the full set of advanced options.

The Output Window

The Output window (see Figure 2-17) resides at the bottom of the IDE. When you run a Visual Basic .NET program, information about the compilation process is displayed in the window. You can also write to it programmatically in your code using the Debug.Write statement, as described in Chapter 7.

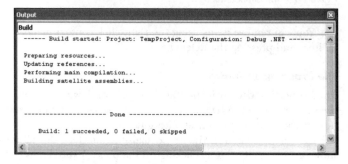

Figure 2-17: Successful build output

The drop-down list box at the top of the Output window allows you to display the Build or Debug information.

The Task List

The Task List (see Figure 2-18) is a new convenience that helps you manage programming tasks while working on a project. To determine what types of items are displayed in the task list, right-click on it, select Show Tasks, and choose a view option. Use View All to see all types of tasks. To add a new task, click "Click here to add a new task," and type a task description.

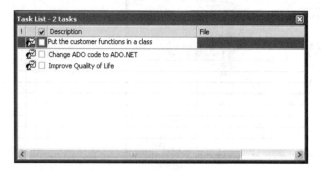

Figure 2-18: The Task List

The most interesting feature of the Task List is how Visual Studio .NET can manage it for you. For example, if you ignore an underlined syntax error in your code, the error will be automatically added to the Task List with an informative description. You can jump to the corresponding point in your code by double-clicking on the task. Similarly, certain predefined comments will be automatically added to the list as well. By default, anytime you enter a comment that starts with 'TODO it will be automatically added to the list. This allows you to keep track of locations in code where further work or revision is required.

You can set the predetermined comment types that will be added to the list. Select Tools • Options, and then choose the Environment folder and the Task List entry. You can add a new type of comment (called a "comment token") by typing in the special word the comment must start with (leave out the apostrophe), setting the default priority, and clicking Add (Figure 2-19).

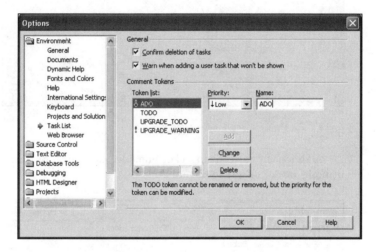

Figure 2-19: Adding custom comment tokens

The Code Display

The code display windows in Visual Studio .NET have some impressive refinements of their own. One of these is the new auto-formatter, which automatically applies the correct indenting to block structures. The most innovative change, however, is the new collapsible display, which allows you to choose portions of the code to view, while hiding those that don't interest you. This allows you to control screen clutter and navigate through your code files more easily.

There are two ways to collapse a section of code. One way is to place code in a #Region block. These blocks have no effect on the function of your code, and are ignored when the code is compiled. The # sign indicates that this is a special instruction for the IDE.

For example, Visual Studio .NET automatically places all the form code that it generates automatically in a special region (Figure 2-20).

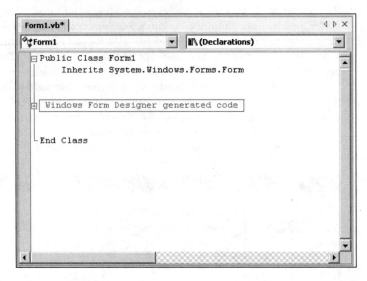

Figure 2-20: The collapsed windows designer region

Additionally, any code in a class, module, subroutine, or function is automatically made collapsible (Figure 2-21).

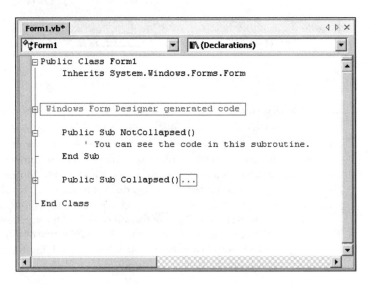

Figure 2-21: Collapsible code

The Dynamic Help Window

The Dynamic Help window is an interesting feature designed to provide links to useful topics in the MSDN help while you work (see Figure 2-22), so that you don't have to interrupt a task to perform a time-consuming search operation.

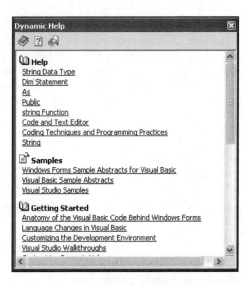

Figure 2-22: Dynamic Help analyzes "Dim X As String"

The idea is grand: Supposedly, Visual Studio .NET will use factors like the selections you make, the placement of your cursor, and the item that currently has focus in the IDE to filter out the most relevant information, and display a list of matching topics in the Dynamic Help window. However, in practice Dynamic Help falls somewhat short of the mark, rarely displaying the relevant information it promises. It also devours extra working memory and imposes a noticeable slowdown on the IDE. For that reason, most developers close the Dynamic Help window, and rely on their searching skills rather than the IDE's guessing skills to find information in the MSDN help. Future Visual Studio .NET upgrades and enhancements will probably make the Dynamic Help feature more valuable, but right now it's more trouble than it's worth.

Using Macros

Macros are a new and welcome feature for Visual Basic .NET users. At their simplest, macros are little pieces of functionality that help you automate repetitive coding tasks. For example, consider the following code example. (I've abbreviated it considerably to save space, but you get the idea.)

```
' Assigning to oddly named controls.
FirstNamelbl.Text = FirstName
LastNamelbl.Text = LastName
Streettxt.Text = Street
Countrycbo.Text = Country
```

The programmer who wrote these lines made a common naming mistake, and put the control identifier (for example, txt for text box) at the end of the name instead of the beginning. In this case, using Visual Studio .NET's Find and Replace feature isn't much help, because though the mistake is repeated, many different variables are incorrectly named. If you're a seasoned coder, you may already realize that this mistake can be fixed with a repeated set of steps that works something like this:

1. Start at the beginning of the line.
2. Press CTRL and the right arrow to jump to the position right before the period.
3. Highlight the last three letters (hold down SHIFT and press the left arrow three times).
4. Use CTRL+X to cut the text.
5. Press HOME to return to the front of the line.
6. Press CTRL+V to paste the variable prefix in the right position.

Easy, right? Just repeat these steps for each of the next dozen lines, and the problem is solved. Of course, now that we've realized that the process of editing a line is just a sequence of clearly defined steps, we can automate the whole process with a macro.

To do this, select Tools • Macros • Record TemporaryMacro (or press CTRL+SHIFT+R). Follow the steps, enter the appropriate key presses, and then click the Stop button on the macro toolbar. Now you can play the temporary macro (CTRL+SHIFT+P) to fix up the following lines.

The Macro IDE

When you record a macro, Visual Studio .NET stores a series of instructions that correspond to your actions. If you've created macros in other Microsoft applications like Microsoft Word or Microsoft Access, you'll already be familiar with this system. The interesting thing in Visual Studio .NET is that the macro language used to record your actions is exactly the same as ordinary Visual Basic .NET code. The only difference is that it has special built-in objects that allow you to interact with the IDE to do things like insert text, open windows, and manage projects. In fact, an entire book could be written about the object model used in Visual Studio .NET's macro facility.

To view the code you created with your temporary macro, select Tools •
Macros • Macro Explorer. In the Macro Explorer window (which is paired with
the Solution Explorer by default), find the TemporaryMacro routine in the
RecordingModule, as shown in Figure 2-23.

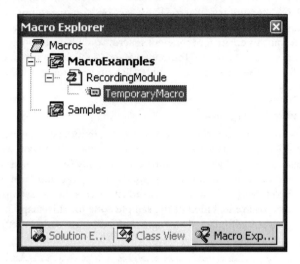

Figure 2-23: The Macro Explorer

Right-click on the TemporaryMacro routine, and select Edit to view the
code, which looks like this:

```
Sub TemporaryMacro()
    DTE.ActiveDocument.Selection.StartOfLine(VsStartOfLineOptionsFirstText)
    DTE.ActiveDocument.Selection.WordRight()
    DTE.ActiveDocument.Selection.CharLeft(True, 3)
    DTE.ActiveDocument.Selection.Cut()
    DTE.ActiveDocument.Selection.StartOfLine(VsStartOfLineOptionsFirstText)
    DTE.ActiveDocument.Selection.Paste()
    DTE.ActiveDocument.Selection.LineDown()
End Sub
```

This code is bound to look a little unfamiliar, as it uses the special DTE
object model, which allows you to interact with the IDE. The key understanding
you should have is that every macro corresponds to a special subroutine, and all
recorded actions are defined in code. To interact with the IDE, you use special
DTE commands.

The Temporary Macro

Macros help you while you are writing a program. In fact, most macros have a limited usefulness: they are created to solve a specific problem, and are not used once that problem is solved. For that reason, a Visual Studio .NET macro is recorded as a "temporary" macro. There can only be one temporary macro at a time, and when you create a new temporary macro the old one is replaced.

If you want to create a permanent macro, you'll have to open the macro editor and move the code in the TemporaryMacro subroutine into a different subroutine. To run this new macro, double-click on its name in the Macro Explorer window.

Macros with Intelligence

In practice, macros often take over where more mundane find-and-replace or cut-and-paste operations leave off. For example, you might want to make a macro that could intelligently examine the currently selected text, and decide what correction or insertion to make based on it. You could even build an entire wizard complete with Windows forms and file access. Some examples of advanced macros are included in the sample code for this chapter.

Below is a straightforward example that swaps the code on either side of an equal (=) sign.

```
Public Sub InvertAssignmentLine()

    ' Retrieve the text.
    Dim str As String
    Dim i As Integer
    DTE.ActiveDocument.Selection.SelectLine()
    str = DTE.ActiveDocument.Selection.Text

    ' Trim the final hard return.
    str = Left(str, Len(str) - 2)

    ' Find the equal sign.
    i = InStr(str, "=")

    ' Reverse the text if it had an equal sign.
    If i > 0 Then
        str = Mid(str, i + 1) & "=" & Left(str, i - 1)
        DTE.ActiveDocument.Selection.Text = str & vbNewLine
    End If

    ' "De-select" the current line.
    DTE.ActiveDocument.Selection.Collapse()

End Sub
```

The structure of this code should be clear, but the DTE commands will be new. A good way to start learning about DTE commands is to record a task in the IDE, and then look at the automatically generated code. For comprehensive information about the DTE, check out the MSDN help files.

Incidentally, the code above also uses traditional Visual Basic 6 string manipulation functions like Len and Left that are still supported, but their use is discouraged in favor of VB .NET's new object-oriented equivalents. The online samples for this chapter include a rewritten version of this macro that uses .NET-style string manipulation. After you've read the next chapter and learned the basics of .NET, you might want to take a look at that sample.

Macros and Events

Visual Studio .NET also provides a special EnvironmentEvents macro module, which contains macros that react to IDE events for windows, documents, and build and debugging operations. Once again, you need to know some non-VB features to perfect this type of macro—namely, the object model for the IDE.

The next macro example uses the WindowActivated event. Whenever you change focus to a new window, this macro closes all the other windows that are a part of your project (the dockable VS .NET windows and the Start page won't be closed) in an attempt to reduce screen clutter. It may seem a little foreign because we haven't yet explained how .NET handles events, but it gives you an interesting idea of what is possible with the IDE. For example, you could create a macro that executes every time a user starts the IDE or a new project and pre-configures the toolbox or initial code files.

```
Public Sub WindowEvents_WindowActivated(GotFocus As EnvDTE.Window, _
    LostFocus As EnvDTE.Window) Handles WindowEvents.WindowActivated

    ' Exit if the current window doesn't correspond to a document.
    If GotFocus.Document Is Nothing Then Exit Sub

    Dim Doc As Document
    Dim Win As EnvDTE.Window

    ' Scan through all the windows.
    For Each Win In DTE.Windows
        ' Ignore the window if it doesn't correspond to a document
        ' or is the currently active window.
        If Not Win.Document Is Nothing And Not Win Is GotFocus Then
            Win.Close()
        End If
    Next

End Sub
```

NOTE *These macro examples are by no means comprehensive. Visual Studio .NET allows you to write and integrate all sorts of advanced add-ins, control designers, and macros. Macros can even use the .NET class library, display a Windows interface, and examine your code.*

Configuring IDE Settings

While you're getting comfortable with your new work environment, you may want to take a look at the full list of options and settings it provides, and start tweaking the IDE to work exactly the way you want it to. Even if you don't want to change anything, looking at the list of settings helps you understand why the IDE does what it does. For example, when you create a new project, the files are automatically created and stored in a default directory, and remain there even if you abandon the project without saving it. How does Visual Basic .NET decide where to store your files? The default path is set in the Options window, along with a number of other user-configurable settings.

The Options Window

To change settings, select Tools • Options from the menu. Settings are grouped into folders, which are subdivided into numerous items (see Figure 2-24).

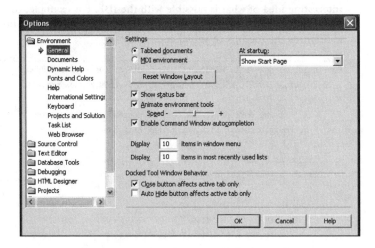

Figure 2-24: Visual Studio .NET options

Before you start experimenting, refer to the following brief descriptions, which outline some of the highlights.

Environment • General

These settings allow you to reset the window layout, configure what Visual Studio .NET does at startup, and determine how many entries are shown in the recent projects list.

Environment • Documents

Use these settings to determine how Visual Studio .NET deals with the individual items in your project. For example, you can configure Visual Studio .NET to open a new window every time you open a different file, or just load the file into the first available open window. You can also set options that determine whether you can edit read-only files and save them with a new name, and whether changes to currently open files made in other programs are automatically read and used to refresh the Visual Studio .NET copy.

Environment • Dynamic Help

These settings determine the types of topics that can be included in the dynamically generated topic list in the Dynamic Help window.

Environment • Fonts and Colors

These settings configure the appearance of text for the code display, printer, or other windows.

Environment • Help

These settings allow you to switch between external and internal help, and apply a default filter to restrict unrelated topics.

Environment • Keyboard

This section allows you to assign shortcut keys to any IDE command. To see what a key is currently assigned to, click in the "Press shortcut keys" box, and press the appropriate shortcut key. For example, if you press CTRL+C you will see that it is assigned to the command labeled Edit.Copy. To assign a new shortcut key, enter it (SHIFT+ALT+Letter and CTRL+ALT+Letter are often good choices), select a command from the list, and click Assign. It may take a while to review all the options on the list, though—they include everything from macros to IDE menu commands. Additionally, you can specify that shortcut keys should only be used in certain views by choosing an option for "Use new shortcut in" other than Global. For example, you could create a shortcut key that is only active when you are using Visual Studio .NET's built-in HTML file editor.

Environment • Projects and Solutions

This section contains the setting that configures whether your application will be saved automatically when you run it or left as it is. It also contains the default location for all projects (each project will become a subdirectory inside this directory).

Environment • Task List

Use this window to specify the comment types that will automatically be added to the task list, along with their default priorities.

Source Control

These options are used to configure version management when multiple programmers are working on the same source code and using a shared code database.

Text Editor • Basic

Use these settings to configure IntelliSense features like automatic indenting. You can also enable the display of margin line numbers, which can be useful for error handling, as we'll see in Chapter 7.

Windows Forms Designer

These settings configure the grid size used for the Windows Forms Designer, which determines how exactly controls can be placed. A small grid size gives you more flexibility when placing a control, but makes it harder to line up controls by hand.

Personalizing Your Environment

Visual Studio .NET also provides some additional options that let you configure the IDE's interface. Select Tools • Customize to choose what toolbars should be displayed, and to add and remove buttons from any toolbar (see Figure 2-25). You can also click Keyboard to jump to the shortcut key settings in the Options window.

Figure 2-25: Customizing the interface

The Simplest Possible .NET Program

The simplest possible .NET program doesn't use any Windows forms. Instead, it is a *Console* or *command-line* application. This type of application takes place in something that looks like an old-fashioned DOS window, but it is really just a special kind of text-based Windows program. Console applications are sometimes used for batch scripts and other extremely simple utilities. Mainly, though, Console applications are used to create every computer writer's traditional favorite: the "Hello World" program.

To create a Console program, just start a new project, and select Visual Basic Projects • Console Application (Figure 2-26).

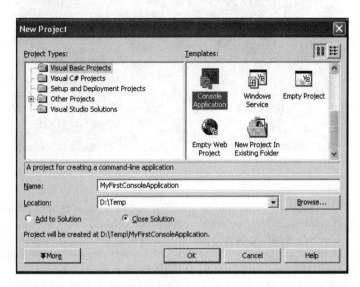

Figure 2-26: Creating a Console application

The following sample program, called MyFirstConsoleApplication, uses the Console object (found in the System namespace) to display some basic information on the screen. The project is configured to run the Main subroutine at startup.

```
Imports System
Public Module MyFirstApplication

    Public Sub Main()
        Console.WriteLine("What is your name?")
        Dim Name As String = Console.ReadLine()
        Console.WriteLine()
        Console.WriteLine("Hi " & Name & ". I feel like I know you already.")
        Console.ReadLine()  ' To stop the window from closing right away.
    End Sub

End Module
```

The result looks like Figure 2-27.

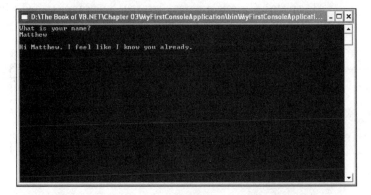

Figure 2-27: An unimpressive .NET application

This book won't feature anything more on Console applications, because Windows and Internet applications provide much richer interface options. The only significance of MyFirstConsoleApplication (and the only reason it's included in this book) is the fact that it shows you a complete Visual Basic .NET application in its simplest form. That application is made up of an implicit namespace (the only thing that doesn't appear in code), a module (although a class could be substituted), and a single subroutine that contains all of the program's operations. Nothing is hidden in this example. You could write this program in a text file, give it the .vb extension, and compile it the old-fashioned way using the vbc.exe command-line compiler.

MyFirstConsoleApplication Files

The essential logic for this application is contained in a single .vb file. However, Visual Studio .NET uses a few extra files to keep track of additional information about your solution.

- MyFirstConsoleApplication.sln contains information about the projects in the solution, and their build settings (which determine if the project is compiled or ignored when you click the start button).

- The MyFirstConsoleApplication.suo file contains binary data that preserves your view settings for the solution, making sure that task list items, breakpoints, and window settings are retained between sessions. This is a major improvement over Visual Basic 6.

- The AssemblyInfo.vb file is essentially used to specify project properties that are compiled into your final executable (like the company name and version number). It's described in Chapter 11.

- The MyFirstConsoleApplication.vbproj file is the most interesting. It uses an XML format to store information about your application, like the assemblies it needs, the configuration settings it uses, and the files it contains. This information is only required when programming and testing your application—as you'll see in Chapter 11, all the necessary details are embedded into the final executable when you compile it.

MyFirstConsoleApplication.vbproj

Although you don't need to work with the .vbproj file directly, you can read it easily in Notepad, and even use it to gain some useful insights about how Visual Studio .NET project configuration works. In this section, we'll consider a slightly abbreviated MyFirstConsoleApplication.vbproj file. Omissions are indicated with <!– XML comments –> (like that).

TIP   *If you're new to XML, the format of the .vbproj file will make much more sense after you read the quick XML primer in Chapter 8. You can return here later when you're an accomplished XML devotee.*

All the file's information is enclosed in a root <VisualStudioProject> node, and then one level deeper in a <Visual Basic> node. The file begins with a section that identifies the version of VB used.

```
<VisualStudioProject>
    <VisualBasic
        ProjectType = "Local"
        ProductVersion = "7.0.9246"
        SchemaVersion = "1.0"
        ProjectGuid = "{474C85BB-A0E1-4C3E-A13C-2A3A06DB3EC7}"
    >
```

There are two other significant groups: <Build> and <Files>. The <Build> node starts with some generic settings that configure the root namespace, the assembly name and type (which in this case is an executable file), and the startup object.

```
    <Build>
        <Settings
            <!-- Some settings omitted. -->
            AssemblyName = "MyFirstConsoleApplication"
            OutputType = "Exe"
            OptionCompare = "Binary"
            OptionExplicit = "On"
            OptionStrict = "Off"
            RootNamespace = "MyFirstConsoleApplication"
            StartupObject = "MyFirstConsoleApplication.MyFirstApp"
        >
```

The next section defines two configuration profiles. One is named Debug (and is used for development testing) and one is named Release (which is used to create the final executable). The main difference is that a file that is compiled in Debug mode uses debug symbols, which allows you to use all the neat debugging tricks you'll see in Chapter 7, like breakpoints and single-step code execution.

```
<Config
    <!-- Some settings omitted. -->
    Name = "Debug"
    DefineDebug = "true"
    DefineTrace = "true"
    DebugSymbols = "true"
    OutputPath = "bin\"
    RemoveIntegerChecks = "false"
    TreatWarningsAsErrors = "false"
/>
<Config
    <!-- Some settings omitted. -->
    Name = "Release"
    DefineDebug = "false"
    DefineTrace = "true"
    DebugSymbols = "false"
    OutputPath = "bin\"
    RemoveIntegerChecks = "false"
    TreatWarningsAsErrors = "false"
/>
</Settings>
```

The final part of the <Build> section lists referenced assemblies and project-wide imports. Both of these new .NET concepts are explained in the next chapter. Quite simply, assemblies are .NET DLLs, while imports allow you to access assembly objects without needing to type long fully qualified names.

```
<References>
    <Reference
        Name = "System"
        AssemblyName = "System"
    />
</References>
<Imports>
    <Import Namespace = "System" />
</Imports>
</Build>
```

The final part of the .vbproj file is the <Files> nodes, which identify the associated files, and what happens to them when you start the application. For example, code files will be compiled, unlike a bitmap or text file you may have added as a resource.

```
        <Files>
            <Include>
                <File
                    RelPath = "AssemblyInfo.vb"
                    SubType = "Code"
                    BuildAction = "Compile"
                />
                <File
                    RelPath = "MyFirstApplication.vb"
                    SubType = "Code"
                    BuildAction = "Compile"
                />
            </Include>
        </Files>
    </VisualBasic>
</VisualStudioProject>
```

Debugging Files

You can compile your application by clicking the start button on the toolbar. You should make sure that Debug mode is selected (Figure 2-28) while testing the application, and Release mode is used to create the final distributable product.

The executable will be created in the bin subdirectory of your project.

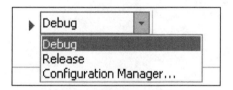

Figure 2-28: Choosing the Debug mode

NOTE *Unlike in Visual Basic 6, all programs are fully compiled before you can run them. When debugging Visual Studio .NET will create a special .pdb file along with the executable. This file contains the debug symbols that allow you to pause, resume, and debug your application.*

What Comes Next?

In this chapter you learned about Visual Studio .NET, the integrated environment where you will perform all your programming. Visual Studio is an indispensable tool, correcting simple mistakes, making code easily readable and navigable, organizing resources, and providing designers for HTML pages, XML documents, graphics, and icons.

Though the focus of the remainder of this book is on the Visual Basic .NET language, an entire book could easily be written on the features in Visual Studio .NET. The customization and macro features alone are probably the most sophisticated ever bundled into a Windows application, and it will take some time before developers have explored all the benefits and possibilities they can provide. If these features have captured your interest, go ahead and start experimenting! You can download some sample macros and interesting add-ins from Microsoft at http://msdn.microsoft.com/vstudio/nextgen/automation.asp.

3

VB .NET BASICS

So far you've read about the fundamental goals of the .NET platform, and learned how to work in the remodelled Visual Studio .NET programming environment. But before you can start creating *real* VB .NET programs, you need a basic understanding of some new .NET concepts. These concepts—the basics of Visual Basic .NET—range over every aspect of the language. They include everything from small details, like changes to assignment syntax and variable scoping, to the new namespace feature, which is the basis of .NET's overall organization. Understanding how namespaces work is your key to accessing the common class library—the all-in-one repository of functionality used for everything from downloading a file from the Internet to printing a document.

We'll begin this chapter with an introduction to namespaces, the common class library, and Visual Basic .NET's new file format. These are the aspects of Visual Basic programming that have changed the most, and will shape all .NET development. Next we will examine how the basic data types have evolved, and expose their hidden object structure. Finally, we'll explore the changes that have been made to assignment syntax and functions, and conclude by introducing delegates, another .NET newcomer. By the end of the chapter you'll be familiar with .NET's most fundamental changes, and you'll be ready to get to work with the Visual Basic .NET language.

New in .NET

You might wonder what a chapter on basics is doing in a book designed for developers who already understand details like functions, variables, and events. The answer? VB .NET represents a complete overhaul of the Visual Basic language. The changes range from minor tweaks all the way to a radical new programming model based on the class library. Some of the new features you'll read about in this chapter include:

The Common Class Library

Java has one. Windows programmers have had dozens, ranging from C++ tools like MFC and ATL to Visual Basic's own built-in Ruby engine. Unfortunately, none of these class libraries has offered a truly complete and integrated solution, so developers have been forced to constantly work with a mix of different components, and even resort to the Windows API. With .NET, developers finally have a complete, modern class library providing all the programming capabilities that were previously available only in countless different bits and pieces.

Redefined Arrays

Arrays are the most obviously changed basic elements in Visual Basic .NET. Unfortunately, gone are the days when arrays could take any shape and size. In order to work with the Common Language Runtime and be consistent, VB .NET arrays always begin at element 0. And that's only the start. Be sure to review the data type descriptions in this chapter to learn why arrays now act like objects, not like structures.

Shortcuts and Cosmetic Changes

Facing the need to implement sweeping changes to support the Common Language Runtime, the VB .NET design team decided to revise the whole language, introducing minor refinements like new assignment shortcuts, mandatory function parentheses, better support for optional parameters, and a Return keyword that allows you to quickly exit a function.

Procedure Overloading

You can now use the Overloads keyword to create multiple functions that have the same name, but different parameters. Visual Basic .NET will decide which procedure to use depending on the variables you supply.

Delegates

A delegate is a new type of variable that can store a reference to a function or subroutine. You can then use this variable to execute the procedure at any time, without needing to call it directly. Delegates help you write flexible code that can be reused in many different situations.

Namespaces, Types, and the Class Library

Every piece of code in a .NET program exists inside a *namespace*. Namespaces prevent .NET from confusing one program with another. For example, suppose the Acme Insurance Company uses a namespace called AcmeInsurance for all of its programs. The code for a program that provides insurance policy information might then exist in a namespace called AcmeInsurance.PolicyMaker (which is really a PolicyMaker namespace inside the AcmeInsurance namespace).

Namespaces are hierarchical, like directories on a computer hard drive. AcmeInsurance is a company-specific namespace that can contain other namespaces representing programs; those namespaces can themselves include still more namespaces. This is useful because Acme's PolicyMaker program might use an object called Policy. Somewhere in the world, another program probably uses a Policy object. However, there's no chance of confusion, even if you install both of these programs at once, because Acme's Policy object really has the full name AcmeInsurance.PolicyMaker.Policy, which is almost certainly unique.

You might recognize this format if you used COM objects in earlier versions of Visual Basic. However, in .NET the concept is vastly extended. For example, as you'll discover in Chapter 11 (which focuses on setup and deployment), namespaces are used with assemblies as the basis for all applications. In other words, you no longer need to add extra information into the registry, and hope that your chosen filename won't collide with that of another application developer.

NOTE *A more dramatic comparison can be made between namespaces and the Windows API. Essentially, all the capabilities of the Windows API exist in a single namespace that is stuffed full of hundreds of functions. Without a very thorough cross-referenced guide, there is no way to tell which functions belong together. The problem is compounded by the fact that procedures in the Windows API are forced to have less-than-ideal names just to avoid colliding with existing function names. This is one of the main reasons that using the Windows API is the secret nightmare of many VB programmers (combined with the fact that a slight mistake can crash the IDE).*

Introducing the Class Library

Namespaces are your gateway into .NET's common class library, which provides several thousand useful *types* (programming objects) that you can drop directly into a Visual Basic .NET program. Essentially, the class library is filled with pre-built pieces of functionality, and replaces entire collections of separate Microsoft components and categories of functions from the Windows API. For example, the System.Windows.Forms namespace contains all the types you need to create graphical controls for Windows applications.

The class library is enormous. Even after you have finished this book and learned VB .NET programming style and syntax, you will continue to return to new parts of the class library as you add new features to your applications.

To review the full details of class library namespaces, you can refer to the MSDN class library reference (you can find this under the topic Visual Studio .NET • .NET Framework • Reference • Class Library). The class library is arranged like a giant tree structure, and each branch contains a few dozen or a few hundred types.

Adding References

The power of the class library comes from different *assemblies,* which are the .NET equivalent of DLLs. Before you can use the objects provided in a name-space, you must make a reference to the appropriate assembly. These assembly references are similar to the references used in earlier versions of Visual Basic to access third-party components and other libraries.

You can use the Solution Explorer to see a list of all the references used by your project. The references shown in Figure 3-1 are added, by default, to all new Windows applications.

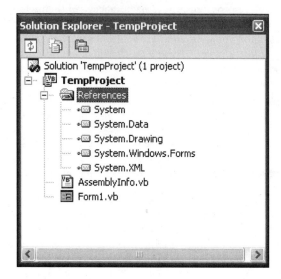

Figure 3-1: Basic references

Usually, these will be all you need. Of course, sometimes you will decide to use a component of the class library that exists in a different assembly. The process works like this:

1. You find an exciting component in the class library that does exactly what you need.

2. You scroll to the bottom of the topic to find out which assembly you need. For example (Figure 3-2), the System.Xml.Node class lives in the assembly named System.Xml.dll.

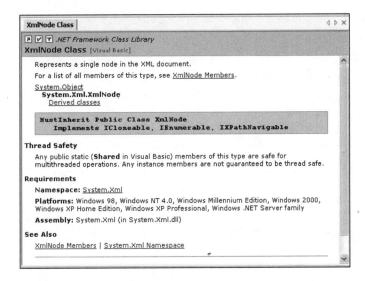

Figure 3-2: MSDN assembly information

3. Then, you right-click on the References item in the Solution Explorer, and select Add Reference.

4. Lastly, you find the appropriate file in the list under the .NET tab, and double-click it.

5. The assembly will be added to the selected components list. Click OK.

Now the components in that part of the class library are available for you to use, as described in the next section.

TIP *Don't become confused between assemblies and namespaces. Logically speaking, the objects in the class library are grouped and stored in namespaces. Physically speaking, the actual code that supports these objects and allows you to use them is stored in assemblies. Once you have the correct assemblies referenced for your project, you can forget about them entirely, assume the point of view of your code, and start thinking in terms of namespaces.*

What Exactly Is in the Class Library?

Namespaces include types, a .NET concept that includes classes, events, structures, and more exotic creations such as enumerations and delegates. In Chapters 5 and 6 we'll get to the technical details of this arrangement, but for now you can think of the class library as a collection of objects you can use in your programs.

You probably remember that Visual Basic 6 provided a few built-in objects that you could use (such as Printer, Screen, App, and Err), and allowed you to add special objects by adding references to COM libraries (like those used for databases or XML support). Visual Basic .NET, on the other hand, provides hundreds of objects that are sorted into namespaces according to function.

If you aren't quite clear on what an object is, keep reading. I'm about to explain the bare minimum you need to know to start using objects.

Objects are programming constructs that contain properties, methods and events (all of which are called members).

Properties

Properties store information about objects. For example, you could use `str = Text1.Text` to copy the text out of a text box and into a variable named str. The property that is being used here is called Text, and the object is Text1. A *control* is really just a special type of object that provides a graphical representation in a window.

Methods

Methods are commands that cause an object to do something. For example, MessageBox.Show uses the Show method of the MessageBox object to display a message, and MyDoc.Print uses the Print method of the MyDoc object to send some data to the printer.

Events

Events are notifications that an object sends you, which you can then either listen to or ignore. For example, a button object sends a Click event, which gives you the chance to respond and perform an operation in your code.

Instance Objects and Shared Objects

One of the most confusing aspects of object-oriented programming, at least for the newcomer, is that some objects need to be created while others don't. The reason for this difference is that objects can have both shared members, which are available even if you haven't created an object, and normal members, which force you to create an object before you can use them. In Visual Basic 6, for example, the App object consists of shared properties and methods, and you don't need to create the App object yourself to use its properties. On the other hand, the Active Data Objects (ADO), which represent database connections and commands, must be explicitly created before they can be used. This is because the properties of these objects (for example, the name of a field in a database) don't have any meaning until you have defined the object and connected it to a specific database.

In VB .NET you don't have this distinction between shared objects and instance objects. Instead, any class can have a combination of shared members and instances members. For example, we'll consider the DateTime object a little later in this chapter. It provides a shared Now property that you can use to retrieve the current date and time, without manually creating an object. It also contains more ordinary instance properties, like Day, which returns the Day component of an existing DateTime object.

Accessing the Objects in a Namespace

As long as you have the appropriate assembly loaded, you can access an object in a namespace by writing its fully qualified name (as in Namespace.Class). This can be cumbersome, though, as many objects are stored several levels deep, in namespaces with long names. For example, the .NET version of the App object is called Application, and is found in the System.Windows.Forms namespace. This means, for example, that in order to retrieve the product version of your application, you have to write code like this (note that ProductVersion is a shared property):

```
VersionString = System.Windows.Forms.Application.ProductVersion
```

Admittedly, the line looks far more complicated than it should. To improve on this, you can make things simpler by using the Imports statement.

Imports

The Imports statement doesn't cause any additional code or information to be added to your program. It's strictly a time-saver to help reduce the number of long, fully qualified names you have to type. You use it in much the same way that you might use a With block, except that the Imports statement must occupy the first line in your code window, before any classes or modules are defined, and the Imports statement doesn't use a block structure.

The Imports statement is shown in action in the following example. Note that one other change has been made: The traditional built-in Visual Basic MsgBox function has been replaced with the equivalent MessageBox class from the class library. Instead of using special constants (such as vbOKOnly), this class uses the MessageBoxButtons object, which provides special properties that represent all the common styles of message boxes. (Technically, MessageBoxButtons is a special type called an enumeration, but we'll get to that in Chapter 6.)

```
' This code has no Imports statement.
' A reference to the System.Windows.Forms assembly exists in the project.
' (VB .NET added it automatically because we chose to create a Windows
'  application.)

Public Module MyModule
    Public Sub Main
        Windows.Forms.MessageBox.Show("You must enter a name.", _
          "Name Entry Error", Windows.Forms.MessageBoxButtons.OK)
    End Sub
End Module
```

The Imports statement saves us some typing in two places:

```
Imports System.Windows.Forms
Public Module MyModule
    Public Sub Main
```

(continued on next page)

```
          MessageBox.Show("You must enter a name.", _
            "Name Entry Error", MessageBoxButtons.OK)
      End Sub
End Module
```

Aliases

You can also use the Imports statement to create an *alias,* which is typically a short form that you can use to refer to a namespace. For example:

```
Imports System.Windows.Forms = Wn
' Now we can use statements like Wn.MessageBox.Show
```

An alias is useful if you want to import namespaces that have the same object names. Using an alias, you can still make it much easier to work with these objects (and ensure that the resulting code is much more readable), but you won't have to worry about conflicts between identically named objects.

Project-Wide Imports

An Imports statement only applies to the file that it's used in. You can also create project-wide imports that apply to all the files in your project. In fact, if you create a new Windows project, you'll find that System.Windows.Forms is already imported at the project level, so you can write code like the preceding Message-Box.Show example *without* typing the Imports statement or using a fully qualified object name.

To see all the project-wide imports, right-click on your project in the Solution Explorer, and select Properties. Then select the Common Properties • Imports option (as shown in Figure 3-3).

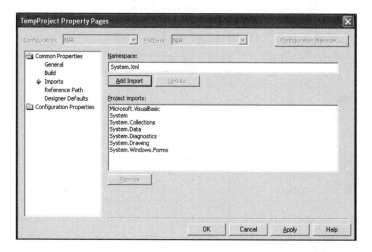

Figure 3-3: Project Imports

From the window that appears, you can easily add, edit, and remove any of the project-wide imports.

Exploring Namespaces

Throughout this book you will discover various parts of the class library and learn how to use them in your programs. To help you understand the structure of the class library, the following is a quick overview of some of the more important namespaces.

System

This is the core namespace that you'll begin learning about in this chapter. The System namespace includes the definitions of basic data types like strings, arrays, and events. It also introduces exceptions, which we'll study in Chapter 7.

Microsoft.VisualBasic

This tiny namespace contains the Visual Basic runtime, which .NET uses to compile your code and provide the traditional built-in VB functions (like the string manipulation functions Left and Mid). You don't use this namespace directly.

Microsoft.Win32

This is a small namespace that lets you access the registry and respond to certain global system events. We'll cover the registry in Chapter 8.

System.Collections

This namespace provides *collection objects*—objects that can contain groups of objects. We'll explore these in Chapter 6, which focuses on object-oriented programming.

System.Data

This namespace includes the types needed for ADO.NET, which is discussed in Chapter 9. Other namespaces that start with System.Data are used for specific parts of ADO.NET, such as SQL Server and OLE DB support.

System.Drawing

This namespace provides types that allow you to draw directly on a form. These features go under the collective name of GDI+, and are quite a bit different from the drawing features provided in Visual Basic 6. They aren't described in this book, however, because manually drawing a form's interface in code is an unsatisfying experience for almost all programmers. It's nearly impossible to produce content that looks attractive, and it's extremely difficult to generate anything like an animation program that works with respectable speed. (In truth, GDI+ does enter into this book briefly in Chapter 4 and in Chapter 8, with printing.)

System.Drawing.Printing

This is a namespace used to support print and print preview features, which we'll explore in Chapter 8.

System.IO

This namespace is used for file access, including reading and writing to your own proprietary files. It is also covered in Chapter 8.

System.Net

This namespace contains low-level network communication classes, as well as some useful objects you can use to retrieve information from the web without delving into ASP. A taste of these features is provided in Chapter 8.

System.Reflection

This namespace provides support for *reflection*, which allows you to do various interesting and slightly unusual things, such as examining a class you don't have information about and finding out what it is ("reflecting" on it), and creating a late-bound object for a type determined at run time. Reflection is further discussed in Chapter 11.

System.Runtime.InteropServices

This namespace, with its rather foreboding name, is used for some important pieces of backward compatibility with COM, the standard used for creating and sharing pluggable components and ActiveX controls. Because COM has existed so long, many products depend on it. If you need to interact with a COM component, VB .NET will make it almost effortless, as you'll see in Chapter 14.

System.Runtime.Serialization

This branch of the class library contains several namespaces that allow you to serialize and restore objects painlessly. These impressive features make an appearance in Chapter 8.

System.Threading

This namespace provides the tools you'll need for creating multithreaded programs. Chapter 10 will give you a solid grounding in threading.

System.Web

This is the namespace to use for ASP.NET applications. The root System.Web namespace provides the basic built-in ASP.NET objects. Other namespaces that start with System.Web include additional important types, such as those used to create the Web Forms interface. You'll learn about ASP.NET in Chapters 12 and 13.

System.Windows.Forms

This namespace includes all the types you need for building the user interface in a Windows program, including classes that support forms, text boxes, and countless other controls. You'll learn all about Windows programming in Chapter 4.

System.Xml

This namespace contains objects that allow you to interact with XML data and create your own XML documents. You'll be introduced to XML in Chapter 8.

Other Namespaces

Of course, the class library provides many more capabilities that can't possibly all be covered here, including advanced string manipulation, regular expressions, sockets and other tools for FTP-type programs, and low-level classes for managing the sticky details of security and COM. There are even whole namespaces of classes that do little more than support features in the Visual Studio .NET IDE, and that provide design-time support for controls and the Properties window.

The class library integrates features that used to be provided only through a combination of dozens of separately developed components and the Windows API. In this book, I'll introduce you to the most exciting parts of the class library, the Visual Basic .NET programming language, and the Visual Studio .NET interface where you'll do your work, all at once.

The New File Format

In previous versions of Visual Basic, several custom file types were used. Form files (.frm) contained the graphical layout and event handling code for a form. Class files (.cls) contained individual classes that you created on your own. Module files (.mod) contained variables and functions that could be made globally accessible. The whole collection of files was grouped into a project, which was described by the familiar Visual Basic project file (.vbp) and could be further bundled into project group files (.vbg).

Visual Basic .NET takes a different approach.

- When you start a new application you create a solution file (.sln), as shown in Figure 3-4.

- Each solution can hold one or more project files (.vbproj).

- All the other files are code files (.vb). These code files can contain multiple classes, modules, and forms (which are really just a special type of class). In other words, the logical grouping of your program into classes, modules, and forms doesn't necessarily determine the physical division of your code into files on the hard drive.

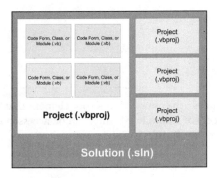

Figure 3-4: A solution file

NOTE *As you'll discover in Chapters 12 and 13, Internet applications are a little different from other programs, and contain a variety of distinct file types.*

Class and Module Blocks

In order to support the new file system, Visual Basic .NET adds new block structures to hold classes, modules, and forms. Here's an example of a code file that contains a class and a module:

```
Public Class MyClass
    ' Code here.
End Class

' No man's land . . . code can't exist here.

Public Module MyModule
    ' Code here.
End MyModule
```

Once you are inside a class or module definition, you can write your code the same way that you did in Visual Basic 6 (although form classes are a little different, as you'll learn in Chapter 4). However, you can't place any type of variable or procedure declaration outside of these definitions.

```
Public i As Integer                ' This is not allowed!

Public Class MyClass
    Public j As Integer            ' This is OK.
    Public Sub MySub()             ' This is also fine.
    End Sub
End Class

Public Sub MySub2()                ' This has no meaning!
End Sub

Public Module MyModule
    Public Sub MySub3()            ' This is OK.
    End Sub
End Module
```

All classes and modules are contained in a root element that you don't see: your project's namespace. For example, MySub3 can be accessed using the fully qualified name MyProject.MyModule.MySub3.

Part of Visual Basic .NET's flexibility stems from the .NET team's increasing drive to make VB code files more transparent, and hide fewer details. Visual Basic 6 used the same sort of system, but it defined modules and classes implicitly, based on files.

TIP   *Bear in mind that Visual Basic .NET's multipart file format should not be seen as a good reason to combine dozens of classes and modules into a single file. Organization at the file level still makes sense. The only difference is that now you have the ability to group together small, interconnected classes and functionally related blocks of code.*

Changing and Extending Your Project's Namespace

All the code you enter in your project is contained in a *root namespace*. By default, Visual Basic .NET will assign it the name of your application. To rename or otherwise change your project's root namespace, right-click on it in the Solution Explorer and choose Properties. The root namespace can be configured under the Common Properties • General tab (Figure 3-5).

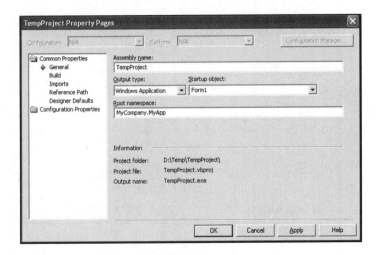

Figure 3-5: Setting the root namespace

You can also create subnamespaces to help you organize the procedures in a large project. To do this, use the Namespace/End Namespace block. Namespaces have to be defined outside all other constructs. This means that you can't create a namespace inside a class or a module; it has to be the other way around.

```
Namespace Configuration
    Module ConfigTools
        Public Sub UpdateSettings
            ' Some code goes here.
        End Sub
    End Module
End Namespace
```

In this example, you can access the UpdateSettings namespace from another namespace in your project as Configuration.ConfigTools.UpdateSettings, or from another project in your solution as ProjectName.Configuration.ConfigTools.UpdateSettings.

Other Resources

Visual Basic .NET projects aren't limited to code files. They can also include such resources as bitmap files, HTML pages, and icons. Visual Studio .NET even provides a designer that lets you modify simple graphics pixel by pixel, and design HTML pages in a drag-and-drop interface. The ability to add files directly into your project ensures that you can keep track of important resources, rather than trusting that they'll be present in the correct directory.

To add a resource file, right-click on your project in the Solution Explorer, and select Add • Add Existing Item. Alternatively, you can create some common file types right inside the designer by choosing Add • Add New Item and selecting the appropriate file type (as shown in Figure 3-6).

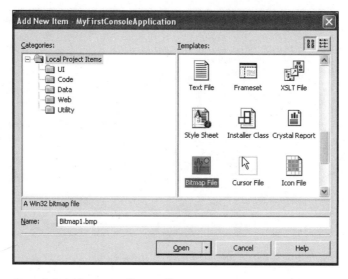

Figure 3-6: Adding a miscellaneous file

Data Types

Most Visual Basic data types remain the same in VB .NET, at least on the surface. For example, all of the following statements are still valid:

```
Dim MyInteger As Integer
Dim MyString As String
Dim MyDate As Date
```

These may look the same as the built-in data types in Visual Basic 6, but in fact they are not. Each one of these variable types is mapped to a corresponding type in the System namespace. For example, the Date keyword really corresponds to System.DateTime, and the String keyword represents System.String.

System Types

The types in the System namespace are shared by every .NET language, and they form part of the infrastructure that lets you integrate code components written in different languages without running into any trouble. Of course, in order for this integration to work, the built-in variable types in Visual Basic 6 had to be harmonized with those from other programs to create the best possible common type system. This is the reason for most of the data type changes that you'll find in VB .NET. For example, Integer now maps to System.Int32—a 32-bit integer that can store a number as great as 2,147,483,647—rather than Visual Basic's traditional 16-bit integer, which could only accommodate numbers up to 32,767.

```
Dim MyInteger1 As Integer        ' This is a 32-bit integer.
Dim MyInteger2 As System.Int32   ' This is also a 32-bit integer.
```

This is quite a convenience for new VB developers, who often use integers as loop counters without realizing that integers have size limitations. One manifestation of this problem used to be the report-generating program that failed with an overflow error if it found more than 32,767 records in a database.

Another change is that the Currency data type is no longer available. You'll have to use Decimal instead, which is optimized for financial calculations that require exact fractions.

Strings work more or less the same way that they did in VB 6, although you can't create a fixed-length string anymore. User-defined types (those created with Type/End Type statements) are another casualty, but they can be replaced by structures and classes, as you'll see in Chapters 5 and 6.

Arrays

Arrays in Visual Basic .NET always start counting at element 0. The types in the class library also follow this convention. (This is a change from earlier versions of Visual Basic, where some collections were base 0 and others base 1, with little real consistency.)

When declaring an area, you specify only the upper boundary, as shown in our next example. The total number of elements in the array is always one greater than the number you specify.

```
Dim MyArray(10) As String  ' This creates an array with 11 elements,
                           ' numbered from 0 to 10.
Dim MyArray(0 To 10) As String ' This doesn't work!
                           ' The "To" statement is not supported.
```

Opinions vary about this change. Many programmers resent the fact that arrays have been limited, while other developers have accepted it as a cost of integration with the Common Language Runtime. It also adds a level of commonality that helps programmers share code and know what to expect.

TIP *It is technically possible to create a .NET array with a lower bound other than zero by resorting to some very strange commands. I certainly don't recommend this ugly workaround. Instead, if you need a more flexible type of array, consider a more object-oriented solution, and create a custom collection class. This trick is described in Chapter 6.*

Arrays and IEnumerable

One useful addition to arrays is the IEnumerable interface, which lets you move through an array with a For Each command, instead of looking up the appropriate upper and lower boundaries and then specifying the coordinates. The following example shows how you can examine every string in an array with a few lines that are very light on manual code. The only drawback is that you receive a read-only element from the array, which is suitable for a display or print operation, but not for a modification.

```
Dim MyString As String
For Each MyString In StringArray
    ' Display it in a list box.
    lstStrings.Add(MyString)
Next
```

Arrays as Reference Types

Another interesting detail about arrays is that they are actually reference types, not value types like the other simple variables. This means that the code used for copying arrays and testing equality has slightly different effects than it would with integers and dates.

To be more specific, setting two arrays equal to each other doesn't copy the contents of an array, only the reference. You end up with two array variables that access the same array. If you modify one of these variables, the other will be updated as well. In order to create a real copy of an array, you have to use its built-in Clone method.

```
MyIntegerA = MyIntegerB   ' Copies the value of B into A.
                          ' We end up with two copies of the same information.
MyArrayA = MyArrayB       ' Copies the reference of B to A.
                          ' We end up with two variables accessing the same array!
MyArrayA = MyArrayB.Clone()  ' A duplicate copy of B goes into A.
                             ' We have two copies of the array.
```

All this nifty sleight of hand raises a couple of puzzling questions. Why does MyArrayB have its own Clone method? Who created that?

The answer is that arrays are really objects. In fact every data type, even a value type, leads a double life as an object.

Data Types "Under the Hood"

Visual Basic .NET is object-oriented to the core. If you haven't had any experience with object-oriented programming and design, you may have to wait until Chapters 5 and 6 before the .NET picture really becomes clear. However, I can't wait that long to divulge one more unusual secret: Every variable type in Visual Basic .NET is really a full-fledged object.

It's All Objects

They don't look like objects. In some ways, they don't even act like objects. (We usually expect an object to behave like a reference, as arrays do in VB .NET. However, .NET includes objects for strings, numbers, and dates that act like value types, which is more useful for those types of data.) But objects they are. All of which raises another excellent question: What is the point of something that looks like an object but doesn't act like one?

In one respect, variable types do act like objects. That is, they have built-in methods for handling associated procedures. For example, you may remember that Visual Basic 6 included a whole host of functions for calculating such things as the length of a string or the upper boundary of an array. One of the goals of .NET was to remove this collection of disorganized language-specific functions and provide equivalent or better capabilities through the elegant class library. Accordingly, you might expect to find classes in the System library that contain similar helper methods, organized according to function. But what's the point of including a special class that does nothing but calculate the length of a string? In fact, isn't the length of a string an important characteristic of a String object?

Consider this example:

```
' The old fashioned way, which is still supported in VB .NET
StringLength = Len(MyString)

' The new .NET way, which treats the string as a System.String object.
StringLength = MyString.Length
```

In VB .NET, every String object contains all the basic procedures that it needs, bundled right with it. These techniques work for string variables, or string literals (text enclosed in quotation marks). Consider a couple of more examples for parsing a string:

```
' Capitalize a string and trim spaces, all in one line.
MyString = "lower case   ".ToUpper().Trim()        ' = "LOWER CASE"

' Get the portion of the string that starts at the second character
' and is four characters long. Note that strings start numbering at 0,
' which represents the first character.
MyString = MyString.Substring(1, 4)                ' = "OWER"
```

(continued on next page)

```
' Replace all occurrences of the characters "W" with "LD".
MyString = MyString.Replace("W", "LD")                ' = "OLDER"

' Get a string from an integer.
Dim MyInteger As Integer = 42
MyString = MyInteger.ToString()                       ' = "42"
```

These examples only scratch the surface. To find out more about what a String object can do, including information about the Split method (which creates an array of substrings by dividing a string based on a specified character) and the Insert method (which adds another string into the middle of the current string), refer to the System.String class in the MSDN class library reference.

Visual Studio .NET is helpful enough to provide a list of matching properties and methods when you press the period after typing a recognized variable name (see Figure 3-7).

Figure 3-7: IntelliSense for a String

Arrays

Of course, it's also interesting to look at some of the built-in features of an array. For example, you can iterate over an array like this:

```
For i = MyArray.GetLowerBound(0) To MyArray.GetUpperBound(0)
    ' Some code here.
Next i
```

The methods shown here replace the old UBound and LBound functions, although those functions are still supported if you want to code in the traditional (and slightly outdated) way. The 0 in this example specifies the first argument. Remember, VB .NET starts counting at 0, so 0 means "first." Note that we don't really need to check the lower boundary, because we know that all arrays start numbering at 0.

The Array class also includes shared methods. The methods and properties shown so far use instance methods, which means you need to create an array in order to use them. Shared methods, however, can be used independently. To use a shared method, you use the name of the class, which in this case is Array.

For example, you can reverse an entire array in one blow with the following code:

```
MyReversedArray = System.Array.Reverse(MyArray)
```

(Technically, you don't need to specify the System namespace before Array, because the System namespace is always imported into your project.)

You can use similar shared methods for even more value-added features:

```
' This code works as long as the array contains elements that can be sorted
' and has only one dimension. Examples include numbers or strings.
MySortedArray = Array.Sort(MyArray)
```

Even array searching is automated:

```
Dim Foods() As String = {"cheese", "meat", "sugar", "soy milk"}
Dim MeatPostion As Integer
MeatPosition = Array.IndexOf(Foods, "meat")
' MeatPosition is set to 1, representing the second element.
' If you receive -1, the item could not be found.
```

Dates

Date types also have some interesting features that make it easy to retrieve portions of a date and perform date calculations. You can also use the TimeSpan class to store a measured interval of time, instead of a specific date. Here's an illustrative example that gets straight to the point:

```
Dim MyDate As Date, MySpan As TimeSpan

' Set the date to today and the timespan to one day.
MyDate = Date.Now
MySpan = TimeSpan.FromDays(1)

' This displays the current hour.
MessageBox.Show(MyDate.Hour)

' This moves the date to tomorrow.
MyDate.Add(MySpan)

' Here's another way to modify dates, which moves us back to today.
MyDate.AddDays(-1)
```

Summary

The preceding examples show the most important methods and properties of the common data types, but there are still many more useful features. If you want to examine them, refer to the MSDN class library reference. Remember, many traditional Visual Basic functions are still supported for backward compatibility. However, the object-oriented way of doing things is often more elegant and organized.

You'll learn far more about objects and how to use them in Chapters 5 and 6 of this book.

Changes to Operations

Operations look the same in Visual Basic .NET as they did in previous releases, so you won't have any trouble combining strings and adding numbers. However, you can make use of a few elegant shortcuts.

Syntax Changes

Syntax changes are designed to make your life easier. In many cases, these changes are conveniences that have been "borrowed" from other languages.

Initializers

Initializers let you assign a value to your variable on the same line where you define it:

```
Dim i As Integer = 1
```

This technique even works with objects and arrays (which are enclosed in curly braces):

```
' Define and initialize an array all at once.
Dim NumberArray() As Integer = {1,2,3,4}

' Define and initialize an object in one step, using its constructor.
Dim MyFile As System.IO.FileInfo = New System.IO.FileInfo("c:\readme.txt")
```

You can also create new variables inside other code statements, such as function calls, by using the New keyword:

```
MyValue = MyFunction(New JustInTimeVariable As Integer = 5)
```

Don't overuse this convenience though, as it can make your code difficult to read.

Assignment Shorthand

Visual Basic .NET also provides timesaving ways to increment values. They look a little strange at first, but they let you save a few extra keypresses and condense overly verbose code.

```
intA += 1             ' Equivalent to intA = intA + 1
intA += intB          ' Equivalent to intA = intA + intB
strName &= "End"      ' Equivalent to strName = strName & "End"
```

You can use this trick with all the basic numeric operators, including addition (+), subtraction (-), multiplication (*), division (/), and exponents (^).

Multiple Variable Declaration

Visual Basic has always allowed you to create more than one variable on a single line. In the past, however, the results weren't always what you might have expected. Consider the following example:

```
Dim intA, intB, intC As Integer
```

In Visual Basic 6, this line of code would create one integer (intC), and two variants. (A variant was the default variable type in VB 6.) In Visual Basic .NET, however, all the variables in this line will become integers.

In fact, Visual Basic .NET no longer supports variants. If you want to create a variable that can accommodate different data types, you will need to use the generic System.Object type, which can hold any kind of variable or object reference. You'll also need to convert your generic variable to the appropriate data type before you can use it in any operations (such as math calculations, or method invocations).

Generally, this will be more work than you'll want to do, but in certain situations it can be a valuable feature. For example, you might be calling a function that returns a "mystery" object. You can catch this object in a generic System.Object variable, and then check its type using the TypeOf keyword.

```
Dim MysteryObject As Object
Dim Number As Integer

' You can place any type of data in a mystery object. You just can't use it.
MysteryObject = 10

' It's easy to find out what MysteryObject really is.
If TypeOf MysteryObject Is Integer Then
    ' Now we know that this will work.
    Number = CType(MysteryObject, Integer)
End If
```

Converting Variables

Most professional applications will use the Option Strict statement to prevent automatic variable conversions. Automatic variable conversions (famously called "evil type coercion" in previous versions of Visual Basic) are dangerous because they may work under some circumstance and fail under others. The problem is explored in much more depth in Chapter 7, which deals with bugproofing your code. For now, it is enough to know that conversions that might fail, such as converting a string to a number or a 32-bit integer to a 16-bit integer, can't occur automatically if you have Option Strict enabled. You have to do the work manually, using either the shared functions of the System.Convert class, or the CType function that is built into Visual Basic .NET.

CType works by taking two arguments: the variable you want to convert, and the type that you want to convert it to. Consider this example:

```
' This converts a string to a number.
MyInteger = CType(MyString, Integer)
```

Here is another example that uses conversion with basic objects, VB .NET's replacement for the variant:

```
Dim objA As Object, objB As Object
objA = 3
objB = "3"

' Will not work! VB .NET doesn't know how to add mysterious objects.
objA = objA + objB

' This works, provided the objects can be converted to integers.
objA = CType(objA, Integer) + CType(objB, Integer)
```

> **NOTE** *You also use CType in a process called casting. It's essentially the same operation, except you are converting one object into another type of supported object. More information about casting is divulged in Chapter 6, which explores interfaces and advanced object-oriented programming.*

Math

The math class contains a number of shared properties and methods that support mathematical operations. For example, you can get the constant pi from Math.Pi. A few other examples are shown here:

```
MyValue = Math.Sqrt(81)        ' MyValue is 9.
MyValue = Math.Abs(-42)        ' MyValue is 42.
MyValue = Math.Round(4.779, 2) ' MyValue is 4.78.
MyValue = Math.Log(4.22)       ' I'll leave you to calculate this one.
```

Random Numbers

Random numbers are easily generated in Visual Basic .NET. They continue the trend of moving programming capabilities out of the dark alcoves of specific languages and into the common class library. This example uses the System.Random class to automatically generate an integer between 0 and 5:

```
Dim MyNumber As Integer
Dim RandomGenerator As Random = New Random()

' Retrieve a random number from 0 to 5.
' (You can add one to get a random number from 1 to 6.)
MyNumber = RandomGenerator.Next(5)

' Retrieve another random number, but this time make it an integer from 1 to 6.
' (VB .NET interprets this as a value of 1 or larger, but always less than 7.)
MyNumber = RandomGenerator.Next(1, 7)
```

Some New Rules for Scope

Scope is the measure of a variable's life, and of the ability of other parts of your code to access it. You are probably familiar with the fact that a Private variable in a module or class can't be accessed by any code outside of that module or class. Similarly a variable created inside a procedure exists only as long as the procedure does, and can't be accessed in any other routine.

Visual Basic .NET tightens scoping another notch. Variables defined inside block structures (such as loops and conditional blocks) can't be reached from outside the block. This probably won't affect you, but it is still good to know.

```
If MyCondition = True Then
    ' Create a variable with If-block scope.
    ' (This scoping behavior is automatic and unchangeable.)
    Dim NewInteger As Integer = 12
End If
' NewInteger cannot be accessed here.
```

Enhanced Functions

Just as in previous versions of Visual Basic, VB .NET incorporates two types of procedures: the function, which returns a value, and the subroutine, which does not.

One nice addition to functions is the Return keyword, which allows you to write this kind of code:

```
Public Function Add(intA As Integer, intB As Integer)
    Return(intA + intB)   ' Instead of Add = intA + intB
    ' Any code here will not be executed.
End Function
```

The Return command combines two actions together: setting the function's result to the specified value, and exiting the function immediately (as though an Exit Function statement had been used). The nicest thing about using Return is that you don't need to specify the function's name to provide the return value. This allows you to sidestep some minor but annoying problems, such as mistyping the function name, or having to update your function code if you change the name of the function.

Optional Parameters and Defaults

A procedure can still use optional values by incorporating a parameter array. A *parameter array* is an array provided to your function that contains "everything extra" that was added in the function call. For example, this function:

```
Public Function GetRecordCound(EndDate As Date, _
    ParamArray OtherOptions() As String) As Integer
```

could be called with this statement:

```
NumberOfRecords = GetRecordCount(Date.Now, "John", "California")
```

The OtherOptions array would contain the string "John" at index 0, and the string "California" at index 1.

Parameter arrays allow you to collect any extra information that a user wants to send, and that makes them very flexible, especially when the procedure being called doesn't need to know a lot about the extra information, and can just write it to disk, pass it to another function, or use it in a predefined way. However, a procedure with a parameter array can be difficult to use, particularly for other users, because it doesn't define what information is required or provide any type checking. Consequently, the function might easily end up with a lot of mysterious information that it can't interpret.

Generally, parameter arrays are an awkward means of using optional values. Visual Basic .NET provides two other options: *default values* and *overloaded procedures,* both of which are more convenient and aesthetically pleasing.

Default Values

With default values, you explicitly mark parameters that are optional. These can be included, or just left blank by the calling code. If they are left blank, the default value that you have specified will be used automatically.

For example, this function:

```
Public Function GetRecordCount(EndDate As Date, Optional Person As String = "", _
    State As String = "Kentucky") As Integer
      ' Some code here.
End Sub
```

can be called like this:

```
NumberOfRecords = GetRecordCount(Date.Now)
```

or like this:

```
NumberOfRecords = GetRecordCount(Date.Now, , "California")
```

or like this:

```
NumberOfRecords = GetRecordCount(Date.Now, "John", "California")
```

Default values may seem just about perfect. They allow you to create functions that accept a variety of different information, but they also define all the possible pieces of information. In practice, however, optional values aren't always ideal. One problem is that they sometimes allow too *much* flexibility. The function might end up making assumptions about what information will be supplied, or you might end up using default values that are inappropriate for certain situations. There is also no way to find out if a value hasn't been supplied, or if the user has supplied a value that is identical to the default value.

Procedure Overloading

The preferred way to handle situations where the supplied information varies is with overloaded functions. This technique has long been the standard in other programming languages, but it makes its VB debut in Visual Basic .NET.

Procedure overloading allows you to provide different versions of the same function or subroutine. These procedures have the same name, but they have different argument lists (and are preceded with the Overloads keyword). For example, consider the following Combine functions:

```
Public Overloads Function Combine(intA As Integer, intB As Integer) As Integer
    Return(intA + intB)
End Function

Public Overloads Function Combine(strA As String, strB As String) As String
    Return(strA & strB)
End Function
```

In this scenario, if you were to call a Combine function in your code, Visual Basic .NET would look at the argument list you provide, and match it with the appropriate version of Combine.

```
IntegerValue = Combine(1, 2)      ' Uses the first version to return 3.
StringValue = Combine("1", "2")   ' Uses the second version to return "12".
```

In this case, we overload the Combine function because "combine" means two different things, depending on the type of value used.

This type of differentiation already existed in the Visual Basic language with the addition operator (+), which adds numbers but concatenates strings, just like our function. This is an example of operator overloading, which is built into the Visual Basic language.

VB .NET doesn't currently support custom operator overloading. Custom operating overloading, which is occasionally used in C/C# applications, changes the meaning of basic operators (like + or *) when using specific types of objects.

Procedure Overloading and Data Access

Another common use of procedure overloading is to provide database access routines that work with different criteria. For example, if you have ever created a database program, you've probably used such functions as GetRecordByID, GetRecordByName, and GetRecordsByDate. There is nothing wrong with this system, but it can get awkward when you have several different databases and need to create long function names, such as GetClientSalesByClientName.

You can provide the same solution with overloaded functions:

```
Public Overloads Function GetUser(ID As Integer) As UserObject
    ' Code here.
End Function

Public Overloads Function GetUser(Name As String) As UserObject
    ' Code here.
End Function

' And so on . . .
```

However, you will need to make sure that the data types are all different. (Assigning them different parameter names isn't enough.) A common technique is to provide a basic function, and then overload versions that add new information bit by bit.

TIP *There's another good reason to learn about procedure overloading: The .NET library uses this technique extensively in its own classes (and never uses optional parameters). This allows you to concentrate on the information you need from a function, rather than worry about the information you can supply as parameters.*

Calling a Procedure

One minor change with procedure calls is that they now require parentheses. In the past, parentheses were only used when a return value was needed:

```
' Visual Basic 6 code
MsgBox "Hi there!", vbOKOnly                    ' No parentheses allowed here.
Response = MsgBox("Delete file?", vbYesOrNo)    ' Parentheses required here.
```

Visual Basic .NET always uses parentheses. It's only a cosmetic change, but it makes code a little more consistent, and it aids readability because you can distinguish a procedure call from another type of statement at a glance:

```
' Visual Basic .NET code
MessageBox.Show("Hi there!" , MessageBoxButtons.OK)
Response = MessageBox.Show("Delete file?", MessageBoxButtons.YesNo)
```

Notice here that the MsgBox function has also been replaced with the MessageBox object.

Parentheses are even used when a function or subroutine doesn't require parameters, as in this line:

```
Form1.Show()
```

ByVal and ByRef

ByVal is the new default for procedure parameters, and Visual Studio .NET inserts that keyword automatically and incessantly to emphasize the point. ByVal parameters are passed as copies. Any changes to a ByVal parameter affects the copy, not the original. The procedure below, for example, is free to change the Number parameter without affecting the variable that was supplied in the calling code.

```
Public Function CheckForPrimeNumber(ByVal Number As Integer) As Boolean
    ' If we change Number here, no one else will know.
End Function
```

That said, there are some subtleties that you need to be aware of when passing values by value. With reference values (i.e., objects), a copy of the memory reference is passed for a ByVal parameter. However, this copy still refers to the same object. If you change the reference, the change won't be propagated back to the calling code. However, if you keep the reference, access the object, and change it in some way, the change will still affect the one and only original object, contrary to what you might expect!

In other words, changes you make to simple data types won't return to your calling code. However, any object type (including arrays) will be modifiable when passed by reference or by value.

```
Public Function CheckForPrimeNumber(ByVal Number() As Integer) As Boolean
    ' If we change a value in the Number() array, it will affect the original
    ' array in the calling code, even though it was passed ByVal.
End Function
```

You could take extra, potentially painful steps to change this behavior. For example, you could copy the object, or use the array's built-in Clone method.

Delegates

Visual Basic .NET also introduces an interesting feature called delegates, which give you another way to work with functions and subroutines. A delegate is a special type of variable that can store the location of a procedure. Before you can create a delegate, you have to define its type, in a statement like this:

```
Public Delegate Function ProcessFunction(StringIn As String) As String
```

This statement doesn't create a delegate variable. Instead, it defines a type of delegate. Based on this definition, the ProcessFunction delegate type can be used to store the location of a function that accepts a single string argument and that has a string return value. (The actual names you give the parameters in the declaration really don't matter.)

You declare the delegate variable as you would any other variable:

```
Dim ProcessDelegate As ProcessFunction
```

The delegate will be able to store references only to procedures that have the exact same signature (parameter and return value types). This is how delegates enforce type safety, and prevent you from referring to the wrong function or subroutine by accident.

```
Public Function CapitalizeName(Name As String) As String
   ' A reference to this function can be stored in ProcessDelegate.
End Sub

Public Function MyFunction(Name As String, Optional ID As Integer = 0) As String
   ' This function is different. It cannot be stored in ProcessDelegate.
End Sub

Public Sub Process(Name As String)
   ' This won't work either. It's a subroutine, not a function.
End Sub
```

Once you create a variable based on a delegate, you can assign a function to it by using the AddressOf operator. The AddressOf operator lets Visual Basic .NET know that you are using a reference to a procedure, not trying to run it directly.

```
ProcessFunction = AddressOf CapitalizeName
```

Once you set a delegate, you can run the procedure later, just by using the delegate:

```
' Calls the CapitalizeName function and assigns its return value to UCaseName.
UCaseName = ProcessFunction(LCaseName)
```

This is a useful technique, because it allows what programmers call an *extra layer of indirection*. This means that the code you create is more generic and has a better chance of being reused.

Here's a function that accepts a delegate as an argument, and uses the function specified by the delegate to perform a task:

```
Public Sub ProcessArray(MyArray As String(), FunctionToUse As ProcessFunction)
    Dim i As Integer
    For i = 0 to MyArray.GetUpperBound()
        MyArray(i) = FunctionToUse(MyArray(i))
    Next i
End Sub
```

You call the subroutine like this:

```
ProcessArray(CustomerArray, AddressOf CapitalizeName)
```

The result of this sleight of hand is that each element of CustomerArray will be modified according to the CapitalizeName function.

By using a delegate, you can create a single ProcessArray subroutine that can process array elements in a variety of different ways, depending on the FunctionToUse reference that you supply.

Delegates won't receive much more attention in this book for two reasons. First of all, delegates can often be replaced by objects and methods. For example, we could rewrite the preceding ProcessArray example to use a collection of special Customer objects that support a Process method. (If the following example is a little perplexing, don't worry; all will be explained in Chapters 5 and 6.)

```
Public Sub ProcessArray(MyArray As Customer())
    Dim MyCustomer As Customer
    For Each Customer In MyArray
        Customer.Process()
    Next
End Sub
```

You can also use delegates to allow communication between different objects, by having one object store a delegate that contains a method in another object. However, this type of communication is better handled with events, which are really just delegates with some added conveniences.

An interesting real-world example of delegates and threading is provided in Chapter 10.

What Comes Next?

This chapter has provided a whirlwind tour through dozens of different language changes. The fundamental new concept presented here was the common class library, a complete programmer's toolkit stocked with most of the features you could ever need in any language.

This chapter also explained how and why many of the features that VB programmers have relied upon for years are now changing from stand-alone functions into class methods, and being grouped with the objects that they relate to. The key to understanding the new .NET world is realizing that *everything* is an object. The next step, if you weren't already acquainted with class-based programming, is to dive right in with the new few chapters. Additionally, you might want to start making forays into the MSDN class library reference to find out what methods and properties are exposed by the common data types.

Lastly, if you are interested in string manipulation, you might want to check out the special StringBuilder class from the System.Text namespace. It provides similar features to the String object, but it's optimized for speed. This could become important if you are performing a long series of intensive string operations (for example, if you are coding a word processor from scratch).

4

WINDOWS FORMS

Windows Forms are the building blocks of the traditional graphical programs designed for the Windows operating system. Most of the applications you use, from office productivity software, like Microsoft Word, to interactive games and multimedia products, can be considered Windows Forms applications. The defining characteristic of a Windows Forms program is that every part of its interface is built out of windows.

Windows Forms applications are all-purpose solutions to most programming problems. Though the latest version of Visual Basic puts the Internet squarely in focus with the .NET moniker, support for traditional Windows application programming has also been revitalized. It's now easier than ever to design a rich interface with Visual Basic .NET's new support for resizing forms, splitting windows, and anchoring and docking controls. VB .NET also takes the confusion out of MDI (Multiple Document Interface) applications, adds enhanced designers that let you build tree views and list views by hand, and lets you lock individual controls into place so they can't be accidentally moved while editing.

Perhaps the most remarkable shift is the fact that every form, and all the controls on it, is now completely defined in Visual Basic code. This means that as you use the designer to rearrange your user interface and set properties, the IDE is actually quietly adding the corresponding information into your .vb code file. This makes it easy if you want to tweak these settings by hand, or even create a portion of user interface dynamically while the application is running. Best of all, it gives you greater control over your application.

New in .NET

.NET introduces a whole new model for working with forms. It saves C++ developers the effort of wrestling with the MFC framework, and gives Visual Basic programmers a level of control they've never had without delving into the low-level Windows API. If you are a seasoned VB developer, you'll find many pleasant surprises in this chapter.

The Component Tray

In earlier versions of Visual Basic, controls were such a popular and easy way to add functionality to a program that they were used even when the "control" (a timer, for instance) didn't require any user output at all. In VB .NET, these invisible controls are no longer placed on a form's drawing area. Now they are organized in a special component tray.

Anchoring and Docking

They're the kind of little frills that win the hearts of developers. Anchoring and docking let you make controls move and change size automatically, so that you never need to write resizing code again.

Forms Are Classes

Forms in Visual Basic 6 had a dual identity, acting like live objects and classes at the same time. In Visual Basic .NET, a form is just another type of class—one that inherits from System.Windows.Forms.Form. Even better, all of its characteristics—including such details as the position and properties of contained controls—are included automatically in the class definition.

Extender Providers

In a bid for even greater organization, Visual Basic .NET introduces the concept of *providers*, which are controls that enhance other controls on the same form with additional properties. For example, if you want your controls to have tooltips, add a ToolTip control to the component tray, and voilà! Every control has a new ToolTip property.

MDI Enhancements

.NET removes many old restrictions on your ability to work with windows, and nowhere is that more apparent than with MDI windows. Not only can you turn any form into an MDI parent by setting a simple property, but with a single command, you can also turn any other Windows form into a child at run time.

System Tray Icons

Previously, creating system tray icons was an unpleasant, error-prone chore involving the Windows API. In Visual Basic .NET, adding icons to the system tray is just a matter of dragging the appropriate control to the component tray.

Getting Started

Windows Forms applications get their name from the fact that they are built out of numerous windows, or forms. Different applications use windows differently. For example, multiple document (MDI) applications, such as Visual Studio .NET, can designate that several windows be manipulated inside a larger "container" window. Other applications—Windows Explorer, for example—use a single window that divides itself into several resizable panes. Both these types of interfaces are easy to create with Visual Basic .NET.

Before continuing any further, it's probably a good idea to start a Windows Forms project and try adding some controls. Much as in earlier VB versions, you add a control by selecting the icon and drawing it onto the design surface. You can also add more forms by right-clicking on your project in the Solution Explorer, and choosing Add • Add Windows Form.

TIP *In this section, we explore how you can design the interface for a project with a single form. As you start adding more forms, and writing code to handle events and communicate information from one form to another, the VB .NET world takes a couple of new twists. We'll explore the implications of multiple forms, and the real architecture of forms, a little later in the chapter.*

The new Windows Forms engine works like the traditional Visual Basic 6 Form Designer when it comes to creating and designing forms. Properties are still configured in a Properties window. Controls can be moved, copied, and aligned with the grid, exactly as they could in previous versions of VB.

The Component Tray

In previous versions of Visual Basic, some features were implemented through "invisible" controls, the most common example being the Timer control. This was a convenient way to add functionality, but it was a little messy—after all, controls were designed to provide user interface, not to replace DLLs and other code components. Visual Basic .NET provides a cleaner implementation through a tool called the *component tray*.

You'll notice this new addition as soon as you try to draw an "invisible" control on the design surface. Instead of appearing on the form, where it might be obscured by other legitimate controls, invisible components will appear in a special area of the window, as shown in Figure 4-1.

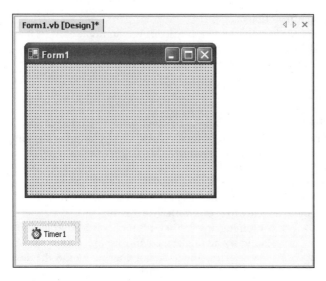

Figure 4-1: A timer in the component tray

This added clarity lets you easily add support for menus, timers, and standard Windows dialog boxes (such as Open, Save, and Print, and selection windows for Font, Color, and Print settings). You could create these controls directly through the System.Windows.Forms namespace using just a couple of lines of code, but the component tray makes the process effortless.

Custom Designers

Some controls have complex properties that can't be set through the Properties window. A typical example is the TreeView control, which contains a hierarchy of different elements (called *nodes*), although simpler controls like the ListBox also share this drawback. On the other hand, you may have noticed that certain controls, like the TabControl, have special features that let you modify them at design time. That's because these controls are paired with special custom designers that provide this enhanced flexibility.

Visual Basic .NET brings a new level of consistency to control design, and adds even more custom designers, allowing you to easily configure complex properties for most controls. For example, a ListBox control can be filled at design time. Just find the Items property in the Properties window, and click on the ellipsis (. . .) next to the word Collection. A special window will appear where you can enter your list items (see Figure 4-2). A similar tool is available for the Items property in the ListView control, and for the Nodes property in the TreeView control.

Figure 4-2: Configuring list items with the designer

These custom designers are lightweight and straightforward. The designers for the ToolBar and StatusBar controls have also been given a clean and consistent new look (Figure 4-3), which replaces the old cluttered, multitabbed approach.

Figure 4-3: Configuring ToolBar buttons

The best way to get used to this new system is to try it out. The basic principle is that items (for example, individual nodes and buttons) are added to the list on the left. To configure the properties for an individual item, select the item from the list, and then modify the property list that appears on the right. And remember, if you want to add an image to an item, you'll need an associated ImageList control, which will provide a collection of pictures to choose from. Thankfully, the ImageList control also has its own new designer, so now inserting and rearranging graphics files is a breeze.

Locking Your Controls

It used to be that getting controls to line up perfectly in a complex interface could be a slow and tricky process. It sometimes involved turning off the Snap to Grid feature in order to position some of the controls exactly, and then re-enabling it so that other controls could easily be placed in consistent positions that lined up properly. And once you finally had your controls perfectly arranged, you risked scattering them with an accidental mouse click.

Locking is a convenient design-time feature that can help you prevent this type of accident. It existed in Visual Basic 6, but only in a crude, "all or nothing" form. As soon as you locked a VB 6 form, you couldn't change anything until you unlocked it, which often didn't allow you enough flexibility. The locking feature still exists in Visual Basic .NET—just right-click on your form and select Lock Controls (and do it again to unlock them).

However, VB .NET also provides a more useful version of this feature that allows you to lock individual controls. To use it, select the control and change its Locked property to True. You can now add new controls and rearrange existing ones, without having to worry that you'll accidentally move a control that you've positioned perfectly.

Basic Form Properties

As you look through the list of properties provided by the Windows Forms engine, you will probably notice that a few changes have taken place. Two useful introductions are the MinimumSize and MaximumSize properties. When these properties are set, they stop a user cold if he or she tries to resize a form beyond its pre-established dimensions.

MinimumSize and MaximumSize offer a great improvement over the manual techniques that Visual Basic programmers have traditionally resorted to, which involved reacting to a form's Resize event, determining whether the form had been made too small or too large, and then manually resizing it if necessary. There were two significant problems with that approach. First of all, the Form Designer had to be careful not to trigger an extra Resize event and get trapped in an endless loop. Secondly, code in the Resize event handler reacted only *after* the form had been changed to an invalid size. This meant that, depending on the user's display settings, the window sometimes flickered noticeably as it fought between the user's attempted change and the programmer's stubbornly resistant code.

Forms also have an AcceptButton and a CancelButton property, which indicate the button that will be "clicked" automatically when the user presses the ENTER key (to "accept" the window) or the ESC key (to "cancel" it). The same potential existed in Visual Basic 6, but it was implemented in the Default and Cancel properties for button controls. This state of affairs was a little confusing, as it didn't clearly indicate that a form could have only one Default and one Cancel button.

Anchoring

Anchoring is a simple idea that saves a lot of trouble. The best way to understand anchoring is to see it in action. Examine the window shown in Figure 4-4.

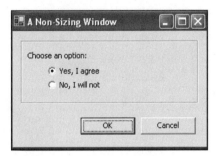

Figure 4-4: An ordinary window

By default, Windows controls are "anchored" to the upper-left corner of a form. This used to mean that as a form was resized, the controls stayed put, because the position of the upper-left corner does not change. As a result, unless you wrote explicit resizing code, the embarrassing blank borders at the bottom and right edges of your form would grow wider, as shown in Figure 4-5.

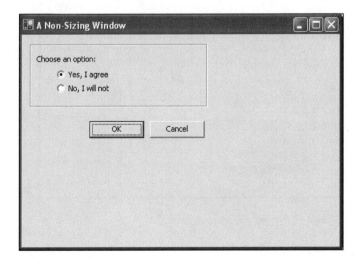

Figure 4-5: An embarrassment

If, on the other hand, a control could be anchored to the bottom of the form, its position would drop as you lengthened the form, guaranteeing that the distance between the control and the bottom edge of your form always remained constant. This is exactly the ability that .NET forms provide.

To change a control's anchoring, find its Anchor property in the Properties window; then change it using the special drop-down control (see Figure 4-6). Click to select the edge or edges that your control should bind to. For example, you might want to anchor a control to the lower-right corner, thus ensuring that the control will always be a fixed distance away from the bottom and right edges of your form.

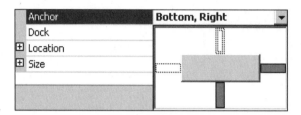

Figure 4-6: Anchoring options

You can even anchor a control to more than one side. In this case, the control has to grow automatically to maintain a consistent distance away from the form edges as the form is resized. In our sample resizable form shown in Figure 4-7, the command buttons are anchored to the bottom right, the group box is anchored to the left, right, and top (so it will grow to fit the form width), and the radio buttons are anchored to the top left (the default). A checkbox allows you to test anchoring by turning it on and off (and then setting the anchor properties manually in code).

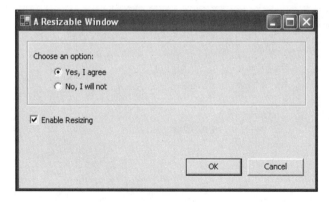

Figure 4-7: A respectable resizable form

There are some controls that you'll never want to be resized. For example, buttons should always be a standard, consistent size—they look bizarre if they start to grow as a form changes size. This is one of the main problems with many of the commercial add-ins for automatic resizing.

A sophisticated program will resize the areas of its interface that can benefit from more screen real estate. For example, if you are creating a window with a group of checkbox settings, you should probably give it a fixed border, because the window will not need to change size. On the other hand, if you have a window that contains a control with a lot of scrollable information (a RichTextBox, a ListView, or a DataGrid, for example), you should allow it to grow when resized, by docking it to opposite sides.

Docking

Docking allows a control to latch onto an edge of a window and resize itself automatically. To add docking to a control, find the Docking property in the Properties window, and choose an edge to dock on (Figure 4-8). You can only dock against a single edge (or choose to fill the entire form), and you can't dock *and* anchor a single control.

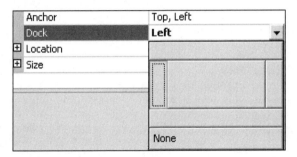

Figure 4-8: Docking options

The first time you use docking, you're likely to become slightly frustrated. While docking does what it claims, it also forces the control to sit flush against the docked edge and take its full width. This often means that your control is squeezed up against the side of the form, without enough of a border, as shown in Figure 4-9.

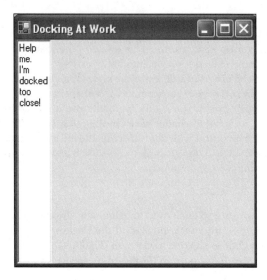

Figure 4-9: Docking problems

Thankfully, there is a way to fine-tune control docking and create a perfectly resizable form.

Making Docking Work

The secret to successful docking is *padding*. Padding allows you to insert a buffer between the docked control and the form that it's docked to (see Figure 4-10).

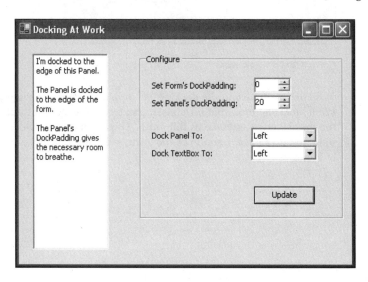

Figure 4-10: Integrating Docking and DockPadding

To set some extra padding for your form, find the DockPadding property, expand it, and set All to 15. Now the docked control will still bind to the side and be resized, but it will have some much-needed spacing around it.

Of course, form padding doesn't help you if you are trying to dock multiple controls next to each other and you want to increase the spacing between them. To have more fine-grained control over spacing and docking, place your controls inside separate Panel controls. The Panel control provides its own Dock-Padding property. The process works like this: You dock the Panel to the side of the form, and then you configure the Panel's padding to make sure the control it contains is placed perfectly. The sample code includes a simple application that allows you to play with different docking settings.

It will take some experimentation before you master this system well enough to create the interfaces you want. Most articles about Visual Basic .NET just gloss quickly over the whole affair, and don't admit that fine-tuning an interface is still a labour of love, even with Visual Studio .NET's enhanced anchoring and docking features. To get started, you might want to start experimenting with the sample code included for this chapter, which shows some examples of how you can use panels to help organize groups of controls.

Splitting Windows

The split-window interface is one of the hottest design features these days, and the applications that use it are replacing traditional MDI programs. For example, the system utilities component included with Windows 2000, which is used for everything from configuring your hardware to adding user accounts, now uses a Windows Explorer–like interface that divides a single window into multiple, sizable components. Even applications (such as Visual Studio .NET) that still use the MDI paradigm usually combine it with dockable windows and other split-window displays.

Split-window designs have been somewhat of a rarity in Visual Basic programs, however, because traditionally they have been a chore to program, sometimes requiring reams of extra resizing code. One of Visual Basic .NET's best-kept secrets is that it can not only dock and anchor controls, it can also create resizable split-window programs that require no extra code.

To create a split window, you need to start by docking a control to one side of the window. For this example, try using a TreeView control. Then add a Splitter control, and make it dock to the same size. Now add another control—this time PictureBox. The new control acts as though the window is filled entirely with available space; it ignores the position occupied by the other two controls. This means that if you've docked the Splitter and TreeView controls to the left, and then dock the PictureBox control to the left, it will dock against the edge of the splitter bar. Or, you could set the PictureBox docking to Fill, and it will occupy all the remaining space on the right side of the window, as shown in Figure 4-11.

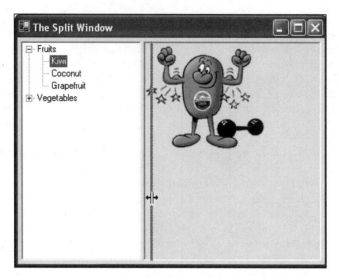

Figure 4-11: Configuring a split window

The application user can move the splitter bar at run time to change the size of the PictureBox and the TreeView controls. You can also set the Splitter-Bar's MinSize property to configure the smallest size (in pixels) to which the TreeView can be resized. You can set the SplitterBar's MinExtra property to configure the minimum size for the controls on the non-docked side (in this case, the PictureBox control).

Once again, you'll have to experiment with these techniques in order to master them, but you now understand the fundamental concepts.

Form Oddities

Forms have a few unusual extra properties. You probably won't need to use them, but they can provide a few hours of design-time fun. All of these strange behaviors are on display through the FormOddities project included with the sample code.

Opacity

One of these interesting features is *opacity,* which allows you to make a form partially transparent (see Figure 4-12). For example, if you change a form's Opacity setting to 10% (actually 0.10), the form and all its controls will be almost completely invisible, and the background window will clearly show through. If you set the background window's Opacity to 10%, the background will show through only slightly. This feature is supported only in Windows 2000 and later operating systems. (In other words, it doesn't work in Windows 98.) For this reason, the Opacity feature should never be used indiscriminately in business applications. A master user interface designer might be able to use it to create floating controls, or menus that don't mask underlying content—or to enable some nifty effect in a logo animation or graphic display. In general, however, such enhancements won't be supported by older computers, and will do little more than complicate an application.

Figure 4-12: A transparent window

TransparencyKey

You can use the TransparencyKey property to make portions of a window invisible. The color that you specify with this feature will become transparent when your program is running (much as a form does when you alter its opacity). For example, if you choose light red, any occurrence of light red in your form—whether it is in the form's background, in another control, or even in a picture contained in a control—will become invisible, and the application behind your program will show through. However, unlike sections altered with the Opacity feature, transparent areas act like "holes" in your application's window (see Figure 4-13). A user can even click to activate another window if it's visible through a transparent region.

The sample code uses a form with three red PictureBox controls, which disappear at run time.

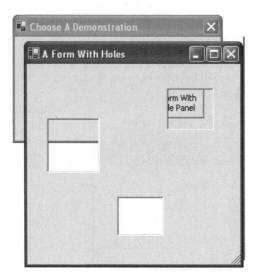

Figure 4-13: Cutting out bits of a form

Once again, this feature is only supported in Windows 2000 or later. Can it be useful? It's hard to say, as it depends in part on the performance of the GDI+ drawing functions in the .NET class library, and on which version of Windows your user is running. Judging from my own tentative experimentation, it will probably be a long time before this feature turns up in any games or next-generation application interfaces.

AutoScroll

If you set the AutoScroll property to True, and you resize your form so that some controls "fall off the edge," scrollbars will be provided automatically so that the user can scroll the form and access the hidden controls. AutoScroll provides a very crude solution for resizable windows, and is generally far inferior to the more professional results you can achieve with anchoring and docking. However, if you use your imagination, you may find some interesting uses for Auto-Scroll forms.

More useful is the Panel control, which includes a similar AutoScroll feature that you can use to create list controls. For example, Visual Basic .NET now includes checkbox lists, which allow you to scroll through a list of items that can each be checked or unchecked. Instead of using this control in a configuration window, you could create your own list of scrollable options that might contain other controls, such as buttons and labels. Figure 4-14 shows the difference between a scrollable form and a scrollable panel.

Once again, this tool is best reserved for experienced interface designers, as it is usually a better idea to use standard Windows conventions, such as split windows, lists, and tab controls, to organize information.

 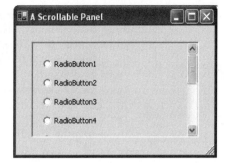

Figure 4-14: Two ways to scroll

Exploring .NET Forms

Forms have existed in Visual Basic since its first release, and along the way, they've evolved from static templates to full-featured objects. Unfortunately, this evolution has led to a few inconsistencies. A form in Visual Basic 6 is both a class and a special kind of ready-made object.

TIP *If you haven't used classes before, you may wonder what the difference is between a class and an object. Essentially, a class is a definition that you create an object from. For example, there is one text box class (System.Windows.Forms.TextBox) that provides all the features that let a text box work the way it does, including properties such as Text that your program can interact with. There may be many text box objects in your program that are built with this class. For all the explicit details about classes and objects, be sure to read Chapters 5 and 6.*

The fact that a form plays a strange dual role as a class and an object means that you can display a form in the traditional way (using MyForm.Show), or you can create a new form programatically, based on your form class, and then use that:

```
' VB 6 code to create a form dynamically.
Dim MyDynamicallyCreatedForm As MyForm
Set MyDynamicallyCreatedForm = New MyForm
MyDynamicallyCreatedForm.Show
```

This procedure allows you a lot of flexibility when creating multiple-document applications. For example, you could use this technique in a word processing application to create a window whenever the user opens a new document. Best of all, you don't need to hard-code an upper limit. Code like this can handle as many simultaneous windows as you want, with no extra programming required.

Of course, this dual usage of forms can be somewhat confusing. For example, a common error is to create a new form as shown in the preceding example, but to mistakenly end with MyForm.Show instead of MyDynamicallyCreatedForm.Show. In this case a form is still displayed (because MyForm is both an object and a class), but the newly created MyDynamicallyCreatedForm drifts off into memory, abandoned.

Another limitation with this technique is that you have to work extra hard if you want to create multiple forms that are similar, but not entirely identical. For example, in the word processing application we discussed earlier, you might want to have a slightly customized interface for editing XML documents. To accomplish this, you have to write some code that identifies the type of form you're trying to create and changes the interface accordingly.

The .NET Way: Forms as Classes

In Visual Basic .NET, forms are classes. If you try to write `MyForm.Show()`, you'll get an error. This is because MyForm is a class, but Show is an instance method, which means that it's only valid for the objects you create out of that class. On its own, without an object, an instance method can't do anything. (This is different from shared methods, which provide some functions that you can use without creating an object. For example, the MessageBox class we looked at in Chapter 3 has a shared Show method, which means that you can display the message without going through the work of creating a MessageBox object.)

The only valid way to create an object is by using the form you've defined, as shown here:

```
' VB .NET code to create and show a form.
Dim MyFormObject As New MyForm()
MyFormObject.Show()
```

This example saves a line by using the New keyword in the declaration of MyFormObject. If it didn't, you'd need to add `MyFormObject = New MyForm()` to initialize the form before it could be used. Otherwise you'd get a "null reference" error indicating that MyForm is uninitialized.

TIP *There is one time that you don't need to explicitly create a form. That's when you make it the startup object for your project. In this case, Visual Basic will automatically create an object, based on your form, and display it.*

The form creation process in Visual Basic .NET is very similar to dynamic form creation in Visual Basic 6. It protects us from the potential "null reference" error I pointed out earlier, but it doesn't allow us much more flexibility when it comes to tailoring dynamic forms—or does it? To answer this question, we have to peer under the hood of a form class.

Form Inheritance

As in Visual Basic 6, every .NET form comes with some built-in capabilities. If you look at the code that makes up a custom form class, you'll find out why. Every form begins with lines like this:

```
Public Class HelloForm
    Inherits System.Windows.Forms.Form
```

In other words, your form inherits all the features of a prebuilt Form class that can be found in the System.Windows.Forms namespace. *Inheritance* allows an object to access the features of another class. This means that your form gets the basic functions that it needs in order to look and act like a form from System. Windows.Forms.Form. In addition, it possesses other features all its own (depending on the controls you've added). The hierarchy is shown in Figure 4-15.

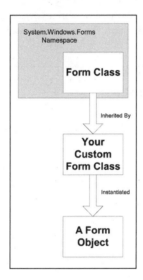

Figure 4-15: Form inheritance

I've simplified the relationships a bit here. In fact, the System.Windows. Forms.Form class itself inherits qualities from other, more basic classes in the .NET class library.

Modal Forms

The preceding example uses the Show method, which displays a *non-modal* form. Quite simply, a non-modal form is one that doesn't disable other forms in your application. This means that a user can still access different windows and enter information into them. Sometimes, non-modal forms have to be built with custom communication and refresh routines, which allow them to update themselves in response to changes in other currently open forms. Interaction between different forms is examined a little later in this chapter.

Some parts of an application's interface are, by convention, *modal*. For example, About windows, Open/Save windows, and Preferences windows are always modal. Once a modal window appears, the user cannot access any other part of the application until the window has been dealt with and closed. (Usually, the user does this by entering or selecting any necessary information, and then clicking OK or Cancel.)

To create a modal form in Visual Basic 6, you used the Show method with a special parameter. In Visual Basic .NET, you use the ShowDialog method instead:

```
Dim MyFormObject As New MyForm()
MyFormObject.ShowDialog()
```

Visual Basic 6 Forms "Under the Hood"

In Visual Basic 6, every form is stored in a file with the extension .frm, and any binary information (pictures, for example) is stored in a corresponding file with a .frx extension. If you've ever opened a .frm file in a text editor, you've seen information like this:

```
Begin VB.Form frmHello
    Caption         =   "Hello World Program"
    ClientHeight    =   3195
    ClientLeft      =   60
    ClientTop       =   345
    ClientWidth     =   4680
    LinkTopic       =   "frmHello"
    ScaleHeight     =   3195
    ScaleWidth      =   4680
    StartUpPosition =   3  'Windows Default
    Begin VB.CommandButton cmdQuit
        Caption     =   "Quit"
        Height      =   495
        Left        =   1440
        TabIndex    =   1
        Top         =   2520
        Width       =   1815
    End
    Begin VB.Label lblHello
        Caption     =   "Hello World (of Visual Basic 6)!"
        Height      =   495
        Left        =   1080
        TabIndex    =   0
        Top         =   960
        Width       =   2535
    End
End
```

```
Attribute VB_Name = "Form1"
Attribute VB_GlobalNameSpace = False
Attribute VB_Creatable = False
Attribute VB_PredeclaredId = True
Attribute VB_Exposed = False
Option Explicit

Private Sub cmdQuit_Click()
    Unload Me
End Sub
```

This code was generated when I created the simple "Hello World" form shown here in Figure 4-16, with a label control and a Quit button.

Figure 4-16: A basic VB 6 form

If you've never looked at your code before, it might come as a bit of a surprise. At the end of this file is all the Visual Basic event handler code that you created (in the preceding example it's just the Click event handler for the cmdQuit button). But before that is a great deal of information that sets the properties and position of all the interface elements in your program. This code resembles Visual Basic code somewhat, but closer examination shows that it's actually sort of a strange hybrid. For example, controls are defined with a Begin VB.Label lblHello statement, which follows the C style of syntax by indicating the type of element to be created (VB.Label), followed by the name of the item (lblHello). More significantly, though this code is clearly present and accessible, it's not provided anywhere inside the Visual Basic IDE.

The "code" in a VB 6 .frm file is untouchable, because there is no guarantee that your changes won't break it. If you want to modify your user interface, you have to do it manually, using the built-in Form Designer. Usually, this is the most convenient option; however, every once in a while a problem appears that could easily be solved by tweaking a few values if you have direct access to the form file. Instead, these changes always require time-consuming manual repositioning or resizing.

Visual Basic .NET handles this kind of situation quite a bit differently.

Visual Basic .NET Forms "Under the Hood"

Every Visual Basic .NET file has the extension .vb, whether it is a form, a class, or a module. When you create a form, VB .NET creates a corresponding class with prebuilt infrastructure code. This code is similar to the code in the .frm file we looked at earlier, except that it's valid Visual Basic code. It's also provided right inside the IDE, in the form's InitializeComponent procedure. This infrastructure code is automatically contained in a Region labeled "Windows Form Designer generated code," which is collapsed by default so you won't see it while you write your program (Figure 4-17).

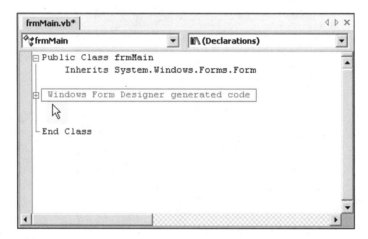

Figure 4-17: The location of the concealed form code

This code frees Visual Basic from its dependence on the IDE. Visual Basic code is now pure Visual Basic code, and can be created with nothing more than a text editor. For most of your life, you'll want to stay away from this prebuilt infrastructure code, because it can quickly grow into a large amount of unimportant boilerplate. Generally, the Windows Forms engine provides the easiest way for you to configure your interface.

However, if you're an advanced user, you may find that going behind the scenes to see how Visual Basic creates your interface not only provides some interesting information, but also allows you to perform some otherwise time-consuming rearrangements just by modifying a few automatically generated values. For example, if you've been forced to adopt a new naming convention, you can quickly change all the names of your interface elements with a simple Find and Replace operation in your code display. In other words, you *won't* need to click on each control in the Form Designer and manually make the change to the Name property through the Properties window.

Stepping Through the "Muck and Goo"

Some developers refer to this portion of the Visual Basic code as "muck and goo" (and others have likely invented less flattering euphemisms). Once you learn to understand it, however, you'll gain a unique programming edge, and a better understanding of the .NET framework.

In the sample .frm file shown earlier, I showed the code that would be needed for a simple "Hello World" form. In Visual Basic .NET, the same window would create code like this:

```
Friend WithEvents lblHello As System.Windows.Forms.Label
Friend WithEvents cmdQuit As System.Windows.Forms.Button

'Required by the Windows Form Designer
Private components As System.ComponentModel.Container

'NOTE: The following procedure is required by the Windows Form Designer
'It can be modified using the Windows Form Designer.
'Do not modify it using the code editor.
<System.Diagnostics.DebuggerStepThrough()> Private Sub InitializeComponent()
    Me.lblHello = New System.Windows.Forms.Label()
    Me.cmdQuit = New System.Windows.Forms.Button()
    Me.SuspendLayout()
    '
    'lblHello
    '
    Me.lblHello.Location = New System.Drawing.Point(80, 40)
    Me.lblHello.Name = "lblHello"
    Me.lblHello.Size = New System.Drawing.Size(208, 40)
    Me.lblHello.TabIndex = 1
    Me.lblHello.Text = "Hello World"
    '
    'cmdQuit
    '
    Me.cmdQuit.Location = New System.Drawing.Point(128, 264)
    Me.cmdQuit.Name = "cmdQuit"
    Me.cmdQuit.Size = New System.Drawing.Size(80, 40)
    Me.cmdQuit.TabIndex = 0
    Me.cmdQuit.Text = "Exit"
    '
    'HelloForm
    '
    Me.AutoScaleBaseSize = New System.Drawing.Size(5, 13)
    Me.ClientSize = New System.Drawing.Size(440, 373)
    Me.Controls.AddRange(New Control() {Me.lblHello, Me.cmdQuit})
    Me.Name = "HelloForm"
    Me.Text = "Hello World Program"
```

(continued on next page)

```
Me.ResumeLayout(False)

End Sub
```

Notice that I've left out two prebuilt methods, New and Dispose. The New method calls the InitializeComponent method shown here, and it can also be used for your own initialization. The New method is similar to the Initialize event in Visual Basic 6, but it takes place before the form has been created and displayed.

Looking at this code, you can make the following observations:

- Every control is defined as a variable in a form. The special Friend keyword is used, which means that other forms in your program can access these controls.

- All these controls are initialized in a special InitializeComponent subroutine that is called automatically when the form is loaded. This subroutine has a special attribute (the text enclosed in the < > brackets) that tells Visual Studio how to treat the code during debugging.

- The properties of each control are set in separate blocks, each identified with a comment indicating the control name.

- All the controls are added to the form at once with the Me.Controls. AddRange statement. The Me keyword represents the current form, which has a Controls property that represents all the controls it contains.

- At the end of the InitializeComponent subroutine, some additional properties are set for the current form.

Perhaps the most useful thing you can do once you understand the infra-structure code is to copy and paste parts of a user interface from one form to another. With the Form Designer, you have to manually select the correct con-trols—and positioning them on another form can be tricky. If you understand the muck and goo, however, it's just a matter of copying text.

What About Binary Information?

Not all information can be represented in code. For example, you might load a picture into a picture box, a form, or an image list at design time. When you do this, Visual Basic .NET stores the appropriate information in a resource file, and then writes the code needed to read the information from that file. As with Visual Basic 6, each form can have a resource file, but instead of having the extension .frx, every VB .NET resource file ends with .resx.

In this case, what you don't know probably won't cause you any problems. You can remain blissfully unaware of the whole coding process, and Visual Basic .NET will take care of the details for you automatically, even compiling the resource file into your final executable. In fact, .resx files are contained in your project, but hidden by default (Figure 4-18). To display them, select Project • Show All Files. Now you can expand each .vb form file in the Solution Explorer and see the corresponding .resx file.

Figure 4-18: Hidden files in the form oddities project

Handling Control Events

An event handler allows you to respond to notifications from a control. To chose a control event to handle, select the control from the control list in the code display window; then select the appropriate event from the list on the right (see Figure 4-19).

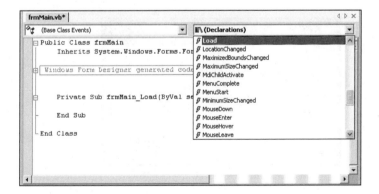

Figure 4-19: Creating an event handler

TIP *Don't despair if you can't find the events for your form object. Remember, all the code you are writing is inside the form class. To access its events, you have to choose Base Class Events from the drop-down control list.*

Here is a sample event handler for a button's Click event:

```
Private Sub Button1_Click(ByVal sender As System.Object, _
  ByVal e As System.EventArgs) Handles Button1.Click
    ' Do something here.
End Sub
```

All Visual Basic .NET event handlers look pretty much the same—another valuable break from Visual Basic tradition, in which every event had its own unique collection of parameters. This new uniformity allows you to write event handlers that can deal with more than one type of event, and guarantees that you'll know the correct standard to use when creating and handling events.

The .NET convention for events states that they must have two parameters. One, called *sender*, provides a reference to the object that sends the event. The advantage here is that you can always examine the *sender* parameter to find out where the event originated. The other parameter, called *e*, is an object that bundles together any additional information that you need from the event. Different events may differ slightly in that they will use different objects for *e*, depending on their needs. The default event style, which is used for a button's Click event, doesn't require any additional information, and so it sends an empty *e* object.

On the other hand, the MouseMove event does include important extra information: the current coordinates of the mouse pointer. In the following example (see Figure 4-20), the event handler retrieves and displays this information.

```
Private Sub frmMouseTracker_MouseMove(ByVal sender As Object, ByVal e As _
    System.Windows.Forms.MouseEventArgs) Handles MyBase.MouseMove
    lblPosition.Text = "The mouse is at X: " & e.X & " Y:" & e.Y
End Sub
```

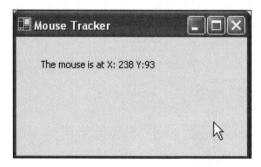

Figure 4-20: Tracking the mouse

Handling More Than One Event

Another profound change in Visual Basic .NET is the way that an event handler works with multiple different controls. In Visual Basic 6, you had to create a control array. Then, each time an event was called for one of the controls in the array, you would be provided with an index number that identified the control that sent the event. This system did a nice job of letting you reuse code, but it had some quirks, which you may have encountered if you've ever had to re-index individual controls.

In VB .NET, an event handler is connected to an event through the Handles keyword, which appears at the end of the definition. By default, functions use VB 6 naming conventions, so a Click event for Button1 is named Button1_Click. However, Button1_Click is only a name, and you can change it, or modify the name of the control it works with, without causing any problem. This is because the actual link between an event and a control is specified explicitly with the Handles keyword.

One advantage of this system is that it's easy to create event handlers that work with more than one control. All you have to do is add their names to the Handles clause. Consider our next example (see Figure 4-21), which receives Click events from three different buttons, and examines the *sender* object to find out where the event occurred:

```
Private Sub ClickHandler (ByVal sender As System.Object, _
  ByVal e As System.EventArgs) Handles cmdA.Click, cmdB.Click, cmdC.Click
    Dim ctrl As Control

    ' Convert the unidentified sender object to a more useful form.
    ctrl = CType(sender, Control)

    MessageBox.Show "You clicked the button called " & ctrl.Name
End Sub
```

Notice that before this code can use the *sender* object, it has to convert it into a recognized type. In this case, we could convert the *sender* object to the Button class, but instead we use the more generic Control class, which supports some basic properties that are shared by all controls. This includes the Name property. If the code didn't make the conversion, and tried to use the *sender* object directly, it would cause an error, because the System.Object class only supports a few basic operations.

Figure 4-21: A generic event handler

Adding Controls Dynamically

A common question from Visual Basic programmers is how to add controls to a form *dynamically*—in other words, while the program is running. For example, you might want to create a diagramming program that allows users to drag and drop various symbols onto a form. Rather than manually painting the individual graphics, a better way to handle this problem is to use button or picture controls. With this technique, you can easily move pictures using their properties, and let the Windows operating system worry about painting the form in such a way that the existing controls aren't overwritten. This approach also allows you to easily capture mouse clicks, and allow the user to drag and move your icons after they have been placed.

In Visual Basic .NET, the distinction between controls added at run time and those added at design time has been blurred. All the controls that you add using the Windows Form Designer are really created by the code in the InitializeComponent routine when your form is first loaded. This code looks almost exactly the same as the code you would use to add a control later in a program's execution. The only difference is its location in your program.

Thus, one easy way to dynamically add a control is to add it at design time and configure its properties. Then, find the corresponding automatically generated code, and cut and paste it into another method. Be aware that this code may exist at several different places in the Windows Designer code region.

Examine the following infrastructure code, which is used to create a new label:

```
' The declaration in the class:
Friend WithEvents Label1 As System.Windows.Forms.Label

' From the InitializeComponent subroutine:
Private Sub InitializeComponent
    Me.Label1.Location = New System.Drawing.Point(96, 100)
    Me.Label1.Name = "Label1"
    Me.Label1.Size = New System.Drawing.Size(112, 48)
    Me.Label1.Text = "Permanent label"
    ' (Code for other controls has been left out.)
    Me.Controls.AddRange(New Control(){Me.Button1}, Me.Label1)
End Sub
```

This code, with some minor modifications, could be inserted into a button's Click event to create the label dynamically, as shown in our next example. There are two significant changes. First, the Controls.AddRange method, which adds a whole group of controls from an array, has been replaced with the Controls.Add method, which adds only a single control. Secondly, the declaration for the label has been changed to a Dim statement, because the Friend and WithEvents keywords are not valid inside a subroutine.

```
Private Sub Button1_Click(ByVal sender As System.Object, _
   ByVal e As System.EventArgs) Handles Button1.Click

    Dim LabelNew As System.Windows.Forms.Label
    Me.LabelNew.Location = New System.Drawing.Point(96, 200)
    Me.LabelNew.Name = "LabelNew"
    Me.LabelNew.Size = New System.Drawing.Size(112, 48)
    Me.LabelNew.Text = "Dynamically created label"
    Me.Controls.Add(LabelNew)

End Sub
```

This code does have a couple of drawbacks, however. For one thing, the control variable is created inside the button's Click event, so it is destroyed as soon as the Click event is over. Does this mean that the control itself disappears? In fact, the control remains, but it's a little bit more difficult to access. The only way you can reach it is through the Controls property of your form (with `MyForm.Controls("LabelNew")`, for instance), which contains a collection of *all* the controls on the form. A better solution is to use your own collection for groups of dynamically added controls. To use your own collection, add this line to your form class:

```
Private DynamicControls As Collection
```

Then use the following line to add a reference to your label, and then store it:

```
DynamicControls.Add(LabelNew)
```

Of course, if you are creating a control that you won't need to access again, these lines aren't necessary.

Dynamic Event Hookup

Alternatively, you might be adding a control whose prime purpose is receiving events (such as a button control). In this case, you may not need to explicitly keep track of the control, but you do need a way to receive its events. Unfortunately, controls that are created at run time can't be defined with the With-Events keyword. Even if they could, it wouldn't help you; all WithEvents really does is make it easy for you to write event handlers by choosing the appropriate control and event in the code display window.

You can solve this problem by dynamically "wiring up" a new control at run time with the special AddHandler statement. Consider the following example, which adds a new button at a random location, and sets it to use the same event handler as the first button. Every time you click on this button, you add a new button which, when clicked, adds yet another new button.

```
Private Sub Button1_Click(ByVal sender As System.Object, _
  ByVal e As System.EventArgs) Handles Button1.Click

    ' Create a random number generator for choosing the new button's position.
    Dim Rand As New Random()

    ' Generate and configure the new button.
    Dim NewButton As System.Windows.Forms.Button
    NewButton = New System.Windows.Forms.Button()
    NewButton.Left = Rand.Next(Me.Width)
    NewButton.Top = Rand.Next(Me.Height)
    NewButton.Size = New System.Drawing.Size(88, 28)
    NewButton.Text = "New Button"

    ' Add the button to the form.
    Me.Controls.Add(NewButton)

    ' Wire up the new button's Click event.
    AddHandler NewButton.Click, AddressOf Button1_Click

End Sub
```

To see this random button reproduction in action, try out the DynamicRandomButtons sample program (Figure 4-22).

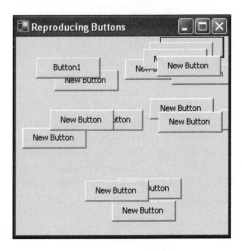

Figure 4-22: Buttons that spawn other buttons

Assigning dynamic event handlers is another technique that you can use to replace control arrays.

Interaction Between Forms

Every form in Visual Basic .NET is created manually, based on a form class. You *cannot* access a form by using its class name. For example, you could create a form class called Form1 using the following code:

```
Dim Form1 As New MainForm()
Form1.Show()
```

However, you could not access the form later using the class name MainForm:

```
MainForm.Hide()   ' Won't work.
```

Similarly, you couldn't use code like this from another form:

```
strName = MainForm.txtName.Text
```

Instead, you would need to keep the form variable stored somewhere. In simple situations, this isn't required. For example, consider a preferences window that allows your user to configure some basic options and then click OK or Cancel. No other windows or code modules need to communicate with this window. When the user clicks the OK or Cancel button, the code inside the event handler just uses the Me keyword to refer to the current instance (as in Me.Close). Ideally, this will be the way that all your forms work, minimizing interaction and making your windows more self-sufficient.

However, in some cases, you may need to read a value directly from another form. In these cases, you have to use a variable that refers to the form. For example, Visual Basic .NET automatically launches the first window in your program when you run the program. The result is that you have a form, but no variable to use to access it from another form's code.

Consider an example where the automatically loaded form (called Main) presents a list of information that can be edited in a second form (called Edit-Info). The second form needs to call the custom Refresh subroutine in the Main form so that it can update its display accordingly, but it has no way to do so.

To solve this problem, you could change your project options so that your program is started in a module, with a Main subroutine. This module could retain the form variable and make it globally accessible, as shown here:

```
Public Module Startup
    Public frmMain As Form    ' Can be accessed in your app as Startup.frmMain
    Public Sub Main()
        frmMain = New MainPolicyForm()
        frmMain.Show()
    End Sub
End Module
```

Another solution would be to add code into the form's load event handler that automatically sets the global form variable with the current instance of the form:

```
Public Class MainPolicyForm
    ' (Windows Designer code left out.)

    Public Sub Form_Load(ByVal sender As System.Object, _
     ByVal e As System.EventArgs) Handles MainPolicyForm.Load
        ' Set the reference so others can access this form.
        Startup.frmMain = Me
    End Sub

End Class
```

Dialog Windows

Dialog windows offer another way to communicate basic information. The MessageBox object is a special kind of built-in dialog window. You choose the options you need, display them in the window, and then examine the user's choices through the convenient return value:

```
Dim Result As DialogResult
Result = MessageBox.Show("Is this a yes or no question?", _
                         "Question", MessageBoxButtons.YesNo)

If Result = DialogResult.Yes Then
    ' The user clicked Yes.
Else
    ' The user clicked No.
End If
```

A custom Windows form isn't this convenient. You can display the window, but you then have to rely on global variables, or check the state of other variables in the form to find out what choices the user had made.

Visual Basic .NET provides a new model for dialog windows that lets you get simple results from a custom form without needing to maintain extra variables. It also gives you the ability to put code where it belongs rather than scattering it among various event handlers. This method won't help you if you must have complex or detailed information returned from a window, but if all you need is a simple Yes or No, your code will be cleaner and more standardized than it could have been in the past.

A good example of a dialog window is a custom confirmation window. For example, you may have an email feature in your application that allows the user to send you a purchase order. Before sending the order, a confirmation window might display additional information and ask whether or not the user wants to proceed. In reality, this window does very little (besides giving your users the chance to double-check their data). Essentially, it displays some information, and then closes when the user clicks OK or Cancel. However, you also need a special control or format to display the required information, so you can't use the typical MessageBox object.

To solve this problem select the OK button, and set the DialogResult property to OK. This is the value that will be returned from your window automatically if the user clicks this button. Now select the Cancel button, and set the DialogResult property to Cancel. There's no need to write any extra code, or even to add an event handler. Once the user clicks one of these buttons, Visual Basic .NET will automatically close the form and return the result to you.

The code for displaying your custom confirmation window will look something like this:

```
Dim Result As DialogResult
Dim frmConfirm As New ConfirmationForm()
Result = frmConfirm.ShowDialog()

If Result = DialogResult.OK Then
    ' The user clicked your OK button.
Else
    ' The user clicked your Cancel button.
End If
```

If necessary, you can add additional code to the button event handlers to store extra information on the form, and you can check those variables from within your calling code. Keep in mind that even after the window is closed, the form object remains in memory, along with all its information, until the form variable goes out of scope.

The dialog model is extremely convenient. However, it may not work for more complicated scenarios—for example, when a user has a variety of different options that aren't covered by the preset DialogResult variables.

Owned Forms

Visual Basic .NET introduces the concept of *owned forms*. An owned form belongs to another form. When the owner window is minimized, all of its owned forms are also minimized automatically. When an owned form overlaps its owner, it is always displayed on top. Owned forms are usually used for floating toolbox and command windows. One example of an owned form is the Find and Replace window in Microsoft Word.

Any form can own another form, and you don't need to set up the relationship at design time. Instead, you just set the Owner property, as shown here:

```
' Show the main window.
Dim MainForm As New frmMainForm()
MainForm.Show()

' Create and display an owned form.
Dim SearchForm As New frmSearchForm()
SearchForm.Owner = MainForm
SearchForm.Show()
```

MDI Interfaces

An MDI (Multiple Document Interface) program is generally based on a single parent window that can contain numerous child windows (see Figure 4-23). Usually, this model is used to allow a user to work with more than one document at a time. (A document might be a report, a data grid, a log, a text listing, or something entirely different.)

Any window can become an MDI parent (container) if you set the IsMdi-Container property to True. Many of the restrictions that were placed on MDI parents in previous versions of Visual Basic have now been lifted. For example, parent windows can now contain regular controls, such as buttons, along with the standard menus and command bars. This makes it possible to create a wide variety of bizarre forms that look nothing like a conventional window should. For respectable interfaces, an MDI parent should contain only dockable controls, such as status bars and menu bars, which latch onto an edge of the window and provide a clear working area for any child windows.

Turning a window into an MDI child is similar to making it an owned form.

```
Private Sub NewChild(ByVal sender As System.Object, _
  ByVal e As System.EventArgs) Handles cmdNewChild.Click
    Dim frmChild As New DateForm()
    frmChild.MdiParent = Me
    frmChild.Show()
End Sub
```

Figure 4-23: MDI children are locked inside MDI parents

Of course, at the end of this subroutine, the frmChild variable will be lost, and you won't be able to use it to access the MDI child. However, MDI forms include some extra conveniences that make them easy to work with, and free you from manually keeping track of forms. Every MDI parent has a special MdiChildren collection, which contains all of the currently opened MDI forms. Every MDI parent also has an ActiveMdiChild property, which tells you which child window currently has focus. This allows the following kind of information exchange:

```
' This code is in the MDI child class.
Public Sub RefreshData()
    ' Some code here to update the window display.
End Sub

Private Sub InfoChanged(ByVal sender As System.Object, _
  ByVal e As System.EventArgs) Handles cmdRefresh.Click
    ' Calls a function in the parent.
    CType(Me.MdiParent, ParentForm).RefreshAllChildren()
End Sub
```

Note that in order to call the RefreshAllChildren subroutine, the code needs to convert the reference to the MDI parent form into the appropriate form class. Otherwise, you'll only be able to access the standard form properties and methods through the reference, not the custom ones you may have added to the class.

The RefreshAllChildren subroutine is found in the parent:

```
' This code is in the MDI parent class.
Public Sub RefreshAllChildren()
    Dim frmChild As DateForm
    For Each frmChild in Me.MdiChildren
        If Not Me.MdiChildren Is Me.ActiveMdiChild
            frmChild.RefreshData()
        End If
    Next
End Sub
```

This form has an extra feature that determines whether an MDI child is the one that called it, and doesn't bother to call the refresh procedure if it is. The reasoning here is that the active MDI child will already be up-to-date, as it is the one that originated the refresh request. Of course, the real reason I've included this code is to demonstrate the ActiveMdiChild property. Notice that the code uses the Is statement, instead of an equals sign, to compare the forms. This is because both forms are objects (reference types), which cannot be compared with an equals sign.

To see this logic in action, try out the MDIForms project, which automatically refreshes all windows when you click a button in any one of the child forms (see Figure 4-24).

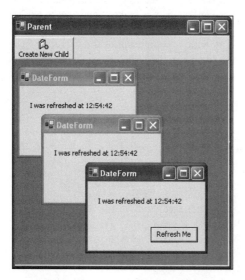

Figure 4-24: Coordinated child forms

A Gallery of VB .NET Controls

So far this chapter hasn't described the individual controls that you can work with. For the most part, there is no need to—most of these controls are similar to those provided in earlier versions of Visual Basic, and are fairly straightforward, with similar sets of properties, events, and methods. The basic controls, including Button, TextBox, CheckBox, PictureBox, RadioButton, and Label, are almost unchanged. The only obvious difference is that controls that display text now always have a Text property. (For some controls, Visual Basic 6 used a Caption property instead.)

A few other select changes are highlighted in the following sections. Some controls are discussed in later chapters (for example, the printing controls are featured in Chapter 8, the DataGrid control is discussed in Chapter 9, and the Timer control makes an appearance in Chapter 10).

List Controls

The traditional ListBox and ComboBox controls continue on in Visual Basic .NET, along with a CheckedListBox control. This control provides a special CheckedItems collection that contains the selected items. It allows you to check for specific checked items, as follows:

```
' Display all the checked items.
Dim i As Integer
For i = 0 To MyCheckedList.CheckedItems.Count - 1
    lblDisplay.Text &= MyCheckedList.CheckedItems(i)
Next i

' Check if a specified item is checked.
If MyCheckedList.CheckedItems.Contains("Paper Bag") = True Then
    lblDisplay.Text = "Paper Bag is checked."
End If
```

One nice addition to list-based programming is that you can now databind a simple array to a list control. This can save you from typing a few extra lines of code, or from using a For/Next loop.

```
Dim FoodChoices() As String = {"squash", "banana", "lentils", "salt"}
lstFood.DataSource = FoodChoices
```

Keep in mind, however, that once you bind an array, you can't directly add or remove items from the listbox. To get around this limitation, you can just copy the array into the listbox, with the help of the new AddRange method.

```
Dim FoodChoices() As String = {"squash", "banana", "lentils", "salt"}
lstFood.Items.AddRange(FoodChoices)
```

Finally, you can also use the NumericUpDown and DomainUpDown controls to provide similar list functions. For example, DomainUpDown typically provides a small series of different preset options. The user can move from one option to another using the included up-arrow and down-arrow buttons.

Organization Controls

The GroupBox, a traditional Visual Basic control for assembling other controls, is still available in .NET. Along with it is the Panel control, a versatile control that automatically supports scrolling and dock padding, as described earlier in this chapter. A Panel can have a border, but does not require one. Unlike the Group-Box, it has no Text property, and therefore cannot have an associated caption.

Other organization controls are quite straightforward. You'll find TabControl extremely easy to use. The Splitter control was discussed earlier in this chapter. The HScrollBar and VScrollBar controls have really just remained for the sake of backward compatibility; they have little to offer the .NET world, which supports automatic scrollbars in most controls, and offers the AutoScroll property for forms and panels.

Menu Controls

Menu controls haven't changed much, although they now have a new designer that allows you to type in menu items without needing to use a separate window (see Figure 4-25). You can use the Properties window to configure the properties for each menu item.

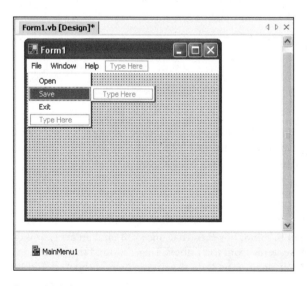

Figure 4-25: Designing a menu

I won't bother to walk you through this process, as it is very intuitive. However, one change that you need to be aware of is that context menus (the kind that appear when a control is right-clicked) are no longer taken from a form's main menu. Instead, you now add a separate ContextMenu control for each context menu. To edit a context menu, click to select the corresponding ContextMenu control from the component tray. The menu will appear at the top as though it were a normal drop-down menu, except that you'll be able to edit it as needed.

Modern Controls

The modern controls include many of the hallmarks of Windows application design, including the ListView and TreeView controls (as featured in Windows Explorer), the common ToolBar and StatusBar controls, and the ImageList control, which stores pictures and icons that you can use in all the other modern controls. These controls work much the same way as they did in Visual Basic 6. The most obvious change is that they now sport new, enhanced designers that allow you to configure their collections (of list items, tree nodes, buttons, or pictures) without writing a line of code (see Figure 4-26). One minor difference that might throw you off is that modern controls are now all 0-based. This means, for example, that the first element in a collection of list items is always at position 0 in the collection.

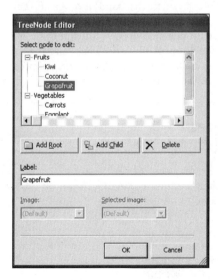

Figure 4-26: The TreeView node designer

The NotifyIcon Control

At last, Visual Basic provides an easy way to add and use a system tray icon. All you need to do is place the NotifyIcon control on your component tray, and associate an appropriate icon. The icon will appear immediately when the form is displayed (Figure 4-27), and will disappear when the form is unloaded.

Figure 4-27: A system tray icon

A more useful way to use the NotifyIcon control is by creating it in code. This allows you to use an application-wide system tray icon even when no corresponding forms are visible. For example, you might have a utility application that loads an icon onto the system tray when it starts, but displays no other user interface. Instead, it might linger in the background performing periodic tasks automatically, or allow you to display forms or choose functions from a context menu when you need them.

The following example is exactly that kind of program. The startup object for the project is the Main subroutine of the App module, not a form, so no windows are displayed. Instead, a system tray icon and the required context menu elements are created manually in code. Then, all the program needs to do is wait for a context-menu click. If the user clicks Exit, the program ends, and if the user clicks Show Clock the current time is displayed.

```
Public Module App
    Public AppIcon As New NotifyIcon()
    Public SysTrayMenu As New ContextMenu()

    ' Our menu items are defined using WithEvents to receive the Click event.
    Public WithEvents DisplayClock As New MenuItem("Show Clock")
    Public WithEvents ExitApp As New MenuItem("Exit")

    Public Sub Main()

        ' Assign an icon from a file.
        Dim ico As New Icon("c:\myicon.ico")
        AppIcon.Icon = ico

        ' Place the menu items in the menu.
        SysTrayMenu.MenuItems.Add(DisplayClock)
        SysTrayMenu.MenuItems.Add(ExitApp)
        AppIcon.ContextMenu = SysTrayMenu
```

```
        ' Set the tooltip text.
        AppIcon.Text = "My .NET Application"

        ' Show the system tray icon.
        AppIcon.Visible = True

        ' Because no forms are being displayed, you need this
        ' statement to stop the application from automatically ending.
        Application.Run()
    End Sub

    Public Sub ExitApp_Click(ByVal sender As Object, _
     ByVal e As System.EventArgs) Handles ExitApp.Click
        Application.Exit()
    End Sub

    Public Sub DisplayClock_Click(ByVal sender As Object, _
     ByVal e As System.EventArgs) Handles DisplayClock.Click
        MessageBox.Show(Date.Now.ToString, "Date", MessageBoxButtons.OK)
    End Sub

End Module
```

The possible uses for an application like this are countless. For example, you could create a task-logging program that records the amount of time spent on each project. All you would need to do is "punch in" and "punch out" on the system tray icon menu. The program would then take care of writing the appropriate information to a file or database.

Providers

Providers extend the properties of other controls on the current form. For example, to add a tooltip to a button, just drag a ToolTipProvider onto the component tray, and modify the corresponding ToolTip property for the button control. You can also tweak various ToolTipProvider properties to configure global tooltip settings, such as how many milliseconds your program will wait before showing the tooltip, or how long the tooltip will remain displayed if the user doesn't move the mouse. Usually, however, the default settings are best.

TIP *Remember that tooltips should be reserved for graphical controls such as toolbar buttons, not label controls or ordinary buttons.*

HelpProvider
Another provider is HelpProvider, which allows you to add context-sensitive help to every control through the SetHelpNamespace property (which specifies the help file) and the SetHelpKeyword property (which specifies the topic, or uses a built-in value to show the contents tab or index tab). Most applications use form-specific help, and only set these properties for the form.

Visual Basic .NET's help features now support the HTML Help standard (.CHM files), and allow you to specify a help string right in your program for use in a simple pop-up message. In order to use this text string instead of a help file, use the SetHelpString method, and leave the HelpNamespace property empty.

Dialog Box Controls

Dialog box controls allow you to display standard Windows dialog boxes, such as those for font or color selection. These controls really don't need to be added to the component tray, as it is more intuitive to define them in your code just before you display them, as shown here:

```
Dim dlgFile As New OpenFileDialog()
dlgFile.InitialDirectory = "c:\"
dlgFile.Filter = "txt files (*.txt)|*.txt|All files (*.*)|*.*"
dlgFile.FilterIndex = 2

' Here the code shows the dialog in the same line that it checks the result.
' This trick means that you don't need to declare a separate results variable.
If dlgFile.ShowDialog() = DialogResult.OK Then
    ' You can now open the selected file, which is dlgFile.FileName.
End If
```

Notice that you no longer have to perform error trapping to determine whether a user has clicked the OK button or the Cancel button. Instead, you use the familiar DialogResult object discussed earlier in this chapter.

More information about using the print dialog controls is included in Chapter 8.

Windows XP and Visual Styles

By this point, you have probably noticed that all the screenshots in this book are taken using Windows XP, which automatically applies a new appearance to the non-client region (the form border and title bar) of all windows. If this annoys you, Windows XP makes it easy to disable these new Visual Styles, and return to the traditional Windows look.

By default, when you create a .NET application it will have the Windows XP window border, but it won't use the Windows XP styles in its client region. That means that buttons, checkboxes, and other user interface elements will be trapped in the past, and won't have the new colored look.

You can enable Windows XP Visual Styles for the controls in your application, but it requires a little bit of grunt work. Essentially, you need to create a special *manifest file* for your application, and place it in the same directory as your executable. This manifest always has the name of your exe file, with the .manifest extension added on the end. Note that the .exe extension is also retained, so if you are creating MyApp.exe, the manifest file *must* be called MyApp.exe.manifest.

This file can be created using Notepad. Its role is to declare that your application has shown an interest in the new version of the Comctl32.dll file, and is hoping to use it to apply Visual Styles. If your application is not running on a Windows XP computer, this request will be harmlessly ignored, and the ordinary control appearance will remain.

The manifest file for an application called WindowsXPTest is shown below. I've highlighted the only portion that you will need to change in your own application. You can ignore the rest of the settings, as long as they are present.

```
<?xml version="1.0" encoding="UTF-8" standalone="yes"?>
<assembly xmlns="urn:schemas-microsoft-com:asm.v1" manifestVersion="1.0">
<assemblyIdentity
    version="1.0.0.0"
    processorArchitecture="X86"
    name="WindowsXPTest"
    type="win32" />

<dependency>
<dependentAssembly>
<assemblyIdentity
    type="win32"
    name="Microsoft.Windows.Common-Controls"
    version="6.0.0.0"
    processorArchitecture="X86"
    publicKeyToken="6595b64144ccf1df"
    language="*" />

</dependentAssembly>
</dependency>
</assembly>
```

You might recognize that this file uses an XML tag-based format (XML is discussed in Chapter 8). The only line that you really need to be concerned with is the line that specifies the name of your application.

Once you have created the manifest file, copy it into the bin subdirectory for your application. If you copy it into the main project directory, it won't work, because Visual Studio .NET creates the compiled .exe file in the bin directory when you are testing the application, and runs it from there.

By this point, you've accomplished most of the work, but you still need to make a few minor adjustments for button-style controls like Button, CheckBox, and RadioButton. These controls provide a FlatStyle property, which you must change from Standard to System in order for Windows XP to take over. The changes won't appear inside the Visual Studio .NET designer, but they will appear when you run the application. The differences are more noticeable in real life than in print, as the new controls use a special colorful shading (see Figure 4-28).

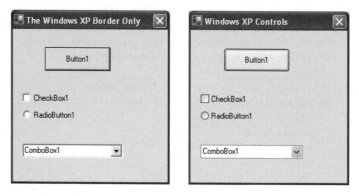

Figure 4-28: Enabling Windows XP visual styles

What Comes Next?

The future is bright for user interface programming with Windows Forms. All .NET languages share the same WinForm technology, which means that Microsoft won't be introducing new controls that are only available to developers using a certain language. In the past, Visual Basic developers have run into this kind of trouble, being denied new cutting-edge interface elements, such as special toolbars, until a C++ programmer could bundle them into an ActiveX object. But with the .NET platform, just as all languages share the same common run time, they also use the exact same user interface engine.

In the future, new third-party components and advanced user interface add-ins will start to appear for .NET. Right now, your best bet is to master the full-featured suite of controls bundled with Visual Basic .NET. Complete reference information for every control can be found in the class reference portion of the MSDN help feature, in the System.Windows.Forms namespace.

5

OBJECT-ORIENTED PROGRAMMING

Visual Basic first introduced support for object-oriented programming in version 4.0, and the response was varied. Some cutting-edge developers began to push forward with object-oriented concepts, using them to build sophisticated component-based programs that could scale to serve thousands of simultaneous users, while the rest of the developer community continued as it always had. As time went on, the group of object-oriented programmers grew larger, and most books about Visual Basic programming began to include at least some reference to its OOP features. With Visual Basic .NET these features are greatly expanded—in fact, they've swallowed the entire language!

If you want to do anything in .NET, you'll need to use objects. You create and manage files by using File and Directory objects, print out reports by using the Printer object, and interact with databases by using the DataSet and DataReader objects (as you'll discover in Chapter 9). In fact, in Visual Basic .NET *everything* is an object, whether you realize it at first or not. We had a glimpse of this in Chapter 3, which examined how fundamental Visual Basic .NET data types, such as arrays, strings, and even integers, are actually full-featured objects. In Chapter 4 the plot thickened with forms, which were also exposed as a special type of object. As this book continues, you'll learn how to create your own custom objects and use them for a variety of programming tasks. But before we can get there, we need a crash course in object-oriented programming. That's where this chapter comes in.

To make the best use of .NET objects, and to enhance your own applications, you should develop a good understanding of object-oriented concepts. You may have already learned how to use classes and objects with a previous version of Visual Basic. Even still, you'll probably want to read through the majority of this chapter and the next to put Visual Basic's new object-oriented features into context, and to get the big picture of the world of classes, interfaces, and object relationships.

New in .NET

Visual Basic .NET's enhanced OOP features are the most hotly anticipated part of the .NET release. For the first time, Visual Basic has all the hallmarks of a true object-oriented language. In this chapter, you'll see some of the following changes:

The Class Keyword

In the past, each class was placed in a separate file. Now, you can group your classes any way you want, as long as you place all classes inside declarations (for example, start with `Public Class MyClassName` and end with `End Class`).

No More Set Statement

It used to be that object assignment was done with a statement like this: `Set objMyData = New MyData`. Now VB .NET can recognize object operations automatically, and the Set statement is no longer supported.

It's Safe to Use the New Keyword

In previous versions of Visual Basic, using the New keyword in a Dim statement could get you into trouble by defining a dynamically creatable object that could spring to life at any moment, and just wouldn't stay dead. Now the syntax `Dim VarName As New ClassName` instructs Visual Basic to create and instantiate an object immediately, just as you would expect.

The Is Keyword

In VB .NET, you test whether two objects are the same by using the Is keyword (for example, `If objOne Is objTwo Then`), not the equals sign.

Constructors

You can now use constructors to preload information into a class in a single line, just as you can define and initialize variables at once.

Garbage Collection

Garbage collection replaces deterministic finalization. When you set an object to Nothing, it doesn't disappear until the next time the garbage collector runs, which means that you can't use a Class.Terminate event handler to do cleanup.

Introducing OOP!

Visual Basic is often accused of being a loosely structured language, and many VB developers lapse into an event-driven style of programming that scatters code fragments everywhere. If you want to write a program that has any chance of being extensible, reliable, and even fun to program, it's up to you to adopt a programming methodology—and none is nearly as powerful, or as natural to the way Windows works, as object-oriented programming.

I can't imagine anything in the past ten years that has so completely caught the imagination of developers as object-oriented programming. What started off as an obscure philosophy for "language nerds" has grown into a whole assortment of nifty, easy-to-use techniques that can transform a complex, bloated application into a happy collection of intercommunicating objects. Quite simply, object-oriented programming makes it easier to debug, enhance, and reuse parts of an application. What's more, object-oriented principles are the basis of core pieces of the Windows operating system—first with COM, and now with the .NET framework.

What Is Object-Oriented Programming?

One of the more intimidating aspects of object-oriented programming is the way its advocates tout it as a philosophy (or even a religion). To keep things straight, it's best to remind yourself that object-oriented programming really boils down to the best way to organize code. If you follow good object-oriented practices, you'll end up with a program that's easier to manage, enhance, and troubleshoot. But all these benefits are really the result of good organization.

The Problems with Traditional Structured Programming

Traditional structured programming divides a problem into two things: data, and the ways that you process it. The problem with structured programming is that unless you've put a lot of forethought into it, you'll probably end up with a program that has its functionality scattered in a number of different places.

Consider a simple database program for sales tracking that includes a basic search feature. Quite probably, at some point, you'll need to add the ability to search on slightly different criteria. If you're lucky, you've built your search routine out of a few general functions. Maybe you'll be really lucky, and your changes will be limited to one function. Now consider a more drastic upgrade. Maybe you need to add a logging feature that works whenever you access the database, or perhaps your organization has expanded from Access to Oracle and you now have to connect to an entirely new and unfamiliar type of database. Maybe you need to have your program provide different levels of access, to radically change the user interface, or to create a dozen different search variants that are largely similar, but slightly different. As you start to add these enhancements, you'll find yourself making changes that range over your entire program. If you've been very disciplined in the first place, the job will be easier. But by the end of the day, you'll probably end up with a collection of loosely related functions, blocks of code that are tightly linked to specific controls in specific windows, and pieces of database code scattered everywhere.

In other words, the more work you do with a structured program, the more it tends toward chaos. When bugs start to appear, you'll probably have no idea which part of the code they live in. And guess what happens when another programmer starts work on a similar program for inventory management? Don't even dream of trying to share your code. You both know that it will be more difficult to translate a routine into a usable form for another program than it will be to rewrite the code from scratch.

In Chapter 6 you'll see some examples that explain how object-oriented programming overcomes these disasters. But for now, it will help if you get a handle on how you can create an object in Visual Basic .NET.

First There Were Structures...

The precursor to objects was a programming time-saver called *structures*. (In earlier versions of Visual Basic, it was called *types*.) A structure is a way of grouping data together. For example, consider a case where you need to store several pieces of information about a person. You could create separate variables in your code to represent birth date, height, name, and taste in music. If you leave these variables separate, you've got a potential problem. Your code becomes more complicated, and it's not obvious that these separate variables have anything to do with each other. And if you have to work with information for more than one person at a time, you have to create a frightening pile of variables to keep track of all the information. It's likely that you'll soon make the mistake of changing the wrong person's age, forgetting to give someone a birth date, or misplacing their favorite CD collection.

A Very Simple Person Structure

To group this information together, we can create the following structure:

```
Public Structure Person
    Dim FirstName As String
    Dim LastName As String
    Dim BirthDate As Date
End Structure
```

Where can we place this code? In the Visual Basic 6 world, we were limited to the general declarations area, but in VB .NET we can put Public structures anywhere at the file or module level. (They can't be inside a function or a subroutine.) If we define a Private structure, we can put it inside the class or module where we want to use it.

Now we can create a Person object in some other place in our code, and set that Person's information like so:

```
Dim Lucy As Person
Lucy.FirstName = "Lucy"
Lucy.LastName = "Smith"
Lucy.BirthDate = DateTime.Now
```

(In this case, we set the birthday to the current time to indicate that Lucy has just been brought to life.)

The preceding code is easy to read. When you change a variable, you know which person it relates to. If you want to create more than one Person object, it's easy, and there will be a lot less code. Best of all, you can pass an entire Person to a function or subroutine through just one parameter, as in the function shown here:

```
Public Sub GoShopping(ByVal Shopper As Person)
        ' Some code here to manage the mall process.
End Sub
```

Structures are really "super variables." You're probably familiar with this concept from having worked with databases, even if you've never actually created a structure or a class. In a database, each person is represented by a record (also known as a row), and each record has the same series of fields to describe it.

Basically, there is one important similarity between structures and classes: Both are defined only once, but can be created as many times as you want, just about anywhere in your code. This means you only need to define one Person object, but you can build families, convention centers, and bowling clubs without introducing any new code.

Making a Structure That Has Brains

What about a structure with built-in intelligence? For example, what if we could make a Person object that wouldn't let you set a birth date that was earlier than 1800, could output a basic line of conversation, and would notify you when its birthday arrives?

This is what we have with a class: a structure that can include data and code. (In actual fact, Visual Basic .NET structures can have some code in them, though there are subtle differences between structures and classes, which we'll explore a little later in this chapter. In practice, classes are usually the way to go. Most programmers see structures simply as examples of backward compatibility—little pieces of living history accessible from the modern Visual Basic programming language.)

Consider our Person as a genuine class:

```
Public Class Person

    ' Data for the Person
    Public FirstName As String
    Public LastName As String
    Public BirthDate As Date

    ' Built-in feature to get the Person object to introduce itself.
    Public Function GetIntroduction() As String
        Dim Intro As String
```

(continued on next page)

```
        Intro = "My name is " & FirstName & " " & LastName & ". "
        Intro &= "I was born on " & BirthDate.ToString()
        Return Intro
    End Function

End Class
```

Notice that our class looks similar to the Person structure we created earlier. It has the same three variables, except that now we must be careful to mark them Public. (By default, class variables are Private, which means that only the code inside the class can see or change them.) We've also added a function called GetIntroduction right into our class. This means that every Person object is going to have a built-in feature for introducing itself.

Similarly, if we were to make a class modeling a microwave, we might have data such as the microwave's manufacturer and the current power level, along with a CookFood function. Now you can see how classes help us to organize code. Functions that are specific to a particular object are embedded right in the class.

Instantiating an Object

Returning to our Person object, you'll find that it's quite easy to make a legitimate object out of our class:

```
Dim Lucy As New Person()
Lucy.FirstName = "Lucy"
Lucy.LastName = "Smith"
Lucy.BirthDate = DateTime.Now
MessageBox.Show(Lucy.GetIntroduction(), "Introduction")
```

This code produces the output shown in Figure 5-1.

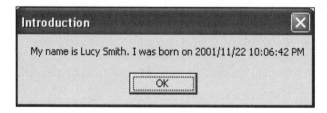

Figure 5-1: An introductory class

Notice that to create an object based on a class, we use a Dim statement with the New keyword. The New keyword is required to actually create the object. Alternatively, we could have written the following:

```
Dim Lucy As Person    ' Define the Lucy object variable.
Lucy = New Person()   ' Create the Lucy object.
```

This code is almost exactly the same. The only difference is that it gives us the ability to separate the two lines, and ends up defining the Lucy variable in a different spot from where we actually create the Lucy object. Notice that there is no Set statement used. (The Set statement was a hallmark of objects in Visual Basic 6.)

To release an object, we set it equal to Nothing, as shown here:

```
Lucy = Nothing
```

This tells Visual Basic that the object is no longer needed. Strictly speaking, you won't often need to use this statement, as the variable will be automatically cleared as soon as it goes out of scope. For example, if you define a variable in a subroutine, the variable will be set to nothing as soon as the subroutine ends. If you want to clear an object variable before this, you can use the Nothing keyword, as shown in this example.

What Is an Object, Really?

An object uses a special kind of variable that acts a little differently than ordinary simple variables. This unusual behavior was introduced with arrays in Chapter 3, although it is significant enough to examine in more detail here.

Consider the following code:

```
' Create two people.
Dim Lucy, John As New Person()

' Enter information in the Lucy object.
Lucy.FirstName = "Lucy"

' Copy the reference, not the value. The original John object is abandoned.
John = Lucy
```

The last line is the most significant. If you were expecting objects to behave like numbers and strings, you might think that this line copies Lucy's information into John. Instead, the existing John object is abandoned, and replaced by a reference to the Lucy object. At the end of the last line, there is really only one object (Lucy) remaining, with two different variables that you can use to access it.

Let's continue with the following code:

```
John.FirstName = "John"
' Now Lucy.FirstName is also John!
```

This is an example of *reference equality*. It tends to be more useful than value equality for working with objects.

This is the basic difference between VB .NET structures and classes: Structures are value types, while classes are reference types. As with all value types, assignment and comparison operations work on the contents of the object, not the memory reference. This can make large structures much slower and less efficient to work with than classes.

Many classes support cloning, which allows you to copy the contents of an object when needed by calling a Clone method. The familiar Array class is an example. In order to create an object that supports cloning, you need to go to a little extra work and implement a special interface. The next chapter explains interfaces and demonstrates this technique.

Object Comparison

Objects also have their own rules for comparison. Notably, you can't use the equals sign (=). This is to eliminate confusion regarding the true meaning of an "equals" comparison. With two variables, a comparison determines whether the values of both variables are the same. With two objects, a comparison doesn't determine whether the contents are the same, but rather, whether both object *references* are pointing to the same object. In other words, if objOne Is objTwo, there really is only one object, which you can access with two different object names. If intOne = intTwo, however, it means that two separate variables are storing identical information.

```
If Lucy Is John Then
    ' Contrary to what you might expect, the Lucy and John
    ' variables are pointing to the same object.
End If


' This won't work, because you can't compare object contents directly.
If Lucy = John Then
    ' This comparison can't be made automatically.
    ' Instead, the object would need to provide a method that manually compares
    ' every property (or just the important ones that are necessary to define
    ' equality).
End If
```

The Null Value Error

The most common error you will receive while working with objects is the common System.NullReferenceException, which warns you that "Value null was found where an instance of an object was required." What this means is that you've tried to work with an object that you have defined, but have not instantiated. Typically, this is caused when you forget to use the New keyword.

```
Dim Lucy As Person        ' No New keyword is used; this is a definition only.
Lucy.FirstName = "Lucy"   ' Won't work because Lucy doesn't exist yet!
```

It's a small mistake that you will soon learn to avoid, but being able to recognize it ensures that it will never frustrate you again.

Enhancing a Class with Properties

A class provides another important ingredient called *properties*. Right now, our Person class uses three variables. All of these variables are exposed to the outside world, which makes life convenient, but dangerous. It's the equivalent of removing the control panel on a microwave object, and allowing a user to control it directly through the circuitry in the back. In such a situation, numerous problems could occur, ranging from user errors (for example, accidentally setting a power level too high and damaging the microwave) to safety violations (such as running the microwave with the door open).

In order for an object to be a legitimate, well-encapsulated black box, its developer has to provide it with a control panel, and hide as much of the internal details as possible. This means that every object should perform its own basic error checking. It also means that an object should use only private variables that are hidden from the outside world. To let the calling code change a private variable in a class, you use properties.

Properties are really special procedures that allow a private variable to be changed or retrieved in a more controlled way. Let's look at our replacement for the FirstName variable:

```
Private _FirstName As String

Public Property FirstName() As String
    Get
        Return _FirstName
    End Get

    Set(ByVal Value As String)
        _FirstName = Value
    End Set
End Property
```

Our FirstName variable has been broken into two parts: the private _First-Name variable that works "behind the scenes," and the FirstName property that the class user sees. The internal _FirstName variable uses an underscore in its name to distinguish it. This is a common technique, but is definitely not your only possible choice.

The code for setting and retrieving FirstName is still exactly the same. In fact, the property procedure hasn't introduced any new code, so we haven't gained anything. But let's look at what we can do with the BirthDate variable:

```
Private _BirthDate as Date

Public Property BirthDate() As Date
    Get
        Return _BirthDate
    End Get
```

(continued on next page)

```
    Set(ByVal Value As Date)
        If BirthDate > Now Then
            MessageBox.Show("You can't create an unborn person")
        ElseIf IsDate(BirthDate) = False Then
            MessageBox.Show("That date is invalid.")
        Else
            _BirthDate = Value
        End If
    End Set
End Property
```

Be aware that displaying message boxes in response to invalid input is a clear violation of encapsulation. A Person object has nothing to do with your program's user interface, and should limit its functions to setting and retrieving data. To correctly handle invalid input, you should throw an exception, which would be received by the code setting the property, and would be interpreted as an error. The code where the class properties are being set could then decide how to handle the problem. (Throwing and catching exceptions is discussed in Chapter 7 of this book.)

You may have also noticed that the limitations imposed by this code don't necessarily make a lot of sense. For example, assigning the Person a birth date in the future might make a lot of sense for performing certain types of calculations. The restrictions in the preceding code example are really just designed to give you an idea of how a class can review data and refuse to accept information that is not appropriate.

Properties also provide another layer of abstraction. For example, when you set a microwave to defrost, several different internal properties are set, including settings for a maximum and a minimum power level, and a frequency between which the two are alternated. These details are hidden from the user. If the user had to set all this information directly, not only would a typical microwave operation take a lot more effort, but different microwave models would require different programming.

ReadOnly Properties

Sometimes you might want a property to be visible, but not directly changeable. For example, in our microwave analogy, there could be a LastServiceDate property that indicates when the microwave was most recently repaired or examined. We wouldn't want the microwave user to change this date, although the microwave class itself might update it in response to its ServiceMicrowave method.

To make a property read-only, you leave out the Set procedure, and add the keyword ReadOnly to the definition. In the case of the Person object, you might want to make the BirthDate property read-only, because this value can't be changed at will:

```
Public ReadOnly Property BirthDate() As Date
    Get
        Return _BirthDate
    End Get
End Property
```

You can also use the WriteOnly keyword to include a property with only a Set procedure, and no Get procedure; this rarely makes sense, however, and is not usually what an ordinary programmer expects from an object.

The preceding code example raises an interesting question. The program has been restricted so that the value of BirthDate can't be changed, which is a reasonable restriction. However, it also prevents us from assigning a BirthDate in the first place. In order to solve this problem, we need a way to load basic information when the Person object is first created, and *then* prevent any future changes to values (such as BirthDate) that can't ordinarily be modified. The way to accomplish this is to use a ReadOnly property procedure, as shown in the preceding example, in combination with a custom *constructor*.

Enhancing a Class with a Constructor

In Chapter 3 you learned that with initializers, you can preload variables with information using the same line that you use to create them. Initializers allow you to convert this:

```
Dim MyValue As Integer
MyValue = 10
```

into this:

```
Dim MyValue As Integer = 10
```

Constructors work the same kind of magic with objects that initializers do with variables. The difference is that objects, being much more complex than simple variables, can require significantly more advanced initialization. For example, you will typically have to set several properties, and in the case of a business object, you might want to open a database connection or read values from a file. Constructors allow you to do all this and more.

A constructor is a special subroutine that is invoked automatically in your class. This subroutine *must* have the name New—that's how Visual Basic .NET identifies it as a constructor.

Consider the following Person class:

```
Public Class Person
    ' (Variable definitions omitted.)
    ' (Property procedures omitted.)
```

(continued on next page)

```
    Public Sub New()
        _BirthDate = DateTime.Now
    End Sub

End Class
```

Notice that we've included a constructor that assigns a value for the internal _BirthDate variable. Now every time you create a Person object, a default birth date will be automatically assigned. This technique can allow for some shortcuts in your code if you frequently rely on certain default values.

Constructors That Accept Parameters

The previous example only scratches the surface of what a well-written constructor can do for you. For one thing, constructors can require parameters. This allows for a much more flexible approach, as shown here:

```
Public Class Person
    ' (Variable definitions omitted.)
    ' (Property procedures omitted.)

    Public Sub New(ByVal FirstName As String, ByVal LastName As String, _
    ByVal BirthDate As Date)
        _FirstName = FirstName
        _LastName = LastName
        _BirthDate = BirthDate
    End Sub

End Class
```

The constructor in this example allows you to preload information into a Person object in one line. Best of all, it's done in a completely generic way that lets you specify each required piece of information.

NOTE *You might notice that the parameter names in the previous example conflict with the property names of the class. However, the parameter names have precedence, so the code will work the way it is written. To refer directly to one of the properties with the same name in the New subroutine, you would need to use the Me keyword (as in Me.FirstName).*

```
Dim Lucy As New Person("Lucy", "Smith", DateTime.Now)
' This can also be written with the following equivalent syntax:
' Dim Lucy As Person = New Person("Lucy", "Smith", DateTime.Now)
```

Bear in mind that it makes no difference in what order you place your methods, properties, variables, and constructors within a class. Typically, you should standardize on a set order; this will help make it easy to read your code.

A good standard is to include all of an object's private variables first, followed by property procedures, then constructors, and then other methods. Visual Basic .NET gives you as much freedom to arrange the internal details of a class as it gives you to arrange different classes and modules in a file.

To try out the Person class, and see how a simple client interacts with it, you can use the Object Tester sample included with the online code for this book (see Figure 5-2).

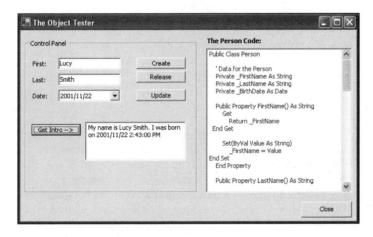

Figure 5-2: Testing the Person object

Multiple Constructors

Another exciting feature of VB .NET is the ability to define multiple constructors for an object. Once you've done this, then when you create an instance of that object, you can decide which constructor you want to use. Each constructor has to have its own distinct parameter list. (In other words, multiple constructors can't share the same signature.)

How does it work? Conceptually, it's the exact same process as for overloading procedures, which was demonstrated in Chapter 3. The only difference is that you don't use the Overloads keyword.

Here's a Person class with more than one constructor:

```
Public Class Person
    ' (Variable definitions omitted.)
    ' (Property procedures omitted.)

    Public Sub New(ByVal FirstName As String, ByVal LastName As String, _
    ByVal BirthDate As Date)
        _FirstName = FirstName
        _LastName = LastName
        _BirthDate = BirthDate
```

(continued on next page)

```
    End Sub

    Public Sub New(ByVal FirstName As String, ByVal LastName As String)
        _FirstName = FirstName
        _LastName = LastName
        _BirthDate = DateTime.Now
    End Sub

    Public Sub New(ByVal FirstName As String, ByVal LastName As String, _
      ByVal Age As Integer)
        _FirstName = FirstName
        _LastName = LastName
        _BirthDate = DateTime.Now.AddYears(-Age)
    End Sub
End Class
```

These overloaded constructors allow you to create a Person by specifying all three pieces of information or by specifying only the name, in which case a default date will be used. You can also use a variant of the constructor that calculates the BirthDate using a supplied *Age* parameter.

The technique of multiple constructors is used extensively in the .NET class library. Many classes have a range of different constructors that allow you to set various options or load information from different data sources. Overloaded constructors are also much more flexible than optional parameters, which are never used in the .NET class library.

When you create an object that has more than one constructor, Visual Studio .NET shows you the parameter list for the first constructor in a special IntelliSense tooltip (see Figure 5-3). This tooltip also includes a special arrow icon that you can click on to move from constructor to constructor (you can also use the up and down arrow keys).

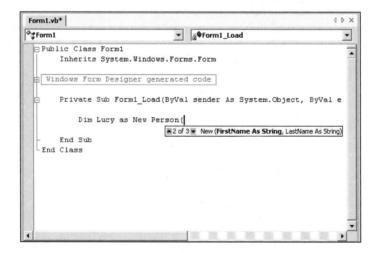

Figure 5-3: Constructor IntelliSense

Multiple constructors are a way of life in .NET. The concept is fairly straightforward, but as you learn about the .NET class library you'll realize that creating classes with the perfect set of constructors is as much an art as a skill.

> **TIP** *You can create multiple versions of any method in a class. You just need to use the Overloads keyword, along with the techniques that were introduced in Chapter 3. Overloading methods is another trick that makes a frequent appearance in the .NET class library, and provides your objects with increased flexibility.*

The Default Constructor

One other detail about constructors is worth noting. Even if you don't create a constructor, your class has one. In the case of a class without a specified constructor in code, your object will use a default constructor that doesn't require any arguments and doesn't do anything special. However, as soon as you add a custom constructor to your class, Visual Basic .NET will stop generating this default constructor for you. This means that if you add a constructor that requires parameters, you will then be forced to specify values for those parameters when creating an object based on the class. This restriction can come in very handy, ensuring that you create your objects successfully with valid data.

If you want to be able to create objects without any special parameters, just include the default constructor manually in your class. The default constructor looks like this:

```
Public Sub New()
    ' Initialize variables here if required.
End Sub
```

Destructors

With all this talk about constructors, it might have occurred to you that it would be useful to have a complementary *destructor* method that is automatically invoked when your class is destroyed. A destructor method might allow a lazy programmer to create an object that automatically saves itself just before it is deallocated, or—more usefully—one that cleans up after itself, closing database connections or open files. However, Visual Basic .NET has no direct support for destructors. That's because .NET uses garbage collection, which is not well suited to destructors. Quite simply, garbage collection means that you can't be sure when your object will really be cleared.

Garbage Collection

It's worth a quick digression to explain garbage collection. Garbage collection is a service used for all languages in the .NET framework, and it's radically different than the way things used to work in Visual Basic 6.

Object Death in Visual Basic 6

Visual Basic 6 uses reference counting. Behind the scenes, it keeps track of how many variables are pointing at an object. (As you've already seen in this chapter, more than one object variable can refer to the same object.) When the last object variable is set to Nothing, the number of references to an object drops to zero, and the object will be swiftly removed from memory. At the same time, the Class.Terminate event will occur, giving your code a chance to perform any related cleanup. This process is called *deterministic finalization* because you always know when an object will be removed.

As with many characteristics of Visual Basic 6, this system had some problems. For example, if two objects referred to each other, they could never be removed, even though they might be floating in memory, totally detached from the rest of your program. This problem is called a *circular reference*.

Object Death in VB .NET

In .NET, objects always remain in memory until the garbage collector finds them. The *garbage collector* is a special .NET runtime service that works automatically, tracking down classes that aren't referenced any more. If the garbage collector finds two or more objects that refer to one another (known as a *circular reference*), and it recognizes that the rest of the program doesn't use either of them, it will remove them from memory.

This system differs from Visual Basic 6. For example, imagine a Person object that has a Relative property that can point to another Person object. A very simple program might hold a couple of variables that point to Person objects, and these Person objects may or may not point to still more Person objects through their Relative property. All these objects are referenced, so they will be safely preserved.

On the other hand, consider a Person object that you use temporarily, and then release—let's call this object PersonA. The twist is that the PersonA object itself points to another object (PersonB), which points back to PersonA. In Visual Basic 6, this circular reference would force the abandoned Person objects to remain floating in memory, because neither one has been fully released. With VB .NET garbage collection, the garbage collector will notice that these objects are cut off from the rest of your program, and will free the memory (as shown in Figure 5-4).

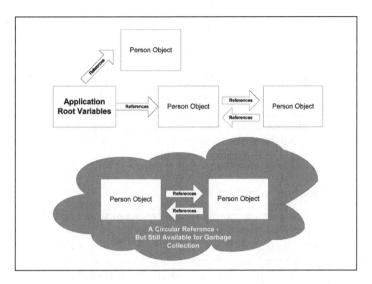

Figure 5-4: Garbage collection and .NET objects

A side effect of garbage collection is *nondeterministic finalization;* in other words, in Visual Basic .NET, you *don't* know exactly when an object will be removed. This is because the garbage collection service, handy as is, doesn't run continuously. Instead, it waits for your computer to be idle, or for memory to become scarce, before it begins scanning. This often allows your program to have better all-around performance. However, it also means that any code in a Finalize event (the VB .NET equivalent of Terminate) may not be executed for quite some time. This can be a problem. If you are relying on using the Finalize event to release a limited resource, such as a network database connection, the resource remains active for a longer time, thus increasing the resource cost of your application—and potentially slowing life down dramatically.

Object Cleanup

You can manually trigger the garbage collection process by using the following code:

```
System.GC.Collect()
```

However, this technique is strongly discouraged. For one thing, it will cause an immediate performance slowdown as .NET scans the entire allocated memory in your application. A much better approach is to create your own "destructor" type of method for classes that use limited resources. This method will have to be called manually by your code. By convention, this method should be named Dispose.

Generally, most classes won't need a Dispose method. However, a few classes might—for example, a business object that represents a record from a database. When adding a Dispose method, ask yourself if it is really required. A class that reads information from a database should probably open and close the database connection from within its constructor. A separate method would be used to update database information, and that method would also open and close a database connection. These measures will ensure that no matter how you write the code that uses the class, there will be no possibility of accidentally holding a database connection open for too long. Careful programming design can prevent limited resources from being wasted.

Enhancing a Class with Events

Events are notifications that your class sends to the code that created it. These notifications are often ignored. (Consider, for example, the many different events that are fired from a typical form.) However, the client can choose to pay attention to important events, and write an event handler to respond to them.

You can define an event with the Event keyword. An example is shown below in the Person class:

```
Public Class Person
    ' (Other class code omitted.)
    Public Event DataChanged()
End Class
```

Once you have defined an event, you can fire it at a later time from inside any code in your Person class. For example, you can use the DataChanged event in any part of your Person class to notify the rest of your code that a piece of information has changed.

The following code demonstrates the inclusion of a DataChanged event in the FirstName property procedure:

```
Public Property FirstName()
    Get
        Return _FirstName
    End Get

    Set(ByVal Value As String)
        _FirstName = Value
        RaiseEvent DataChanged()
    End Set
End Property
```

An Event in Action

These are the ingredients: an event definition and a RaiseEvent command to fire the event when needed. So how do we link it all together? Events used in classes work the same way as the control events that you are already familiar with. As with control events, you can create an object using the WithEvents keyword, and then attach event handlers to its events using the Handles keyword for a subroutine. You can also hook up event handlers dynamically using the AddHandler command, as you saw in Chapter 4.

Our example uses a simple program that creates a Person object, and displays its information in a window. The fields that show this information are read-only, and can't be modified. However, the user can change the first name through another avenue: an additional text box and an update button in a group box with the caption "Apply For a Name Change," as shown in Figure 5-5.

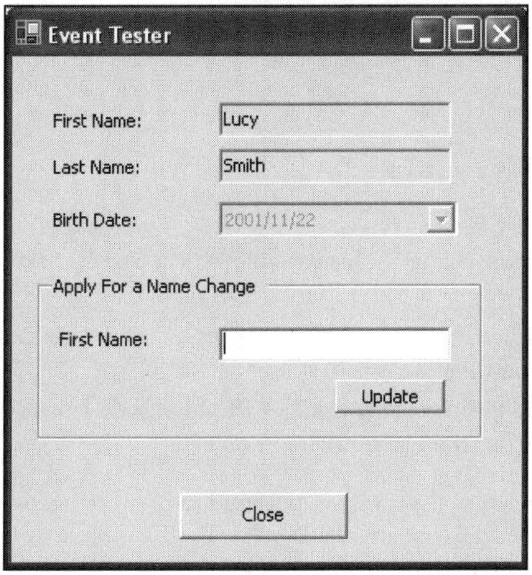

Figure 5-5: The event tester

The form class looks like this:

```
Public Class EventTester
  Inherits System.Windows.Forms.Form
    ' (Windows Form designer code omitted.)

    ' Create the Person as a form-level variable.
    Private WithEvents CurrentPerson As New Person("Lucy", "Smith", DateTime.Now)

    ' This event handler updates the window when the form is loaded.
    Private Sub frmClassTester_Load(ByVal sender As System.Object, _
```

(continued on next page)

```
      ByVal e As System.EventArgs) Handles MyBase.Load
          RefreshData()    ' Call the RefreshData subroutine.
      End Sub

      ' This event handler allows the user to update the class.
      Private Sub cmdUpdate_Click(ByVal sender As System.Object, _
        ByVal e As System.EventArgs) Handles cmdUpdate.Click
            CurrentPerson.FirstName = txtNewFirst.Text
      End Sub

      ' This procedure must be called manually.
      Private Sub RefreshData()
          txtFirstName.Text = CurrentPerson.FirstName
          txtLastName.Text = CurrentPerson.LastName
          dtBirth.Value = CurrentPerson.BirthDate
      End Sub

End Class
```

Here's a quick summary:

- A Person object is created as a form-level variable named CurrentPerson when the form is created. This variable is declared WithEvents, which means that its events are automatically available.
- An event handler for the form's Load event calls the RefreshData subroutine when the form is first loaded.
- The RefreshData subroutine updates the on-screen controls with the information from the CurrentPerson object.

We are now just a step away from putting the DataChanged event to good use.

First, we can modify the RefreshData method so that it is invoked automatically in response to our DataChanged event:

```
Private Sub RefreshData() Handles CurrentPerson.DataChanged
```

Now, when you click on the cmdUpdate button, the CurrentPerson object is modified, the event is fired, and the data is refreshed automatically.

Clearly, the preceding example doesn't *need* an event. You could accomplish the same thing by calling the RefreshData procedure manually after you make your changes. To make life a little more confusing, there's no single rule to determine when you should use events and when you should do the work in your client code. In fact, a lot of thought needs to go into the process of modeling your program as a collection of happily interacting objects. There are many different design patterns for communication, and they are the focus of frequent debate and discussion. A good way to get started is to start thinking of your objects as physical, tangible items. In the case of events, ask the question, "Which object has the responsibility of reporting the change?"

Events are very flexible because they allow multiple recipients. For example, you could add a Handles clause for the CurrentPerson.DataChanged event to several different subroutines. If these subroutines are all in the same form, they will be handled one after the other, although the order can vary. Events can also be fired across projects, and even from event definition code in one language to event handler code in another.

Events with Different Signatures

You can also create an event that supplies information through additional parameters. Remember, the recommended format for a .NET event is a parameter for the sender, combined with a parameter for the additional information. The additional information is provided through a special class that derives from System.EventArgs. For example, our DataChanged event might require a special object that looks like this:

```
Public Class PersonDataChangedEventArgs
  Inherits EventArgs

    Public ChangedProperty As String

End Class
```

With this example, we're getting slightly ahead of ourselves. It introduces the concept of inheritance, which Chapter 6 delves into in more detail. The important concept here is that PersonDataChangedEventArgs is a special class used to pass information to our DataChanged event handler. It is based on the standard EventArgs class, but it adds a new property that can hold additional information.

The event definition will now need to be adjusted to the typical .NET format:

```
Public Event DataChanged(ByVal sender As Object, _
 ByVal e As PersonDataChangedEventArgs)
```

Note that the standard names—*sender* and *e*—are used for the parameters. The event can be raised like this:

```
' This code would appear in the FirstName Set property procedure.
Dim e As New PersonDataChangedEventArgs
e.ChangedProperty = "FirstName"
RaiseEvent DataChanged(Me, e)
```

This system introduces a few problems. First, the RefreshData method can no longer receive the event, because it has the wrong signature. We must rectify this before we can use RefreshData. Second, the process of creating the Person-DataChangedEventArgs object and filling it with information adds a few more lines to our code. In short, we may have added more functionality than is required, and needlessly complicated our code.

In a sophisticated scenario, however, multiple parameters can be invaluable. For example, as soon as you create an event handler that can receive events from several different objects, you'll need to make sure it can distinguish which object is sending it the notification, and take the appropriate action. In this case, the end result will be shorter and clearer code. The preceding example above might be useful if the refresh operation required is particularly time-consuming. Depending on which information has changed, the event handler might refresh only part of the display:

```
Private Sub RefreshData(ByVal sender As System.Object, _
 ByVal e As PersonDataChangedEventArgs) Handles CurrentPerson.DataChanged

    Select Case e.ChangedProperty
        Case "FirstName"
            txtFirstName.Text = CurrentPerson.FirstName
        Case "LastName"
            txtLastName.Text = CurrentPerson.LastName
        Case "BirthDate"
            dtpBirth.Value = CurrentPerson.BirthDate
    End Select


End Sub
```

This type of design could bring about a significant increase in performance. Of course, the approach of including the property values as strings isn't very efficient, as it leaves the door wide open to logic errors caused by mistyped variable names. A better way of passing information to a function is to use enumerations, which make their appearance in Chapter 6.

Assessing Classes

Let's take a step back and answer our original question: Just what is a class? A class is a template we use to create objects. A class consists of three things: properties that contain information about it, methods that we use to make it take actions, and events that it uses to notify our program about certain changes. Some classes might only have properties. In that case they resemble our Person structure. Other classes might consist almost entirely of methods that allow us to process information, or to perform such tasks as writing to a file. An example of a class like this is the Math class featured in Chapter 3. It is made up entirely of shared methods that perform mathematical operations.

The amazing thing about our Person class is the way that we, or other programmers, can reuse and expand upon it. Other programmers don't have to understand how the Person class works in order to use it. To them, it's just a black box. Can you imagine the excitement you'll feel when a colleague tells you he's taken your Person class and incorporated it in a collection within a NuclearFamily object that has additional properties such as Address and additional functions such as FindYoungestMember?

What Comes Next?

Objects are central to the philosophy of .NET, and we continue to explore them in Chapter 6. In the meantime, you can get started looking at the object structure of your application with the Class View window, seen here in Figure 5-6.

Figure 5-6: An application's class structure

This window provides a tree showing all the classes you use, and includes information about the properties, methods, events, and private variables contained in each one. Together, these details make up the *members* of the class.

You can see a similar view of namespaces and the class library using the Object Browser. To display the Object Browser, choose View • Other Windows • Object Browser. Each member has a brief associated description. However, you'll probably find that it's easiest to learn about .NET classes by consulting the MSDN class library reference.

6

MASTERING OBJECTS

This chapter continues our exploration into the world of objects. In Chapter 5 we covered the basics of how to define a class, enhance it with properties, methods, events, and constructors, and use it to create live objects. This chapter begins by explaining some more of the philosophy behind *why* you should go to all this trouble, and outlining the principles that can guide you to good object-oriented design.

Of course, the bulk of the chapter is spent examining some additional types of objects and the classy tricks needed to master OO programming. Some of these concepts have been available in previous versions of Visual Basic, but are now substantially changed; these include enumerations (objects that contain a list of options as constants), collections (used to group objects together), and interfaces (which allow you to "lock down" class design). Many other object features are completely new to Visual Basic .NET. These include shared members (class members that can be used without creating an object) and inheritance (the ability for a class to acquire and extend the functionality of another class).

As you read this chapter, you'll realize that these ingredients aren't just new features for advanced OO programming—instead, they are organizing principles that shape the entire .NET framework and the Visual Basic .NET language. The more you learn about objects, the more you'll understand about the .NET class library, and the easier you'll find it to learn about new classes and integrate them into your program to provide additional features. In short, if you only have time to learn about one VB .NET concept, I heartily recommend the theory and practice of using objects. No other topic is as integral to the workings of the Visual Basic .NET language.

New in .NET

Visual Basic .NET has a whole new perspective on objects. Classes and interfaces are no longer just two more features pasted onto the language—now they represent the underlying philosophy of the whole .NET framework. Here are some of the minor changes, along with some of the more seismic ones:

Shared Members

The Shared keyword allows you to create properties, variables, and methods that are always available, even when no instance object exists. Visual Basic 6 allowed you to create global classes that were entirely made up of shared methods, but it didn't provide anything close to the features and fine-grained control afforded by the Shared keyword.

Inheritance

Inheritance, perhaps the most anticipated feature to ever enter into the Visual Basic language, allows you to create sophisticated objects that share features and functions. In fact, if you've worked through the examples in the preceding chapters of this book, you've already been using inheritance in Visual Basic .NET, most notably to create your own Windows forms.

Interfaces

Interfaces are now directly supported as a separate code construct, instead of a special type of class. This makes using them more straightforward and convenient than ever.

Collections

The Visual Basic collection remains more or less unchanged in .NET, but thanks to the class library and inheritance you can now create your own custom collection classes without having to resort to strange, undocumented commands to provide support for the For Each/Next block.

The Philosophy of OOP

Making the shift from traditional programming to an object-oriented approach is a significant adjustment. Before we plunge back into the technical details of Visual Basic .NET's support for object-oriented design and development, it may help to review some of the reasons why object-oriented design and programming is held in such high esteem.

Object-oriented programming encompasses several principles that contribute to reusable, efficient design. Taken together, these principles allow you to create programs and components built out of tightly organized, extremely reusable components.

The "Black Box" Idea

Classes in your program should behave as much as possible like *black boxes*—"black" meaning that you can't see inside them to puzzle out what's going on. Imagine the difficulty you would have if using your microwave to defrost chicken required you to take the Microwave object, peer into its circuitry, and make alterations. Clearly, you would have quite a problem on your hands. If you look at the program as a black box (which conceptually it is), you are only concerned with the inputs and outputs: Frozen chicken goes in, defrosted chicken comes out. The process of defrosting is "abstracted away," which is a fancy way of saying that the microwave manufacturer worries about it so you won't have to. And I'm sure you'll agree that as a result, your kitchen experience is much more productive.

Similarly, if an entirely new microwave were to come onto the market tomorrow, you wouldn't need to change your cooking habits to accommodate it. You could still rely on it having the same *interface*, which is another important object-oriented concept. The microwave would plug into the same outlet, accept food through a similar door, and require the same information (cooking time and power level) in order to perform its tasks.

The programming analogue of this microwave is any component that can be updated in a program without "breaking" the existing code that uses it.

This chapter frequently refers to "the client code" as though the programmer writing an object and the programmer using it are not the same. In fact, this is not a strange example of multiple personalities, but a healthy way to approach object-oriented design. In order to make sure your applications are built out of complete, well-encapsulated objects that can be reused in different scenarios and even different programs, you should start thinking of each object as its own individual program. Every object should receive all the information it needs through clear, standardized methods and properties, and provide capabilities that can be used directly, without requiring additional processing or the use of specific conversions and undefined rules.

Loose Coupling

In the preceding example, we started to drift into another principle of good object-oriented design: *loose coupling*. In a loosely coupled system, the various components in your application are as independent as possible. Consider the Microwave object again. It's quite reasonable to expect that the Microwave object is built out of smaller objects like an "electrical system interface," or Plug object, a FoodHeating object, and a Door object. And while the microwave and the oven both process food, it doesn't follow that the microwave can rely on the oven's CookFood method. If it did, the microwave and the oven would be tightly coupled; in other words, they would be interdependent. So if you moved the oven out of the kitchen, the microwave would suddenly stop working.

When designing classes, it will help for you to think about yourself as a component designer, and to imagine that another programmer will use your classes in his own highly customized programs. The more interdependencies and requirements you incorporate in your work, the harder it will be to move a component into another program. In the worst-case scenario, you'd have to bring along a whole class of unrelated objects, global variables, and helper functions before the object could work properly.

> **TIP** *It's worth noting that although loose coupling is credited as an object-oriented design principle, it isn't really anything new. The best traditional structured programs also incorporate this principle, and their creators design functions that are highly generic. The more generic the code is, the easier it is to reuse, whether it's inside your own program or someone else's.*

Cohesion

A related idea is *cohesion*. In a well-designed, highly cohesive program, every portion of code is responsible for one—and only one—task. In traditional structured programming, this means that you carefully separate functions so as to isolate small, reusable units of logic. In object-oriented programs you should apply this principle as rigorously as possible, dividing objects and their methods into the smallest useful components, and clearly making a distinction between the types of tasks that each method performs. For example, you would never include presentation-layer code in an object. An object should return information to the calling code, which you can then format and present to the user. If you were to include user interface code in an object, it would be tied to a specific window, and hard to reuse for different windows or in other programs.

You've probably come across nightmarish situations where user interface, data access, and business logic code were all intermingled in a single procedure. This is part of the reason that Visual Basic has a bad reputation in some circles: It's just too easy to put data access and processing code in an event handler (such as the Click event for a button) where it's hard to find, debug, and reuse.

> **TIP** *It may help to remind yourself: The object consumer (that is, the program) shouldn't need to know anything about how an object works.*

What Do Objects Represent?

When introducing objects, most programming books use examples with classes that represent concrete, physical *things* in the real world. For example, our Person object is clearly designed to model a real-world person. Similar concrete objects might have names like Invoice, Product, TextBox, and Calculator.

However, you should remember that programming objects don't need to correspond to something real. Objects might just represent a programming abstraction. For example, objects like Rectangle, FontUnit, Buffer, and Version just represent a useful way to combine together related bits of information. Similarly, objects might just group together useful related functionality—Console and Math are two .NET classes that do exactly that.

Types in .NET

So far, we have discussed classes (the definitions of objects) and objects (examples of classes in action). In reality, the class library consists of *types,* a catch-all term that includes the following species of object templates:

Classes

This is the most common type in the class library, and the one that we examined in Chapter 5. The word *classes* is often used interchangeably with *objects* or *types,* because classes underlie the most important features of any object-oriented framework (such as .NET). Classes are the basic ingredient for creating a wide array of flexible objects.

Structures

Structures are simpler classes that closely match a specific type of data. Structures can be defined in Visual Basic .NET, as you learned in Chapter 5. One of the main differences between structures and classes is that structures act more like simple data types for comparison and assignment operations. For example, assigning one structure variable to another copies the entire structure, not the object reference.

Delegates

Delegates are the definitions for type-safe function pointers. They are used behind the scenes to support .NET events, which are generally more convenient. Delegates were explained in Chapter 3, and they make a repeat appearance in Chapter 10, which explores multithreaded programming.

Enumerations

An enumeration is a simple object that allows a user to choose from a list of constants. Enumerations are described in this chapter.

Interfaces

An interface is a special contract that provides a partial class definition. This allows more sophisticated object design, and is particularly useful when a class needs to be deployed and enhanced without breaking existing clients. Interfaces are discussed in this chapter.

Enumerations

Chapter 5 presented an example which used the Person class and a DataChanged event that fired every time a change was made. The DataChanged event contained extra information, namely the name of the variable that had changed. Unfortunately, a string was used to identify the variable name; this made it all too easy to cause an error by using the wrong case, or by misspelling a word. Even worse, an error like this would have no chance of being caught by the compiler.

Instead, it would probably become a hard-to-detect logic error, propagating deep within your application and causing all sorts of mysterious problems.

The problem exposed by the Person's DataChanged event is not at all unusual. A similar error can occur if you are creating a special function that can perform one of a set number of different tasks. For example, consider a Person object with a more advanced GetIntroduction function that allows us to specify the type of environment:

```
Public Function GetIntroduction(EnvironmentType As String) As String

    Dim Intro As String
    If EnvironmentType = "Business"
        ' Set Intro accordingly.
    ElseIf EnvironmentType = "Home"
        ' Set Intro accordingly.
    ElseIf EnvironmentType = "Formal Occasion"
        ' Set Intro accordingly.
    End If

    Return Intro
End Function
```

In this example, the GetIntroduction function uses a string value, which is set equal to a specific predetermined value to designate the type of introduction required. The same type of logic could be used with an integer variable using a predetermined number. However, there are several drawbacks to this approach:

- A mistake is easy to make, because no checking is performed to make sure that the parameter has a supported value (unless you add such logic yourself).

- The client code has no idea what logic your function uses. If you use an integer, it may be easier to code accurately, but harder to guess what each value really represents to your function.

- The code is difficult to read and understand. It may make sense when you code it, but it might become much less obvious a few months later.

- The approach is not standardized. A hundred different programmers may solve similar problems a hundred different ways, with hundreds of different predetermined values; as a result, integration and code sharing can become very difficult.

A somewhat better approach is to define special constants. Then you can pass the appropriate constant to the function. This approach prevents casual mistakes from being made, because the compiler will catch your mistake if you type the constant name incorrectly. However, it doesn't really solve the consistency problem. It also introduces a new problem: Where should the constants be stored? If a program is not carefully designed, the constants can be lost in a separate file, or they might even conflict with the names of constants used for different functions!

Creating an Enumeration

Enumerations are designed to solve such problems. An enumeration is a special object that groups a set of constants together. For example, the following enumeration could help with our GetIntroduction example:

```
Public Enum EnvironmentType
    Business
    Home
    FormalOccasion
End Enum
```

In your code, you would use this enumeration with the name you have created. For example, here's the new GetIntroduction function:

```
Public Function GetIntroduction(Environment As EnvironmentType) As String

    Dim Intro As String
    If Environment = EnvironmentType.Business
        ' Set Intro accordingly.
    ElseIf Environment = EnvironmentType.Home
        ' Set Intro accordingly.
    ElseIf Environment = EnvironmentType.FormalOccasion
        ' Set Intro accordingly.
    End If

    Return Intro
End Function
```

And here's how we could call the function:

```
ReturnedMessage = GetIntroduction(EnvironmentType.Business)
```

Notice that we don't have to create an instance of an enumeration object. Its values are automatically available.

One other nice feature is the way that IntelliSense automatically prompts you with possible values from your enumeration, as shown in Figure 6-1.

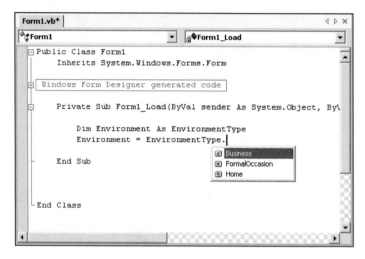

Figure 6-1: IntelliSense with enumerations

Enumerations "Under the Hood"

Behind the scenes, each entry in the enumeration is given its own integer value. In our previous example, Business was given the value 0, Home was 1, and FormalOccasion was 2. This means that the comparison in the GetIntroduction function is really just examining a number value and comparing it to the values defined in our EnvironmentType definition.

In fact, if you were to look directly at the Environment value you received (by displaying it on screen in a label control or message box without using the ToString method), you would see that it is really an ordinary number. The use of the enumeration in your code just makes the logic more clear and understandable. It also makes it much more difficult to make a mistake, because there is only a small group of enumerated values, while there is no practical limit to the number of different integer values you could use.

```
Dim Environment As EnvironmentType = EnvironmentType.Home
Dim EnvironmentString As String

EnvironmentString = Str(Environment)          ' EnvironmentString = "1"
EnvironmentString = Environment.ToString()    ' EnvironmentString = "Home"
```

In some cases, you might want to define specific number values for your enumerations. This might be required if you are migrating a segment of code from a system of hard-coded integer values or constants to a more modern approach with enumerations. In this case, you might have procedures in your code that still expect certain specific values, and that check for these values instead of comparing a value to your enumeration definition.

To create a backward-compatible enumeration for this situation, you could specify values in your enumeration definition, like this:

```
Public Enum EnvironmentType
    Business = 50
    Home = 51
    FormalOccasion = 52
End Enum
```

You could also use this approach if you need an enumeration to correspond to some other value. For example, you might want to create an enumeration that allows you to examine error codes. You would create the enumeration using the error codes with the appropriate values, and use it to make your code more clear.

In other words, this:

```
ReturnValue = OpenDB("mydb")
If ReturnValue = 34 Then
    ' Database already open error.
End If
```

Would become this:

```
ReturnValue = OpenDB("mydb")
If ReturnValue = DBErrors.AlreadyOpen Then
    ' Database already open error.
    ' You could also still use the old code and check that ReturnValue = 34.
    ' Essentially, ReturnValue is a named numeric constant.
End If
```

With the help of this enumeration:

```
Public Enum DBErrors
    AlreadyOpen = 34
End Enum
```

Organizing Enumerations

Enumerations can be placed just about anywhere in your code, but they generally belong in the class that uses them. That prevents them from conflicting with other enumerations, and makes sure they will always be available if you copy a class into another project. For example, the Person class could use the following enumeration for the PersonChanged event:

```
Public Class Person
    ' (Code omitted.)
    Public Enum ChangedProperty
        FirstName
        LastName
        BirthDate
    End Enum
End Class
```

Next, a good idea is to create a standard EventArgs class that stores the changed property. This PersonChangedEventArgs class will be used to pass the required information with the PersonChanged event.

```
Public Class PersonChangedEventArgs
  Inherits EventArgs

    Public _ChangedProperty As Person.ChangedProperty
    Public Property ChangedProperty() As Person.ChangedProperty
        Get
            Return _ChangedProperty
        End Get
        Set(ByVal Value As Person.ChangedProperty)
            _ChangedProperty = Value
        End Set
    End Property

    Public Sub New(ByVal ChangedProperty As Person.ChangedProperty)
        _ChangedProperty = ChangedProperty
    End Sub
End Class
```

This example is very similar to what you saw in the last chapter, with a couple of minor refinements. Though the PersonChangedEventArgs class only stores one important piece of information (the changed property), the code is more lengthy because it uses a full property procedure. The class also adds a special constructor that allows the property to be specified when the object is created.

You would also need to update the PersonChanged event definition:

```
Public Event PersonChanged(ByVal sender As Object, _
  ByVal e As PersonChangedEventArgs)
```

And the code that raises the event:

```
' Raise the PersonChanged event to indicate that the LastName was modified.
' This also involves creating a new PersonChangedEventArgs object to send.
RaiseEvent PersonChanged(Me, _
  New PersonChangedEventArgs(ChangedProperty.LastName))
```

The fully revised code is available as an online example for this chapter.

Keep in mind that to use an enumeration in a class, you will have to specify its full name. Interestingly enough, enumerations are always available, even if you don't have a live object. For example, we could use the following code to examine the enumeration in the PersonChanged event handler:

```
Private Sub RefreshData(ByVal sender As System.Object, _
 ByVal e As PersonChangedEventArgs) Handles CurrentPerson.PersonChanged
    Select Case e.ChangedProperty
    Case Person.ChangedProperty.FirstName
        txtFirstName.Text = Lucy.FirstName
    Case Person.ChangedProperty.LastName
        txtLastName.Text = Lucy.LastName
    Case Person.ChangedProperty.BirthDate
        dtBirth.Value = Lucy.BirthDate
    End Select
End Sub
```

This example takes the ChangedProperty value returned in the special PersonChangedEventArgs object, and compares it to the different possible values in the enumeration. The interesting detail about this code is that the enumeration is accessed directly through the class (Person) instead of through a live object. This is possible because all public enumerations are created as shared members that are always available, even if you haven't created an object.

Visual Basic .NET provides this ability because enumerations are part of the basic set of information that you need in order to interact with an object. Because enumerations are essentially unchangeable constants, they don't need to be linked to a specific object instance. Also, because enumerations are shared, you can easily use them in constructors, and other shared methods, when you might not have an object instance available.

The next section examines shared members in more detail, and describes how you can manually create your own shared properties and methods.

Shared Members

When we discussed objects in Chapter 3, we briefly explored how objects can be potentially confusing because they can have both shared and instance members. So far, all the properties, methods, and events we have created in the Person class have been instance members. These members have no meaning until you create an instance of the class.

```
Person.FirstName = "Lucy"    ' Has no meaning and will cause an error!

Dim Lucy As New Person()
Lucy.FirstName = "Lucy"       ' FirstName is an instance member, so this will work.
```

We examined a similar distinction with Windows forms in Chapter 4. Windows forms also need to be instantiated from the class description before you can access any members.

Shared members allow you to circumvent these rules. A shared member can be used directly, without requiring a live object.

Shared Methods

Shared methods (also known as *helper methods*) allow you to provide useful functionality related to an object. Many classes in the .NET class library use shared methods. For example, the System.Math class is composed entirely of useful functions for performing advanced mathematical operations. You never need to specifically create a Math object.

```
' Works even though Math is the class name, not an instance object!
MyVal = Math.Sin(AngleInRadians)
```

Another commonly used class with shared members is the MessageBox class.

Shared methods have a wide variety of possible uses. Sometimes they provide basic conversions and utility functions that support your class. For example, you might have a special class that reads information from a file and provides it through properties. This class might benefit from a shared IsFileValid function that takes the name of the file you plan to open, determines whether it is in the correct format, and returns True or False. You could then make a decision about whether to use the file by creating an instance of the class.

The following example uses a shared method to enhance our Person class:

```
Public Class Person
    ' (Code omitted.)

    Public Shared Function CalculateBirthDate(AgeInYears As Integer) As Date
        ' The following line takes the current date (using a shared method
        ' of the DateTime class), subtracts the number of specified years
        ' (using a built-in method), and returns the result.
        Return DateTime.Now.AddYears(-AgeInYears)
    End Function
End Class
```

This function is useful if you want to create a new Person, but you don't know the appropriate BirthDate to use. Using this shared function, you could supply the age in years, and receive a date value that you could use to create a new Person. (In practice, this function isn't required, because the Person class provides an additional constructor that accepts an Age parameter instead of a BirthDate.)

```
Dim BirthDate As Date
' Calculate the appropriate birth date for a 25-year-old using the shared method.
BirthDate = Person.CalculateBirthDate(25)

' Now create the person.
Dim CurrentPerson As New Person("Lucy", "Smith", BirthDate)
```

The Shared keyword is the only new addition; it indicates that this method is "shared" among all instances of this class, and will always be available.

A shared method can't access an instance member, such as a nonshared property or variable. In order to access a nonshared member, it would need an actual instance of your object—in which case it would also have to be an instance method.

```
Public Shared Function GetAgeInYears() As Integer
    ' This will not work because there is no current object!
    ' It would work perfectly well for a non-shared
method.
    Dim Age As TimeSpan
    Age = DateTime.Now.Subtract(Me.BirthDate)
    Return (Age.TotalDays \ 365)
End Function
```

Even so, a shared method can still be used with an instance object. In practice, it's best to use the class name instead of a live object when invoking a shared method. That way, it's obvious to anyone looking at your code that the particular procedure you are using does not require a live object.

Shared Properties

Just as you can create shared methods, you can create shared variables and properties by adding the Shared keyword. Once again, the possibilities are profound. Here is a simple example:

```
Public Class Person
    Private Shared _Count As Integer
    Public Sub New()
        _Count += 1
    End Sub
    Public ReadOnly Property Count() As Integer
        Get
            Return _Count
        End Get
    End Property
End Class
```

Here I've left out the other Person code to illustrate a new concept: A class can count how many objects have been created. It works like this:

- A shared variable, _Count, is used to keep track of the number of objects in use.

- Every time an object is created, the _Count variable is incremented in the constructor. The variable exists as long as the program is running, regardless of whether or not there are currently any Person objects in use.

- Remember that Count is read-only, and doesn't have a corresponding Set procedure.

Keep in mind that there is no code to subtract from _Count when an object is destroyed. This means that the counter won't be accurate in the long run unless you add additional features, such as a Dispose method that subtracts one from _Count.

Modules "Under the Hood"

You probably remember that classes aren't the only place to put code in Visual Basic .NET—you can also use modules, which provide procedures and variables that can be accessed at any time.

Modules are usually used for *helper functions*—routines that perform basic conversion or utility functions that may be required in numerous different places in your application. For many Visual Basic programmers, modules were the first tool they had to reuse code in several different places in an application.

If all this sounds oddly familiar, it's because modules perform the same role as shared methods. You might think that modules are a simpler way to share functionality, but in fact, there is really no difference at all. If you were to peer into the innards of your code, you would see that modules are really special classes that are made up entirely of shared members.

That's right—modules are classes! Because every member is shared, you don't need to create an instance of a module before you use it. This also means that you can work with only a single copy of your module, and that any information stored in its variables is available to any code using that module.

Here's an example of a module:

```
Public Module FileAccessTools
    Public FileName As String

    Public Sub OpenFile(File As String)
        ' Open the file here and set the FileName variable.
    End Sub

    Public Sub CloseFile
        ' Close the current file (indicated by FileName).
    End Sub
End Module
```

This module is identical to the class shown next. There is not a single difference, other than syntax.

```
Public Class FileAccessTools
    Public Shared FileName As String

    Public Shared Sub OpenFile(File As String)
        ' Open the file here and set the FileName variable.
    End Sub

    Public Shared Sub CloseFile
        ' Close the current file (indicated by FileName).
    End Sub
End Module
```

The more you understand about Visual Basic .NET, the more you will realize that the language is completely built around objects and the principles of object-oriented programming. Some of the conventions of traditional Visual Basic remain, but really just as a thin veneer over the OO reality.

Inheritance

Inheritance, consistently the most requested addition to Visual Basic, finally makes its debut in Visual Basic .NET. Inheritance allows you to define a basic set of features and procedures, and then create new classes that use this functionality and extend it with their own members. There are two main uses for inheritance:

- Inheritance allows code to be reused. For example, you might create an application with several data objects that read information from various files. The file access code would probably be almost identical, but the data objects would have different procedures and properties, depending on the types of information they represented. In this case, you could create a base class with basic file access code, and then create specific data classes that would inherit from the base class. They would gain all the file access code, and could add their own specific functionality.

- Inheritance is required to use key components of the .NET class library. For example, you create a form by inheriting from the System.Windows. Forms.Form class and adding your own code elements, such as control variables and event handling procedures. If you didn't use inheritance, you would have to use the default form that the class library provides to you, unchanged.

If you have read the preceding chapters, you've already had an introduction to a few important examples of inheritance at work, and more will be explored throughout the book. Some examples where inheritance is used with the .NET class library include:

- Forms, which derive all their basic functions from System.Windows. Forms.Form.

- Web Services, which derive from System.Web.Services.WebService.

- Custom collections (System.Collections.CollectionBase), exceptions (System.Exception), event argument objects (System.EventArgs), and many more.

Inheritance Basics

Here's an example of inheritance at its simplest:

```
Public Class Politician
   Inherits Person

    Private _Elected As Boolean
    Private _Party As Party

    ' Include some sample political parties.
    Public Enum Party
        Independent
        Communist
        National
    End Enum

    Public Property PoliticalParty() As Party
        Get
            Return _Party
        End Get
```

```
        Set(ByVal Value As Party)
            _Party = Value
        End Set
    End Property

    Public Property IsInOffice() As Boolean
        Get
            Return _Elected
        End Get
        Set(ByVal Value As Boolean)
            _Elected = Value
        End Set
    End Property

End Class
```

This Politician class inherits from the original Person class. (We can also say that the Politician class *derives* from the Person class, which is an example of a *base* or *parent* class.) This design is used because politicians have all the basic properties of people, including a first and last name and a birthdate. In addition, there is some information that applies only to politicians, such as Political-Party and the IsInOffice boolean variable used above.

If we create a Politician, you'll see that it has all the events, subroutines, and properties defined for a person, as shown in Figure 6-2.

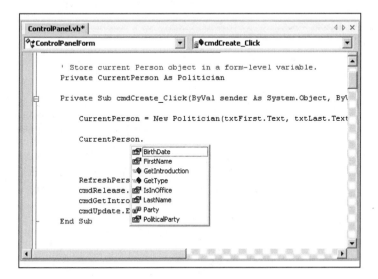

Figure 6-2: Events, subroutines, and properties of a Politician

This means that we can easily work with the full set of properties:

```
Dim President As New Politician()
President.PoliticalParty = Politician.Party.National
President.FirstName = "Lucy"
President.LastName = "Smith"
```

Inheritance in Action

The sample code for this chapter includes an InheritedObjectTester utility that shows the Politician class in action (see Figure 6-3).

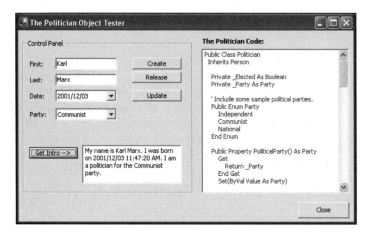

Figure 6-3: The Politician object tester

One interesting feature of this program is how it works with enumerations. The main window displays a listbox that allows the user to set the political party for the Politician object. However, the political parties are not added to the list by hand—to do so would violate encapsulation, and mingle Politician details with the user interface code.

Instead, the code uses a special shared method that is built into the System.Enum class—the GetNames method. This method provides an array of strings that represents all the constant names in the enumeration.

```
Private Sub ControlPanelForm_Load(ByVal sender As System.Object, _
  ByVal e As System.EventArgs) Handles MyBase.Load
    ' AddRange adds a whole array of string items at once.
    lstParty.Items.AddRange(System.Enum.GetNames(GetType(Politician.Party)))
End Sub
```

Note that in order the use the GetNames method, you need to retrieve a special object that represents the Party enumeration type. This Type object is obtained with the built-in GetType function.

Once a user has chosen a value from the listbox, the string has to be reconverted to the appropriate enumerated value (which, as you'll remember, is really just an integer). To perform this magic, you can turn to another piece of functionality that's built into every enumeration. In this case, it's the Parse method that converts a string name to the appropriate number.

```
Dim PartyChoice As Politician.Party
PartyChoice = System.Enum.Parse(GetType(Politician.Party), lstParty.SelectedItem)
```

Constructors in Inherited Classes

There are a couple of interesting quirks associated with derived classes. First of all, constructors are not directly inherited. Instead, as with any other class, Visual Basic .NET automatically provides a default constructor that takes no arguments for your derived class. This constructor automatically calls the constructor of your base class (Person, in our example). But our Person class has several different constructors. How does it know which one to call?

By default, the Politician constructor calls the matching Person constructor with no arguments. If our Person class doesn't have a constructor with no arguments, Visual Basic .NET will generate an error when you try to run the program.

Of course, there's no good reason to add a constructor with no arguments to the Person class just to fix this problem. Quite simply, the default constructor just doesn't provide enough information to create a new Person object. To get around this deficiency, you have to create at least one custom constructor for the Politician object. Once you add this constructor, you are off the hook. However, you are left with the dismal prospect of either writing additional, repetitive code to set the appropriate properties, or allowing the class user to create a half-initialized politician that is missing important information, such as a name and birthdate. Fortunately, derived classes provide a solution in a special property called MyBase.

MyBase represents the current instance of the class that you are inheriting from, just as Me represents the current instance of the derived class. One useful thing that MyBase allows you to do is invoke the constructor from the parent class.

Here's an example of a custom constructor in the Politician class that uses a constructor from the Person class:

```
Public Sub New(ByVal FirstName As String, ByVal LastName As String, _
   ByVal Age As Integer)
    MyBase.New(FirstName, LastName, Age)
End Sub
```

The parameter list for this constructor is the exact same as that for the constructor in our Person class. Once the constructor receives the information, it passes it along to the Person class to set up the basic Person values. This approach is extremely powerful, for the following reasons:

- You control exactly which constructors are available. For example, a constructor from the Person class that does not apply for a politician doesn't need to be available.
- You can use all the constructor logic from the parent class without having to repeat your code in the derived class.
- You have the chance to perform any additional politician-specific setup or error checking that is required. For example, you can ensure that a politician can't be created with an age less than 18.
- You can use a constructor from the parent class, but extend it with politician-specific information, as shown here:

```
Public Sub New(ByVal FirstName As String, ByVal LastName As String, _
 ByVal Age As Integer, ByVal PoliticalParty As Party)
    MyBase.New(FirstName, LastName, Age)
    _Party = PoliticalParty
End Sub
```

It's good practice to always begin a constructor in a derived class by calling one of the parent constructors. If you don't, you are at the risk of creating too much specific code, and creating a class that doesn't cleanly inherit from its parent. As a rule, if inheritance is difficult, or requires a great amount of special code to alter or override the original behavior, it isn't a good solution for your programming problem.

Protected Members

When you inherit from a class, all the public members are available, and all the private members—such as the variables used to store internal details—are hidden. This is generally good encapsulation. If your derived class wants to modify one of these variables, it should go through the appropriate property procedure, or call a method in the base class. It all boils down to an issue of responsibility. The derived class is responsible for managing all the additional information it supplies. The base class is responsible for managing its own internal workings and basic set of data. In order to be able to do this with confidence, it needs to be assured that no other piece of code can arbitrarily reach in and modify internal variables.

Sometimes, however, you might want to make a variable available to all derived classes, but not to any other code. This could allow some optimizations among a tightly linked group of related classes. To make a variable available, use the keyword Protected, instead of Private or Public.

The name Protected is a bit of a misnomer. As with a Private variable, a Protected variable is protected from careless client code, but is not protected from abusive code in the derived class. Here is an example:

```
Protected _BirthDate As Date
```

This variable will be accessible only to code in the Person class and any other derived class, such as Politician.

```
Public Class Politician
    ' (Code omitted.)
    Public Sub ChangeBirthDate(ByVal NewDate As String)
        ' Note that the MyBase keyword isn't required, but it makes it clear
        ' that you are modifying a value from the parent class.
        MyBase._BirthDate = NewDate
    End Sub
End Class
```

The same principle can be applied to methods, which can also be protected. This is generally a more useful technique. For example, you might have a special function that allows certain properties to be modified in your Person class. This utility method shouldn't be made directly available to the client code—instead, it should be available for use by other class methods or constructors when needed. However, the protection method might be useful for a derived class, and you can probably trust a derived class, such as Politician, to use it for the right reasons. Inside the actual method, you can still perform any required error checking to create a basic level of protection, thus ensuring that no invalid data is supplied.

Overriding Methods

Sometimes, the behavior of a parent class may not suit a derived class. For example, consider the GetIntroduction function in our Person class. While this is a nice starting point for a conversation, it may not be the most suitable choice for a politician's introduction. We could create a new method (GetPoliticianIntroduction) in the derived class, but this would mean that the client code would have to treat Politician objects and Person objects differently. One of the goals of using object-oriented design with inheritance is to create objects that have the same interface and that can be manipulated with the same code. Once you've done this, a client programmer needs to modify only one definition in order to create a program that can use Politician objects just as easily as it can use Person objects, with no coding changes required.

To help facilitate this vision, you can use overridable methods. *Method overriding* allows you to replaced a method in the base class with a more suitable method in a derived classes. For example, we could make our GetIntroduction function overridable:

```
Public Class Person
    ' (Code omitted.)
    Public Overridable Function GetIntroduction() As String
        Dim Intro As String
        Intro = "My name is " & FirstName & " " & LastName & ". "
        Intro = Intro & "I was born on " & BirthDate.ToString
        Return Intro
    End Function
End Class
```

Then we could create a specialized version for a Politician:

```
Public Class Politician
  Inherits Person
    ' (Code omitted.)

    Public Overrides Function GetIntroduction() As String
        ' Make use of the original GetIntroduction function.
        Dim Intro As String = MyBase.GetIntroduction()

        ' Add some additional politician-specific content.
        Intro &= " I am a politician for the " & _Party.ToString & " party."
        Return Intro
    End Function

End Class
```

This example gets the original introduction (using the MyBase keyword) and extends it. Alternatively, we could have skipped this step and just substituted an entirely new custom introduction.

Overridden Methods in Action

The technical details of overridden methods are fairly straightforward, but you may not realize the real benefit they provide until you see them in action. The advantage of overridden methods is that they allow a class to continue to interact with code in the way that the original parent class would, but with customized results.

For example, a programmer might have made a simple program using a Person class:

```
Dim CurrentPerson As New Person("Lucy", "Smith", 44)
' Call a custom procedure to print out the introduction to a printer.
PrintIntro(CurrentPerson)
```

This programmer uses a custom PrintIntro subroutine:

```
Public Sub PrintIntro(ByVal P As Person)
    Dim StringToPrint = P.GetIntroduction()
    ' Insert special code here to send the StringToPrint string to the printer in a
    ' nicely formatted page output.
End Sub
```

Now, perhaps the programmer wants to update the program to use the new Politician class. The following change is made:

```
Dim CurrentPerson As New Politician("Lucy", "Smith", 44)
```

And the program is now complete and fully functional. The PrintIntro procedure does *not* need to be changed, even though it expects a Person object. Because the Politician object is really a special kind of Person, it can be converted automatically.

The PrintIntro function won't be able to use any Politician-specific features, because it is treating the Politician object as a simple Person. However, when it calls the GetIntroduction method, it is the Politician object's version of the method that will be invoked! This is because in Visual Basic .NET, the bottommost version of a method is always used in a class, regardless of how the variable is defined (whether as a Politician or a Person, in our example).

Technically, no conversion takes place when the Politician object is passed to PrintIntro function. Instead, a special process called *casting* occurs.

Casting

When you use casting, you don't lose any information. Instead, you are just changing the way that Visual Basic .NET looks at an object. For example, you might receive a basic Object type from some sort of generic function. Essentially, an object is a reference to a blob of memory. When you receive an Object type, there's not much that you can do with it. If, on the other hand, you know what the object is really supposed to be, you can use CType to cast it, and start using your object's properties and methods immediately. You can't use these properties and methods without casting it, because Visual Basic .NET can't verify whether the object will really support them, and that violates type safety.

The key to understanding this process is realizing that casting is *not* conversion. No matter how you cast an object, it is still an identical blob of memory. The only change is what methods and properties are available. Of course, you can't cast an object to a different type unless it supports it. The only supported types of casting are from an object to an object's parent (for example, from a Politician to a Person) or from an object to one of its supported interfaces (which is discussed later in this chapter).

Here's a more direct example of casting, in action with the Politician class:

```
Dim CurrentPerson As New Politician("Lucy", "Smith", 44)
lblIntro.Text = CurrentPerson.GetIntroduction()

' Now convert the reference to a Person object.
CurrentPerson = CType(CurrentPerson, Person)

' GetIntroduction still works the same as it did before,
' with the political introduction, because CurrentPerson is a Politician object.
lblIntro.Text = CurrentPerson.GetIntroduction

' This doesn't work, because though CurrentPerson is a Politician,
' the code is treating it as a simple Person, and so the Party property is not available.
Lucy.Party = Politician.Party.Communist
```

MustOverride and MustInherit

There are a couple of additional tools you can use when modeling objects. One is *abstract classes*, which are defined with the MustInherit keyword. You cannot create objects out of the MustInherit class. All you can do is derive new classes based on it. An abstract class is often used to represent an entity that doesn't have any real meaning on its own.

```
Public MustInherit MyAbstractClass
    ' Ordinary class code goes here.
End Class
```

For example, you might have an application that uses several data objects that retrieve information from a database. These objects could share a common set of characteristics by inheriting from a DBRecord class. However, DBRecord methods have no meaning on their own. For example, a SaveData or LoadData method may use common operations; however, without information to store or load, there is no logical implementation for these methods.

Another related tool is the MustOverride keyword, which is used to create a method that has no implementation, but most be overridden by a base class. When you define a method with MustOverride, you do not add any code other than the method definition. You don't even include a final End Sub statement. Also note that a derived class *must* override all MustOverride methods; it can't simply ignore them.

The following code shows how you might model the DBRecord class:

```
Public MustInherit Class DBRecord

    Public Sub Connect(ByVal ConnectionString As String)
        ' Code goes here.
    End Sub

    Public MustOverride Sub LoadData()
    Public MustOverride Sub SaveData()

End Class
```

The Connect method is generic enough that it can be coded directly into the DBRecord class. However, the other methods have no default implementation, and must be replaced with overridden methods in derived classes.

You can use MustOverride to create a class template that specifies the types of methods that a class should use, and their parameter lists. Such a class template can be used for several different classes, ensuring consistency. This is a powerful approach, but the same result is often better accomplished through interfaces, which are designed specifically for this purpose.

Multiple Inheritance

Visual Basic .NET allows you to use unlimited layers of inheritance. For example, we could create a new class called DemocratPolitician, or even President, that inherits from the Politician class. The multiple inheritance feature is used to great effect in the class library. For example, every .NET type originates from the ultimate base type System.Object. Some classes pass through multiple levels of inheritance to build up all their features. For example, look at the inheritance diagram for a common Windows form shown in Figure 6-4.

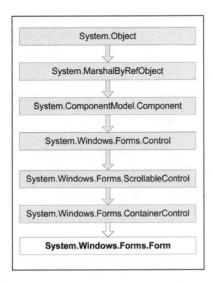

Figure 6-4: The lineage of a Windows form

Of course, the architects of the .NET class library are experienced OO developers. Multiple inheritance in a program should generally be viewed with skepticism. As a rule of thumb, try to keep the levels of inheritance to as few as possible (or just to a single level), particularly if there are multiple intermediate levels that you don't use. For example, if your application uses only Politicians, it's best that you create only a Politician class, not a base Person class and a derived Politician class.

Visual Basic .NET does *not* allow you to inherit from more than one class at the same time. If you have multiple, related sets of procedures that you want to combine in a class, it's often best to create a compound class that contains multiple objects. These objects will "plug in" to provide additional capabilities. For example, you could create a Person class that can contain an instance of an Occupation class to specify job-related information, and a Car object that describes the primary vehicle used by that person.

Is Inheritance a Good Idea?

In fact, inheritance can be a bit tricky, and with overuse, can lead to more problems than it's worth. A common problem with inheritance is *fragile classes*. These can emerge when you have a complex hierarchy of objects, and multiple layers of inheritance. In such a situation, it's often extremely difficult to change any characteristics of your base classes, because the changes would affect countless derived classes. In other words, your program reaches an evolutionary dead end, because any enhancement would break existing classes and cause a series of interrelated changes that would be difficult to track down and deal with.

When using inheritance, you should ask yourself if there are other available solutions to your problem. In some cases, you can also handle shared code by creating a utility class with appropriate functions. For example, we might solve our data object problem by placing file access routines into a common class or code module. Another way to avoid inheritance is to design more flexible objects that can contain other objects. For example, a data object could contain a special DBAccess object, and use it to communicate with the database. This technique is called *containment,* and it's usually used in combination with a technique called *delegation.*

Delegation is the process of a class passing information on to a contained class. For example, suppose you create a data object with a Connect method. When this method is called, the data object will call the contained Connect method in the contained DBAccess object, as follows:

```
Public Class SalesDataObject
    Private objDB As New DBAccess
    ' (Other code ommitted.)

    Public Sub Connect(ByVal ConnectionString As String)
        objDB.Connect(ConnectionString)
    End Sub

End Class
```

Using Inheritance to Extend .NET Classes

This chapter has concentrated on using inheritance with business objects. Business objects tend to model entities in the real world, and consist of data (properties and variables) and useful functions and methods that allow you to process and manipulate that data.

Inheritance also allows you to acquire features and procedures from the .NET class library for free. You've already seen how to do this with Windows forms, but we haven't discussed the full range of possibilities. This section provides two quick examples designed to illustrate the power of inheritance.

Visual Inheritance

Every form inherits from System.Windows.Forms.Form. However, you can also make a form that inherits from another form. As a sample exercise, create a form named frmBase, and add a couple of buttons. Now create a new form called frmDerived. Change the definition of frmDerived from this:

```
Public Class frmDerived
    Inherits System.Windows.Forms.Form
```

to this:

```
Public Class frmDerived
    Inherits frmBase
```

Before going any further, run your application to make sure that frmDerived is updated. (Otherwise, the changes described here may not be immediately visible in Visual Studio .NET.)

Your new form, frmDerived, will contain all the controls you created on frmBase (see Figure 6-5). In fact, frmDerived will look exactly the same as frmBase, because it will have inherited all of frmBase's controls and their properties. What's more, any time you make changes to frmBase, frmDerived will be updated automatically (although you may have to build the project before Visual Studio .NET will update the display). None of the code will be repeated in the frmDerived form class code, but it will all be available. For example, if you code a button click event handler in frmBase, it will take affect in frmDerived as well.

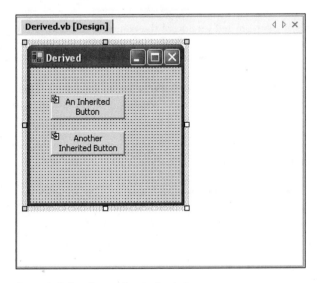

Figure 6-5: An inherited form in the designer

The only difference between frmBase and frmDerived is that you won't be able to move or alter the controls on frmDerived. However, you can still add new controls to frmDerived, and you can also change form-level properties (like the form caption or dimensions).

Visual inheritance is a strict and somewhat limiting tool. However, if you need to create several extremely similar windows, such as a series of windows for a custom Wizard, you can make good use of it.

Subclassing a Control

You can use a similar technique to extend a .NET control. To try this, add the following code:

```
Public Class CustomTextBox
  Inherits Windows.Forms.TextBox

    Public ReadOnly Property ReversedText() As String
        Get
            Dim Reversed As String
            Dim i As Integer
            For i = 1 To Text.Length
                Reversed &= Text.Chars(Text.Length - i)
            Next
            Return Reversed
        End Get
    End Property
End Class
```

This is a customized version of the common text box. It inherits everything that the TextBox control has to offer, and adds an additional read-only property. This property—ReversedText—returns the text in the text box backward (so that "TextBox1" becomes "1xoBtxeT").

To use this class, add a normal text box to your form. Then, examine the automatically generated Windows Designer code, and change the following line:

```
Friend WithEvents TextBox1 As System.Windows.Forms.TextBox
```

into this:

```
Friend WithEvents TextBox1 As MyProjectNamespace.CustomTextBox
```

Then change this:

```
Me.TextBox1 = New System.Windows.Forms.TextBox()
```

into this:

```
Me.TextBox1 = New MyProjectNamespace.CustomTextBox()
```

You will need to replace MyProjectNamespace with the root namespace of your project (which is, by default, the name of your project). To check this namespace, right-click on your project in the Solution Explorer, and select Properties.

If you've followed these instructions, you have converted the text box on your form into an instance of your custom text box. This means that it now supports the property you added (see Figure 6-6). To test it, try out the following line of code:

```
MessageBox.Show(TextBox1.ReversedText, "Custom TextBox Test")
```

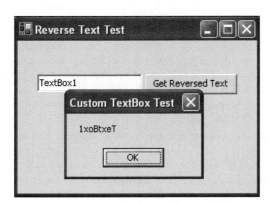

Figure 6-6: The reversible TextBox

TIP *You may notice that Visual Studio .NET is a little temperamental in this situation, making the custom text box disappear until you recompile the program, and providing misleading warnings at compile time. If you want to subclass a control in a professional application, the best approach would be to create a class library project, add the CustomTextBox class to that project, and then compile it as a DLL (Chapter 11 provides information about this process). You could then add a reference to this DLL in any project that needs to use the subclassed control. This approach, while technically the same, tends to provide better behavior in Visual Studio .NET.*

Interfaces

The *interface* is a cornerstone of object-oriented design, particularly for large-scale applications that need to be deployed, maintained, and enhanced over long periods of time. Interfaces require a bit of extra effort to use, and they are often avoided because they provide few immediate benefits. However, over the long term, they help solve common problems that make an application difficult to extend and enhance.

The goal of an interface is to allow you to separate a class definition from its implementation. An interface defines a small set of related properties, methods and events. By convention, interfaces always start with the capital letter I.

For example, you could create an interface to represent file access operations:

```
Public Interface IFileAccess

    Property IsFileOpen() As Boolean

    Sub Open(ByVal FileName As String)
    Sub Close()

    Sub LoadData()
    Sub SaveData()

End Interface
```

An interface contains absolutely no real code. In that sense, it's a bare skeleton of the members needed to support a specific feature or procedure. In that respect, an interface is very similar to an abstract class that is entirely composed of empty MustOverride methods. Note that interfaces don't use the Public or Private keyword when defining members. All the elements in an interface are automatically public. You'll also notice that interfaces don't use the full syntax for the members they define—mainly, they leave out the End statement and only include the property or method definition.

To use an interface in a class, you use the Implements statement. A class can implement as many interfaces as it needs. However, the class needs to provide its own code for every member in the implemented interface. Consider this example:

```
Public Class PersonData
    Implements IFileAccess
End Class
```

As soon as you enter this information in Visual Studio .NET, the IntelliSense feature will underline the word IFileAccess to indicate that your class cannot be considered complete, as one or more member from IFileAccess has not been implemented in PersonData (see Figure 6-7).

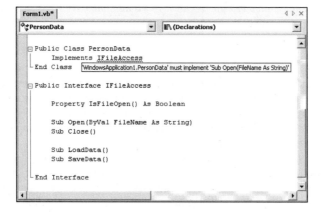

Figure 6-7: An unimplemented interface

To implement an interface, you need to provide code for every method. Here is an example of how you would implement the Open method:

```
Public Sub Open(ByVal FileName As String) Implements IFileAccess.Open
    ' (Code omitted.)
End Sub
```

Inheritance versus Interfaces

The difference between inheritance and interfaces is that inheritance allows code reuse. Interfaces guarantee that a class works a certain way, but the technical details are specific to the class. In our IFileAccess example, this may be a good idea, because the SaveData and LoadData methods will be completely different for each data object that uses them. To guarantee consistency, these methods might need to use a common .NET component or a custom file access class.

Using Interfaces

If you are new to interfaces, you're probably wondering why you should use them at all when they clearly require so much work. Unlike inheritance, interfaces do not let you reuse blocks of code; in order to reuse shared code, you have to make careful use of utility functions or inheritance in addition to interfaces. Interfaces also have the drawback of inflexibility (you always have to implement *every* member) and extra syntax (every member requires an appropriate Implements statement to match it to the appropriate method, property, or event that it is implementing). So what good can an interface do?

In fact, interfaces aren't nearly as crazy as they look. First of all, you need to understand that interfaces are not designed to solve problems of code reuse. Instead, an interface is a contract that guarantees that a certain set of features is available to an object. A client program may not know anything about a new SalesInfo class, but as long as it implements the IFileAccess interface, it knows how to use the LoadData and SaveData methods. Or, consider a Microwave and a ToasterOven object, both of which use a similar control panel to cook food. This could be implemented as an interface (ICookFood), which would allow a calling program to make dinner without necessarily needing to use any microwave-specific or toaster oven–specific functions.

Remember, with inheritance you can cast an object to its parent's type to provide a basic set of functions and features. The same is true with interfaces. Imagine the following class:

```
Public Class SalesInfo
    Implements IFileAccess
        ' (Code omitted.)
End Class
```

This class could be passed to a function, as shown here:

```
Public Sub PrintFileInfo(DataObject As IFileAccess)
    DataObject.Open()
    DataObject.LoadData()
    ' (Printing code omitted.)
    DataObject.Close()
End Sub
```

In other words, any class that implements IFileAccess can be cast to IFileAccess. This allows generic functions to be created that can handle the file access features of any class.

This ability is called *polymorphism*. Polymorphism is a feature that lets you use the same method name for multiple different types of objects. The corresponding method that is defined for a particular object is used automatically.

Interfaces and Backward Compatibility

Interfaces are designed as contracts. Once you create and implement an interface, you don't change it. For example, if you decide you need to create new LoadData and SaveData methods that accept different parameters (for example, a key for encryption, or a boolean value indicating whether compression should be used), you have to create a new interface, such as IFileAccess2. This new interface will apply to every single member of the class, even the members that haven't changed.

You may be able to simplify your life somewhat by using same method to implement more than one version of the interface, but this is only possible if the code hasn't changed:

```
Public Sub Open(ByVal FileName As String) _
  Implements IFileAccess.Open, IFileAccess2.Open
    ' (Code omitted.)
End Sub
```

Why go through all this trouble? By following this strict versioning policy, you create a new class that can be used by existing programs that still require the IFileAccess interface, and by new programs that have been upgraded to recognize the IFileAccess2 interface. If you just change the object and the interface, any existing programs will need to be recompiled with the new object; otherwise, they will stop working.

COM and Interface-Based Programming

All this interface-based programming may seem like a lot of extra work (it is). At this point, you may be tempted to forget about backward compatibility and just recompile all the programs that use an object whenever you change it. In truth, this isn't such a bad idea. In many cases it may even be the best idea. But in some situations, this approach isn't a valid option. The most common example is when you are developing a class for use in other programs. Once your class is distributed in a component, you can't simply modify it and break all the existing client applications.

Interface-based programming is the default method for creating old-fashioned COM-based applications. All COM components require interfaces, and they don't support inheritance. In many cases, a COM component requires a fixed interface for compatibility, because it is designed to be shared and used in countless programs.

For example, in previous versions of the Visual Basic language, the user interface controls provided by many features were ActiveX controls. If Microsoft had developed a new ActiveX component that broke its interface contract, or that didn't support previous interfaces, numerous existing applications would have been immediately broken when this component was installed on a client computer.

Other Reasons to Use Interfaces

Interfaces aren't just used for version compatibility. They also allow an object to standardize several different feature sets. Remember, you can only inherit from one class at a time. However, a class can implement all the interfaces that it needs. Interfaces are used extensively in the .NET framework, and they represent the handiwork of master OO designers. For example, arrays implement ICloneable (to provide a custom Clone method that copies the elements of an array), IList and ICollection (which allow an array to act like a collection), and IEnumerable (which allows an array to provide For Each enumeration support). In the next few sections, we'll consider some of .NET's most useful interfaces.

Cloneable Objects

Every class you create actually has the built-in intelligence to copy itself. It acquires this feature from the MemberwiseClone method, which every class inherits from the base System.Object class.

However, you can't access this method directly, because it is marked as Protected, which means it's only available to code inside the class, not code *using* the class. This is designed to impose some basic order on object copying. Because the MemberwiseClone method is not right for all objects, .NET forces you to go through a little bit of extra work to enable it explicitly.

You could create your own class method to use MemberwiseClone. The recommended approach, however, is to use the ICloneable interface, which is designed for this purpose. The ICloneable interface defines one method: Clone. Your object provides the code for this method, which can then use the internal MemberwiseClone method for a simple copy, or add some additional logic.

Here's a Clone method that could be used for the Person class:

```
Public Class Person
  Implements ICloneable
    ' (Other code omitted.)

    Public Function Clone() As Object Implements ICloneable.Clone
        ' Return a duplicate copy of the object using the MemberwiseClone method.
        Return Me.MemberwiseClone()
    End Function

End Class
```

The client would then need to call the Clone method, and use the CType function to convert it to the appropriate class type.

```
Dim CurrentPerson As New Person("Matthew", "MacDonald")
Dim NewPerson As Person

' Clone the author.
NewPerson = CType(CurrentPerson.Clone(), Person)
```

Cloning Compound Objects

One of the reasons that the MemberwiseClone feature is hidden from client use is because of the difficulty involved in cloning a compound object. For example, consider the following cloneable family class:

```
Public Class Family
  Implements ICloneable
    ' (Other code omitted.)

    Public Mother As Person
    Public Father As Person

    Public Function Clone() As Object Implements ICloneable.Clone
        Return Me.MemberwiseClone()
    End Function

End Class
```

When this object is cloned, the Mother and Father object references will be copied. That means that a duplicate Family class will be created that refers to the same Mother and Father. To modify this behavior so that the contained Mother and Father objects are also cloned (as shown in Figure 6-8), you would need to add additional code:

```
Public Function Clone() As Object Implements ICloneable.Clone

    Dim NewFamily As Family
    ' Perform the basic cloning.
    NewFamily = Me.MemberwiseClone()

    ' In order for this code to work, the Person object must also be cloneable.
    NewFamily.Father = Me.Father.Clone()
    NewFamily.Mother = Me.Mother.Clone()

    Return NewFamily

End Function
```

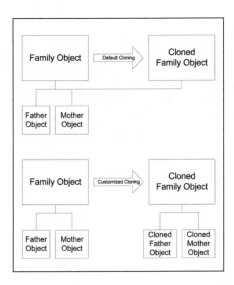

Figure 6-8: Two ways to clone

> **TIP** *In this example, it's fairly obvious that the Family class is a compound object. Compound objects are not always this recognizable. For example, an object might store information in a collection or an array. Collections and arrays are both reference type objects, which means that MemberwiseClone will copy the reference, not duplicate the object. You need to be extra vigilant when adding cloning capabilities to a class in order to avoid this sort of subtle error.*

Disposable Objects

From the last chapter, you'll remember that because of garbage collection, you can't rely on code that runs when an object is destroyed. If your class uses a limited resource (like a file or database connection), you should provide a method that allows this limited resource to be released. The recommended, standardized way to do this is to implement the IDisposable interface, which contains a single method called Dispose.

```
Public Class PersonFile
  Implements IDisposable

    Public Sub New()
        ' (Add code here to open the file.)
    End Sub

    Public Sub Dispose() Implements IDisposable.Dispose
        ' (Add code here to release the file.)
    End Sub

End Class
```

There's not much to using IDispose. Just remember that the calling code needs to call the Dispose method; it will not be invoked automatically. A good safeguard is to write code that overrides the Finalize method and checks that the finalization was carried out properly. (You can use a boolean class variable like Disposed, and set it to True when disposal is complete.) The Finalize method will be called automatically when the object is garbage collected.

```
Public Class PersonFile
  Implements IDisposable
    Private Disposed As Boolean = False
    ' (Other code omitted.)

    Public Sub Dispose() Implements IDisposable.Dispose
        ' (Add code here to release the file.)
        Me.Disposed = True
    End Sub

    Protected Overrides Sub Finalize()
        If Me.Disposed = False
            ' The object wasn't properly cleaned up. You might want to log this
            ' error to a file, because it can harm application performance.
            Dispose()
        End If

        ' Perform the .NET finalization.
        MyBase.Finalize()
    End Sub

End Class
```

Comparable Objects

By implementing the IComparable interface, you allow .NET to compare objects based on your class. One common reason that you might want to implement IComparable is to allow your classes to be sorted in an array or collection.

The IComparable interface has a single method called CompareTo. In the CompareTo method, your code examines two objects based on the same class, and decides which one can be considered "greater than" the other. The CompareTo method then returns one of three numbers: 0 to indicate equality, -1 to indicate that the compared object is less than the current object, and 1 to indicate that the compared object is greater than the current object.

Following is an example that shows how you can implement custom comparisons with the Person object. In this case, the programmer decided that the criteria for comparing Person objects would be their age. Thus, in a sorted list the youngest people would appear first, and the oldest would appear at the bottom.

```vb
Public Class Person
  Implements IComparable
    ' (Other code omitted.)

    Public Function CompareTo(ByVal Compare As Object) As Integer _
      Implements IComparable.CompareTo
        Dim ComparePerson As Person = CType(Compare, Person)
        If ComparePerson.BirthDate = Me.BirthDate
            Return 0    ' Represents equality.
        ElseIf ComparePerson.BirthDate < Me.BirthDate
            ' The compared object's age is greater than the current object.
            ' (Remember, the greater the birth date, the smaller the age.)
            Return 1
        ElseIf ComparePerson.BirthDate > Me.BirthDate
            ' The compared object's age is less than the current object.
            Return -1
        End If
    End Function

End Class
```

The built-in Sort method in the Array class recognizes the IComparable interface and uses the CompareTo method automatically. You can also use the CompareTo method directly in code.

TIP *Sometimes you need to provide a class that can be sorted in several different ways. In this case, you need to create separate sorting classes (like SortByName, SortByDate, and so on). Each of these sorting classes will implement the IComparer interface. This interface is similar to IComparable, and provides one method, CompareTo, that compares two objects and returns an integer indicating 0, 1, or –1. To use a special sorting method with the Array class, use the overloaded Sort method that allows you to specify an additional parameter with the appropriate IComparer object.*

Collection Classes

Inheritance is a relatively strict type of relationship, referred to as an *is-a* relationship. For example, a Politician is a Person (or at least most would agree). However, there are many other types of relationships in the world of objects. One of the most common is the *has-a* relationship—and as many can attest, in the materialistic world of today, what a person has is often more important than who they are. So too it is with classes, which can contain instances of other classes, or even entire groups of classes. This section jumps directly to the latter case, and introduces the *collection class,* which is an all-purpose tool for aggregating related objects, particularly for inclusion in a class.

A collection is similar to an array, but much more flexible. An array requires that you specify a size when you create it. A collection, on the other hand, can contain any number of elements, and allows you to add or remove items as you see fit. An array requires that you specify the data type of the information it will contain (or specify an object, if you want to be able to hold variables of different data types). A collection can contain any type of object. Lastly, while an array uses an index to identify its elements, a numeric index is of little use for a collection, because items can be added and removed at any point, thus changing the indices of all subsequent items. Instead, when you need to find a specific item in a collection, you either search through every element, or use the key you defined when you added the item.

> **TIP** A key *is a short, unique string description. Collections that use keys are sometimes called* dictionaries, *because they store information under specific key headings, like a dictionary does.*

A Basic Collection

Here's a simple collection:

```
Dim People As New Collection()
People.Add(Person1, "First")          ' Add a Person object with the key "First"
Person2 = People.Item("First")        ' Will set Person2 to Person1.
MessageBox.Show(People.Count)         ' Will display 1 (the number of items).
```

A NuclearFamily Class

Now it's time to jump right into a full-fledged example: the NuclearFamily class. I'll break down the elements of this example to explain how it uses a collection.

Here is the definition for our NuclearFamily class:

```
Public Class NuclearFamily
    Public Father As Person
    Public Mother As Person
    Public Children As New Collection()
```

```
Public Sub New(ByVal Father, ByVal Mother)
    Me.Father = Father
    Me.Mother = Mother
End Sub

Public Function FindYoungestChild() As Person
    Dim Child As Person
    Dim Youngest As Person

    For Each Child In Children
        If Youngest Is Nothing Then
            Youngest = Child
        ElseIf Youngest.BirthDate < Child.BirthDate Then
            Youngest = Child
        End If
    Next

    Return Youngest
End Function

End Class
```

Here's the rundown:

- The NuclearFamily class *has a* Father and a Mother variable, which point to corresponding Person objects. These variables are defined without the New keyword. This means that blank Father and Mother objects aren't created when you create a NuclearFamily. Instead, you must assign preexisting Person objects to these properties. (In the interest of shorter code, our example takes a shortcut by using variables instead of full property procedures.)

- All the children are contained in a collection called Children. This collection is defined with the New keyword, because it needs to be created before any Person objects can be added to it.

- A single constructor is used for the class. It requires parameters identifying both parents. In other words, you won't be able to create a NuclearFamily without a Father and Mother. Notice that the names of the parameters in the constructor are the same as the names of the variables in the class. This may seem confusing, but it's actually a common technique used to avoid needlessly creating new variable names. In this case, the parameter name has priority over the class name, so you need to use the Me keyword to refer to the current class in order to directly access the variables.

- A FindYoungest function searches through the Children collection and compares each child until it finds the one with the most recent BirthDate (and hence, the youngest age).

To use our NuclearFamily class, you need to create and add the family members:

```
' Create four distinct people.
Dim Lucy As New Person("Lucy", "Smith", 43)
Dim John As New Person("John", "Smith", 29)
Dim Anna As New Person("Anna", "Smith", 17)
Dim Eor As New Person("Eor", "Smith", 15)

' Create a new family.
Dim TheFamily As New NuclearFamily(John, Lucy)

' Add the children.
TheFamily.Children.Add(Anna)
TheFamily.Children.Add(Eor)

' Find the youngest child.
MessageBox.Show("The youngest is " & TheFamily.FindYoungestChild.FirstName)
```

The result of all this is shown in Figure 6-9.

Figure 6-9: Finding the youngest member

There isn't much new material in this example. What's important is the way everything comes together. Our NuclearFamily class is a compound class that contains two Person objects and its own collection.

A traditional structured program would probably model a family by creating a bunch of different information. Maybe it would keep track of only the children's birthdays, or even hard-code a maximum number of children in a fixed area. Along the way, a structured program would probably also introduce fixed assumptions that would make it difficult to expand the program and keep it clear. The NuclearFamily class, on the other hand, is built out of Person objects. Every family member is treated the same way, and the family is broken down into equivalent objects. You could even create multiple NuclearFamily classes that assigned the same family member (Person object) different roles—for example, as a child in one class and a parent in another.

In short, everything is consistently well organized. We change the Person class, and any part of our code that uses it automatically benefits. Code that deals with people is contained inside the Person class, so we always know where to find it. Life is good.

To try out the NuclearFamily class, run the CollectionTester utility from the sample code (see Figure 6-10).

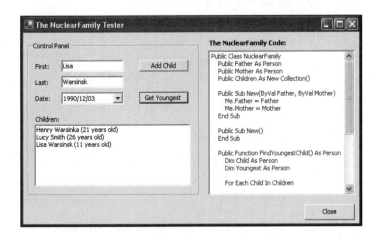

Figure 6-10: The NuclearFamily test utility

Creating a Custom Collection Class

One drawback with our NuclearFamily.Children collection is that it isn't type-safe. Though our respectful program only adds children into the collection, poorly written code could easily throw in strings, numbers, and other complex objects, which could cause all sorts of problems. Remember, when creating a component, you should always imagine that it is a separate program that may be thrust out into the world on its own and used by a variety of programmers, who may have little knowledge about its inner workings. For that reason, a class has to carefully protect itself against incorrect input.

One way to do this is through property procedures, as you saw in Chapter 5. In the NuclearFamily class, we could create a property procedure or a special method that accepts an object, checks its type, and then adds it to the Children collection. However, this approach has a significant drawback. Because the collection is no longer directly exposed, the client doesn't have any way to iterate through it. (*Iteration* is the handy process that allows a programmer to use a For Each/Next block to move through all the items in a collection without worrying about indexes or keys.)

A better solution is to create a custom collection class that is fine-tuned for a specific type of object. We can do this using inheritance and the System.Collections.CollectionBase class, which contains the basic procedures used to build a do-it-yourself collection that incorporates a built-in List collection. It also uses the IEnumerable interface, which means that it supports For Each iteration.

```
Public Class ChildCollection
    Inherits System.Collections.CollectionBase

    Public Sub Add(ByVal P As Person)
        Me.List.Add(P)
    End Sub

    Public Sub Remove(ByVal Index As Integer)
        ' Check to see if there is a Person at the supplied index.
        If Index > Count - 1 Or Index < 0 Then
            Throw New System.IndexOutOfRangeException()
        Else
            List.RemoveAt(Index)
        End If
    End Sub

    Public ReadOnly Property Item(ByVal Index As Integer) As Person
        Get
            ' The appropriate Person is retrieved from the List object and
            ' explicitly cast to the Person type.
            Return CType(List.Item(Index), Person)
        End Get
    End Property

End Class
```

Every collection class should have an Item property, and an Add and Remove method. The only change that our custom class introduces is that it restricts the Add method to valid Person objects. Many other customizations are possible. For example, if you're particularly sharp, you may have already realized that the FindYoungest method introduced in our earlier NuclearFamily example really belongs in this collection, because it acts only on the children.

To use the ChildCollection class, just change the data type of the Nuclear-Family.Children collection:

```
Public Children As New ChildCollection()
```

What Comes Next?

This chapter has discussed a wide range of object-oriented techniques. However, now that you have the knowledge, you still need the experience to learn how to implement object-oriented designs.

A substantial part of the art of using objects is deciding how to divide a program into classes. That question has more to do with the theory of application architecture than with the Visual Basic .NET language. Here are two starting points, based on some well-worn lingo often associated with object-oriented programming:

Three-tier Design

Three-tier design is the idea that applications should be partitioned into three principle levels: the user interface, the business objects or data processing procedures, and the back-end data store (a relational database or a set of XML files, for example). Three-tier design has caught on because it allows extremely scalable applications. With clever design, all three levels can be separated, upgraded or debugged separately, and even hosted on different computers for a potential performance boost. The concepts of three-tier design are also important when you are creating simpler client-server or desktop applications. By remembering that database access, data processing, and user interface are three different aspects of a program, you can get into the habit of separating these functions into different groups of classes. For example, your form classes all reside at the user interface level. This means that they shouldn't contain any code for processing data; instead, they should make use of a business object. Similarly, a business object shouldn't display a message directly on the screen, or access a form. It should be completely isolated from the user interface, and should rely on receiving all the information it needs through method parameters and properties. Understanding three-tier design can help you ensure that even your most straightforward programs are more encapsulated and easier to enhance and troubleshoot. To learn more about three-tier design, refer to topics in the MSDN website.

Business Objects

Essentially, *business objects* are the objects that exist in the middle tier of three-tier design (see Figure 6-11). They interact with your program on one side, and with the database or data objects on the other:

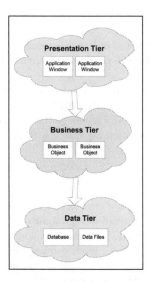

Figure 6-11: Three-tier design

Business objects encapsulate business rules: the specific operations and calculations in practice at an organization. Ideally, business objects contain almost no other information, because all the user interface and database code is taken care of on the other two levels. If you follow this system, you can create a powerful and reusable infrastructure. You can easily respond to changes in business rules, and you can reuse database or user interface code for other projects, because much of your project-specific content will be delegated to business objects. Of course, business objects don't necessarily look like the objects we've been creating. For example, many business objects use a transactional style of programming that emphasizes performance by eliminating procedures, and by using methods that require all the information to be submitted in parameters. This makes for uglier object-oriented design, but better performance in distributed applications, which may need to serve hundreds of users simultaneously.

For more information about business objects, you may want to read the MSDN topics related to MTS (the Microsoft Transaction Server) and distributed programming.

7

BUGPROOFING

Bugs—flaws in a program's logic, design, or syntax—have crashed everything from personal computers to a $125 million Mars orbiter. This chapter examines how you can code defensively, restrict possible problems, and protect yourself from bugs. You'll also learn how to handle common problems by using Visual Basic .NET's new structured exception handling, which replaces the well-worn On Error Goto statement. This new error-handling infrastructure allows you to filter out specific errors, pass error information in exception objects, and use a modern Try/Catch block structure.

Traditional VB error handling used a sort of "traffic redirection" to deal with problems. That made it very difficult to isolate error-handling code from application code, and the resulting spaghetti-like tangle could actually make errors more likely. VB .NET exception handling works like a handcrafted net. You design this net to catch specific error types, and then handle them appropriately if they occur.

Of course, even the best error-handling methods won't stop every potential problem. Eventually a bug will slip into your program, producing an error that you can't fix, or some data that just doesn't make sense. VB .NET continues to offer the wide range of debugging tools found in earlier versions of Visual Basic, with some additional refinements. In this chapter, you'll learn how to use these tools to track down and exterminate any bug that's loose in your software. You'll also learn some debugging techniques that will help you peer into the low-level gears and wires of your applications and uncover what's really taking place while your code executes.

New in .NET

Visual Basic has always provided a rich set of debugging tools, and these tools are still available in the latest .NET release, with a few helpful tweaks and improvements. The real story, however, is Visual Basic's new error-handling syntax, which modernizes VB to match other .NET languages.

Some of the changes you'll see in this chapter include:

Structured Exception Handling

Finally, you can remove the last Goto statement from your application and clean out spaghetti code for good. Visual Basic .NET's structured exception handling helps you ensure that your application's error recovery logic is as clean and well organized as the rest of your code.

Error Highlighting

Visual Basic has always been famous for catching errors as you type, and with the .NET platform, its intelligence has grown. Now troublesome code will be automatically underlined in blue, identifying where you've tried to use a method or variable that doesn't seem to exist, or where you've performed an illegal data conversion.

Type Safety

Accidental conversion errors are no longer a silent killer. VB .NET allows you to forbid dangerous conversions, thus giving you tighter control over your code.

Improved Debugging Tools

With Visual Basic .NET, the great gets better. Enhanced debugging tools, including an improved Call Stack display and a Breakpoints window, make it a breeze to hunt down troublesome code. You can even set different debugging options (like break or continue) for different types of errors.

The End of the "Run-Fix-Continue" Pattern

Sadly, not all .NET changes are good news. Visual Basic .NET uses the same debugging tools as every other .NET language, and these tools don't allow your programs to be modified "on the fly." If you change a line of code while debugging, you won't see the effect of your change until you rebuild your code and start over.

Anatomy of an Error

Bugs exist in many different varieties—some exotic, others as well known as the common housefly. Some of the species you'll see include:

Editor Mistakes

Visual Basic .NET is unique among languages because it includes a sophisticated error checker that works as you type, often identifying mistyped words and syntax errors. This tool is your first defense against errors, and one of the best ways to catch minor mistakes and save time.

Compile-Time Errors

When you run a program from the Visual Studio .NET IDE, any compile-time errors are reported to you in the Output window and on the Task List. *Compile-time errors* can result when you ignore an editor mistake, or if you make some other type of minor error—such as trying to perform a math operation with a string—that may not be caught until the program is being built.

Runtime Errors

Runtime errors are problems that occur while the program is being used. Usually, a runtime error is an unhandled error that propagates back to the user and ends the program. For example, if you try to open a file that doesn't exist, and don't provide any error-handling code, the Common Language Runtime will provide an error message and your code will stop abruptly. A compile-time error usually cannot become a runtime error, because Visual Basic .NET will refuse to compile the offending code, and will continue using an older version of your program. However, a code statement that is syntactically correct but could result in a problem—for example, trying to access a web page on a computer that may or may not have an Internet connection—can cause a runtime error.

Logic Errors

This is the most insidious type of bug, because it is often difficult to determine what part of the code is responsible. Code containing a *logic error* runs without generating any warning or error messages. However, the information or behavior that results is clearly not what is expected. A good example is an investment program that automatically *subtracts* 1.5 percent interest on existing balances.

Errors That Can't Happen

One of the goals of the .NET platform is to make your life easier. There are entire classes of errors that have troubled generations of earlier programmers but are now impossible. Memory leaks, pointer errors, and other types of fiendish problems that have plagued our programming ancestors are carefully defended against in the .NET world.

The Principles of Bugproofing

The earlier an error is detected, the better. You should celebrate when Visual Basic .NET generates a build error and refuses to compile your code. When a compile-time error occurs, it means that Visual Basic .NET's automatic error checking has found a potential problem that you've missed, and has identified it so that you don't have to spend hours trying to troubleshoot a mystery in the future. Visual Basic .NET improves on Visual Basic 6 by detecting many common errors earlier—finding missing variables while you type, for instance, instead of when you compile, and flagging data type conversion problems with compile-time errors instead of runtime errors.

Expect the unexpected. Later in this chapter, we'll consider some basic techniques for coding defensively. Once you start expecting users to enter strange and possibly illogical input, you are ready to prepare and prevent possible catastrophes. Often you can tell the novice programmer from the expert not by how fast an application is completed, but by how well the application stands up after a few months of intensive use in the field.

Don't ignore the compiler. Once your program gets into the hands of users, and inexplicable errors start to occur, a trivial problem that once seemed to be fixed by a randomly changed line may keep you awake for a few sleepless nights.

Test early and test often. I won't spend much time in this chapter talking about testing, because it really is a straightforward process. Still, it is amazing how many programmers don't try out their own creations, thus missing mistakes that can hurt their pride and careers once they deliver the code. None of the great tools in Visual Basic .NET can remove the inevitability of human error, so be thorough, and make use of the debugging tools discussed in this chapter. Some programmers even insist that they won't let any code out of their hands until they've single-stepped through every line in every function.

How Visual Basic .NET Treats Errors

Visual Basic .NET's treatment of errors is straightforward, but slightly different than in previous releases. In Visual Basic 6, the editor would interrupt you every time you made a mistake with an intrusive message box (as seen in Figure 7-1).

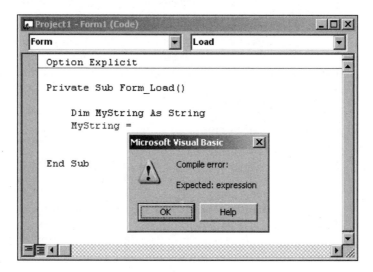

Figure 7-1: The intrusive editor in Visual Basic 6

Visual Basic .NET takes a friendlier approach, working as your partner, not your prosecutor. The process works like this:

- First, if you've made an obvious, clear-cut mistake, the editor tries to correct it for you automatically. For example, you'll notice that if you start an If block and leave out the word Then, the editor will add it for you. It will also add details (such as the closing End If, in this case) to prevent you from making other possible mistakes.

- If the editor can't correct the mistake, it will underline the offending code in blue. Common reasons for blue underlining include using a variable, method, or property that's not defined, calling a method with the wrong number of arguments, or using a language construct with syntax that just doesn't make sense (for example, writing "If End" instead of "End If"). If you have Option Strict enabled (and you should), invalid variable assignments and conversions will also be highlighted. If you're wondering why a line is underlined in blue, place the mouse over the line and read the corresponding tooltip text (see Figure 7-2).

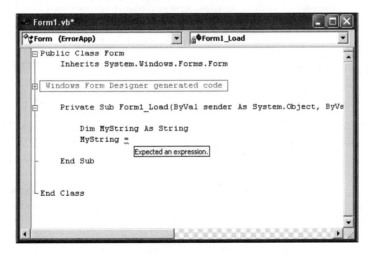

Figure 7-2: The polite editor in VB .NET

- When you compile a program, either for debugging or as a release, any editor errors you've ignored will become compile-time errors. An overview will be provided in the Output window (as shown in Figure 7-3), and you'll be asked if you want to continue. If you continue, part of your application may not be recompiled, and you may end up testing the preceding version of your code, without all your recent changes.

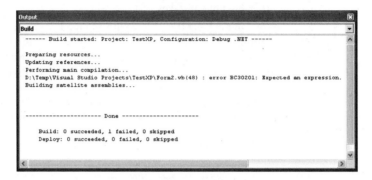

Figure 7-3: Output for a failed build

- Instead of continuing with compile-time mistakes, you should cancel the build process and review the list of errors (see Figure 7-4). Visual Basic .NET makes it easy for you: Just double-click on an entry in the task list and you'll be brought to the appropriate spot in your code, with the error highlighted. This is a big improvement over Visual Basic 6, where you were told about errors one by one, and you had to fix the current error before finding out about the rest.

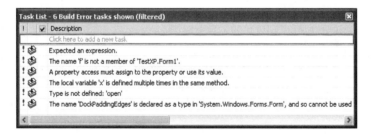

Figure 7-4: Problems tracked in the task list

- When a runtime error occurs, Visual Basic .NET searches your code for an error handler that can deal with the problem. If none is found, it presents an error message with basic information, and ends the program. If you are debugging in the development environment when the problem occurs, you will be given the option to go directly to the line of code where the error occurred. You can then fix the problem, but you will have to restart (and rebuild) the program before your correction will take effect. Unlike Visual Basic 6, Visual Basic .NET cannot compile your code dynamically in debug mode.

Option Explicit and Option Strict

These two life-saving options should always be enabled. Option Explicit stops you from using a variable without creating it, and thus prevents the mistakes that can occur when a new, empty variable is automatically created after you misspell the name of an existing variable. Option Explicit is enabled by default.

Option Strict is new to Visual Basic .NET, and it prevents the runtime overflow errors that can result from automatic variable conversions. For example, converting an Int32 into an Int16 is a "narrowing" conversion, and it may or may not succeed. With Option Strict off, you are free to try. . .

```
Option Strict Off

Private Sub SwapNumbers(BigNumber As Int32, SmallNumber As Int16)
    Dim Swap As Int32
    Swap = BigNumber
    BigNumber = SmallNumber   ' This is a widening conversion; it always works.
    SmallNumber = Swap        ' Sure, it works now, but it could become a fatal
                              ' runtime error under the right circumstances.
End Sub
```

In this example, Visual Basic won't complain, and you'll be blissfully unaware of the potential time bomb—until you submit a value for BigNumber that is larger than 32,767.

With Option Strict on, it's a different story. The code will be underlined in blue, and an error will be generated at compile time. You won't be allowed to use the code without modifying it to perform an explicit (manual) conversion. At that point, you'll probably realize the potential problem, and either change SmallNumber to an Int32, or rewrite the code with an extra safeguard:

```
Option Strict On

Private Sub SwapNumbers(BigNumber As Int32, SmallNumber As Int16)

    Dim Swap As Int32
    Swap = BigNumber
    BigNumber = SmallNumber     ' This is a widening conversion; it always works.

    If BigNumber > SmallNumber.MaxValue Then
        MessageBox.Show "Sorry, this number doesn't fit."
    Else
```

(continued on next page)

```
    ' The CType function manually converts the number.
    SmallNumber = CType(Swap, Int16)
End If

End Sub
```

This example makes use of the MaxValue constant that is built into many
simple data types, including integers. It indicates the largest number that the
current variable can hold (which is 32,767 in this case). By using the MaxValue
constant, you can avoid coding the number directly into the program, and you
allow the program to continue working even if you change the data type of
SmallNumber.

If you suspect that Option Strict or Option Explicit is not enabled for your
project, right-click on your project in the Solution Explorer, and select Properties. The Option Strict and Option Explicit settings are configured under the
Common Properties • Build folder (see Figure 7-5).

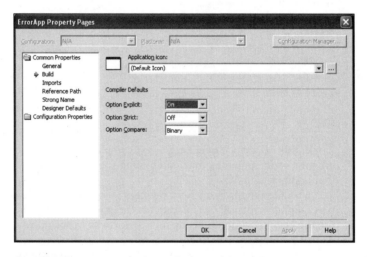

Figure 7-5: Project settings for Option Explicit and Option Strict

Line Numbers

Line numbers used to be the hallmark of old-fashioned programming languages—such as the original DOS version of BASIC. In Visual Basic 6, you were
able to optionally add numbers to specific lines. In Visual Basic .NET, you can't
even do that. Line numbers have vanished. Or have they?

One well kept secret is that you can enable a line number display for your
code by selecting Tools • Options to display the Options window, and then
selecting the Text Editor • Basic • General tab. Click on the Line Numbers
checkbox, and Visual Studio .NET will display a margin that numbers every line
in the file, including blank ones (see Figure 7-6).

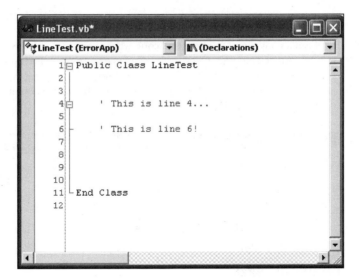

```
LineTest.vb*

LineTest (ErrorApp)          (Declarations)

    1 Public Class LineTest
    2
    3
    4         ' This is line 4...
    5
    6         ' This is line 6!
    7
    8
    9
   10
   11 End Class
   12
```

Figure 7-6: Line numbers return from the past

You can't directly enter or change these numbers. So why use them? As you'll see later in this chapter, Visual Basic errors include line number information that pinpoints where an error has occurred. If an unhandled error occurs at a client site, you can customize your error message to display or record the corresponding line number. Then you can track down the corresponding code at your desk, without needing to recreate the problem.

Visual Studio .NET's Debugging Tools

It's bound to happen eventually. Illogical data appears. Strange behavior occurs. It looks as though information that you've never entered is appearing out of thin air, and code is being executed in a different order or in a different way than you expected. In other words, you've got a bug. So what should you do about it?

This section walks you through Visual Basic .NET's debugging tools, including *breakpoints* that let you study code flow, *watch windows* that let you examine variables in action, and the *call stack history,* which gives additional information about your program's place in the overall order of procedures.

Watching Your Program in Action

One of the greatest tools in any programming language is the ability to *step through* an application. This feature allows you to watch the action and study the flow, or the path of execution your program takes, through the classes and functions that you provide it with. When you step through your code, you test the assumptions that you have about how it will work. You determine the order in which statements are executed, and the values that are recorded in your variables. Single-stepping allows you to spy on what your program is really up to.

To single-step through a Visual Basic .NET program, follow these steps:

1. Find a convenient spot in your code where you want to pause execution and start single-stepping. Click in the gray margin next to the appropriate line to insert a red breakpoint (Figure 7-7). (You can put a breakpoint on any *executable* line of code. It cannot be put on a blank line, comment, or variable declaration.)

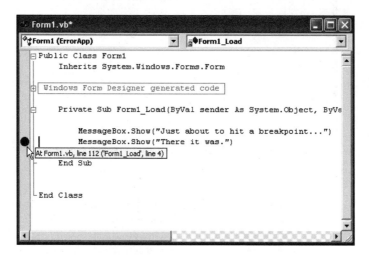

```
Form1.vb*

Form1 (ErrorApp)                    Form1_Load

Public Class Form1
    Inherits System.Windows.Forms.Form

    Windows Form Designer generated code

    Private Sub Form1_Load(ByVal sender As System.Object, ByVa

        MessageBox.Show("Just about to hit a breakpoint...")
        MessageBox.Show("There it was.")
    At Form1.vb, line 112 ('Form1_Load', line 4)
    End Sub


End Class
```

Figure 7-7: Setting a breakpoint

2. Run your program. When it reaches the breakpoint, execution will pause. The statement with the breakpoint will not be executed. This line will have a yellow arrow next to it, indicating that it is the next instruction that will be executed when the program resumes.
3. You can now hover over variables to see their current contents, and run your program one line at a time by pressing F8.

Commands Available in Break Mode

While your program is paused, you can use the following commands.

Step Into (F8)

This command executes the currently highlighted line, and then pauses again. If the currently highlighted line calls a method or a function, execution will pause at the first executable line *inside* the method or function (which is why this feature is called *stepping into*).

Step Over (SHIFT-F8)

This command works the same as Step Into, except that it runs methods and functions as though they are a single line. If you press Step Over while a procedure call is highlighted, the entire method or function will be executed, and execution will pause at the next executable statement in the current procedure.

Step Out (CTRL-SHIFT-F8)

This command executes all the code in the current procedure, and then pauses at the statement that immediately follows the one that called the executed method or function. In other words, it allows you to *step out* of the current procedure in one large jump.

Continue (F5)

This command resumes the program and continues to run it normally, without pausing until another breakpoint is reached or you click on the Pause button.

Run To Cursor (CTRL-F8)

This command lets you run all the code up to a specified location (where your cursor is currently positioned). Run To Cursor is often used to skip a time-consuming loop, and is a little bit like creating a temporary breakpoint. You can also use this feature by right-clicking on a line of code in break mode and choosing Run To Cursor from the context menu.

Set Next Statement (CTRL-F9)

This command causes your program to mark the line where your cursor is positioned as the current line for execution. When you resume execution, that line will be executed, and the program will continue from that point. Essentially, Set Next Statement allows you to change your program's path of execution while you are debugging. This useful feature allows you to repeat a section of code, or to skip a section that is potentially problematic or requires some sort of validation that would ordinarily prevent you from continuing. For example, you may have code that only runs in a certain situation. Rather than trying to recreate this situation, you can use the Set Next Statement command to jump directly to the appropriate section and run it.

Show Next Statement

This command displays the current statement, which will be executed when you next press F8 or F5. The line will be marked by a yellow arrow. Show Next Statement is useful if you lose your place while editing, and you can choose it quickly from the right-click context menu.

Customizing Breakpoints

Visual Basic .NET provides you with additional options for setting up breakpoints. To configure these options, right-click on a breakpoint, and select Breakpoint Properties from the context menu as shown in Figure 7-8.

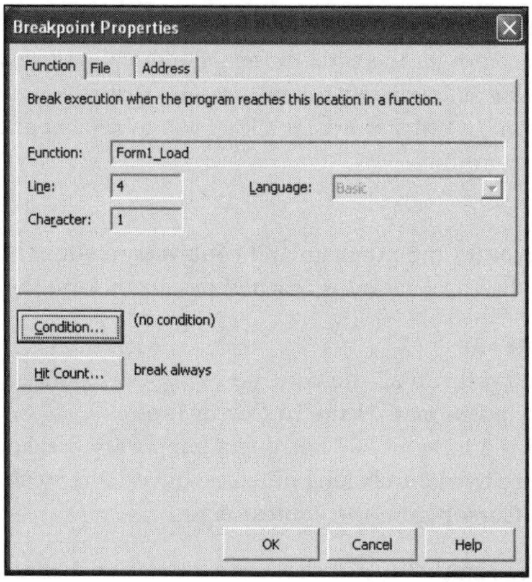

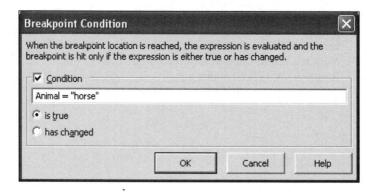

Figure 7-8: Breakpoint properties

Condition

Use the Condition button to set extra criteria that will be used to decide whether or not execution should pause at the breakpoint. For example, the following condition will stop execution at the specified point when the variable Animal contains the string "horse" (see Figure 7-9). Otherwise, the breakpoint will be ignored. You can use a condition to filter out a problem, and then halt the program immediately when a specific piece of invalid data appears.

Figure 7-9: A sample breakpoint condition

Hit Count

The Hit Count window allows you to specify whether or not execution should pause at a breakpoint, depending on how many times the program has executed the line of code. This feature is useful when you create a breakpoint on a frequently executed line, such as one inside a loop. In this case, you may want to stop execution after a certain number of passes through the loop, rather than every time the statement is encountered.

Depending on the Hit Count options you set, you can configure your program to pause only after a breakpoint has been encountered a certain number of times, after a certain multiple of times (for example, every third time), or when the hit count is exactly equal to a specified number.

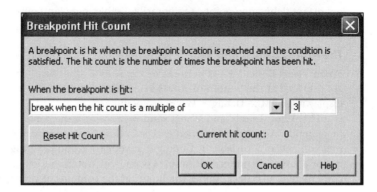

Figure 7-10: A Hit Count breakpoint condition

The Breakpoints Window

You can take a quick look at all your breakpoints by using the Breakpoints window; simply choose Debug • Windows • Breakpoints (see Figure 7-11). In the Breakpoints window you will see a list of all the breakpoints defined in your project. You can jump to the corresponding location in code by double-clicking on a breakpoint.

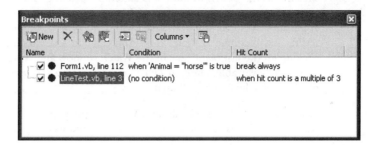

Figure 7-11: The Breakpoints window

If you uncheck a breakpoint, it appears in the code editor as a transparent gray circle with a red outline. This means that the breakpoint is disabled and will be ignored. However, you can quickly re-enable it from the Breakpoints window when it is needed again. The Breakpoints window also provides the hit count, showing the number of times a breakpoint has been encountered. The hit count is reset every time the program is stopped and restarted.

You can also configure breakpoint properties from this window by right-clicking on an individual breakpoint.

Saving Breakpoints

Unlike earlier versions of Visual Basic, VB .NET automatically saves your break-points with your application. This means that you can insert breakpoints at important debugging points, temporarily disable them, and quickly enable them from the Breakpoints window at a later date when they are needed.

The Autos, Locals, and Watch Windows

When Visual Basic .NET is in break mode, several additional tabbed windows are provided at the bottom of your screen. If any of these is not visible, you can display it using the Debug • Windows menu.

The Autos, Locals, and Watch windows show you the contents of variables in break mode. As you have learned earlier in this chapter, you can inspect the current contents of a variable by finding it in your code and hovering your mouse cursor above it. However, the Autos, Locals, and Watch windows provide a more convenient way to peer "under the hood" at the contents of your variables.

- The **Autos** window is automatically set to variables that Visual Basic .NET determines are probably important for the current breakpoint. Usually, these include only the variables that were accessed or changed in the previous line.

- The **Locals** window displays all the variables that are in scope in the current procedure. This window offers a quick summary of important variables.

- The **Watch** window is quite similar to the Autos and Locals windows. However, its list contains only the variables that you have specifically added. This makes the Watch window well suited for prolonged testing, when you want to keep track of a specific variable or object during the lifetime of an application. Watches are even saved with your project, so you can pause testing and continue at a later time. You can add a watch quickly by double-clicking on the last blank row in the Watch window and typing in an appropriate variable name, or by right-clicking on a variable in your code display and selecting Add Watch.

Each row in the Autos, Locals, and Watch windows provides such information as the type or class of the variable or object, and its current value.

Object Structure

One of the most impressive features of the Autos, Locals, and Watch windows is that you can see the object structures of the classes and procedures in your program. For example, in the Locals window you'll see the term Me, which is a reference to the current class. Next to the word Me is a box with a plus sign (+), indicating that more information is available. Click on this box to expand the Me reference and display all of its properties.

TIP *The Watch window also shows information about nested objects. For example, an ordinary Form class contains a variable for each control displayed in the window. You can expand these variables to find out information about the properties of your textboxes, buttons, and labels.*

A good example of how to use a Watch window with an object is shown here. Using the Locals window on my Person class, I'm able to spot a potential mistake: The LastName property has not been initialized (Figure 7-12).

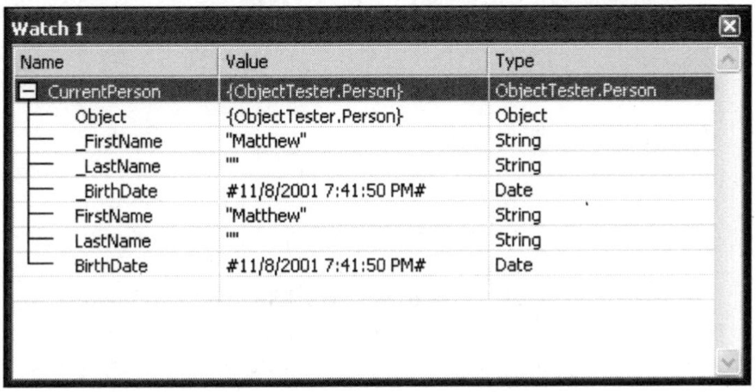

Name	Value	Type
☐ CurrentPerson	{ObjectTester.Person}	ObjectTester.Person
⎯ Object	{ObjectTester.Person}	Object
⎯ _FirstName	"Matthew"	String
⎯ _LastName	""	String
⎯ _BirthDate	#11/8/2001 7:41:50 PM#	Date
⎯ FirstName	"Matthew"	String
⎯ LastName	""	String
⎯ BirthDate	#11/8/2001 7:41:50 PM#	Date

Figure 7-12: The object structure of a Person

Notice that the Watch window knows no boundaries—it fearlessly displays both public data (the properties like FirstName, LastName, and BirthDate) and private data (the internal member variables that are preceded with an underscore).

Modifying Variables During Break Mode

The Autos, Locals, and Watch windows don't just display variables; they also allow you to change them while a program is in break mode. This allows you to easily re-create specific scenarios. For example, you might run a test to determine what happens when an invalid value is set in one of your variables.

To set a value, double-click on the value in the Value column, and type in the new value.

The Command Window

The Immediate window is alive and well in VB .NET, although it has been renamed to be the Command window. It doesn't retain the full range of power that it had in Visual Basic, but it still allows you to print out the contents of specific variables by using the question mark (?), as shown in Figure 7-13. One nice touch is that you can use the question mark (or the full command, Debug.Print) to print out the full contents of an object just by specifying the variable name.

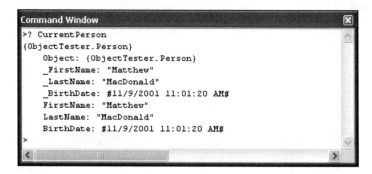

Figure 7-13: Printing an object's contents

One of the strangest twists is that the Command window can be used at design time, but not to evaluate expressions or run code. Instead, it allows you to perform IDE commands (see Figure 7-14). For example, instead of selecting Print from the File menu, you can type the File.Print command into the Command window. You can access just about any part of Visual Studio .NET, and there's even some rudimentary statement completion to help you out. However, you are almost certain to find this interesting quirk to be more trouble than it's worth.

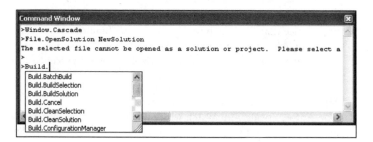

Figure 7-14: Typing IDE commands—the return of DOS?

The Call Stack Window

The Call Stack window shows you the currently executing procedure, and a history of recent procedures that have not yet completed. When in break mode, the current procedure is marked with a yellow arrow. If you double-click on a procedure, the editor will display the line in your code that called that procedure.

Procedures are added to the call stack history as they are started, and removed from the call stack history once they are completed. For example, in Figure 7-15, the current procedure is the method Calculate, which was called by the event handler for the cmdCalculate button. Once the Calculate method finishes and returns a result, it will disappear from the Call Stack window.

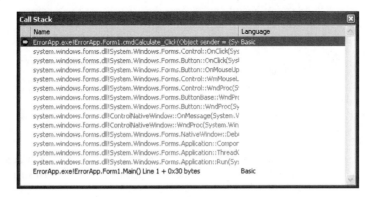

Figure 7-15: The Call Stack after a button click

You'll notice that the Call Stack includes not only the methods and functions in your own application, but also parts of the Common Language Runtime that are executed automatically. Sections of your program are displayed in black, while external CLR procedures are shown in light gray.

There is actually quite a lot of information packed into the Call Stack window. For example, the parameters that were used for every procedure call are displayed, giving you a history of the different values that your program has passed to different routines. (If you can't read the full parameter list, hover your mouse cursor over it to display a tooltip window.)

Structured Exception Handling

Not every bug can be tracked down and removed from your program. In fact, there are some cases where an error can occur through no fault of your own. For example, if your program uses file input, when you open a file you are assuming that it is accessible to you, that the disk has not been corrupted by media failure or a virus, and that the file won't be deleted between the time the user selects it and the time your code attempts to read it.

Your application can and should handle basic verification procedures, such as checking that the file exists before attempting to open it, and checking that it contains the header that your program created to indicate that the file is valid.

However, you can't defend yourself against all the possible problems that might occur. This is why Visual Basic .NET provides *structured exception handling*.

Here's an example of structured exception handling in a file access routine:

```
Dim FileLine As String
Dim FileStream As System.IO.StreamReader

Try
    ' This code could cause a problem . . .
    FileStream = System.IO.File.OpenText("does_not_exist.txt")
    FileLine = FileStream.ReadLine()
Catch MyError As Exception
    ' We end up here if an error occurred.
    MessageBox.Show(MyError.Message)
Finally
    ' We end up here no matter what!
    If Not FileStream Is Nothing Then
        FileStream.Close()    ' Close the file.
    End If
End Try
```

The foundation of structured error handling is the Try/Catch/Finally block, which replaces Goto statements with a more modern structure, such as If/End If or For/Next.

In the preceding example, the portion of the code after the Try statement is the code that is being watched for errors. If an error occurs, the Catch portion of the code is executed. And either way, whether a bug occurs or not, the Finally section of the code is executed next. The Finally code allows you to perform some basic cleanup. Even if an unrecoverable error occurs that will prevent the program from continuing, the Finally code will still be executed.

NOTE *Along with this new method of error handling comes some new lingo. You've probably already noticed that it's not an error any more, but an exception. Also, exceptions aren't generated or raised, but thrown by misbehaving code. Your Try/Catch block then catches the thrown exception.*

Understanding the Error Call Stack

When an error occurs in your application, Visual Basic .NET tries to find a matching Catch statement in the current procedure. If none is found, the search continues through the Catch statements in the code that has called the current procedure. This process continues through the entire stack until a Catch block is found that can handle the current error, or until the search feature reaches the uppermost level of the application—at which point a runtime error will be generated, ending the program.

The Evolution from On Error Goto

Up until now, I've glossed over an ugly secret. Visual Basic .NET still supports the On Error Goto command for backward compatibility. All your old programs can continue using it. However, you should adopt the new structured exception handling as soon as you start a new project. Why?

On Error Goto has a number of problems. Almost every other language, from Pascal to C++, has been using more advanced error handling for years. I hate to revisit ancient history, but here is a quick summary of what you are leaving behind when you enter the .NET world:

Spaghetti Code. Error routines in Visual Basic 6 were clear and readable, as long as you were checking for only one type of error in one block of code. If you need to handle multiple different errors, you have to juggle numerous On Error Goto statements directing code to different sections of your program. Otherwise, you could determine the type of error, but not where it occurred.

Error Monogamy. Visual Basic 6 has exactly one error object: the built-in Err. If an error occurs in your error-handling routine, or if you try to examine the error information in another routine, you'll find that all of the error information disappears immediately, leaving you empty-handed. Visual Basic .NET exceptions are full-featured objects that you can catch and throw on your own, and pass from routine to routine.

Language Limitations. Exceptions are built into the .NET runtime. This means that you can throw an exception in Visual Basic .NET and catch it in C# without having to worry about any compatibility code.

Limited Diagnostic Ability. The Err object just doesn't provide enough information. However, even basic exceptions contain a StackTrace property that gives you specific low-level information about where the error originated.

The Exception Object

The cornerstone of structured exception handling is the *exception object*. The basic exception object is System.Exception, and that's the type that we caught in the preceding example. The exception object also exists in many different, more specialized versions that inherit from System.Exception. Usually, when an error is thrown, it's one of these more specific varieties. For example, in the previous file-handling example, the exception that occurred might have been System.IO.EndOfStreamException if the file existed but had no content, or it might have been System.IO.FileNotFoundException if the file had not been found.

To gain some insight into what an exception object is, it helps to examine one close up. A tool you can use for such an examination is the Locals window. To try it out, create a Windows Forms application, and enter the code from the previous file access example in the Load event handler. This code is sure to fail, because the file does_not_exist.txt is not present on your computer. Now, place a breakpoint after the Catch line, on the MessageBox.Show statement. (Alternatively, you can get this program from the online samples. It's in the ExceptionsAndAssertions project.)

When you run your program, the bug will be triggered, and the program will enter break mode. You can now take a closer look at the object structure of the exception you've caught in the Locals window (see Figure 7-16). Remember, we are primarily interested in the public data associated with the exception object. Ignore the information that starts with an underscore.

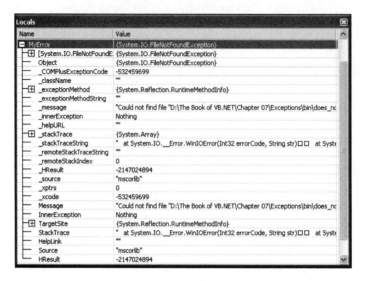

Figure 7-16: The internal structure of an exception

What does this tell us about the error object?

- Its type is indeed System.IO.FileNotFoundException.

- It comes with a Message property that contains the text "Could not find file D:\Temp\Visual Studio Projects\WindowsApplication4\bin\ does_not_exist.txt."

- It has a Source property that tells us which class or application the error occurred in.

- It has a StackTrace property that contains a whole list of information about the recent history leading up to the error. (The easiest way to see this information is usually to display it in the label of a message box.) The last line contains this important piece of information: "at WindowsApplication4. Form1.Form1_Load(Object sender, EventArgs e) in D:\Temp\Visual Studio Projects\WindowsApplication4\Form1.vb:line 73."

- The last part of the StackTrace property indicates a line number that tells us where the problem occurred. This can be a very useful piece of information. For example, you might create a simple logging routine that automatically stores the StackTrace property in a text file when an error occurs. Then, if you have enabled line numbering, which I described earlier in this chapter, you can easily find the corresponding problem.

You can replace the MessageBox.Show statement in the previous example with the following block of code. It reports more information about the exception (see Figure 7-17).

```
Dim Spacer As New String("-", 150)
Spacer = vbNewLine & Spacer & vbNewLine

Dim Message As String
Message = "Exception Type" & Spacer
Message &= MyError.GetType().ToString() & vbNewLine & vbNewLine
Message &= "Message" & Spacer
Message &= MyError.Message & vbNewLine & vbNewLine
Message &= "Stack Trace" & Spacer
Message &= MyError.StackTrace

MessageBox.Show(Message, "Exception Occurred")
```

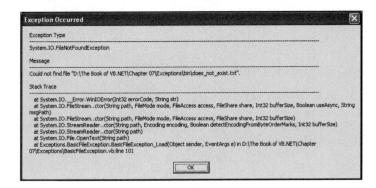

Figure 7-17: Reporting exception details

NOTE *There are some other, less frequently used properties. For example, exceptions automatically have an HResult error code associated with them for backward compatibility with COM, and can store a reference to a specific help file and topic in the HelpLink property.*

Inner Exception

One interesting property, InnerException, doesn't appear in the preceding example. InnerException is used when more than one error happens in quick succession. For example, a FileNotFoundException could trigger a higher-level data processing error, say a NullReferenceException, when you try to access a class that hasn't been initialized because the data couldn't be loaded from the file. In Visual Basic 6, you would lose track of all previous errors whenever a new error occurred. In Visual Basic .NET, however, you can package a previous error into the InnerException property.

In the preceding example, a custom class might return a NullReferenceException with a FileNotFoundException in the InnerException property, thus identifying the exception that started the whole problem. There's no limit to the number of errors you can chain together in this way. However, your code needs to perform this task manually, by creating a new exception object, and assigning the original exception to the InnerException property of this new object. (We'll consider how you can create your own exceptions a little later in this chapter.)

Filtering by Exception

The file access example used a generic error-handling routine that dealt with any error, regardless of the cause. The Try/Catch/Finally structure also allows you to identify specific types of exceptions and handle them separately. To do so, you would write several Catch statements, each designed to handle a different type of exception.

Consider the more sophisticated file access example here, which stores information read out of a file in a collection:

```
Dim FileLines As Collection
Dim FileStream As System.IO.StreamReader

Try
    FileStream = System.IO.File.OpenText("does_not_exist.txt")
    Do
        FileLines.Add FileStream.ReadLine()
    Loop
Catch MyError As System.IO.EndOfStreamException
    ' All the information has been read out of the file.
    ' No other action needs to be taken.
Catch MyError As System.IO.FileNotFoundException
    ' The file was not found.
    ' Add code to request a different file name from the user.
Catch MyError As Exception
    ' Some other error occurred.
    MessageBox.Show(MyError.Message)
Finally
    If Not FileStream Is Nothing Then
        FileStream.Close()    ' Close the file.
    End If
End Try
```

In this case, Visual Basic .NET will automatically use the first matching exception when an error occurs. If an exception occurs, but it is not an EndOfStreamException or a FileNotFoundException, the final, generic Catch statement will handle it.

Exception Types

When writing code, you'll find it helpful to know what types of exceptions you can expect. Select Debug • Exceptions, and a window will appear that shows all the exceptions in the .NET class library, organized by namespace (as shown in Figure 7-18).

Figure 7-18: The .NET exception hierarchy

This window doubles as an extremely useful debugging tool. You probably remember how Visual Basic 6 provided two basic error-handling options: breaking on unhandled errors only, or breaking on all errors. The latter option allowed you to bypass your program's error-handling code when debugging, and be immediately alerted about an error. That meant you didn't need to disable your error-handling code to troubleshoot a problem.

VB .NET goes one step further: It allows you to set this option individually for every type of exception. That means you could choose to allow your program to handle a common FileNotFoundException (which might just be the result of an invalid user selection), but cause it to enter debug mode if it encounters an unexpected EndOfStreamException (which might indicate a more serious error in your file access code). However, in your program you could still provide error-handling code for both situations. This code would alert the end user of the problem or abort the action.

Filtering by Conditions

Filtering out different types of exception objects is the most common way of filtering errors. However, you can also filter your code based on any conditional expression by using the When keyword. This is most useful in higher-level code where you might be dealing with a business object, rather than directly with a file. In the following example, a business object is used to create a new record in the database:

```
Dim NewSale As SaleItem
Try
    NewSale.ID = "sale220"
    NewSale.AddOrderItems(MyCustomOrderCollection)
    NewSale.AddToDatabase()
Catch When NewSale.Items = 0
    ' Error must have occurred when we tried to add the items.
Catch When NewSale.DBConnection = Nothing
    ' For some reason, the database connection couldn't be established.
Finally
    NewSale.Close()
End Try
```

Instead of looking for specific exception objects, this error routine examines properties of the NewSale object. You can accomplish the same sort of higher-level logic by creating your own exceptions, as explained in the next section.

Throwing Your Own Exceptions

In your own classes, you should throw exceptions when problems occur. Remember, a business object should never present an error message directly to the user. Instead, it should alert the calling procedure when invalid data has been supplied, and let the procedure decide how to handle the problem. This is a principle of encapsulation, and it allows your code components to be flexible and highly reusable.

To throw your own exception, you must instantiate a valid exception object, and then use the Throw keyword:

```
Public Sub UpdateFile()
    If IsFileOpen = False The
        ' There is no currently open file to update!
        Dim MyError As New System.InvalidOperationException()
        Throw MyError
    End If
End Sub
```

Every exception object also provides a constructor that allows you to specify a special message.

```
Dim MyError As New InvalidOperationException("You have made a terrible mistake.")
Throw MyError
```

You can also create your own custom exception classes that can assist in providing more detailed information. For example, consider this custom exception, which is designed to identify invalid database information:

```
Public Class ConflictingDBDataException
    Inherits System.ApplicationException

    Public InvalidFields As New Collection()

End Class
```

This custom exception would be useful, for instance, when a user attempts to add a record that has conflicting information to a database. The following block shows the action that the code will take when the user attempts to create a record that has two conflicting fields: an IsPetOwner flag set to False, but a Pet-Breed name set to "Daschund," indicating that there really is a pet. The code responds by creating an instance of the ConflictingDBDataException and adding information about both fields to the InvalidFields collection.

```
Dim MyError As New ConflictingDBDataException()
MyError.InvalidFields.Add("IsPetOwner", IsPetOwner)
MyError.InvalidFields.Add("PetBreed", PetBreed)
Throw MyError
```

You can then consume this exception in the same way you would a natural .NET exception:

```
Try
    ' Try to add a database record here with your data.
Catch MyError As ConflictingDBDataException
    MessageBox.Show("Operation failed. You had " & _
                    MyError.InvalidFields.Count & "conflicting data fields.")
End Try
```

There's really no limit to what you can do with custom exceptions. In highly componentized systems, you might create your own exceptions with special helper functions for performing additional diagnosis, troubleshooting, or cleanup. You can also use the InnerException property to add additional information—for example, to include a more basic exception type representing the origin of the problem.

TIP *All custom exceptions inherit from the ApplicationException class, not the basic Exception class. By inheriting from ApplicationException, you identify that your exception does not represent a Common Language Runtime error. Instead, it represents an application-specific problem.*

Perfecting a Custom Exception Class

In order to make your exception respectable, you should follow the design pattern specified by the .NET framework. All exceptions require two special constructors: one that allows a custom exception message to be specified, and one that allows a nested exception to be inserted. In addition, you need to explicitly add the default parameterless constructor.

```
Public Class ConflictingDBDataException
    Inherits System.ApplicationException

    Public InvalidFields As New Collection()

    Public Sub New()
        MyBase.New()
    End Sub

    Public Sub New(Message As String)
        MyBase.New(Message)
    End Sub

    Public Sub New(Message As String, Inner As Exception)
        MyBase.New(Message, Inner)
    End Sub

End Class
```

All these constructors do is call the base class constructor with the supplied information. The base class performs the required initialization.

Defensive Coding

Defensive coding extends from the philosophy that it's better to prevent an error than to try and compensate for it in your code, or fix it afterward with an update to your application. The goal of defensive coding is to restrict the ways that an error can occur, and to make sure that when an error does occur, it is confined to a limited, diagnosable area in your code.

The Principles of Defensive Coding

Garbage in, garbage out. This is a cliché in today's world, but it highlights an important programming truth. One of the most common sources of error is invalid user input. To compensate for this, many programmers write involved validation routines that verify submitted input and alert the user if an entry is invalid. If you've tried this approach, you know that it can be labor intensive. A better solution is just to restrict input so that invalid options can't be entered.

Make the user choose from pre-filled lists, disable invalid options by setting the Enabled property to False, and restrict input in text boxes using such properties as MaxLength and CharacterCasing. If numeric input is required, use the KeyPress event to check the character before it appears and disallow it if it's invalid.

Reduce your assumptions. Assumptions make your code fragile, and result in code that may work properly at your site, but will break when sent to a user who enters different information. A typical example is division. When dividing numbers, it's a good rule of thumb to check to make sure that the divisor doesn't equal zero, which would cause an infamous divide-by-zero error. Don't assume that just because the variable *must* be greater than zero, it will be. An error or oversight in your code may create a problem that you can easily protect against—*if* you take the time.

Build your code out of independent units. You learned in Chapters 5 and 6 that if you structure your program as numerous independent components, you will simplify the processes of enhancing, troubleshooting, and sharing your code. You will also make it easier to contain your errors. For example, a database error should be caught and trapped in a database access class, so it won't enter into the rest of your program, where it might metamorphose into a data or logic error.

Testing Assumptions with Assertions

One of the reasons that bugs are so difficult to eliminate from applications is because our code often contains well-disguised assumptions. For example, you may assume that a certain object is always initialized, or that a variable is always greater than zero, and then fail to see that a potential error lurks ahead if these conditions are not met.

Visual Basic .NET includes an assertions feature that forces your code to test these assumptions. *Assertions* are statements that you guarantee must be true, otherwise something serious has gone unexpectedly wrong in your application. If Visual Basic .NET tests an assertion and finds out that it is, in fact, false, it will provide an intimidating error message with a pile of diagnostic code, and give you the option to either halt the execution of your program, or ignore the problem and continue.

There's one catch. Assertions only work in debug mode. Once you compile and distribute your program, all the assertions disappear. This means that assertions are designed to help you spot problems while testing your application. They do not take the place of error-handling code; rather, they let you know when your error-handling code has failed and something has gone wrong.

To include an assertion in your code, you use the Assert method of the Debug class (from the System.Diagnostics namespace). Here's an example:

```
Debug.Assert(Balance > 0)
```

If this assertion evaluates to False (that is, if the Balance variable is equal to zero or less), an error message will be displayed, which will look something like Figure 7-19.

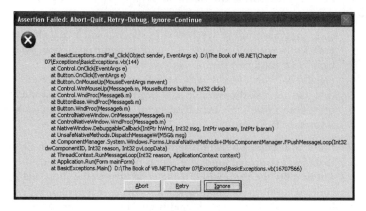

Figure 7-19: Pure intimidation with a failed assertion

Remember, assertions cannot take the place of error-handling code. If it is possible in some way that the user might attempt to specify a balance less than zero, for example, then handle that error appropriately. If, however, you restrict the user from specifying a negative balance, then an assertion is a good place to double-check that the limitation really is in effect. Think of assertions as a form of quality control.

Debug assertions are completely removed from the final release of your program, so you don't have to worry about these checks slowing down your code. You do have to make sure that a debug assertion doesn't call a procedure that might somehow modify a value in your program, because then there might be unintended side effects when you remove it.

Debug.WriteLine

With the WriteLine method, you can use the Debug class to print out diagnostic information to the Output window (as shown in Figure 7-20). For example, you could use WriteLine to explain what your code is doing in a loop:

```
' Leaving out the code to define variables and open the file.
Dim i As Integer
For i = 0 to 100
    Info(i) = TextFile.ReadLine()
    Debug.WriteLine("Iteration number " & i.ToString() & ". Read " & Info(i))
Next i
```

The nice thing about this method is that the information will be there if you need it, but can be easily ignored when you don't need it.

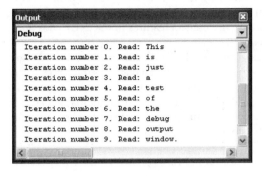

Figure 7-20: Writing debugging information

This kind of information can save a lot of time when you are testing your application, because you can see very clearly what data was being used and what point the application was at when a given error occurred. It can provide a shortcut to solving your problem when manually single-stepping through your code might take a little longer. As with the Debug.Assert method, Debug.WriteLine statements are removed from your code in the final executable version, so they won't slow your application down.

Trace Assertions

Trace assertions work almost exactly like debug assertions. The following example uses a trace assertion to verify that an object has been created:

```
Trace.Assert(Not MyObject = Nothing)
```

The only difference between trace assertions and debug assertions is that trace assertions remain in the final program. Usually you won't need trace exceptions, because you will just use custom error handling. However, they can be useful if you are testing a program at a remote site.

Using Logging and Traces

Picture this situation: A client is having a problem with your Visual Basic program. You could probably fix it, if you could only figure out what it is. The client's memory is a little hazy . . . maybe the trouble occurred when he or she clicked the Submit button, or maybe just after . . . and no one thought to copy down the specific error message or error number that you created.

As you might guess, the scenario I'm describing is quite common. The best solution is often to create a log file. When an error occurs, you can simply instruct the client to email the log file to you for technical review. Depending on your needs, you may want to create your own system for creating text log files, but you can also use the built-in features in the .NET class library. One of these features is *tracing*.

To use tracing, you use the Trace class in the System.Diagnostics namespace. It works very similarly to the Debug class, but trace writes and assertions will be performed even in the release build of your program. To capture trace information to a file, you have to start off by adding a *listener*. In order for tracing to be useful, you will usually use a text file as a listener. This is the file where all output will be stored.

```
Dim FileListener As New TextWriterTraceListener(File.Create("output.txt"))
Trace.AutoFlush = True
Trace.Listeners.Add(FileListener)
```

You can now use the methods of the Trace class to write to the text file.

```
Trace.WriteLine("Starting application")
Trace.Indent    ' This is a nice touch to make well organized output.
Trace.WriteLine("Doing some task . . .")
' Add some code here.
Trace.WriteLine("Finished task")
Trace.Unindent
Trace.WriteLine("All done")
```

The output.txt file would look like this:

```
Starting application
    Doing some task . . .
    Finished task
All done
```

Even if you don't use Trace.WriteLine statements very often, make sure that you use them every time an error occurs. It's a good idea to develop a generic procedure that will take an exception object and write all of its properties to the Trace object (including the properties of any exception stored in the InnerException property). Here is an example:

```
Try
    ' Some code here.
Catch MyError As Exception
    WriteTraceInfo(MyError)
End Try
```

The generic routine would look something like this:

```
Public Sub WriteTraceInfo(Error As Exception)

    Trace.Write(Error.Message)
    Trace.Write(Error.StackTrace)
    ' And so on . . .

    ' Use recursion to get all the information in the entire exception chain.
    If Not Error.InnerException = Nothing Then
        ' Call this subroutine again, with the nested exception.
        WriteTraceInfo(Error.InnerException)
    End If

End Sub
```

Keep in mind that a log file really can't contain too much information about an error, and information such as StackTrace and InnerException can really help track down the root of the problem.

To reap the benefits of tracing in your compiled application, you have to make sure that tracing is enabled. Right-click to display your project properties, and enable the Define TRACE constant flag under the Configuration Properties • Build folder.

What Comes Next?

In this chapter, you've seen how to maintain complete control of your code in .NET, and how to watch its flow, monitor the contents of its variables, and track its performance in the field. The key to successfully using these features is just using them. Take the extra time to add logging instructions to your code. You will more than make up for that time when you are solving the inevitable bugs later on.

You've also learned how to use Visual Basic .NET's structured error-handling feature to catch exceptions, and even to throw your own. You'll find that once you get comfortable dealing with exception objects, you won't ever feel the same thrill of fear when an error occurs. Instead, you'll be ready for it.

To really master exception handling, you should become familiar with the exception classes that .NET uses to notify you about common problem types. It's always better to specifically catch different types of exceptions than to just catch a generic System.Exception object. A good tool for learning about exceptions is the .NET class library reference. Start with the System.Exception class, and browse through any of its descendants that you think may be related to the tasks you are performing.

8

DEALING WITH DATA: FILES, PRINTING, AND XML

Most programs consist of a series of operations for retrieving, processing, and displaying data. A typical example is a reporting program that reads information from a database, compiles it to produce interesting summary information according to the user's selections, and returns a result that can be displayed in a window or sent to a printer. More complicated applications might add considerably more sophisticated interfaces, and might use other .NET features. They might also support various environments, from traditional desktop applications to interactive Internet sites. In the end, however, everything is about data.

This chapter examines some of the nuts and bolts of dealing with data. You'll learn how to store information in the registry and retrieve it as needed, display and print formatted documents, and interact with files in a completely object-oriented way. (No more Input # commands.) You'll also learn about .NET tools that let you work with XML files so easily and painlessly that you might make XML the native format for all your applications.

Most of these capabilities aren't new to the .NET framework. However, traditional Visual Basic is notoriously inconsistent. For example, it provides a variety of different ways to access files—some more flexible than others—and requires separate components for dealing with XML. As always, Visual Basic .NET offers a wealth of refinements. This chapter will teach you the .NET way of dealing with data from the ground up, along with an introduction to streams and serialization.

New in .NET

Data access in Visual Basic .NET provides more refinement than revolution. However, if you are a long-time Visual Basic developer, you'll find many enhancements to be happy about.

Object-Oriented File Access

You may have already seen it with the FSO (File System Object) model in Visual Basic. Or, you may be an unredeemed user of Open and Input # commands. Either way, you'll discover that the .NET class library offers easy and consistent ways to access your computer's file system as a collection of interrelated objects.

Asynchronous Printing

The printing model has been slightly tweaked to make sure that lengthy print operations can't drain the life out of your applications. Now, pages are sent to the printer one at a time, by means of a special PagePrint event.

Print Preview

If you've created a print routine in VB .NET, you've also created a print preview routine—all you need to do is pass your PrintDocument object to the PrintPreviewDialog control that .NET provides for you. If you've ever struggled with third-party components, or tried to draw a dynamic print preview on your own, this feature will be a welcome addition.

Unrestricted Access to the Registry

The built-in registry features in Visual Basic 6 limited you to a small branch of the registry, under the heading "VB and VBA Program Settings." This made life difficult when you wanted to read settings from a third-party program or use a more professional (and standardized) location. Visual Basic .NET now makes it easy for you to read and write to any area of the registry.

XML Access

In Visual Basic 6, reading XML files was just one more activity requiring the help of an additional component, which you had to distribute with your application and register on any computer that used it. VB .NET fills the void with several different classes that allow you to write and read XML with the exact level of sophistication and complexity that you need. For quick and easy XML, you can use a simple XMLTextWriter object. For more advanced applications, you can manipulate XML files with the full XML Document Object Model (DOM), which treats XML data as a collection of interrelated objects.

Interacting with Files

This section provides a quick walkthrough that explains all the basics of reading and writing information to a file. As in the previous chapters of this book, we want to do this the ".NET way"—which means using objects and the class library, of course!

Creating a FileStream

To interact with files in Visual Basic .NET, you use one of the tools provided in the System.IO portion of the .NET class library. So to get off to a good start, import the System.IO namespace so you'll have all of its classes at your fingertips:

```
Imports System.IO
```

A good starting point is the FileStream class. The FileStream class is your gateway to file access: It's an object that connects to a file on your computer. Creating one is easy:

```
Dim fs As FileStream
fs = New FileStream("c:\myfile.txt", FileMode.CreateNew)
' I could also do this in one line like so:
' Dim fs As New FileStream("c:\myfile.txt", FileMode.CreateNew)
```

As you might have guessed, the FileMode.CreateNew argument tells Visual Basic .NET that your program wants this file to be created. If the file already exists, you will receive an error (an IOException object, to be precise). The File-Mode enumeration provides other possibilities. You could instruct Visual Basic .NET to open an existing file or append data to an existing one, or you could even use FileMode.OpenOrCreate, which opens the file if it exists, and creates it if it doesn't.

Before you can do anything with a file stream, you have to attach a stream reader or writer to it. Why the extra step? Even though you have already decided to read or write information using a FileStream, you haven't specified the format in which data will be transmitted inside that stream. Without the format information, your stream can't be used for any practical purpose.

At this point, you have two main options: You can work with binary data using the BinaryWriter and BinaryReader classes, or with plain text information using the StreamWriter and StreamReader classes. The Writer classes are for sending information to a file, while the Reader classes retrieve information *from* a file.

Writing Text to a File

It's comforting to begin with plain text data, because you can open the resulting file in Notepad to ensure that your program is working correctly.

Here's an example that uses the StreamWriter to send two lines of information to a file:

```
' Create the file stream.
Dim fs As FileStream
fs = New FileStream("c:\myfile.txt", FileMode.CreateNew)

' Create a StreamWriter that uses this file stream.
Dim w As StreamWriter
w = New StreamWriter(fs)

' Send some data.
w.WriteLine("First line")
w.WriteLine(40023)  ' Integers work as well as strings.

' Tidy up.
w.Close()
```

If you look at the corresponding myfile.txt file in Notepad, you will see the following information. Notice that there are no quotation marks around the data in the text file. The StreamWriter outputs an entire line of text, not a quote-delimited string.

```
First line
40023
```

The StreamWriter object provides a reasonably straightforward approach to retrieving your data. Using the StreamReader class is just as easy, with a corresponding ReadLine method that returns a string with the information we've placed in the file.

```
Dim r As New StreamReader(fs)
Dim FirstLine As String, SecondLine As Integer
FirstLine = r.ReadLine()
SecondLine = CType(r.ReadLine(), Integer)
```

The StreamWriter class is smart enough that it can handle any simple data type, including numbers, strings, and Boolean (which become the text "True" or "False" when written to a file). When you are retrieving information, though, it always comes out in the form of a string. You then have to convert it to the appropriate type using the CType function.

Writing Binary Information

The BinaryWriter class works in a similar fashion to the StreamWriter, except that it only works with bytes in an encoded binary format. You can use some of the shared methods of the System.BitConverter class to convert data into byte arrays, or you can just use the Write method of the BinaryWriter class, which is smart enough to do all the work for you, as long as you are using simple data types.

In many programs, binary files are the standard way of storing information (although XML is also gaining ground as a popular standard for hierarchical text-based information). One of the advantages of binary information is that it is not easily readable. While the information is still visible in the file if you look for it, novice users are less likely to accidentally change it in Notepad or any other program. Binary storage also makes the best use of space. The only thing you have to remember is that, as with the StreamWriter and StreamReader class, you must read information in the same order that you wrote it in.

The next example is slightly more sophisticated. It presents a custom Person class that has the built-in features needed to serialize itself to a file:

```
Public Class Person
    Public Name As String
    Public Age As Integer
    Public Height As Integer

    Public Sub New()
    End Sub

    Public Sub New(ByVal Name As String, ByVal Age As String, _
                ByVal Height As String)
        Me.Name = Name
        Me.Age = Age
        Me.Height = Height
    End Sub

    Public Sub SaveToFile(ByVal Filename As String)
        Dim fs As New FileStream(Filename, FileMode.CreateNew)
        Dim w As New BinaryWriter(fs)
        w.Write(Name)
        w.Write(Age)
        w.Write(Height)
        w.Close()
    End Sub

    Public Shared Function LoadFromFile(ByVal Filename As String) As Person
        Dim fs As New FileStream(Filename, FileMode.Open)
        Dim r As New BinaryReader(fs)
        Dim NewPerson As New Person()
        NewPerson.Name = r.ReadString()
```

(continued on next page)

```
        NewPerson.Age = r.ReadInt32()
        NewPerson.Height = r.ReadInt32()
        r.Close()
        Return NewPerson
    End Function
End Class
```

This class provides the following elements:

- Three pieces of information—a name, age, and height—all of which would be implemented as full-featured property procedures in a more sophisticated example.

- Two constructors: a basic one that creates an empty person object, and a more useful constructor with arguments to preload the name, age, and height.

- A SaveToFile subroutine that stores the current Person object in a specified file as a bunch of binary information. (Note that both this and the LoadFromFile function are simple examples; they do not incorporate the error checking that you would require in a production-level program.)

- A LoadFromFile function that creates a Person object based on the information in a file. One interesting feature about this function is that it's declared with the Shared keyword, which means that you can use it even if you haven't created a Person object. It will then return a fully loaded Person object for you to work with. This is a common technique for class creation. Another option would have been to supply another constructor that accepted a string specifying the filename, and then loaded data into the new Person object.

To determine whether the class works as expected, we test it like this:

```
' Create Bob and clone a copy of him into a file.
Dim Bob As New Person("Bob", 34, 5.25)
Bob.SaveToFile("c:\bob.dat")

' Erase the current copy of Bob.
Bob = Nothing

' Revive Bob by using the file, and check that his data is correct.
Bob = Bob.LoadFromFile("c:\bob.dat")
MessageBox.Show(Bob.Name)
```

This verifies that we have created an intelligent, self-storing object. The only drawback to this method is the fact that the binary format is specific to the data type. This means that when retrieving information, we have to remember not only the order in which we've stored the information, but also the data type of each variable so that we can use the appropriate method (for example, Read-String instead of ReadInt32). A more powerful and time-consuming system might use XML to describe the data, and more intelligent storage and retrieval routines, which could allow Bob to be revived from older files even if the original class has been modified.

Figure 8-1 shows what the bob.dat file looks like in Notepad.

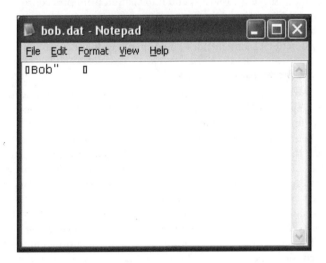

Figure 8-1: The contents of bob.dat

The string is still readable, but the conversion of our integers is quite unintuitive. All the information is packed together, with no spaces.

NOTE *.NET automatically adds information to the beginning of the string that indicates its length in characters. This lets the ReadString method know how much information it should retrieve (and once again shows us the built-in cleverness of the .NET framework).*

The last thing you should know about binary files is that you can use the Seek method to move directly to a specific position. However, this technique isn't used very much these days. It used to be important for creating files that held different records, but now databases are a much more powerful and flexible alternative. The process of moving manually through binary information in a file is frustrating, time-consuming, and prone to error.

Visual Basic–Style File Access

There is one ugly secret I should admit. VB .NET still provides Visual Basic's old-fashioned file access routines—in a slightly recast form. The Open statement was removed because its name is potentially confusing: Why assume that the only thing that can be opened is a file? The equivalent is the FileOpen statement, which closely parallels the archaic Open. The Input statement remains (along with LineInput), and Get and Put have been renamed FileGet and FilePut.

If you are an experienced Visual Basic developer, your first instinct may be to return to these well-known functions. I strongly discourage it. The file access classes in the System.IO namespace provide all the convenience of modern object-oriented programming. In addition, they settle issues of scope and code readability, make it easier to send information from procedure to procedure, and help you catch errors. If you want your program to have the greatest standardization, and you are thinking the .NET way, then you will use the compatibility functions I have just described sparingly, for compatibility *only*.

A Little More About Streams

Our discussion so far has focused on the practical steps you need to follow when accessing a file. However, there are also some interesting concepts at work that aren't immediately obvious.

You'll remember that to access a file, you first create a stream, and then attach the appropriate writer and reader. Streams are an important concept in .NET, and they aren't just limited to files. Instead, streams represent a generic way to access many different data sources (also known as *backing stores*). This philosophy means that you can read information from a memory stream, a network stream, or a file stream using conceptually similar techniques. The .NET framework even uses streams behind the scenes for tasks like saving a bitmap.

For most programmers, file access will be the most common use of streams. But consider the next example, which retrieves a web page (the eBay home page), and displays the HTML text stream in a text box (see Figure 8-2).

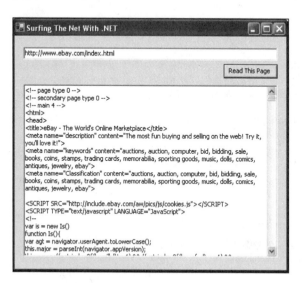

Figure 8-2: Reading from the Web

The nice thing about this application is that it uses streams with a little help from the System.Net namespace to do its work. And, because you now understand streams, you can probably already interpret how this code works.

```
Me.Cursor = Cursors.WaitCursor

Dim PageRequest As HttpWebRequest = WebRequest.Create(txtURL.Text)
Dim PageResponse As WebResponse = PageRequest.GetResponse()
Dim PageReader As New StreamReader(PageResponse.GetResponseStream())
Dim PageString As String = PageReader.ReadToEnd()
PageReader.Close()
txtHTML.Text = PageString

Me.Cursor = Cursors.DefaultCursor
```

The basic steps are as follows:

1. Use the shared Create method of the System.Net.WebRequest class to specify the page you want and retrieve an HttpWebRequest object that will do the job for you.

2. Use the GetResponse method of the HttpWebRequest object to return the page as a WebResponse object. The WebResponse exposes a GetResponseStream method that allows you to access the underlying stream.

3. Create a StreamReader for the WebResponse object's stream.

4. Now that you have a familiar Stream object, perform whatever additional steps you want, like writing it to a file or reading it into a variable.

> **TIP** *Retrieving a web page as a stream isn't as useful as it might seem at first. For one thing, it's next to impossible to retrieve any useful information from the page without making assumptions about how it is laid out. The moment the page is slightly changed, your application will fail to get the right data. Instead, a better way to communicate information over the Web is to use Web Services, which we examine in Chapter 13.*

Managing Files and Folders

If you try to use the original Bob program twice in a row, you will receive an error indicating that your program is trying to create a file that already exists. To get around this problem, you could use FileMode.Create instead of FileMode.CreateNew when creating the FileStream object. This instructs Visual Basic .NET to erase the current file, if it exists. However, this is only a partial solution. What if the existing Bob file contains important information? What we need is a way to manage directories and files programmatically.

The File Class

Once again, the System.IO namespace in the .NET class library provides all the tools we need. Let's start with the File class, and add the following code to the beginning of our Person.SaveToFile method:

```
If File.Exists(Filename) Then
    File.Delete(Filename)
End If
```

The File class uses shared methods, which allows us to use the Exists and Delete methods without first needing to create a File object.

This example shows how easy it is to manipulate files with the File object. It's just a matter of finding the specific method that does what you need. There are methods for copying a file (Copy and Move), retrieving and setting its attributes (e.g., GetAttributes), and even some shortcuts (like OpenText and Open-Write) that return StreamReader or StreamWriter classes for the file.

The File class is a utility class. You don't actually create an instance of it; all the features you need are provided through shared methods. This means that for every method you use, you have to supply a string specifying the file you want to work with. If you want to work extensively with a file over the course of a program's lifetime, it will probably be better to use the FileInfo class.

TIP *The FileInfo class is faster for multiple operations. That's because the FileInfo class performs its security checks once, when you first create the object. The shared methods of the File class, on the other hand, need to perform a separate security check with each operation.*

The FileInfo Class

The FileInfo class represents a single file. You might create a FileInfo object that corresponds to a file on your computer, and manipulate its properties accordingly, or you might create a FileInfo object for a file that doesn't exist, in which case its Exists property will return False and you will probably want to use the Create method.

Here is a typical example showing how a FileInfo object might be used. This program retrieves information for an existing file when a button is clicked. A subroutine called Out allows the program to quickly add information to a read-only text box control.

```
Private Sub cmdGetInfo_Click(ByVal sender As System.Object, _
  ByVal e As System.EventArgs) Handles cmdGetInfo.Click
    Dim MyFile As New FileInfo("c:\myfile.txt")

    ' We can now access some of the following properties.
    Out("Length in bytes: " & MyFile.Length)
    Out("Attribute list: " & MyFile.Attributes.ToString)
    Out("Stored in: " & MyFile.DirectoryName)
    Out("Created: " & MyFile.CreationTime)

    ' Any property we can get, we can also change.
    MyFile.LastWriteTime = DateTime.Today.Add(TimeSpan.FromDays(100))
End Sub
```

```
Public Sub Out(ByVal NewText As String) ' Utility for displaying information.
    txtDisplay.Text &= vbNewLine & NewText
End Sub
```

After running this example (shown in Figure 8-3), you can check the
c:\myfile.txt file in Windows Explorer. You will see that it claims to have been
last updated 100 days in the future.

Figure 8-3: Testing the FileInfo class

This FileInfo object is quite versatile. Not only can you easily copy it (with
the CopyTo method), but you can also move it (with the MoveTo method). You
can also work with directories by using analogous Directory and DirectoryInfo
objects.

TIP *The File and FileInfo objects (or the Directory and DirectoryInfo objects) expose very
similar functionality, with similar property and method names. The difference is really
just that of instance objects (FileInfo and DirectoryInfo) versus classes made up of shared
members (File and Directory). The only feature difference worth noting is that the File
class does not provide a way to retrieve size information, while you can count on the
FileInfo.Length property to return the size of a file in bytes.*

File Attributes

There is one interesting trick you should understand with files, and it has to do
with file attributes. File attributes are represented by the FileInfo.Attributes
property (or the GetAttributes and SetAttributes members of the File class).
This property can be set using the FileAttributes enumeration, which includes
enumerated values for hidden files, system files, read-only files, and so on.

However, a file can have *any* combination of these attributes. To evaluate or set a combination of enumerated values, you need to use what is called *bitwise* comparison or assignment.

For comparison, you use the And keyword to filter out just a single attribute. You can then examine if this attribute is set.

```
' This won't work (and least not correctly).
If FileInfo.Attributes = FileAttributes.Hidden Then
End If


' This, on the other hand, does work properly.
If (FileInfo.Attributes And FileAttributes.Hidden) = FileAttributes.Hidden
    ' You have successfully filtered out the hidden attribute, and found
    ' that it is set.
End If
```

With assignment, you use the Or keyword to combine an additional attribute to the current set of attributes.

```
' A fatal mistake that accidentally clears all other attributes:
FileInfo.Attributes = FileAttributes.ReadOnly


' This adds a read-only attribute, and leaves the other attributes intact.
FileInfo.Attributes = FileInfo.Attributes Or FileAttributes.ReadOnly


' This removes a read-only attribute, and leaves the other attributes intact.
FileInfo.Attributes = FileInfo.Attributes Or Not (FileAttributes.ReadOnly)
```

File and Directory Relationships

Another nice detail is the way that the file and directory objects automatically link up together. A FileInfo object provides a link to its current DirectoryInfo object through its Directory property. DirectoryInfo and Directory objects have methods, such as GetFiles and GetDirectories, that provide arrays of all the files or directories in the current directory as FileInfo or DirectoryInfo objects.

```
' Make a DirectoryInfo for c:\
Dim CDrive As New DirectoryInfo("c:\")


' Get all the files.
Dim FileArray() As FileInfo
FileArray = CDrive.GetFiles()


' Display every file's name.
Dim i As Integer
For i = 0 To FileArray.GetUpperBound(0) - 1
    Out(FileArray(i).Name)
Next i
```

It's simple but powerful. You can access your computer's file system as a collection of interrelated objects, and manipulate attributes and names just by changing properties.

A Simple Directory Browser

The next example processes a drive recursively and fills a TreeView control with a complete directory listing. The user can click on any directory to see the list of files it contains (as shown in Figure 8-4).

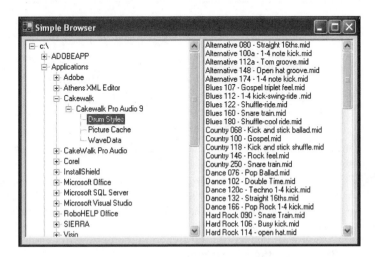

Figure 8-4: A simple file browser

The program begins by filling the TreeView with all the subdirectories on drive C: at startup. It does this with the help of a special Fill method that is called recursively to burrow down the levels of the directory tree.

```
Private Sub Browser_Load(ByVal sender As System.Object, _
  ByVal e As System.EventArgs) Handles MyBase.Load

    Dim RootDir As New DirectoryInfo("c:\")
    Dim RootNode As New TreeNode("c:\")
    treeFiles.Nodes.Add(RootNode)
    Fill(RootDir, RootNode)

End Sub

Private Sub Fill(ByVal Dir As DirectoryInfo, ByVal DirNode As TreeNode)
    Dim FileItem As FileInfo, DirItem As DirectoryInfo

    For Each DirItem In Dir.GetDirectories
        ' Add node for the directory.
```

(continued on next page)

```
        Dim NewNode As New TreeNode(DirItem.Name)
        DirNode.Nodes.Add(NewNode)

        ' Use a recursive call here to get all subdirectories.
        Fill(DirItem, NewNode)
    Next

End Sub
```

When a node is selected, a DirectoryInfo object is created and used to retrieve a list of contained files, which is then added to the list box:

```
Private Sub treeFiles_AfterSelect(ByVal sender As System.Object, _
  ByVal e As TreeViewEventArgs) Handles treeFiles.AfterSelect
    Dim Dir As New DirectoryInfo(e.Node.FullPath)
    lstFiles.Items.Clear()
    lstFiles.Items.AddRange(Dir.GetFiles())
End Sub
```

TIP *It can take quite a long time for the program to start and fill the initial tree on startup. A better approach would be to fill the first level of nodes, and to fill in subdirectories "just in time" as the nodes are expanded. You could do this by responding to the TreeView.BeforeExpand event.*

"Watching" the File System

One other interesting introduction to VB .NET is the ability to "watch" folders for any changes, deletions, or additions. This technique can come in quite handy. For example, you could create a sales fulfilment program that waits for a new order file to be saved in a directory (perhaps after it is received as an email attachment by a sales associate), and then automatically springs into action to process the new file. This technique replaces some of the ugly tricks that programmers resorted to in the past, which include continuously examining a directory for changes, and thereby wasting precious CPU cycles with redundant checks.

To add this functionality to your applications, you just need to use the FileSystemWatcher class, which is found in the System.IO namespace, like all our file access tools. You set the Path property to indicate the directory that you are monitoring (like G:\Orders), and the Filter string to set the file types (like *.xls).

```
Dim Watch As New FileSystemWatcher()
Watch.Path = "d:\Orders"
Watch.Filter = "*.xls"

' You can also allow the FileSystemWatcher to search subdirectories.
' Watch.IncludeSubdirectories = True
```

The FileWatcher produces four events: Changed, Created, Deleted, and Renamed. If needed, you can disable its events by setting the EnableRaisingEvents property to false.

```
' Add an event handler dynamically.
AddHandler Watch.Created, AddressOf NewFile
```

The subroutine below reacts when a new file is added to the monitored directory, and retrieves its name using the supplied parameters. Figure 8-5 shows this logic at work.

```
Public Sub NewFile(ByVal sender As Object, _
  ByVal e As System.IO.FileSystemEventArgs)

    lstNewFiles.Items.Add("New file: " & e.Name)

End Sub
```

Figure 8-5: Monitoring the File System

File System Change Events

It's easy to monitor the Created, Deleted, and Renamed events of the FileSystemWatcher. However, the Changed event is a little trickier, because there are a huge number of different types of possible changes that can be detected as Windows performs its ordinary housekeeping.

In order to properly handle the Change event, you need to set the NotifyFilter property to the type of changes you are monitoring for (using a value from the NotifyFilters enumeration). You can combine several different types of monitored actions using the bitwise Or keyword.

```
' Watch for changes to file size or file name.
Watch.NotifyFilter = NotifyFilters.FileName Or NotifyFilters.Size
```

Object Serialization

The Bob program we looked at earlier used a relatively crude (but effective) mode of handmade *serialization*. The .NET platform also introduces an automatic form of serialization that you can use to persist the information in an object (see Figure 8-6). This technique can be used on your own, or the .NET framework might rely on it to transmit a class to a remote component on another computer if you are designing a distributed application.

Implementing this serialization in one of your classes is extremely easy. All you need to do is flag your class as serializable with a special attribute. The client code (the code using your class) can then decide what type of serialization it wants to use, and store the object in a binary file, an XML file, or something else.

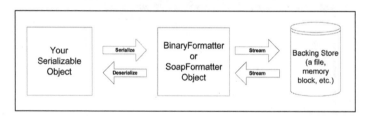

Figure 8-6: .NET serialization

Here is the Person class, simplified and remade to support serialization.

```
<Serializable> Public Class SerializablePerson
    Public Name As String
    Public Age As Integer
    Public Height As Integer

    Public Sub New()
    End Sub

    Public Sub New(ByVal Name As String, ByVal Age As String, _
      ByVal Height As String)
        Me.Name = Name
        Me.Age = Age
        Me.Height = Height
    End Sub

End Class
```

Did you notice the differences? There are exactly two modifications:

- The SaveToFile and LoadFromFile methods were removed. This time, .NET will do the serialization for us automatically.

- The Class now has a <Serializable> attribute in the first line, where it is declared. This tells .NET that it is allowed to persist and restore this class to and from any type of stream.

Storing and Retrieving a Serializable Object

To serialize the class, you need to use a serializer from the System.Runtime.Serialization branch of the class library. There are essentially two choices: the more compact binary format and the text-based XML format, which can be easily transported in places where binary data isn't allowed (like over an Internet firewall). The XML format actually uses a standard called SOAP, which defines how specific data types (like strings and arrays) should be encoded in XML. We'll talk about XML a little later in this chapter—for now, it's enough to know that it is a text-based format.

Storing the Object in Binary

To store the object in a binary format, you use the BinaryFormatter class, which is found in the System.Runtime.Serialization.Formatters.Binary namespace. To get off to a good start, we'll import the namespace:

```
Imports System.Runtime.Serialization.Formatters.Binary
```

The BinaryFormatter class has two important, straightforward methods: Serialize and Deserialize. Serialize takes an object, converts it to a binary format, and sends it to the specified stream.

```
Dim Bob As New SerializablePerson("Bob", 34, 5.25)
Dim fs As New FileStream("c:\bob.dat", FileMode.Create)
Dim bf As New BinaryFormatter()

' Store Bob with the help of the BinaryFormatter.
bf.Serialize(fs, Bob)

fs.Close()
```

Deserialize retrieves the information from the stream, and reconstructs the object. The object is returned to life as the generic System.Object type, so you need to use the CType function to give it back its proper identity.

```
Dim fs As New FileStream("c:\bob.dat", FileMode.Open)
Dim bf As New BinaryFormatter()

' Retrieve Bob with the help of the BinaryFormatter.
Bob = CType(bf.Deserialize(fs), SerializablePerson)

' Verify Bob's information.
MessageBox.Show(Bob.Name)

fs.Close()
```

That's really all you need. It's very simple (although some error-handling code would be nice to guard against any possible file access errors).

Storing the Object in XML

The process is exactly same for XML storage, except now you need to use the SoapFormatter class from the System.Runtime.Serialization.Formatters.Soap namespace. To get off to a good start, you need to import the namespace, and add a reference to the System.Runtime.Serialization.Formatters.Soap.dll assembly (see Figure 8-7).

```
Imports System.Runtime.Serialization.Formatters.Soap
```

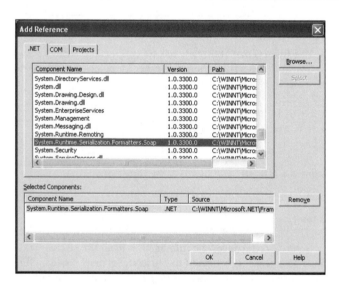

Figure 8-7: Adding the Soap reference

The SoapFormatter class has the same two methods as the BinaryFormatter class—Serialize and Deserialize—and they work exactly the same.

```
Dim Bob As New SerializablePerson("Bob", 34, 5.25)
Dim fs As New FileStream("c:\bob.xml", FileMode.Create)
Dim sf As New SoapFormatter()

' Store Bob with the help of the SoapFormatter.
bf.Serialize(sf, Bob)

fs.Close()
```

When you look at the bob.xml file, you'll find it uses an interesting text-based markup. The file is bound to be longer than the equivalent binary file, but it is also more easily readable.

```
<SOAP-ENV:Envelope >
<SOAP-ENV:Body>
<a1:SerializablePerson id="ref-1">

    <Name id="ref-3">Bob</Name>
    <Age>34</Age>
    <Height>5</Height>

</a1:SerializablePerson>
</SOAP-ENV:Body>
</SOAP-ENV:Envelope>
```

Fine-Tuned Serialization

In some cases, you might have a class that can be partly but not entirely serialized. For example, you might have certain member variables that correspond to information that won't have any meaning on another computer or at another time. For example, you might have a low-level *handle* to a Window. (A handle is a number that the operating system uses to uniquely identify a currently running window. It's abstracted away by .NET, but heavily used by the Windows API.) To deal with this case, just mark the non-serializable information with a <NonSerialized> attribute. This indicates to .NET that it should ignore this value when persisting the class. When the serialized class is reconstructed, this variable will return to its default un-initialized value.

In the PartlySerializablePerson class, any information about Height will not be retained. When a PartlySerializablePerson is retrieved, the Height will return to zero.

```
<Serializable> Public Class PartlySerializablePerson

    Public Name As String
    Public Age As Integer
    <NonSerialized> Public Height As Integer

End Class
```

A more interesting case occurs with an object that contains another object. In this case, the contained object must *also* support serialization, or the whole process will fail. The .NET framework will store and restore all the sub-objects automatically. This can end up persisting a large amount of information. For example, if you have a SerializablePerson class that contains a reference to another SerializablePerson class, which in turn references a third SerializablePerson class, you will end up with three times the data you expected. You should also be careful not to serialize something twice, or you may end up with extra objects floating around in memory with identical data.

In some cases, your object may contain other objects from the .NET class library. These classes *also* need to support serialization. You'll know that they do either through trial and error, or by checking that they implement the ISerializable interface. For example, DataSets implement ISerializable, and can thus be persisted as a part of one of your classes.

Cloning Objects with Serialization

Serialization also provides us with an interesting way to clone an object. You may remember (from Chapter 6) that cloning an object is not always easy, particularly if the class contains multiple sub-objects.

The basic principle to clone an object with serialization is to copy the object into a memory stream, and then retrieve it as a new object. For best performance, you will use the BinaryFormatter, which requires the least amount of space to store data.

You can insert this cloning code directly into your object, as shown below.

```
<Serializable> Public Class ClonableSerializablePerson _
  Implements ICloneable

    Public Name As String
    Public Age As Integer
    Public Height As Integer

    Public Function Clone() As Object Implements ICloneable.Clone
        Dim ms As New MemoryStream()
        Dim bf As New BinaryFormatter()

        ' No more MemberwiseClone!
        bf.Serialize(ms, Me)
```

```
        Clone = bf.Deserialize(ms)
        ms.Close()

    End Function

End Class
```
....

This code will duplicate *every* contained object. In some cases this will be too much, and you'll need a more controlled approach that involves manually copying some objects, as shown in Chapter 6.

Printing and Previewing

Printing in Visual Basic .NET is slightly different than it was in earlier versions. The main difference is that the printing process is now asynchronous. In Visual Basic 6, the computer would be temporarily frozen while output commands were sent to the printer. While this worked fine for most applications, programs that required lengthy print operations would be unresponsive while the information was being sent.

Visual Basic .NET introduces an event-based printing model. Each time a page needs to be printed, the PrintDocument.PagePrint event occurs. This event provides your code with a special object called PrintPageEventArgs, which contains information about the printer, along with methods you can use to print text and pictures. Your code handles the PagePrint event in an event handler, outputs the next page, and then waits for the PagePrint event to occur again. Because pages are printed only one at a time, your program remains more responsive. As a side-effect, you also have to keep track of where you are in the current printout, so that you can resume it at the correct position every time the PagePrint event is fired.

How can you keep track of your position? This part is up to you, but a common way is to use a variable that stores your current page. Then, every time the PagePrint event fires you can check the variable in a conditional block (like If/End If or Select Case) and print the corresponding text. In many programs, a printout actually consists of a single large logical block of information that spans as many pages as needed, in which case it makes more sense to store an offset into that information. For example, if you are printing rows of report information from a database, you might store the current row number. If you are printing a text stream, you might keep track of the character position.

Printing Data from an Array

The following example uses a simple array. The reference to the PrintDocument object and the code for the PagePrint event are contained in a form class named PrintStatus.

```
Imports System.Drawing.Printing
Public Class PrintStatus
  Inherits System.Windows.Forms.Form
    ' (Windows designer code omitted.)

    Private WithEvents MyDoc As PrintDocument
    Private PageNumber As Integer
    Private Offset As Integer
    Private PrintData(100) As String

    Private Sub PrintStatus_Load(ByVal sender As System.Object, _
    ByVal e As System.EventArgs) Handles MyBase.Load
      ' Fill PrintData array with bogus information.
      Dim i As Integer
      For i = 0 To 100
          PrintData(i) = "This is line number " & i + 1 & ". "
          PrintData(i) &= "It originates from the array element number "
          PrintData(i) &= i & "."
      Next
      MyDoc = New PrintDocument()
    End Sub

    Private Sub cmdPrint_Click(ByVal sender As System.Object, _
      ByVal e As System.EventArgs) Handles cmdPrint.Click
        PageNumber = 0
        Offset = 0
        MyDoc.Print()
    End Sub

    Private Sub MyDoc_PrintPage(ByVal sender As Object, _
      ByVal e As PrintPageEventArgs) Handles MyDoc.PrintPage
        ' Print code left out...
    End Sub

End Class
```

This example is based on a single form called PrintStatus. This form contains member variables that store the current page number and print offset, as well as the actual print data. In the Load event, the print data array is filled with sample information, and a printer is selected. Asynchronous printing is started when the user clicks the cmdPrint button.

The actual printing takes place once the PrintPage event occurs. The first PrintPage event will occur almost instantaneously (as you can verify by inserting a breakpoint). Inside the event handler, you use the PrintPageEventArgs object to perform the actual printing:

```
Private Sub MyDoc_PrintPage(ByVal sender As Object, _
   ByVal e As PrintPageEventArgs) Handles MyDoc.PrintPage

      ' Define the font and determine the line height.
      Dim MyFont As New Font("Arial", 10)
      Dim LineHeight As Single = MyFont.GetHeight(e.Graphics)

      ' Create variables to hold position on page.
      Dim x As Single = e.MarginBounds.Left
      Dim y As Single = e.MarginBounds.Top

      ' Increment global page counter and refresh display.
      PageNumber += 1
      lblStatus.Text = "Print Page " & PageNumber

      ' Print all the information that can fit on the page.
      Do
          e.Graphics.DrawString(PrintData(Offset), MyFont, Brushes.Black, x, y)
          Offset += 1
          y += LineHeight
      Loop Until (y + LineHeight) > e.MarginBounds.Bottom Or _
        Offset > PrintData.GetUpperBound(0)

      ' Determine if another page is needed.
      If Offset < PrintData.GetUpperBound(0) Then e.HasMorePages = True

End Sub
```

In our example, the PrintPage event will occur twice—once for each of the two required pages. The event handler code begins by defining a font that will be used for printing, and determining how large the line spacing should be to accommodate that font. The next two lines create variables to track the current position on the page. By default, printing begins at the page margin border. Remember, with printing routines, you need to take care of all the details; for example, you have to break up long strings into multiple lines of text, and explicitly set the position on the page every time you print a new line.

The following two lines increment the page counter, and display the page information in a label control in the window. This keeps the user informed about print progress. The Do/Loop block contains the actual printing code. This code uses the DrawString method to print out a single line of text at the indicated coordinates. The code then increments our Offset value (which represents the line number), and moves the *y* coordinate down one full line space. (Coordinates are measured from zero, starting at the upper-left corner.) Before continuing to print the next line, the event handler checks for two possible conditions.

```
Loop Until (y + LineHeight) > e.MarginBounds.Bottom Or _
  Offset > PrintData.GetUpperBound(0)
```

In order to continue, there must be space left on the current page for the next line, and there must be data left to print. (The value of PrintOffset can't be larger than the upper boundary of our array, because then it would indicate a row that doesn't exist.)

The final line of our event handler determines whether there is still unprinted data left in the array. If there is, the e.HasMorePages property must be set to True. Otherwise, Visual Basic .NET will assume that our printing is completed, and won't bother to call the PrintPage event again.

Printing Pictures

The previous example demonstrates how to print the most common type of information: formatted text. You can also use other methods from the e.Graphics object with equal ease to print different types of information, including basic shapes (through methods like DrawRectangle), lines (DrawLine) and even pictures:

```
e.Graphics.DrawImage(Image.FromFile("C:\MyFolder\MyFile.bmp"), x, y)
```

TIP *When you use the Graphics object, you are actually making use of the GDI+ technology in the .NET framework. The interesting part is that this standard Graphics object is reused in more than one place. For example, the way you use DrawImage and DrawString to place output on a printed page is the exact same way you use DrawImage and DrawString to place output onto a Windows form. Even though you are less likely to use GDI+ to manually create window output, it's good to know that the skills you use in printing can be reused with on-screen graphics if required.*

Print Settings

Our printing example specifies a printer and uses default margin and page size settings. However, this approach is rarely flexible enough for a real application. Most users expect to have control of at least some basic printing options, including the ability to choose the specific printer they want to use. In previous versions of Visual Basic, this was a fairly straightforward but manual task that would involve presenting the user with a Print Options window, retrieving the settings they chose, and applying them to the Print object before a print operation began. In Visual Basic .NET, however, the process has been made much easier.

All the tools you need for displaying standard Print Options and Page Settings windows are provided in convenient classes from .NET's class library. Before you display a Printer Settings window, you associate it with the PrintDocument object that you are using. Then, any configuration that the user performs will be automatically incorporated in the appropriate object (MyDoc in our example) and in the PrinterEventArgs object (called *e*) provided in the PrintPage event.

```
Private Sub cmdConfigure_Click(ByVal sender As System.Object, _
 ByVal e As System.EventArgs) Handles cmdConfigure.Click
    Dim dlgSettings As New PrintDialog()
    dlgSettings.Document = MyDoc
    dlgSettings.ShowDialog()
End Sub
```

With this simple code, we allow the user to set the standard printer options such as Printer and Number of Copies. These settings will be stored in the supplied PrintDocument object. In our example, the MyDoc.PrinterSettings.Printer-Name case will be automatically updated to reflect the selected printer.

In the goal of simplicity, this example creates the PrintDialog object entirely in code. You could also use the component tray to add it to your form, and set its properties at design time. Of course, the end result would be the same. The only difference is that Visual Studio .NET will automatically add the corresponding code for the PrintDialog object to the special Windows Designer region.

Similar code can be used to give the user a chance to modify page settings:

```
Dim dlgSettings As New PageSetupDialog()
dlgSettings.Document = MyDoc
dlgSettings.ShowDialog()
```

These changes will also be reflected automatically throughout related areas of the program. For example, margin selections will affect the e.Margin-Bounds.Top property used in the PrintPage event.

Print Preview

Visual Basic .NET's new print preview feature is almost an example of getting something for nothing. With a few simple lines, you can create a Print Preview screen that displays the exact printed information and pagination, complete with controls for zooming and options for displaying multiple pages at a time.

Here is the code needed to incorporate the print preview feature in our current example:

```
Private Sub cmdPreview_Click(ByVal sender As System.Object, _
  ByVal e As System.EventArgs) Handles cmdPreview.Click

    Dim dlgPreview As New PrintPreviewDialog()
    dlgPreview.Document = MyDoc
    dlgPreview.Show()

End Sub
```

Once again, we create the PrintPreviewDialog control manually at run time, rather than adding it to the component tray (which would work just as well).

When your users click the cmdPreview button, a new non-modal window will appear, as shown in Figure 8-8.

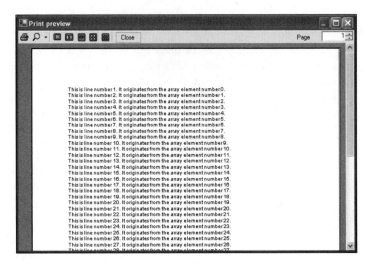

Figure 8-8: The Print Preview

The first amazing aspect of the print preview feature is that it uses all your prewritten printing code, both saving you trouble and eliminating differences in appearance between the Print Preview display and the actual printed copy. Various third-party components attempt to implement this simple but tricky concept, but none do so as simply or as successfully as the .NET framework.

The next great thing about the print preview feature is that it provides a substantial amount of flexibility and customization. Before you display your PrintPreviewDialog object, you can tweak various form properties, including such standards as WindowsState, Size, MaximumSize, MinimumSize, and StartupPosition. You can even set its MdiParent property to make it become an MDI child window inside your program!

The PrintPreview Control

.NET also gives you the ability to create a custom Print Preview window, or integrate the Print Preview display into one of your application windows. This allows you to combine print preview information with other components of the user interface. For example, you could create a program with a customized Print window that lets your users set special options, such as footer and page numbering style. Whenever a change is made, you would update the Print Preview display automatically, to provide a *dynamic preview.*

To incorporate a Print Preview display inside one of your windows, you use the PrintPreview Control, and draw it on your form at design time (see Figure 8-9).

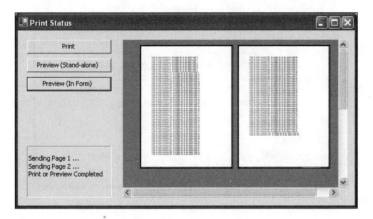

Figure 8-9: Incorporating a Print Preview in a form

To display the preview inside the PrintPreview control, just set its Document property, as you would with the PrintPreviewDialog control. You can also tweak the Zoom property to specify how large the pages should be, and the Columns or Rows property to set the number of pages that can be displayed side-by-side.

```
' The default size zoom is 0.3. 1 is full-size.
Preview.Zoom = 0.2

' The Rows and Columns settings mean 6 pages can be displayed at once (2 x 3).
Preview.Columns = 2
Preview.Rows = 3

' The next line triggers the actual preview.
Preview.Document = MyDoc
```

To recalculate the Print Preview display, set the Document property again.

Parsing Information

Some applications print out extremely long strings of text that break over more than one printed line. There are several different ways to handle this scenario. You can split the text into a series of separate lines before printing, and then load the information into an array or collection. Alternatively, you could parse the information as you print it. This is often the required solution if you are printing mixed information that combines text, graphics, and other data.

The online samples for this chapter include a WrappedPrinting example that demonstrates the difference between wrapping and not wrapping (Figure 8-10).

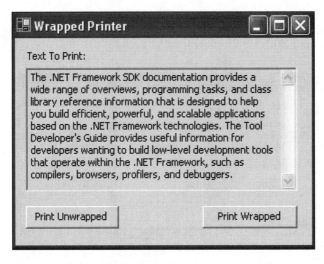

Figure 8-10: The Wrapped Printing utility

In order to print wrapped text, the code breaks down the block of text into a collection of lines, and stores them in an ArrayList collection called Parsed-Lines. The code steps through the text letter-by-letter, looking for a space where wrapping can be performed. When a space is found, the code then checks if the current line is long enough to be printed, by using the MeasureString method and comparing the result to the page width.

```
Private Sub WrappedPrint(ByVal sender As Object, ByVal e As PrintPageEventArgs)

    ' Define the font and determine the line height.
    Dim MyFont As New Font("Arial", 18)
    Dim LineHeight As Single = MyFont.GetHeight(e.Graphics)

    ' Create variables to hold position on page.
    Dim x As Single = e.MarginBounds.Left
    Dim y As Single = e.MarginBounds.Top

    Dim Line As String
    Dim ParsedLines As New ArrayList()
    Dim TextToPrint As String = txtData.Text

    Dim i As Integer

    Do
        ' Add one character to the current line,
        '  and remove it from the text to print.
        Line &= TextToPrint.Chars(0)
```

```
        TextToPrint = TextToPrint.Substring(1)

    If Line.EndsWith(" ") Then
        If e.Graphics.MeasureString(Line, MyFont).Width > _
            (e.PageBounds.Width - 300) Then
            ParsedLines.Add(Line)
            Line = ""
        End If
    End If
Loop While TextToPrint <> ""

ParsedLines.Add(Line)

' Now print the collection of lines.
For Each Line In ParsedLines
    e.Graphics.DrawString(Line, MyFont, Brushes.Black, x, y)
    y += LineHeight
Next

End Sub
```

The wrapped output from this code is shown in Figure 8-11.

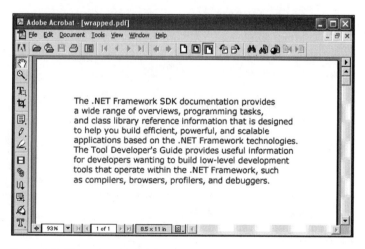

Figure 8-11: The wrapped printout

This type of printing can involve some sophisticated planning. For example, you might want to make sure, whenever possible, that related text appears on the same page. If you are about to start printing a new section, that might be a good point to begin a new printed page, even if it means having a little extra free space at the bottom of the existing page. On the other hand, you might be willing to tolerate a smaller amount of free space when printing a single image, or multiple related lines that you want to have grouped together. In these situations, you wouldn't want your page breaks determined strictly on the basis of a single line-height calculation. Instead, you could write your code to demand more free space when comparing the current position against the bottom page margin.

These print scenarios involve a fair bit of trial-and-error development. A good design pattern is to create one procedure for wrapping multiple text lines, and a separate procedure for determining whether to move to a new page before resuming printing. The logical framework for this type of application is shown here, in pseudocode.

```
Private PageEnd As Boolean   ' Tracks when a new page is needed.

Private Sub PagePrint
    ' Loop through the collection of information to print.
    Do
        If Item Is Picture
            ' Go directly to PrintToPage routine with the picture.
        ElseIf Item Is SingleTextLine
            ' Go directly to PrintToPage routine with the text.
        ElseIf Item Is TextBlock
            ' Call PrintWrappedLine.
        End If

        If PageEnd = True Then
            ' Start a new page.
        End If
    Loop
End Sub

Private Sub PrintWrappedLine(Text As String)
    ' Every time a complete line is built, call PrintToPage with it.
End Sub

Private Sub PrintToPage(ObjectToPrint As Object, Threshold As Integer)
    ' The Threshold determines how close to the bottom of the page the printing
    ' can be before the printing is aborted and PageEnd is set to alert the
    ' PagePrint event handler.
    ' The calling code determines the appropriate threshold value.
End Sub
```

NOTE *Pseudocode is simplified programming logic that needs to be "filled out" before it becomes a real program. We use it in this case because it clearly presents the logic of our program, without extraneous details that might distract us from the overall problem. Pseudocode is also useful in this case because every program that uses the pattern shown here will probably develop its own highly individualized implementation. Note that the syntax used in pseudocode is not necessarily real Visual Basic syntax!*

Working with the Registry

As long as we're on the subject of data, I'd like to slip in a quick discussion of the Windows registry, which is the central repository for storing application settings on a Windows computer. It wasn't hard to use the registry in Visual Basic 6, but you were forced to put your settings into a special area designated for VB programmers. To escape this bizarre (and somewhat insulting) restriction and access the full registry, you had to resort to the Windows API. Thankfully, VB .NET has improved the picture once again.

To access the Windows registry in .NET, you use two classes from the Microsoft.Win32 namespace: Registry and RegistryKey. Registry provides your starting point into one of the main divisions of the registry. Typically, you will use the Registry.CurrentUser property to work with the registry settings that affect the currently logged-on user. On other, rarer occasions, you might use another branch, such as Registry.LocalMachine, which allows you to configure settings that will affect all users.

The registry is a hierarchical repository, containing keys and many levels of subkeys. The usual practice for an application is to store information in either the CurrentUser (HKEY_CURRENT_USER) or LocalMachine (HKEY_LOCAL_MACHINE) branch, in the path Software\CompanyName\ ProductName\ or Software\CompanyName\ProductName\Category. This location is the organizational equivalent of a file folder on a hard drive. The actual information about the application is stored in string values.

The following example shows a generic RegistryReader class that receives a reference to a form, and then either saves its current size and position attributes (SaveSize) or retrieves another set of attributes (SetSize) and applies them instead. The pathname is hard-coded for this application as Software\AcmeInsurance\PolicyMaker. A key is added to the path using the name of the form, to help group the settings for different forms (as in Software\AcmeInsurance\PolicyMaker\Main). Depending on how your application works, this may not be an appropriate way to store information. (For example, if you create different forms dynamically, and are in the habit of giving them the same name, their settings will overwrite each other in the registry.)

Inside each form-specific key, four values are specified: Height, Width, Top, and Left.

```
Imports Microsoft.Win32
Public Class RegistryReader

    Public Shared Sub SaveSize(ByVal frm As System.Windows.Forms.Form)

        ' The next line creates the key only if it doesn't already exist.
        Dim rk As RegistryKey
        rk = Registry.LocalMachine.CreateSubKey( _
            "Software\Acme\TestApp\" & frm.Name)
        rk.SetValue("Height", frm.Height)
```

(continued on next page)

```
        rk.SetValue("Width", frm.Width)
        rk.SetValue("Left", frm.Left)
        rk.SetValue("Top", frm.Top)

    End Sub

    Public Shared Sub SetSize(ByVal frm As System.Windows.Forms.Form)

        Dim rk As RegistryKey
        rk = Registry.LocalMachine.OpenSubKey( _
            "Software\Acme\TestApp\" & frm.Name)

        ' If the value isn't found the second argument is used.
        ' This leaves the size and location unchanged.
        frm.Height = CType(rk.GetValue("Height", frm.Height), Integer)
        frm.Width = CType(rk.GetValue("Width", frm.Width), Integer)
        frm.Left = CType(rk.GetValue("Left", frm.Left), Integer)
        frm.Top = CType(rk.GetValue("Top", frm.Top), Integer)

    End Sub

End Class
```

To use this class, just call the appropriate subroutine with the form that you
want to save or reset. The following example shows two button event handlers
that can be used to make a form automatically save and restore its size and position. (You can run the included RegistryTester program to try this out.)

```
Private Sub cmdSave_Click(ByVal sender As System.Object, _
  ByVal e As System.EventArgs) Handles cmdSave.Click
    RegistryReader.SaveSize(Me)
End Sub

Private Sub cmdLoad_Click(ByVal sender As System.Object, _
  ByVal e As System.EventArgs) Handles cmdLoad.Click
    RegistryReader.SetSize(Me)
End Sub
```

TIP *Registry settings are not case-sensitive, so differences in the capitalization of a key or
value name will be ignored. As you've seen in the preceding examples, you don't need to
worry about missing values. You can use the same command to add a new value or to
replace an existing one. When retrieving a value, you can supply a default, which will be
returned if the specified value does not exist.*

XML Files

The real story with XML and Visual Basic .NET is how the .NET platform uses XML, behind the scenes, as a native format. You'll discover in Chapters 9 and 13 how .NET uses XML to provide communication between Web Services and clients, and to store relational data in ADO.NET. In these cases, the use of XML is automatic and transparent. You won't need to deal with the XML information directly. For many programmers, this will be the closest they get to XML. Sometimes, however, you may want to read or write XML files manually. You might be interacting with data stored by another program, or you may want to use XML to store your own application's data.

For example, you might create a special sales ordering program that allows customers to choose the items they want to order out of a database, and to save their choices to a file if they don't want to order right away. This file will probably contain little more than a list of product IDs that identify the selected items. The corresponding price and product information will reside in corresponding records in the full product database, which is stored on your company's web site. In this case, it would make sense to store the local list of product IDs in a simple format, such as a text file rather than a separate database. An XML file, which is really a text file with an enhanced, standardized organization, may be exactly what you need.

What Is XML, Anyway?

XML code is stored on your computer in a text file, but it looks more like HTML. That's because XML uses tags to "mark up" content. A very basic XML document might look a little like this:

```
<?xml version="1.0"?>
<mydocument>
    <person>
        <name>Matthew</name>
        <phone>555-5555</phone>
    </person>
</mydocument>
```

This XML-like document has four *tags*. As with most XML files, the whole document is contained in a *root tag*, which in this case is called "mydocument." This tag contains a single Person, which contains two additional pieces of information—a name and a phone number—in separate tags called "name" and "phone." The starting and ending tags look the same, except that the ending tag has a special slash (/) character.

As in an HTML document, extra whitespace is collapsed. The different levels of indentation are used to indicate structure, but they have no effect on how the document is read. If this were a text file, you would read it line by line. However, with an XML document you will read it element by element. Even if the document above were condensed to a single line, its elements would be read separately.

Content, Not Format

The preceding example illustrates the primary difference between HTML and XML. In an XML document, tags indicate formatting. For example, <H1>The Title!</H1> tells an Internet browser to place a line of text in a bold font with a larger size than normal body text. An XML document, on the other hand, indicates absolutely nothing about how to format data for appropriate presentation. In fact, if you open an XML document in Internet Explorer, you'll see everything in the same size text, with the tags displayed (Figure 8-12).

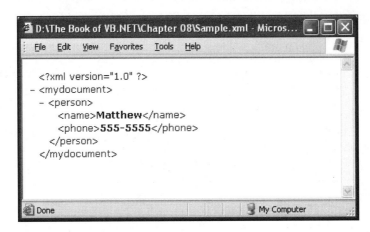

Figure 8-12: XML in Internet Explorer

XML tags indicate content, not format. In fact, XML files are used almost exclusively for storing data, because the data is described in a way that makes it easy for other programs (and even humans) to interpret it.

Part of the complexity of using XML is understanding the many standards for writing XML documents. As you can see, the underlying concept behind XML is pretty general. You can create an XML document pretty much any way you want to. Different standards are used to ensure some consistency, but we won't have a chance to review them in this book.

Attributes and Comments

One other thing you should know about XML is that it doesn't just use *elements*, although those are its primary units for organizing content. You can also use *attributes* and *comments*. Comments go anywhere, and are ignored for data processing purposes. Usually, they just provide additional information that might help a human being understand something about a file. Comments are bracketed by <!- and ->.

Attributes add extra information into an element. A subject of great debate in the XML world is when you should put information into an attribute, and when you should use an element. Generally, an element is preferred for most information, but elements are used to indicate extra descriptive information, not the actual data. Once again, there is no single all-encompassing standard. Attributes appear inside elements, and use a *Name*="*Value*" syntax.

Here is a modified XML example that includes two comments and an attribute:

```
<?xml version="1.0"?>
<mydocument title="MatthewDescription">
<!-- This is the comment. Right above us is the attribute, inside the mydocument
element (attributes are always part of a tag like this). It says that mydocucment
has the title "MatthewDescription". -->
    <person>
        <name>Matthew</name>
        <phone>555-5555</phone>
    </person>
    <!-- It would make sense to add more person tags here, as needed. -->
</mydocument>
```

Writing a Simple XML Document

The easiest and most enjoyable way to write an XML document is to use the no-nonsense XmlTextWriter class, which works a little like the StreamWriter class. This class is designed to let you write a series of XML information from start to finish. If your information needs to be edited, you need to perform the necessary operations with the data in memory before you start writing it to the file.

Our next example shows a block of Visual Basic .NET code that could create the sample XML document we looked at in the previous section. Before beginning, make sure you import the two required namespaces:

```
Imports System.IO
Imports System.Xml
```

The XML writing code is shown below. Indentation is used to help you see the structure of the corresponding XML document.

```
Dim fs As FileStream = New FileStream("c:\myfile.xml", FileMode.Create)
Dim w As XmlTextWriter = New XmlTextWriter(fs, Nothing)
w.WriteStartDocument()
w.WriteStartElement("mydocument")
    w.WriteAttributeString("name", "", "MatthewDescription")
    w.WriteComment("This is the comment, etc.")
    w.WriteStartElement("person")
        w.WriteStartElement("name")
            w.WriteString("Matthew")
        w.WriteEndElement()                 ' Close the name element.
        w.WriteStartElement("phone")
            w.WriteString("555-5555")
        w.WriteEndElement()                 ' Close the phone element.
    w.WriteEndElement()                     ' Close the person element.
```

(continued on next page)

```
' Could add more person elements here ...
w.WriteEndElement()                      ' Close the mydocument element.
w.WriteEndDocument()
w.Close()
```

Notice that we need the root mydocument element. As soon as we close it, our XML file is finished. Visual Basic .NET will not allow us to open another mydocument element, nor write several person elements without any other element containing them, because those actions would violate the XML standard. (This is one of the benefits of using the XmlTextWriter class instead of StreamWriter for XML information: It proofreads your output, and stops you if you try to enter invalid XML.)

Reading XML

To read an XML file, you can use a simple text-reading class called, unsurprisingly, XmlTextReader, or you can use a combination of the XmlDocument and XmlNodeReader classes, which is what this chapter will use. XmlNodeReader is designed to read *nodes*. Each time you use the XmlNodeReader.Read method, it loads the information for the next node in the file into the XmlNodeReader object (using the Name, Value, and NoteType properties). The Read method returns True if the operation is successful, and False if the end of the file has been reached and another node couldn't be found. An XmlError is thrown if the XML file is discovered to contain invalid content, such as a starting tag that doesn't have a corresponding ending tag. To access the actual information for a node, you use the various properties of the XmlNodeReader object.

By this point you may be wondering "What exactly is a node?" and "Is it any different than an element?" The easiest way to answer that question is to show you what an XmlNodeReader will read from the sample myfile.xml file.

The following example uses a subroutine called Out to add some information to a label without overwriting it. (This simple procedure, which isn't shown here, was used in the FileInfo example earlier in this chapter.)

```
Dim doc As New XmlDocument()
doc.Load("c:\test.xml")
Dim r As XmlNodeReader = New XmlNodeReader(doc)
' Use a counter to keep track of how many nodes are found.
Dim ElementNumber As Integer

' Loop until the file is finished.
Do
    ElementNumber += 1
    ' Display each node property, unless it's blank.
    Out(ElementNumber.ToString & ". " & r.NodeType.ToString)
    If Not (r.Name = "") Then Out("  Name: " & r.Name)
    If Not (r.Value = "") Then Out("  Value: " & r.Value)
    Out("")
Loop While r.Read() = True
```

This program performs the simple task of displaying information about each node in the label control. The information that is displayed will look like this:

```
1. XmlDeclaration
   Name: xml
   Value: version= "1.0"

2. Element
   Name: mydocument

3. Element
   Name: person

4. Element
   Name: name

5. Text
   Value: Matthew

6. EndElement
   Name: name

7. Element
   Name: phone

8. Text
   Value: 555-5555

9. EndElement
   Name: phone

10. EndElement
    Name: person

11. EndElement
    Name: mydocument
```

From this listing, it's obvious that our XML file has 11 nodes. There is one node for every starting tag, every ending tag, every comment, and even the XML definition at the top of the file. Elements have associated names, but no values. The data inside an element has no name, but it does have a value. The only potential problem with this system is that attributes don't appear. That's because attributes are actually *properties* of nodes. To check for an attribute, examine the node's HasAttributes property or the AttributeCount property. Then you can use the MoveToAttribute method to jump to the appropriate attribute, and the MoveToElement method to get back to the element. Then you can continue on your way.

It works like this:

```
If r.HasAttributes Then
    Dim i As Integer
    For i = 0 To r.AttributeCount - 1
        r.MoveToAttribute(i)
        ' Display the attribute's properties.
        Out("   Attribute #" & (i + 1).ToString())
        Out("      Name: " & r.Name)
        Out("      Value: " & r.Value)
    Next i
    ' Go back to the start of the original element.
    r.MoveToElement()
End If
```

The full code can be found in the online XML Tester application (shown in Figure 8-13).

This should give you a little taste of what it's like to work with the full XML document object model, in which you navigate through the XML file as a collection of objects. (Of course, you could also just refrain from using attributes altogether, and make your life a little easier.)

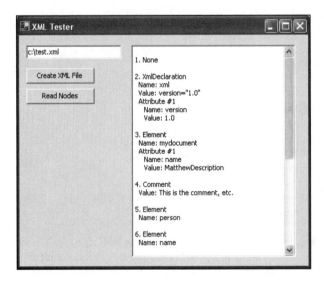

Figure 8-13: The XML tester utility

Advanced XML

The techniques you've learned in this chapter are the most convenient ways to access and create XML documents. However, they are designed for quickly reading from or writing to an entire XML file at once. For example, you might use XmlNodeReader in a FileOpen type of routine, creating the required business objects and setting corresponding properties based on the information that you read. You could then use these objects to manipulate the information, and possibly end by writing a new XML file (or overwriting the existing file) with XmlTextWriter. However, you might prefer that some applications read XML data, and work with the information *as* XML data, not as custom objects. This technique might be useful in a cross-platform project, for example, where XML data is going to be used in several different programming environments, and the features of those environments are known to be incompatible.

In order to work with XML data, you can use the XML DOM (document object model), which looks at your XML document as a collection of related objects, based on their element tags. This model is available in .NET through the XmlDocument class, which has methods for adding nodes in any location, and for navigating through your document. It's similar to working your way through a TreeView control, with properties like FirstChild, NextSibling, and so on.

In this book, we stick to basic XML reading and writing. If you need to store complex and structured information, you should check out ADO .NET, which uses XML natively. If you are working on a cross-platform project that needs more in-depth XML features, refer to the MSDN class library documentation for the XmlDocument class in the System.Xml namespace.

What Comes Next?

In this chapter, we've examined how to reach out from Visual Basic .NET programs and manipulate the data in the registry, as well as in text, binary, and XML files. You have learned how to send data to the printer, build a logical printing framework, configure printing settings, and display a Print Preview window.

Now that you have a good understanding of the fundamental ingredients, it's up to you to discover how to best integrate these features in a live application. It's here where object-oriented design starts to come into play. For example, you might want to create your own class to represent a data file. This class would contain the appropriate StreamReader and StreamWriter objects, but would expose an interface to the rest of your program that is specific to the type of information stored in the file.

For example, a data class might provide specific properties for each piece of data, or a collection representing a list of records or items. It would probably also provide more useful methods for writing to a file—perhaps accepting specific data or business objects from your application, and then deciding how best to write them to disk. Your class might also take care of basic chores, such as writing a special identifying signature at the top of a file when creating the file, and then verifying the signature when reading the file, to make sure that the file really does belong to your application. Or, it might calculate a checksum based on the data in the file. (A simple example would be adding together all the product numbers in a purchase order file, and then storing this total at the end of the file. When reading the file, you could verify this checksum to make sure the data hasn't been tampered with.)

These are all examples of *subclassing*: taking a basic object and wrapping it inside another object to provide more features. It's also an example of *abstraction* at work—your file class handles the low-level text stream features, and your program only has to worry about opening the file, checking for error information, and reading the appropriate properties. This is where the real fun of .NET design begins.

9

DATABASES AND ADO.NET

If you've ever programmed internal projects for tracking customers, sales, payroll, or inventory, you've probably realized that data is the lifeblood of any company. For the Visual Basic programmer, this understanding is particularly relevant, because no other language is used as often to create database applications. In the early days of Windows programming, Visual Basic came to prominence as a simple and powerful tool for writing applications that could talk to a database and generate attractive reports. In some ways, this is still Visual Basic's most comfortable niche.

Over the years, Microsoft has given the world a confusing alphabet soup of database access technologies. Visual Basic programmers first started with something called DAO (Data Access Objects), later upgrading to RDO (Remote Data Objects) to access client-server database products such as SQL, and then migrated to ADO (Active Data Objects), which was supposed to provide the best of both worlds. In many ways, ADO fulfilled its promise, providing a flexible and powerful object model that could be used by programmers in just about any Windows-based programming language. In fact, ADO is still a bit of a newcomer, and has already fragmented into several versions. Some features, such as XML access and disconnected use, have been more or less slapped on as afterthoughts, and more letters have been added to the soup with additional technologies like RDS (Remote Data Service). However, it didn't take Microsoft long to throw in the towel once again and decide with .NET that what everyone needs is yet another entirely new way to access data.

And calling ADO.NET "entirely new" is only a modest exaggeration. While ADO.NET has some superficial similarities to ADO, its underlying technology and overall philosophy are dramatically different. While ADO was a connection-centered database technology that threw in some disconnected access features as an afterthought, ADO.NET is based on disconnected DataSets, and has no support for server-side cursors. While ADO was a "best of breed" standard Microsoft component built out of COM, ADO.NET is an inhabitant of the .NET class library, designed for managed code, and based entirely on XML for storing data. As you'll see in this chapter, ADO.NET is one more .NET revolution.

New in .NET

The .NET languages require a new database technology. ADO, the previous standard, was wedded to COM, and every interaction between .NET-managed code and ordinary code (such as that in a COM component) suffers an automatic performance hit. The surprise is that ADO.NET is not just a .NET version of ADO. Instead, ADO.NET has been redesigned from the ground up.

No Support for Cursors

In ADO, a cursor tracks your current location in a result set, and allows you to perform updates on live data. Cursors have completely disappeared in ADO.NET. They are replaced by a new disconnected model that doesn't maintain connections.

XML-Based Data Storage

In ADO, XML data access is an afterthought. ADO.NET, however, uses XML natively as its own internal format for storing data. In most cases, you won't need to explore the XML internals when dealing with relational data. On the other hand, you might put them to good use by storing data locally in an XML file, or transferring XML data to a component on another computer or operating system.

DataSets and DataReaders Replace Recordsets

Recordsets were the focal point of ADO, but they had some significant drawbacks. ADO.NET replaces the Recordset with the DataSet, which can contain more than one table of data as well as additional information about table relations. For situations where you need fast read-only access, and you don't want to hold onto information for longer than a few seconds, ADO.NET provides a special DataReader object.

New DataAdapters

In ADO, Recordsets were usually directly connected to a data source. In the connectionless world of ADO.NET, DataSets don't directly relate to any data source. Instead, you use a special DataAdapter to pull information out of the database and pop it into a DataSet. You also use the DataAdapter to submit DataSet changes back to the database when you're done.

Introducing ADO.NET

There are essentially two ways that you can use ADO.NET in your applications. First of all, you can use it entirely on its own to create tables and relations by hand. You can then easily store this information in an XML file using ADO.NET's built-in capabilities, and retrieve it later to work with it again. This way of using of ADO.NET, with a dynamically created data file, is described later in this chapter. It provides a simple, no-frills approach to creating and storing single-user information.

However, it's much more likely that you'll use ADO.NET to interact with an underlying database. This database might be a stand-alone Access database, or it might be a multi-user RDBMS (Relational Database Management System), such as Microsoft's SQL Server. No matter what your data source, the way you use ADO.NET will be essentially the same. You can still create your own tables and write an XML file representing the data you retrieve, but your ultimate goal will be to commit any modifications back to the database.

Using Relational Data

ADO.NET picks up where simple file and XML document access end. These techniques, which were examined in Chapter 8, are ideal for simple, small portions of well-contained information. ADO.NET, on the other hand, excels when it comes to dealing with *relational data*: information that is broken down into several separate tables, which are then linked together.

For example, consider an application for tracking staff work hours. In a simple form, this application might be built out of three tables: Employee, Location, and WorkLog. The Employee table would contain all the information related to a specific individual. The Location table would store the information about a work environment. The WorkLog would record a number of hours worked, along with a reference to the appropriate Employee (through an EmployeeID field) and the Location where the work was done (through a LocationID field). This relationship would make it easy to manipulate the data to find out such information as the total number of hours worked at a specific location or by a specific employee. It also wouldn't waste any space, or invite potentially conflicting information by storing employee-specific information (such as the person's name) or location-specific information (such as the address) in the WorkLog table.

The structure would look like Figure 9-1.

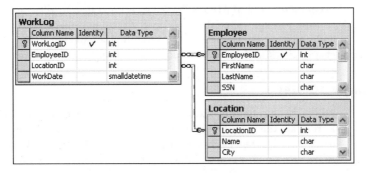

Figure 9-1: Table relations

This, of course, is the typical way you store information in any relational database, whether it is SQL Server, Oracle, MySQL, or something else. Usually, you use a combination of SQL statements and *stored procedures* (miniature programs added to your database) to manage this information. ADO or ADO.NET handles the processes of sending commands to the database and retrieving any resulting information, including the actual data rows, so that you can display them or work with them in your application. Of course, both ADO and ADO.NET allow you to connect to other data sources—even sources that may not be truly relational. But in the majority of cases, you will use ADO or ADO.NET to access a standard database.

The Northwind Database

Incidentally, all the examples in this chapter use tables from the Northwind database, a sample database included with SQL Server to help you test database access code. If you have SQL Server, but for some reason you are missing the Northwind database, you can use the script included with the online samples to install it automatically. You can also use this script to install the Northwind database for MSDE (Microsoft Database Engine).

MSDE is one of Microsoft's best-kept secrets—it's essentially a scaled-down version of SQL that's bundled with Visual Studio .NET. It's completely compatible with SQL Server (in fact, it *is* SQL Server), and free to use for anyone, provided they don't need to support more than five simultaneous database connections. If a client installs MSDE and then wants to upgrade to a system that supports more simultaneous users, SQL Server can be easily installed, and the MSDE databases can be imported in a snap. The only catch is that MSDE, on its own, doesn't provide the nice graphical tools that help you build tables and relations, monitor performance, and perform general database upkeep. To remedy this problem, Microsoft has added some helpful developer database utilities to Visual Studio .NET. Unfortunately, this is a chapter about programming with databases—not how to use database management applications like SQL Server and MSDE. Although I don't have the space to tell you everything you need to know to install and configure MSDE, you can find some information at Microsoft's MSDE site (http://msdn.microsoft.com/vstudio/msde).

TIP *In the Visual Studio .NET setup, even if you select to install MSDE you must complete its setup after Visual Studio .NET is installed. To do so, manually launch the setup.exe program from the \Setup\MSDE\ subfolder under the main Visual Studio .NET installation folder.*

If you have another database product, or you don't want to install the Northwind database, you can tweak the examples to use another data source. Usually you'll only have to adjust the connection string and the names of the tables and fields. Bear in mind, however, that some data sources, such as Microsoft Access databases, don't support all the features we'll discuss (stored procedures, for instance).

SQL Server and OLE DB

Many of the ADO.NET classes are provided in two separate flavors (see Figure 9-2). The standard version works like traditional ADO, and accesses data through something called an OLE DB provider. OLE DB is the layer that lets the data source talk to ADO or ADO.NET. OLE DB providers exist for most relational data products, including Microsoft's own SQL Server.

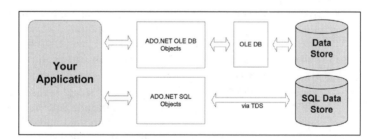

Figure 9-2: Two ways to connect with ADO.NET

NOTE *The only OLE DB provider that ADO.NET can't use is the ODBC provider. Instead, Microsoft plans to make a pre-release managed provider for ODBC available at their web site. I add this as a useful tip if you need it; everyone else should disregard this alphabet soup of database-related acronyms.*

So OLE DB is our old, trusty standard. However, SQL Server also has its own customized .NET provider that's optimized for performance. It interacts directly with SQL Server's Tabular Data Stream (TDS) and bypasses the extra COM and OLE DB layers. To summarize, you use the standard OLE DB providers for all data access in ADO.NET, except when using SQL Server. You could connect to SQL Server using OLE DB, but it wouldn't change the available features you could use, and it would probably slow down performance slightly because of the extra layers.

In the future, other database products will add their own .NET-managed providers for better performance (and some may even be included natively with the .NET framework). Don't worry: The providers for different databases derive from the same classes, implement the same procedures (with the same methods and properties), use the same DataSet object, and work almost exactly the same.

The Basic ADO.NET Objects

All of the ADO.NET features are provided through types in the System.Data branch of the .NET class library. This includes the following five namespaces:

- **System.Data** contains the fundamental classes for managing data, such as DataSet and DataRelation. These classes are totally independent of any specific type of database.

- **System.Data.Common** contains some base classes that are inherited by other classes in the System.Data.OleDb and System.Data.SqlClient namespaces. Essentially, the classes in this namespace specify the basic functionality, while the classes in the other namespaces are customized based on the data source. Thus, you don't use the System.Data.Common classes directly.

- **System.Data.OleDb** contains the classes you use to connect to OLE DB provider, including OleDbCommand and OleDbConnection.

- **System.Data.SqlClient** contains the classes you use to connect to a Microsoft SQL Server database using the optimized TDS (Tabular Data Stream) interface. This includes such classes as SqlDbCommand and SqlDbConnection, which look and act almost exactly the same as their OLE DB counterparts.

- **System.Data.SqlTypes** includes additional data types that aren't provided in .NET, but are used in SQL Server. These include SqlDateTime and SqlMoney. These types can be converted into the standard .NET equivalents, but the process introduces the possibility of a conversion or rounding error that might adversely affect data. Instead, you can create objects based on the structures defined in this class. It might even increase speed a bit, as no automatic conversions will be required.

This chapter uses SQL Server and the associated System.Data.SqlClient namespace. The techniques described here are, without exception, identical for OLE DB providers.

To get off to a good start, you should import the two namespaces you need to use:

```
Imports System.Data           ' Provides common classes like DataSet.
Imports System.Data.SqlClient ' Use System.Data.OleDB instead if using
                              ' an OLE DB provider.
```

Fast-Forward Read-Only Access

There are two ways that you can access data with ADO.NET: as a read-only stream of information, or as a disconnected DataSet that you can examine and manipulate long after the database connection has been closed. In a sense, ADO.NET poses a difficult question that forces you to choose between two dramatically different approaches. The common middle ground found in ADO programming—a live read-write cursor that maintains a connection—just isn't an option in ADO.NET

In the first section of this chapter, we'll explore data access the easy way, and temporarily avoid the thorny issues of disconnected data. As you read ahead, you might want to refer to the diagram in Figure 9-3, which shows you the basic model for this simple type of data access.

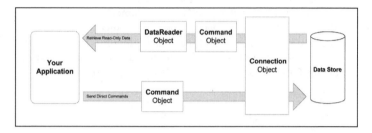

Figure 9-3: Using ADO.NET without disconnected data

Our first task is to introduce the basic ingredients for any type of data access: Connections and Commands.

Connection Objects

You use a connection object to establish a connection to a data source. The only trick is using the right connection string.

The Connection String

The connection string specifies all the information that the database needs in a single line of text. It consists of a string of named parameters and values (for example, user id=sa), each of which is separated by a semicolon.

Below is a sample connection string:

```
Connection = "Data Source=localhost;Initial Catalog=Northwind;user id=sa"
```

This connection string specifies a connection to the SQL Server installation on the local computer (rather than a remote network server), and identifies the database that you want to use (Northwind). It also connects with the user ID *sa*, which is the default system administrator account provided with SQL Server.

If this connection string doesn't work for you, it may be because the *sa* account has been modified since installation, and now requires a password (which is always a good practice). You can specify the password as one additional parameter in the connection string, as in `password=opensesame`.

If you are using SQL 2000, you may have disabled SQL authentication in favor of Windows integrated security, which allows you access based on the currently logged-on user. In this case, you can use a connection string with the following format:

```
Connect = "Data Source=localhost;Initial Catalog=Northwind;" & _
  "Integrated Security=SSPI"
```

In order for this to work, the currently logged-on Windows user must have the required authorization to access the SQL database.

And just for variety, here's how a connection string might look for an OLE DB provider using the OleDbConnection object. The only real difference is the addition of the Provider setting, which identifies the appropriate OLE DB provider. In the following example, the connect string is pointing to the SQL Server OLE DB provider, which you generally won't use.

```
Connection = "Provider=SQLOLEDB.1;Data Source=localhost;" & _
  "Initial Catalog=Northwind;user id=sa"
```

Other providers include MSDAORA (the OLEDB provider for an Oracle database) and Microsoft.Jet.OLEDB.4.0 (the OLEDB provider for Access).

There are several other options you can set for a connection string, and they are all documented in the .NET help files (under the SqlConnection and OleDbConnection references). These options include parameters you can use to specify a few other pieces of information, such as how long you'll wait while trying to make a connection before timing out.

Making a Connection

Once you have created the right connection string, it's easy to create a connection object and establish a live connection. For SQL Server, you use the SqlConnection object. (For an OLE DB provider, you would use the OleDbConnection object.)

It works like this:

```
Dim Connect As String = "Data Source=localhost;Integrated Security=SSPI;" & _
  "Initial Catalog=Northwind;"
Dim con As New SqlConnection(Connect)
con.Open()
```

You can close your connection at any time by calling the Close method.

NOTE *As illustrated in the preceding example,, you don't really use a Connection object. Instead, you use the appropriate derived class (SqlConnection or OleDbConnection). In cases where there is more than one flavor of a class, as with the Connection object, this chapter introduces them with a common (yet fictitious) object name.*

Command Objects

Command objects represent the SQL statements or stored procedures that you can use to retrieve data or submit changes. In order to use ADO.NET, you should have a basic understanding of the SQL language.

SQL Statements

Here's an SQL statement at its simplest. It's used to retrieve data from a single table in the current database (in this case, the Orders table). The asterisk (*) indicates that we want to retrieve all the fields from the table (including OrderID, CustomerID, and so on).

```
SQLString = "SELECT * FROM Orders"
```

Seasoned database programmers will shudder when they see this statement, because it doesn't limit the number of returned records in any way. In other words, it selects all the records in the Orders table, whether there are fifty or five million of them. This type of statement typically goes into an application that works well when it is first deployed, but gradually slows to a crawl as the number of records in the database climbs. Eventually, you may even receive timeout errors.

A safer SQL statement might look like this:

```
SQL As String = "SELECT * FROM Orders " & _
 "WHERE OrderDate < '2000/01/01' AND OrderDate > '1987/01/01'"
```

The Where clause ensures that only certain rows are retrieved. In this case, the OrderDate column must have a value between the two specified dates. (This example uses the international standard date format *yyyy/mm/dd*, which is typically a safe representation.) The values being compared are enclosed in single quotes, unless they are numbers. The And keyword allows us to use more than one criterion in our SQL statement.

Creating a Command

Provided you have a connection, a command is easy to define. If you are using an SQL Server database, you will use the SqlCommand object. OLE DB providers require the OleDbCommand object.

```
Dim SQLString As String = "SELECT * FROM Orders " & _
 "WHERE OrderDate < '2000/01/01' AND OrderDate > '1987/01/01'"
Dim cmd As New SqlCommand(SQLString, con)
```

This example creates an SqlCommand object using a constructor that lets us specify the connection that must be used, and the statement that will be used to select records. We could accomplish the same thing in the more verbose format of our next example. (Like ADO, ADO.NET often provides many paths toward accomplishing the same task.)

```
Dim cmd As New SqlCommand()
cmd.CommandText = SQLString
cmd.Connection = con
' Strictly speaking, the next line isn't required because
' CommandType.Text is the default.
cmd.CommandType = CommandType.Text
```

Notice that these examples don't actually read any data; all either of them does is define a command. In order to use the command, you have to decide whether you want to create a simple DataReader or a full-fledged disconnected DataSet.

DataReader Objects

A DataReader is the equivalent of a *firehose cursor,* which gets its name from the fact that it provides a steady stream of one-way data pouring from the database straight into your program, with few additional frills. A DataReader doesn't provide disconnected access, or any ability to change or update the original data source. You should use a DataReader whenever you need quick, read-only data, as its performance will always beat the full-fledged DataSet. On the other hand, the DataReader provides few features.

There are two types of DataReader objects: SqlDataReader (optimized for SQL Server databases) and OleDbDataReader (for OLE DB providers). Once you've made a connection and defined a Command, you can access the data through a reader.

The heart of our ADO.NET DataReader programming is contained in a single line:

```
Dim reader As SqlDataReader = cmd.ExecuteReader()
```

This defines an SqlDataReader object, and creates it using the ExecuteReader method of our Command object. In order for this to work, you must have already used the code from our earlier examples to create the connection and command that we are using here.

Once you have the reader, you can move through the rows from start to finish, interacting with each row one at a time. This is similar to the way you interacted with a Recordset in ADO, but instead of the MoveNext method you use the Read method. This method returns True as long as there is a row of data at the current position. Once you move past the last row, it changes to False.

The following loop moves through all the rows in the reader. Notice that there is no way to move backward.

```
Do While reader.Read()
    ' Process current row here.
Loop

reader.Close()
con.Close()
```

This loop invokes the reader.Read method in each pass. When the reader has read all the available information, the method will return False, the While condition will evaluate to False, and the loop will end gracefully. Keep in mind that you have to call the Read method before you start processing a row. When the reader is first created, there is no current row.

TIP *Remember, DataReaders maintain a live connection, so you should process the data and close your connection as quickly as possible.*

To access the actual data, you use a field name or an index number (which starts counting at zero). Usually, a field name will be the clearest option, but the index number provides an easy way for you to make sure you use every column in the row.

```
' Put this code inside the reader loop:
lstOrderID.Items.Add(reader("OrderID"))  ' Adds the data from the OrderID field.
lstOrderID.Items.Add(reader(0))          ' The same thing, using the field index.
```

This is just about all that a DataReader allows you to do.

A ListView Example

Our next example uses an SqlDataReader object to move through the returned records and place some basic information into a ListView control (see Figure 9-4). The code looks more complicated because the ListView control requires some special considerations.

The first step is to set up the ListView control so that it displays a multicolumn list:

```
lvOrders.View = View.Details
```

Now we can add a column for every field in the DataReader. There is no quick and easy way to get the field names, so we stick to numbers. FieldCount is one of the few properties provided by the SqlDataReader object, so we can use that to determine how many columns are required:

```
Dim i As Integer
For i = 0 To reader.FieldCount - 1
    lvOrders.Columns.Add("Column " & (i + 1).ToString, 100, _
    HorizontalAlignment.Left)
Next
```

Now that the initial setup is complete, the actual data can be added:

```
Do While (reader.Read())
    Dim NewItem As New ListViewItem()
    NewItem.Text = reader(0)

    For i = 1 To reader.FieldCount - 1
        If reader(i) Is DBNull.Value Then
            NewItem.SubItems.Add("")
        Else
            NewItem.SubItems.Add(reader(i).ToString())
        End If
    Next i


    lvOrders.Items.Add(NewItem)
Loop
```

This example looks more complicated then it actually is. The code is broken into two portions because of the way that the list control works. Every ListView control contains a collection of items. (In our example, each item represents an OrderID.) To put information into additional columns, you have to add subitems to each ListView item.

This example also checks for a null value in the field. In a database, a null value indicates only that the field is empty, and that no information has been entered. You can't change a null value into a string, however, so the Add method will fail if it's used to add a field that contains a null value. The output for this example is shown in Figure 9-4.

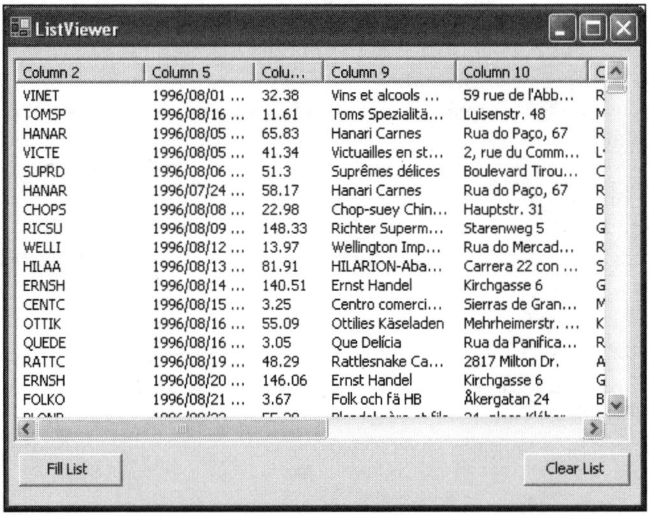

Figure 9-4: Filling a ListView

If you accomplish everything you need to with a DataReader, it's always a good choice. If you need more sophisticated data manipulating abilities, you'll need to step up to the DataSet object, which we'll explore a little later in the chapter.

Updating Data with the Command Object

The DataReader object provides a simple way to pull a stream of data out of a database, but it doesn't allow us to make any changes. What can a programmer do to modify a database? For example, maybe your program needs to record events or transactions without bothering the user with the details. In this case, you need to be able to add a new record to a table in the original database. Or, maybe your program is a more direct database application that presents a record of information, and then allows the user to specify changes. In this case, you need to modify an existing record.

Traditional ADO programming was more flexible than ADO.NET—perhaps too flexible. To update a record, a programmer would usually create a Recordset, select the one relevant row, and then use a direct cursor connection to change values as needed. To add a new record, the programmer would follow more or less the same process involved in creating a Recordset, maybe even selecting some existing records, and would then use the Recordset to add a new row. These techniques won't work in ADO.NET, and it may be worth asking if they were ever a good idea in the first place.

In ADO.NET, you have two options for updating data:

- Updating it directly with a customized Command
- Creating a DataSet, implementing the changes there, and then committing them to the original data source

The next section examines the easier of these two methods: using a Command object.

Why Use a Command Object?

If your application makes relatively straightforward changes, the best way to update the data source is to use a Command object. This object can contain a special SQL statement (such as Update or Delete), or it can run a stored procedure that exists in your database.

Generally, a Command object provides the most straightforward and uncomplicated way to make a change. The only drawback is that it can require some extra work (and code) if your application allows the user to make substantial, varied modifications. This approach—using a Command object to go straight to the data source—was available in ADO. However, ADO developers often fell back on the Recordset object because it was easier to code a solution "on the fly"—in other words, with little planning or forethought. The advantages of the Command approach are:

- No data is returned from the database. After all, why waste time creating a Recordset, and then using a Select statement to put some information into it, if you don't need to?

- If there's a problem following your instruction, you'll know it right away. (With disconnected data and DataSets, however, several changes are usually made at once; this makes it harder to track down what's failed and identify the cause.)

- As long as you understand the SQL language (or have a helpful stored procedure), using Command objects is the most straightforward technique for making changes. Disconnected DataSets require extra planning, because they can apply changes in an unpredictable order, thus causing problems with linked tables.

A Data Update Example

Here's an example that uses a Command object to perform an update operation. For this type of operation, you use the Command object directly, with the help of its ExecuteNonQuery method:

```
' Create connection.
Dim Connect As String = "Data Source=localhost;Integrated Security=SSPI;" & _
  "Initial Catalog=Northwind;"
Dim con As New SqlConnection(Connect)
con.Open()

' Create a silly update command.
Dim SQL As String = "UPDATE Orders SET ShipCountry='Oceania' " & _
  "WHERE OrderID='10248'"
Dim cmd As New SqlCommand(SQL, con)

' Execute the command.
Dim NumAffected As Integer
NumAffected = cmd.ExecuteNonQuery()
con.Close()

' Display the number of affected records.
MessageBox.Show(NumAffected.ToString & " records updated", "Results", _
  MessageBoxButtons.OK)
```

This code creates the standard Connection and Command objects, and then executes the command directly. The update command is an SQL Update statement that finds the record with the OrderID 10248 (which exists in the default Northwind database) and changes the ShipCountry value to Oceania. This record will be updated even if ShipCountry has already been changed, provided it can be found. The message you will see is shown in Figure 9-5.

Figure 9-5: A simple update test

The preceding example uses a fairly straightforward SQL Update statement. However, if you aren't familiar with SQL, it may take a little getting used to. Unfortunately, the SQL language is beyond the scope of this book (although the final section of this chapter will point you to some excellent resources).

Some Real-World Changes

In a more realistic example, the Update statement would be created dynamically using another variable or a control property, as shown here:

```
Dim SQL As String = "UPDATE Orders SET ShipCountry='" & lstCountry.Text & _
  "' WHERE OrderID='" & intCurrentOrder & "'"
```

Be careful to include the single quote marks for non-numeric data! Generally, writing an SQL statement like this in your program is extremely bad form, even if it is generated dynamically. The best alternative is to go through another class that has the appropriate SQL values stored as constants, or to use a function that creates the SQL statement for you based on the corresponding parameters. Either option will make your code much more readable.

For example, a function might use this type of approach:

```
Dim cmd As New SqlCommand(GetSQLToUpdateCountry(OrderID, lstCountry.Text), con)
```

In this case, GetSQLToUpdateCountry is used right in the declaration for the command. It returns the Update string using the specified country and order ID. (You might want to streamline this example with a shorter function name.)

You might find that you are using some common SQL statements repeatedly. If so, a much better approach might be to make them enumerated values.

You could use a helper class, like this:

```
Public Class NorthwindSQL
    Public Enum Queries
        GetAllOrders
        GetAllCustomers
    End Enum

    'A shared method makes this method available even without a live instance.
    Public Shared Function GetSQL(ByVal Query As Queries) As String
        Select Case Query
            Case Queries.GetAllCustomers
                Return "SELECT * FROM Orders"
            Case Queries.GetAllOrders
                Return "SELECT * FROM Customers"
        End Select
    End Function
End Class
```

TIP *Remember, you can access the enumerations in any class by using the class name, even if you haven't created an instance of that class.*

You could use the NorthwindSQL class to create a Command that will select all the records from the Orders table, like this:

```
Dim cmd As New SqlCommand(NorthwindSQL.GetSQL(NorthwindSQL.GetAllOrders), con)
```

At this point, our code savings may not seem that great. But consider some of the advantages:

- In a real application, SQL statements may be much longer and more complex. For example, they will usually specify only the required column fields (rather than using the asterisk (*), which can slow down your application by requesting data that it doesn't need). This list of fields can be quite lengthy—and easily mistyped!

- In a real application you will probably need to set additional information— such as a limiting date range, or other options—for the Where clause. These values can be appended to the returned SQL string, or they can be added by the helper class, provided that you add some extra parameters to your function. Alternatively, you could give your class properties that record extra information (such as the required date range). Then the information would only need to be set once, and could be reused for multiple different commands.

- By having all the SQL statements in one class, you can easily update your application when the database changes.

A Transaction Example

A *transaction* allows you to execute several commands at once, and to be guaranteed that they will all succeed or fail as a unit. The basic principal of a transaction is that if any of the actions in it fails, the whole process is "rolled back" to its initial state. You can appreciate the value of this system if you have ever used an instant bank machine. If, after requesting a withdrawal, the bank machine failed and could not give you any money, you would not be happy if it still deducted the amount from your bank account. In other words, withdrawing money is a transaction made of two steps: your bank account being debited, and you receiving your money. Neither one of these steps should happen without the other.

A database often uses transactions in its stored procedures. They can save you the trouble of coding extra database logic inside your application, and can help separate the basic data management code from the rest of your application. However, in some cases this is not convenient, and you need to be able to create a transaction programmatically in your VB .NET code. To do this, you create a transaction object (either an SqlTransaction or an OleDbTransaction), and use the BeginTransaction method of the Connection object.

To start the process, you need to create and initiate the transaction:

```
' (The code to create the standard Connection and Command objects is left out.)
' Don't need to use New, as this object will be created for us.
Dim tran As SqlTransaction

' Create the transaction and assign it to our Transaction object.
tran = con.BeginTransaction()
```

Now the transaction exists, but it includes no Command objects. To make a Command object a part of this transaction, you can set its Transaction property. Assuming that we've already created two Command objects (cmdOne and cmdTwo), it works like this:

```
cmdOne.Transaction = tran
cmdTwo.Transaction = tran
```

These commands can be executed in the normal way:

```
Dim NumAffected As Integer
NumAffected = cmdOne.ExecuteNonQuery()

' Add the rows affected for the second query to find the total number of rows
' affected by both statements.
NumAffected += cmdTwo.ExecuteNonQuery()
```

However, the changes won't be permanently made to the data source until you commit them:

```
tran.Commit()
```

Alternatively, you can use the Rollback method to reverse changes, and set the data source back to its original state. Usually, you would use the Rollback method in response to an error, as shown here:

```
' Define Connection, Command, and Transaction objects here.
Try
    ' Start the Transaction, execute the Commands, and perform any other
    ' related code here.
    tran.Commit()
Catch err As Exception
    tran.Rollback()
End Try
```

An Example of a Stored Procedure

Stored procedures are miniature programs stored inside a relational database. A typical stored procedure consists of a number of SQL statements that can perform various tasks (such as selecting, updating, inserting, and deleting data).

Here's a sample stored procedure used to add a new customer record to the Customers table. It's not present in the default SQL Server Northwind database, so before you can use the procedure, you have to use the Enterprise Manager to add it. (It will already be added if you used the script provided with this chapter's examples to install the database.)

```
CREATE PROCEDURE AddNewCustomer
    @CustomerID varchar(5), @CompanyName varchar(40), @ContactName varchar(30)
AS INSERT INTO Customers(CustomerID, CompanyName, ContactName)
    VALUES(@CustomerID, @CompanyName, @ContactName)
```

This code looks quite different than anything you could write in VB .NET. The basic details are as follows:

- The procedure is called AddNewCustomer.
- The procedure uses three variables, which are defined in the second line. All SQL variables are identified with an @ symbol at the beginning of their names. The data types for these variables are also unfamiliar to the VB programmer. Varchar is the SQL-specific version of a string (and the number in brackets is its maximum character length).

- The third line features an Insert command, which adds a new row to the Customers table. It also inserts values for the three named fields (using the information on the next line, which is the list of variables). All other values will be left empty—in fact, they will have null values.

You can use the Command object to execute a stored procedure in the same way you would execute an SQL statement. However, there are two differences. First of all, for maximum efficiency, you should set the Command object's CommandType to CommandType.StoredProcedure:

```
' (Code to create a connection omitted).
Dim cmd As New SqlCommand("AddNewCustomer", con)
cmd.CommandType = CommandType.StoredProcedure
```

Secondly, if your stored procedure requires parameters with additional information (as the AddNewCustomer procedure does), you need to create a few OleDbParameter or SqlParameter objects.

Here's how you would create parameters to use with the AddNewCustomer procedure:

```
' Create an SqlParameter object. We don't use the New keyword here because this
' object will only be used to hold a reference to the parameter created with
' the Command object.
Dim param As SqlParameter

param = cmd.Parameters.Add("@CustomerID", SqlDbType.VarChar, 5)
param.Value = "*TEST"
param = cmd.Parameters.Add("@CompanyName", SqlDbType.VarChar, 40)
param.Value = "No Starch Press"
param = cmd.Parameters.Add("@ContactName", SqlDbType.VarChar, 30)
param.Value = "Matthew MacDonald"
```

When a parameter is added, you must specify information about its data type, along with the name of the corresponding stored procedure variable. You can then assign the value of the Parameter object to set the actual information that will be sent.

Once you've added the parameters and assigned the appropriate values, you can execute the stored procedure:

```
Dim NumAffected As Integer
NumAffected = cmd.ExecuteNonQuery()
con.Close()
```

The new record will be added, as shown in Figure 9-6.

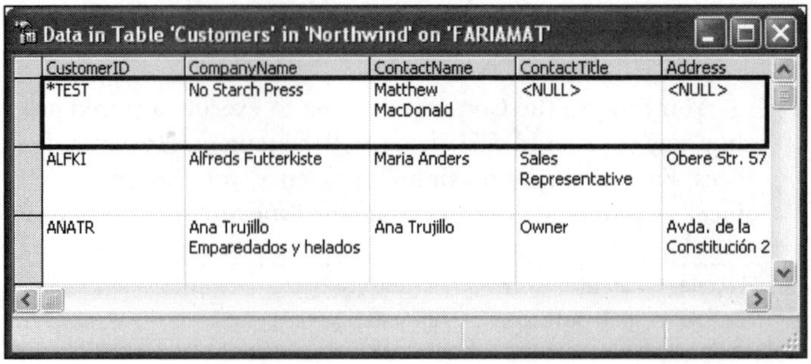

CustomerID	CompanyName	ContactName	ContactTitle	Address
*TEST	No Starch Press	Matthew MacDonald	<NULL>	<NULL>
ALFKI	Alfreds Futterkiste	Maria Anders	Sales Representative	Obere Str. 57
ANATR	Ana Trujillo Emparedados y helados	Ana Trujillo	Owner	Avda. de la Constitución 2

Figure 9-6: The inserted record

Drawbacks to Stored Procedures

Stored procedures are a both a blessing and a curse. Their proponents point out that they let you remove database code from your application, control security (by restricting direct access to the tables, but allowing access to permitted stored procedures), and improve performance (because stored procedures can be pre-compiled, unlike the dynamically-generated SQL statements in your program). All of these advantages are true, and together they mean that you will probably want to use stored procedures in any large, professional business application.

However, stored procedures also have some drawbacks. For one thing, they are based on script-like blocks of code rather than on real objects, which are generally nicer to work with. More importantly, the parameter-based system of using stored procedures requires that you add a lot of extra information into your application about the structure of your database. In reality, your program should not care what the specific data type or string length of a parameter is, as long as it can guarantee that it is submitting a valid value. (And you may have already noticed that SQL statements have all their information in a simple string.) However, when you create a Parameter object, you have to specify all this information, essentially importing database-specific details into your application.

Once again, the best way to handle this is to use an intermediate class to "wrap" the database functions and database-specific details. For example, you could create a function that adds all the parameters for a specific stored proce-dure, using the values you supply, along with the database-specific information about data types stored in the class.

The following example uses a method to add the corresponding parameters and execute the command:

```
NorthwindProcedures.AddCustomer(cmd, "*TEST", "No Starch Press", "Matthew")
```

The database class looks like this:

```
Public Class NortwindProcedures

    Public Shared Function AddCustomer(cmd As SqlCommand, Customer As String, _
      Company As String, Contact As String) As Integer

        Dim param As SqlParameter
        param = cmd.Parameters.Add("@CustomerID", SqlDbType.VarChar, 5)
        param.Value = Customer
        param = cmd.Parameters.Add("@CompanyName", SqlDbType.VarChar, 40)
        param.Value = Company"
        param = cmd.Parameters.Add("@ContactName", SqlDbType.VarChar, 30)
        param.Value = Contact

        ' Execute the Command and return the number of affected rows.
        Return cmd.ExecuteNonQuery()
    End Sub

End Class
```

Stored procedure design can become much more complicated. A stored procedure might perform multiple tasks, and may even return a result set (in which case you need to grab the results with a DataSet). A stored procedure can also send additional information to your program using output parameters. By default all the Parameter objects you add are for input parameters. However, this is easy to change:

```
param.Direction = ParameterDirection.Output
```

When using an output parameter, you don't set the Value property. Instead, you read from the Value property after the Command object has been executed to retrieve your results.

Using DataSet Objects

In many ways, the DataSet object is the focus of ADO.NET programming. Unlike the data reader, a DataSet is disconnected by nature. You can place information into a DataSet, or move information from a DataSet back into a relational database, but the DataSet itself never maintains a connection with a data source—in fact, it doesn't even have a connection property. To shuffle information back and forth between a DataSet object and a data source, you need to use a special DataAdapter object. Figure 9-7 shows how all the ADO.NET objects interact for disconnected access.

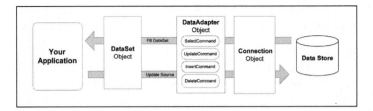

Figure 9-7: Disconnected data access with ADO.NET

When Should I Use a DataSet Object?

A DataReader provides the best possible performance. In general, you should always use a DataReader, unless you need the advanced capabilities of a DataSet. Some of these capabilities include:

- The ability to store data for long periods of time, and transfer it to other classes or components as a neatly packaged object.
- The ability to perform substantial updates and changes to the data, without needing to execute individual SQL statements or stored procedures.
- The ability to save or retrieve data as an XML file.
- Greater flexibility when reading data, such as the ability to move forward and backward through data, and the ability to jump back and forth between distinct, but related tables in the DataSet.

Filling a DataSet with a DataAdapter

As with a DataReader, you need to create a Connection and a Command object before you can retrieve the rows you need:

```
Dim Connect As String = "Data Source=localhost;Integrated Security=SSPI;" & _
  "Initial Catalog=Northwind;"
Dim con As New SqlConnection(Connect)

Dim SQL As String = "SELECT * FROM Orders " & _
 "WHERE OrderDate < '2000/01/01' AND OrderDate > '1987/01/01'"
Dim cmd As New SqlCommand(SQL, con)
```

So far, these lines are the same as those used by our DataReader.

Next, you need to create a DataAdapter. DataAdapters are another example of data source–specific objects. There are two flavors: SqlDataAdapter, shown here, and OleDbDataAdapter.

```
Dim adapter As New SqlDataAdapter(cmd)
```

This statement creates an adapter using our Command object. There are several other equivalent ways that you could accomplish the same thing. For example, you could pass the SQL and Connect strings to the SqlDataAdapter constructor, and coax it into creating an implicit connection and command automatically on its own. However, the approach used in the preceding example is generally more flexible, particularly if you need to reuse the connection or run more than one SQL query in a row with the same adapter.

Next we'll create a DataSet, and fill it with the DataAdapter's Fill method:

```
Dim dsNorthwind As New DataSet()
con.Open()
adapter.Fill(dsNorthwind, "Orders")
con.Close()
```

The Fill method executes the command we've specified, takes the results, and inserts them into the dsNorthwind DataSet in a table named Orders. (In this case, the destination table name is the same as the table name in the data source, but it doesn't need to be.)

NOTE *The DataSet object is generic. Whether you are using an OLE DB provider or the native SQL Server classes, you always create and fill the same DataSet object.*

Accessing the Information in a DataSet

The information in a DataSet is stored in collections. This is quite different from a DataReader, which exposes only one row at a time, forcing you to use the Read method to move from row to row. A DataSet, on the other hand, has a Tables property that contains a collection of DataTable objects. Each DataTable has a Rows property that contains a collection of DataRow objects. You access these DataRows by using the corresponding field names, much as you would with a DataReader. The diagram in Figure 9-8 shows the overall object model.

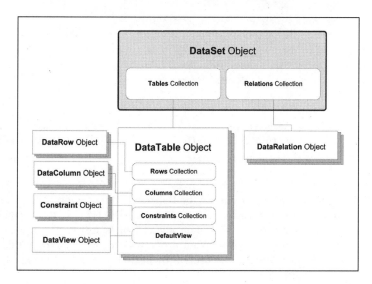

Figure 9-8: The DataSet

You'll notice that the discussion so far has left out a few of the details shown in this illustration. For example, a DataSet can also contain DataRelation objects (which link different DataTables together), and each DataTable can also contain Constraint objects (which specify restrictions on allowable column information) and Column objects (which contain information about the field name and data type of each column). These collections are generally less important, although later in the chapter we will return to the DataRelation object in more detail.

You move through the data in a table using the Rows collection, as shown here:

```
Dim row As DataRow
For Each row In dsNorthwind.Tables("Orders").Rows
    ' Here you can retrieve a value using the current row.
    lstOrderID.Items.Add(row("OrderID"))
    ' Or you can change it.
    row("ShipCountry") = "Lilliput"
Next
```

NOTE *Of course, the DataSet object is always disconnected. This means that any changes you make will appear in your program, but won't affect the original data source unless you take additional steps, which this chapter will delve into a little bit later.*

Deleting Records

You can also delete records from a DataSet using the Delete method. The process is quite straightforward:

```
Dim row As DataRow
Dim colRowsToDelete As New Collection()

For Each row In dsNorthwind.Tables("Orders").Rows
    If row("ShipCountry") <> "Brazil" Then
        ' If the ShipCountry is not Brazil, mark it for deletion.
        row.Delete()
    Else
        ' Otherwise, add it to our list.
        lstOrder.Items.Add(row("OrderID") & " to " & row("ShipCountry"))
    End If
Next
```

However, when you use the Delete method, the row is not actually removed, only marked for deletion. That's because ADO.NET needs to retain information about the record in order to be able to remove it from the original data source when you reconnect later. Your programs need to be aware of this fact, and should include steps that prevent them from trying to use deleted rows:

```
For Each row In dsNorthwind.Tables("Orders").Rows
    If row.RowState <> DataRowState.Deleted Then
        lstOrderID.Items.Add(row("OrderID"))
    End If
Next
```

NOTE *If your program tries to read a field of information from a deleted item, an error will occur. This error is meant to alert you that you are trying to access information that is scheduled for deletion.*

You can also use the Remove method to delete an item completely. However, if you use this method, the record won't be deleted from the data source when you reconnect and update it with your changes. Instead, it will just be eliminated from your DataSet object.

Adding Information to a DataSet

You can also easily add a new row using the Add method of the Rows collection. The trick is to use the NewRow method first to get a blank copy of the row you want to create:

```
Dim rowNew As DataRow
' Create the row.
rowNew = dsNorthwind.Tables("Orders").NewRow()

' Set the information in the row.
rowNew("OrderID") = 12000
rowNew("ShipCountry") = "Lilliput"
' (And so on to add more fields...)

' Add the row to the DataSet.
dsNorthwind.Tables("Orders").Rows.Add(rowNew)
```

Life might not be this easy, depending on your original data source. For example, the database may have other requirements for these columns (such as a maximum length, or a restriction against null values). In addition, most database designs use *auto-incrementing* identity columns. For example, if OrderID were an auto-numbering column, SQL Server would automatically give it a new value when you add a new record. This means that you shouldn't specify any value at all in the OrderID field while you are creating the record, or else you risk specifying a number that will conflict with an existing generated value, thus causing a problem.

Generally, ADO.NET provides one tool that can help you. It's called the FillSchema method, and you can use it before using the Fill method to retrieve a bunch of information about your database, such as column constraints, and add it into your DataTable object.

```
adapter.FillSchema(dsNorthwind, SchemaType.Mapped, "Orders")
adapter.Fill(dsNorthwind, "Orders")
```

The FillSchema method adds the DataTable and all the DataColumn objects, but it doesn't add the actual data. Unlike the Fill method, FillSchema completely configures each DataColumn object with such information as default value, nullability, and maximum length. (For a full list, check the properties of the DataColumn object in the MSDN class library reference.) The primary key requirement is also added as a Constraint object. Foreign keys, which define relationships between tables, are not added, because ADO.NET has no way of knowing whether you have added the required linked tables. When you use the Fill method, the information streams into the ready-made columns without a problem.

The specific details of how to create and modify column constraints and default values are beyond the scope of this chapter. Most programmers will use a visual database design tool (like SQL Server's Enterprise Manager) for this task. Also, keep in mind that it's often a better idea to add a new record directly by using a stored procedure.

Working with Multiple Tables

Sadly, the Fill method can add only one table at a time. If you want to add more than one table, you have to use the Fill method more than once, including more than one Command object (or changing the Command's CommandText property in between).

```
Dim dsNorthwind As New DataSet()
adapter.Fill(dsNorthwind, "Orders")

' This command is still linked to the DataAdapter.
cmd.CommandText = "SELECT * FROM Customers"
adapter.Fill(dsNorthwind, "Customers")

cmd.CommandText = "SELECT * FROM Employees"
adapter.Fill(dsNorthwind, "Employees")
```

After these commands, there will be three tables in the DataSet, each of which can be accessed individually by specifying the appropriate table name (for example, dsNorthwind.Table("Customers") accesses the Customers table).

DataTable Relations

There is no way to import information about linked tables from the data source. Instead, you need to add this information manually if you want to make use of it. To link two tables together, you need to create a Relation object.

Our multi-table example uses three tables that are related. The Orders table has a CustomerID field that corresponds to a CustomerID in the Customers table. To specify this relationship in a DataSet, you can use the following code:

```
' Define the relation.
Dim relCustomersOrders As New DataRelation("CustomersOrders", _
  dsNorthwind.Tables("Customers").Columns("CustomerID"), _
  dsNorthwind.Tables("Orders").Columns("CustomerID"))

' Add the relation to the DataSet.
dsNorthwind.Relations.Add(relCustomersOrders)
```

This code defines a relationship in which the Customers table is the parent and the Orders table is the child. This is because one customer record can have multiple children (orders), but every order has only one parent (customer). This Parent-to-Child relationship is just another way of describing a One-to-Many relationship, which is a basic ingredient in database theory. Once the relationship is defined, our example adds it to the DataSet to put it to work.

As with any relational database, using a relation implies certain restrictions. For example, if you add a relation to the DataSet and then try to create a child row that refers to a nonexistent parent, ADO.NET will generate an error. Similarly, you can't delete a parent that has child records linked to it. These requirements will be enforced already by your data source, but by adding them to the DataSet, you ensure that you will catch any errors as soon as they occur, rather than waiting until an entire batch of changes is committed to the data source later on.

You can also use your relation to provide better record navigation. This technique, shown in the following code, allows you to combine information dynamically from several linked tables, without having to use a join query. It works using the GetChildRows method of a DataRow object. The results are shown in Figure 9-9.

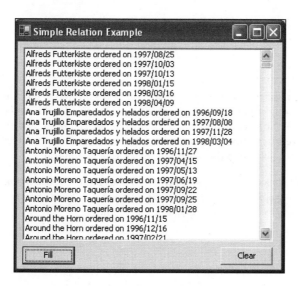

Figure 9-9: A simple example of relational data

```
Dim rowParent, rowChild As DataRow
For Each rowParent In dsNorthwind.Tables("Customers").Rows
    For Each rowChild In rowParent.GetChildRows(relCustomersOrders)
        ' Display combined information using both rows.
        lstOrder.Items.Add(rowParent("CompanyName") & _
        " ordered on " & rowChild("OrderDate"))
    Next
Next
```

An even more useful way to use this relational ability might be to construct a hierarchical TreeView display. The only difference in the code is that you need to make sure to store a reference to the current customer node so you can add order sub-nodes.

```
Dim nodeParent, nodeChild As TreeNode
Dim rowParent, rowChild As DataRow

For Each rowParent In dsNorthwind.Tables("Customers").Rows
    ' Add the customer node.
    nodeParent = treeDB.Nodes.Add(rowParent("CompanyName"))

    ' Store the disconnected customer information for later.
    nodeParent.Tag = rowParent

    For Each rowChild In rowParent.GetChildRows(relCustomersOrders)
        ' Add the child order node.
        nodeChild = nodeParent.Nodes.Add(rowChild("OrderID"))

        ' Store the disconnected order information for later.
        nodeChild.Tag = rowChild
    Next
Next
```

As an added enhancement, this code stores a reference to the associated DataRow object in the Tag property of each TreeNode. When the node is clicked, all the information is retrieved from the DataRow, and then displayed in the adjacent text box. This is one of the advantages of disconnected data objects: You can keep them around for as long as you want.

NOTE *You might remember the Tag property from Visual Basic 6, where it could be used to store a string of information for your own personal use. The Tag property in VB .NET is similar, except you can store any type of object in it.*

```
Private Sub treeDB_AfterSelect(ByVal sender As System.Object, _
  ByVal e As System.Windows.Forms.TreeViewEventArgs) Handles treeDB.AfterSelect

    ' Clear the textbox.
    txtInfo.Text = ""
    Dim row As DataRow = CType(e.Node.Tag, DataRow)

    ' Fill the textbox with information from every field.
    Dim Field As Object
    For Each Field In row.ItemArray
        txtInfo.Text &= Field.ToString & vbNewLine
    Next

End Sub
```

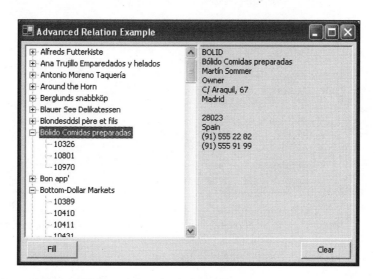

Figure 9-10: An advanced example of relational data

This sample program (featured in the chapter examples as the Relational-TreeView project and shown in Figure 9-10) is also a good demonstration of docking at work. To make sure all the controls stay where they should, and to allow the user to change the relative screen area given to the TreeView and text box, a Splitter control is used along with three Panel controls.

Using a DataSet Object to Update Data

One aspect of the DataSet object that you may not realize at first is that it stores additional information about the initial values of your table and the changes that you have made. You have already seen how deleted rows are left in your DataSet with a special deleted flag (DataRowState.Deleted). Similarly, added rows are given the flag DataRowState.Added, and modified rows are flagged as DataRowState.Modified. This allows ADO.NET to quickly determine which rows need to be added, removed, and changed.

However, in order to modify a changed row, ADO.NET needs to be able to select the original row from the data source. To allow this, ADO.NET stores information about the original field values, as shown in this example:

```
Dim rowEdit As DataRow
' Select the 11 row (at position 10).
rowEdit = dsNorthwind.Tables("Orders").Rows(10)

' Change some information in the row.
rowEdit("ShipCountry") = "Oceania"

' This returns "Oceania".
lblResult.text = rowEdit("ShipCountry")

' This is identical.
lblResult.text = rowEdit("ShipCountry", DataRowVersion.Current)

' This returns the last data source version (in my case, "Austria").
lblResult.text = rowEdit("ShipCountry", DataRowVersion.Original)
```

Ordinarily, you don't need to worry about this extra layer of information, other than to understand that this is what allows ADO.NET to find the original row and update it when you reconnect.

The whole process works like this:

1. Create a Connection object and define a Command object that will select the data you need.

2. Create a corresponding DataAdapter object, using your Command object.

3. Using the DataAdapter, transfer the information into a disconnected DataSet object. Close the Connection object.

4. Make changes to the DataSet (modifying, deleting, or adding rows).

5. Create a Connection object (or reuse the existing one).

6. Create Command objects for inserting, updating, and deleting data. Alternatively, to save yourself some work, you can use the special CommandBuilder class.

7. Create a DataAdapter object using your Command or CommandBuilder objects.

8. Reconnect to the data source.

9. Using the DataAdapter, update the data source with the information in the DataSet.

10. Report any concurrency errors (for example, if an operation fails because another user has already changed the row after you've retrieved it).

You can see why using a simple command with an SQL Update statement is a simpler approach than managing disconnected data!

Using the CommandBuilder Object

Assuming that you have already created the DataSet, filled it with information, and made your modifications, we can pick up with Step 5 of the preceding list. This step involves defining a connection, which is straightforward:

```
Dim Connect As String = "Data Source=localhost;Integrated Security=SSPI;" & _
   "Initial Catalog=Northwind;"
Dim con As New SqlConnection(Connect)
```

The next step is to create a Command. When we selected information from the data source, we needed only one type of command: a Select command. However, when we update the data source, three different tasks could be performed in combination, depending on the changes that we have made, including Insert, Update, and Delete commands. In order to avoid the work involved in creating these three command objects manually, you can use the special CommandBuilder object (which is provided as SqlCommandBuilder and OleDbCommandBuilder). This object has no purpose other than to save you a little manual work when updating a data source.

The CommandBuilder takes a reference to the DataAdapter object that was used to create the DataSet, and it adds the required additional three commands. Assuming that the programmer has been relatively shortsighted, and has already destroyed the Command and DataAdapter objects, we can simply recreate them:

```
' Create the Command and DataAdapter representing the Select operation.
Dim SQL As String = "SELECT * FROM Orders " & _
 "WHERE OrderDate < '2000/01/01' AND OrderDate > '1987/01/01'"
Dim cmd As New SqlCommand(SQL, con)
Dim adapter As New SqlDataAdapter(cmd)
```

At this point, the adapter.SelectCommand property refers to the cmd object. This SelectCommand is automatically used for select operations (such as Fill and ExecuteReader). However, the adapter.InsertCommand, adapter.DeleteCommand, and adapter.UpdateCommand properties are not set.

To set these three properties, you can use the CommandBuilder:

```
' Create the CommandBuilder.
Dim cb As New SqlCommandBuilder(adapter)

' Retrieve an updated DataAdapter.
adapter = cb.DataAdapter
```

Updating the Data Source

Once you have appropriately configured the DataAdapter, you can update the data source in a single line by using the DataAdapter's Update method:

```
Dim NumRowsAffected As Integer
NumRowsAffected = adapter.Update(dsNorthwind, "Orders")
```

The Update method works with one table at a time, so you'll need to call it several times in order to commit the changes in multiple tables. When you use the Update method, ADO.NET scans through all the rows in the specified table. Every time it finds a new row (DataRowState.Added), it adds it to the data source via the corresponding Insert command. Every time it finds a row that is marked with the state DataRowState.Deleted, it deletes the corresponding row from the database by using the Delete command. And every time it finds a DataRowState.Modified row, it updates the corresponding row by using the Update command.

Once the update is successfully complete, the DataSet object will be refreshed, all rows will be reset to DataRowState.Unchanged, and all the "Current" values will become "Original" values, to correspond to the data source.

Reporting Concurrency Problems

Before a row can be updated, the row in the data source must exactly match the "Original" value stored in the DataSet. This value is set when the DataSet is created, and every time the data source is updated. If however, another user has changed even a single field in the original record while your program has been working with the disconnected data, the operation will fail, the Update will be halted, and an exception will be thrown. In many cases, this prevents other valid rows from being updated.

An easier way to deal with this problem is to detect the discrepancy in the DataAdapter's RowUpdated event. This event occurs every time a single update, delete, or insert operation is completed, regardless of the result. It provides you with some special information, including the type of statement that was just executed, the number of rows that were affected, and the DataRow from the DataTable that prompted the operation. It also gives you the chance to tell the DataAdapter to ignore the error, note it, and resolve it later.

The RowUpdated event happens in the middle of DataAdapter's Update method, and so this event handler is not the place to try and resolve the problem or present the user with additional user interface, which would tie up the database connection. Instead, you should log errors, display them on the screen in a list control, or put them into a collection so you can examine them later.

The following example puts errors in one of three shared collections provided in a class called DBErrors. The class looks like this:

```
Public Class DBErrors
    Public Shared LastInsert As Collection
    Public Shared LastDelete As Collection
    Public Shared LastUpdate As Collection
End Class
```

The event handler code looks like this:

```
Public Sub OnRowUpdated(ByVal sender As Object, ByVal e As
  SqlRowUpdatedEventArgs)

    ' Check if any records were affected.
    ' If no records were affected, the statement did not executed as expected.

    If e.RecordsAffected() < 1 Then
        ' We add information about failed operations to a table.
        Select Case e.StatementType
            Case StatementType.Delete
                DBErrors.LastDelete.Add(e.Row)
            Case StatementType.Insert
                DBErrors.LastInsert.Add(e.Row))
            Case StatementType.Update
                DBErrors.LastUpdate.Add(e.Row)
        End Select

        ' As the error has already been detected, we don't need the DataAdapter
        ' to cancel the entire operation and throw an exception, unless
        ' the failure may affect other operations.
        e.Status = UpdateStatus.SkipCurrentRow
    End If

End Sub
```

The nice thing about this approach is that it allows us the flexibility to decide how we want to deal with these errors when we execute the Update method, rather than hard-coding a specific procedure into our event handler.

To bring it all together, we need to attach the event handler before the update is performed. Our next example goes one step further, examining the error collections and displaying the results in three separate list controls in the current window.

```
' Connect the event handler.
AddHandler(adapter.RowUpdated, AddressOf OnRowUpdated)

' Perform the update.
Dim NumRowsAffected As Integer
NumRowsAffected = adapter.Update(dsNorthwind, "Orders")

' Display the errors.
Dim rowError As DataRow
For Each rowError In DB.LastDelete
    lstDelete.Items.Add(rowError("OrderID")
Next

For Each rowError In DB.LastInsert
    lstInsert.Items.Add(rowError("OrderID")
Next

For Each rowError In DB.LastUpdate
    lstUpdate.Items.Add(rowError("OrderID")
Next
```

The ConcurrencyErrors sample project shows a "live" example of this technique. It works by creating two DataSets, and simulating a multi-user concurrency problem by modifying them simultaneously in two different ways (see Figure 9-11). This artificial error is then dealt with in the RowUpdated event handler.

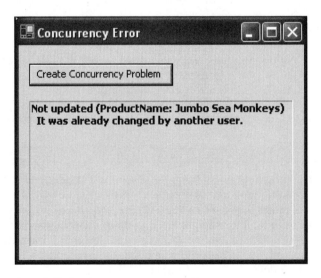

Figure 9-11: Simulating a concurrency problem

Updating Data in Stages

Concurrency issues aren't the only potential source of error when you update your data source. Another problem can occur if you use linked tables, particularly if you have deleted or added records. When you update the data source, your changes will probably not be committed in the same order in which they were performed in the DataSet. If you try to delete a Parent record while it is still being used by a Child record, an error will occur. This error will take place regardless of whether you have defined relations in your DataSet. The problem is that SQL Server will not let you remove a required Parent. Similarly, you won't be able to create a Child record that refers to a Parent that doesn't yet exist. In the case of the Northwind database, you could encounter these sorts of errors by trying to add a Product that references a non-existing Supplier or Category, or trying to delete a Supplier or Category record that is currently being used by a Product.

There is no simple way around these problems. If you are performing sophisticated data manipulation on a relational database using a DataSet, you will have to plan out the order that changes need to be implemented. However, you can then use some built-in ADO.NET features to perform these operations in separate stages.

Generally, a safe approach would proceed in this order:

1. Add any new records to all tables.
2. Modify existing records in all tables.
3. Delete records in all tables.

To perform these operations separately, you need a special update routine. This routine will create three separate DataSets, one for each operation. Then, you'll move all the new records into one DataSet, all the records marked for deletion into another, and all the modified records into a third. To perform this shuffling around, you can use the DataSet's GetChanges method:

```
' Create three DataSets, and fill them from dsNorthwind.
Dim dsNew As DataSet = dsNorthwind.GetChanges(DataRowState.Added)
Dim dsModify As DataSet = dsNorthwind.GetChanges(DataRowState.Deleted)
Dim dsDelete As DataSet = dsNorthwind.GetChanges(DataRowState.Modified)

' Update these DataSets separately, in an order guaranteed to avoid problems.
adapter.Update(dsNew, "Customers")
adapter.Update(dsNew, "Orders")
adapter.Update(dsModify, "Customers")
adapter.Update(dsModify, "Orders")
adapter.Update(dsDelete, "Customers")
adapter.Update(dsDelete, "Orders")
```

Creating a DataSet Object by Hand

Incidentally, you can add new tables and even create an entire DataSet by hand. There's really nothing tricky to this approach—it's just a matter of working with the right collections. First you have to create the DataSet, then at least one DataTable, and then add at least one DataColumn in each DataTable. After that, you can start adding DataRows.

```
' Create a DataSet and add a new table.
Dim dsPrefs As New DataSet
dsPrefs.Tables.Add("FileLocations")

' Define two columns for this table.
dsPrefs.Tables("FileLocation").Columns.Add("Folder", GetType("System.String"))
dsPrefs.Tables("FileLocation").Columns.Add("Documents", GetType("System.Int32"))

' Add some actual information into the table.
Dim newRow As DataRow = dsPrefs.Tables("FileLocation").NewRow()
newRow("Folder") = "f:\Pictures"
newRow("Documents") = 30
dsPrefs.Tables("FileLocation").Rows.Add(newRow)
```

Notice that this example uses standard .NET types instead of SQL-specific or OLE DB–specific types. That's because this table is not designed for storage in a separate data source. Instead, this miniature database stores preferences for a single user. The same information could be stored in the registry, but then it would be hard to move a user's settings from one computer to another. In XML format, these settings can be placed on an internal network, and easily made available to various workstations.

Storing a DataSet in XML

To store the custom data as an XML document, you use the built-in methods of the DataSet object:

```
' Save it as an XML file with the WriteXml method.
dsUserPrefs.WriteXml("f:\MyApp\UserData\" & UserName & ".xml")
dsUserPrefs = Nothing

' And retrieve it with the ReadXml method.
dsUserPrefs.ReadXml("f:\MyApp\UserData\" & UserName & ".xml")
```

The XML document for a DataSet is shown in Figure 9-12, as displayed in Internet Explorer.

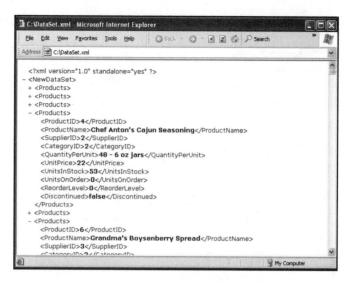

Figure 9-12: A partly collapsed view of a DataSet in XML

Of course, you will probably never need to look at it directly, because the ADO.NET DataSet object handles the XML format automatically. You can text XML reading and writing with the sample project XMLDataSet.

It really is quite easy to use ADO.NET XML in this way. However, keep in mind that this won't compensate for a true relational database. For example, there is no way to manage concurrent user updates to this file—every time it is saved, the existing version is completely wiped out.

If you need to exchange XML data with another program, or if the structure of your DataSet changes with time, you might find it a good idea to save the XML schema information for your DataSet. This document (shown in Figure 9-13) explicitly defines the format that your XML file uses, preventing any chance of confusion. Generally, it is a good safeguard, and easy to implement. All you need to remember is to read the schema into the DataSet before you load the actual data.

```
' Save it as an XML file with the WriteSchema and WriteXml methods.
dsUserPrefs.WriteSchema("f:\MyApp\UserData\" & UserName & ".xsd")
dsUserPrefs.WriteXml("f:\MyApp\UserData\" & UserName & ".xml")
dsUserPrefs = Nothing

' And retrieve it with the ReadSchema and ReadXml methods.
dsUserPrefs.ReadSchema("f:\MyApp\UserData\" & UserName & ".xsd")
dsUserPrefs.ReadXml("f:\MyApp\UserData\" & UserName & ".xml")
```

Figure 9-13: A DataSet schema

Data Binding

Data binding is a powerful way to display information from a DataSet by binding it directly to a user interface control. It saves you from needing to write simple but repetitive code to move through the database and manually copy content from a DataSet into a control. (Our ListView example used this kind of code, but in that case, we had no choice: The ListView control doesn't support data binding.)

Binding a control is usually just as easy as setting a DataSource property.

```
DataGrid1.DataSource = dsNorthwind.Tables("Products")
```

This produces a control with all the columns and data, as shown in Figure 9-14.

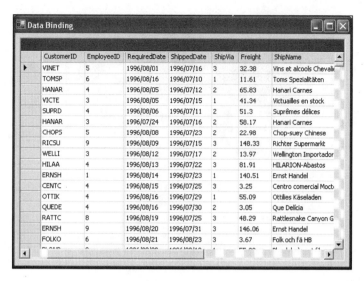

Figure 9-14: A data-bound grid

In its default mode, the DataGrid even allows you to edit a data value by typing in a field, and to add a new row by entering information at the bottom of the row (see Figure 9-15).

	CustomerID	EmployeeID	OrderDate	RequiredDate	ShippedDate	ShipVia	Freight	
	BONAP	4	1998/05/06	1998/06/03	(null)	2	38.28	
	RATTC	1	1998/05/06	1998/06/03	(null)	2	8.53	
▶	NEW	1	2002/01/01	(null)	(null)	(null)	(null)	
*								

Figure 9-15: Adding a new record

When you change or add information to the DataGrid, the linked DataSet is modified automatically, providing some very convenient basic data editing features.

An interesting feature of the DataGrid is that you can use it to display an entire DataSet made up of more than one table.

```
DataGrid1.DataSource = dsNorthwind
```

The DataGrid then adds web-like navigation links that allow the user to move from table to table (Figure 9-16).

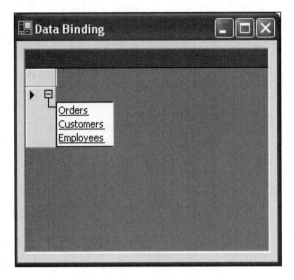

Figure 9-16: A DataGrid with multiple tables

Not all controls support data binding, and few can bind to multiple tables at once. Some, like ListBox controls, can only support binding to one field in a table. In this case, you have to specify two properties: the table data source, and the field that should be used for display purposes:

```
lstID.DataSource = dsNorthwind.Tables("Employees")
lstID.DisplayMember = "EmployeeID"
```

Just about every .NET control supports single-value data binding through the DataBindings property. This property provides a collection that allows you to connect a field in the data source with a property in the control. That means you could have a checkbox control, for example, that has several bound properties, including Text, Tag, and Checked.

The following code binds a generic text box:

```
' Bind the FirstName field to the Text property.
txtName.DataBindings.Add("Text", dsNorthwind.Tables("Employees"), "FirstName")
```

You can bind a DataSet to as many controls as you want, all at the same time (as shown in Figure 9-17). However, only one record can be selected at a time. When you select a value in the ListBox, the corresponding full record row is selected in the DataGrid, and the corresponding values are filled into other bound controls like the text box.

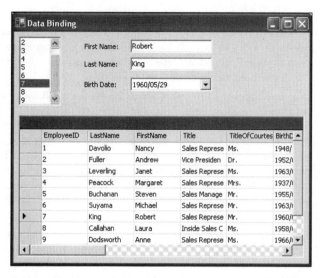

Figure 9-17: Multiple bound controls

This allows you to create windows that contain many different controls, each of which allows you to edit one property of the currently selected record. There's much more that you can do with data binding to configure advanced column display. Using such features as column mapping, you can rename or hide specific columns. ASP.NET even allows you to use templates to configure specifically how a column will look. Unfortunately, we won't get a chance to explore these topics in this chapter. Instead, refer to the MSDN help library.

What Comes Next?

This chapter has tackled a subject that can easily make up an entire book of its own. We've examined all the essentials, with a fairly in-depth look at the best way to organize database code, update information, and manage DataSets. You may want to take the time to work through this chapter again, as many of the insights contained here are the basis for "best practices" and other techniques that can ensure a robust, scalable database application.

There are still many more possibilities left for you to discover with ADO.NET. Here are some of them:

- If you don't already know the SQL language, now is the perfect time to learn. Although you don't need a sophisticated understanding to program with ADO.NET, the difference between a competent database programmer and an excellent one is often an understanding of the limitations and capabilities of SQL. Many excellent SQL resources are available online.

- It also helps to know a specific database product, such as SQL Server 2000, in order to create stored procedures and well-organized data tables. SQL Server provides its own "Books Online" help, which covers advanced tools such as stored procedures, views, column constraints, and triggers, all of which can help you become a database guru.

- Data binding was a dirty word in traditional Visual Basic programming, because it was slow, inefficient, and extremely inflexible. In .NET, data binding has been improved so much that it finally makes sense. Using data binding with the DataGrid, for example, you can automatically provide a sophisticated number of data editing features. The ASP.NET DataGrid is even more impressive, supporting such features as automatic paging (splitting results onto more than one HTML page) and sorting, and advanced selection and editing. It's poised to become the best choice for large-scale Internet applications.

- In the examples in this chapter, we updated our data source using a DataSet and the default UpdateCommand, InsertCommand, and DeleteCommand that ADO.NET generates automatically. You might be able to provide increased performance and some additional options if you learn how to customize these properties with your own commands. For example, you might create a command that can update a record even if it has been changed in the meantime, by making the selection criteria less strict. (You might look the record up just using the ID column, for example.) Or, you could configure the DataAdapter to use a specific stored procedure you have created. See the MSDN help library for more information.

10

THREADING

Threading is, from the logical point of view of your application, a way of running various different pieces of code at the same time. One of the main reasons that people flocked to the Windows operating system and abandoned the DOS world is because Windows provides multithreading, allowing computer users to perform several different tasks at once, albeit with varying degrees of success.

Threading is also one of the more complex subjects examined in this book. That's not because it's difficult to use threading in your programs—as you'll see, Visual Basic .NET makes it absurdly easy—but because it's difficult to use threading *correctly*. If you stick to the rules, and keep your use of threads simple, you will be fine. If, however, you embark on a wild flight of multithreaded programming, you will probably commit one of the cardinal sins of threading, and wind up in a great deal of trouble. Many excellent developers have argued that the programming community has repeatedly become overexcited about threading in the past, and has used it to create endless headaches.

This chapter will explain how to use threading and, more importantly, the guidelines you should follow to make sure you keep your programs free of such troubles as thread overload and synchronization glitches. Threading is a sophisticated subject with many nuances, so it's best to proceed carefully. However, a judicious use of carefully selected threads can make your applications appear faster, more responsive, and more sophisticated.

New in .NET

In Visual Basic 6, there was no easy way to create threads. Programmers who wanted to create true multithreaded applications had to use the Windows API (or create and register separate COM components).

Integrated Threads

The method of creating threads in Visual Basic .NET is conceptually and syntactically similar to using the Windows API, but it's far less error prone, and it's elegantly integrated into the language through the System.Threading namespace. The class library also contains a variety of tools to help implement synchronization and thread management.

Multithreaded Debugging

The Visual Studio .NET debugger now allows you to run and debug multi-threaded applications without forcing them to act as though they are single-threaded. You can even view a Threads window that shows all the currently active threads, and allows you to pause and resume them individually.

An Introduction to Threading

Regardless of how little you may know about threading, you've already seen threads work in the modern Windows operating system. For example, you have probably noticed how you can work with a Windows application while another application is busy or in the process of starting up, because both applications run in separate processes and use separate *threads*. You have probably also seen that even when the system appears to be frozen, you can almost always bring up the Task Manager by pressing CTRL-ALT-DELETE. This is because the Task Manager runs on a thread that has an extremely high priority. Even if other applications are currently executing or frozen, trapping their threads in endless CPU-wasting cycles, Windows can usually wrest control away from them for a more important thread.

If you've used Windows 3.1, you'll remember that this has not always been the case. Threads really came into being with 32-bit Windows and the Windows 95 operating system.

Threads "Under the Hood"

Now that you have a little history, it's time to examine how threads really work.

Threads are created by the handful in Windows applications. If you open a number of different applications on your computer, you will quickly have several different processes and potentially dozens of different threads executing simultaneously. (The Windows Task Manager can list all the active processes, which gives you an idea of the scope of the situation (Figure 10-1). It doesn't list the individual threads used by each process.)

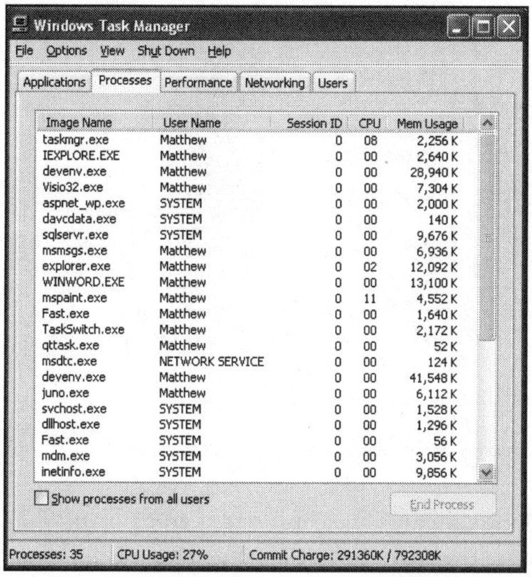

Figure 10-1: Active processes in Task Manager

In all honesty, there is no way any computer, no matter how technologically advanced, can run dozens of different operations at once. If your system has two CPUs, it is technically possible for two instructions to be processed at the same time, and Windows is likely to send the instructions for different threads to different CPUs. At some point, however, you will still end up with many more threads than CPUs.

Windows handles this situation by switching rapidly between different threads. Each thread "thinks" it is running independently, but in reality it only runs for a little while, pauses, and is then resumed a short while later for another brief interval of time. This process is all taken care of by the Windows operating system, and is called *preemptive multitasking*.

Comparing Single Threading and Multithreading

One consequence of thread switching is that multithreading usually doesn't result in a speed increase. Figure 10-2 shows why:

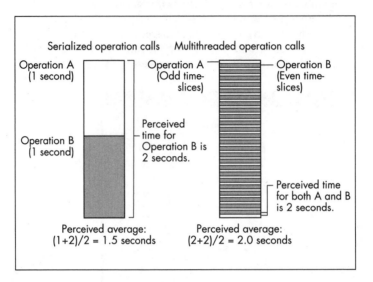

Figure 10-2: Multithreading can make operations appear slower

This illustration compares a *single-threaded* and a *multithreaded* application. Both are performing the same two tasks, but the multithreaded program is working by dividing the two operations into numerous little intervals, and rapidly switching from one to the other. This switching introduces a small overhead, but overall, both applications will finish at about the same time. However, if a user is waiting for both tasks to end, they will both seem to be running more slowly, because both tasks will finish at more or less the same time—at the end of two seconds. At least with the single-threaded approach, Operation A will be completed sooner, after about a second of processing time.

So why use multithreading? Well, if you were running a short task and a long task simultaneously, the picture might change. For example, if Operation B took only a few time-slices to complete, a user would perceive the multithreaded application as being much faster, because the user wouldn't have to wait for Operation A to finish before Operation B was started (technically, Operation B is not *blocked* by Operation A). In this case, Operation A would finish in a fraction of a second, rather than waiting the full one-second period (see Figure 10-3).

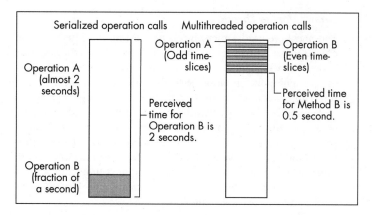

Figure 10-3: Multithreading lets short tasks finish first

This is the basic principle of multithreading. Rather than speeding up tasks, it allows the quickest tasks to finish first, makes an application appear more responsive, and adds only a slight performance degradation (due to all the required thread switching).

Multithreading works even better in applications where substantial waits are involved for certain tasks. For example, an application that spends a lot of time waiting for file I/O operations to complete could accomplish other useful tasks while waiting. In this case, multithreading can actually speed up the application, because it will not be forced to sit idle.

Scalability and Simplicity

There is one other reason to use threading: It makes program design much simpler for some common types of applications. For example, imagine you want to create an FTP server that can serve several simultaneous users. In a single-threaded application, you may find it very difficult to manage a variable number of different users without coding in some preset limit, or creating your own crude thread-switching type of logic.

With a multithreaded application, you can easily create a new thread to serve each client connection. Windows will take care of automatically assigning the processor time for each thread, and you can use the exact same code to serve a hundred users as you would to serve one. Each thread uses the same code, but handles a different client. As the workload increases, all you need to do is add threads.

Timers Versus Threads

You may have used Timer objects in previous versions of Visual Basic. Timer objects are still provided in Visual Basic .NET, and they are useful for a wide variety of tasks. Timers work differently than threads, however. From the program's standpoint, multiple threads work simultaneously. A timer works by interrupting your code for a single task. This task is then started, performed, and completed before control returns to the currently executing procedure in your application. This means that timers are not well suited for long-running processes that perform a variety of different tasks. To use a timer in this way, you would have to fake a thread by performing part of a task the first time a timer event occured, a different part the next time, and so on.

To observe this problem, you can create a project with two timers and two labels, and add the following code.

```
Private Sub Timer1_Elapsed(ByVal sender As System.Object, _
  ByVal e As System.EventArgs) Handles Timer1.Tick
    Dim i As Integer
    For i = 1 To 5000
        Label1.Text = i.ToString()
        Label1.Refresh()
    Next
    Timer1.Enabled = False
End Sub

Private Sub Timer2_Elapsed(ByVal sender As System.Object, _
  ByVal e As System.EventArgs) Handles Timer2.Tick
    Dim i As Integer
    For i = 1 To 5000
        Label2.Text = i.ToString()
        Label2.Refresh()
    Next
    Timer2.Enabled = False
End Sub
```

When you run this program, one timer will take control, and one label will display the numbers from 1 to 5000. The other label will start the same process, but only after the first timer stops. Even though both timers are scheduled to start at the same time, only one can work with the application window at a time. (In fact, if Visual Basic .NET allowed timer events to execute simultaneously, it would lead programmers to encounter all the same synchronization issues that can occur with threads, as you'll see later this chapter.)

Creating a Simple Multithreaded Application

The first type of threaded program we will create is an *unsynchronized* multithreaded application. An unsynchronized application uses multithreading to perform a distinct, independent task. This thread does not have to interact with the rest of your code.

A single procedure is the unit of code you assign to a thread. Before you can create a thread, you start by putting a series of instructions into a procedure. In this example, we will create a couple of simple subroutines in our form class that will perform the same work that our timer did in the preceding example.

TIP *Threads can belong to any object, or, to put it another way, there is no conceptual relationship between threads and objects. A single object can be executed on multiple threads, or a single thread can execute multiple objects.*

```
Imports System.Threading

Public Class ThreadTest
    Inherits System.Windows.Forms.Form
    ' Omitting all the designer code...

    Private Sub RefreshLabel1()
        Dim i As Integer
        For i = 1 To 5000
            Label1.Text = i.ToString()
            Label1.Refresh()
        Next
    End Sub

    Private Sub RefreshLabel2()
        Dim i As Integer
        For i = 1 To 5000
            Label2.Text = i.ToString()
            Label2.Refresh()
        Next
    End Sub

End Class
```

The threads will be created and started in the click event of a button.

```
Private Sub cmdStart_Click(ByVal sender As System.Object, _
  ByVal e As System.EventArgs) Handles cmdStart.Click

    Dim MyThread1 As New Thread(AddressOf RefreshLabel1)
    Dim MyThread2 As New Thread(AddressOf RefreshLabel2)
    MyThread1.Start()
    MyThread2.Start()

End Sub
```

All of our threading logic is contained in just a couple of lines. We declare a thread for the appropriate procedure, and then use the Start method to send it on its way.

TIP *The Start method does not instantaneously start the thread. Instead, it notifies the Windows operating system, which then schedules the thread to be started. If your system is currently bogged down with a heavy task load, there could be a noticeable delay.*

This simple application really demonstrates the power of threading. When you run it, both labels increment at the same time. You (the user) can't really tell that each label is incrementing about half as fast as it did in the timer example, and even if you could, you wouldn't really care. Best of all, the user interface remains responsive, which is not the case with timers. The user can click on other buttons and start other threads while the labels are being incremented, without noticing any slowdown.

One of the reasons multithreading works so well is that modern computers are so fast. Slowing down an application to execute several operations at once is a performance degradation that most applications can easily afford. Also, there's a little human psychology involved—in a user's experience, perception *is* reality.

Witnessing the Difference

To try out the comparison between threads and timers on your own, run the TimersAndThreads sample project (shown in Figure 10-4). It provides some basic timing that tracks the start and stop time for the timer and thread operations. Generally, you'll find the threading operations take the longest amount of time (adding a delay of up to 50 percent), due to the increased overhead generated by the continuous thread switching.

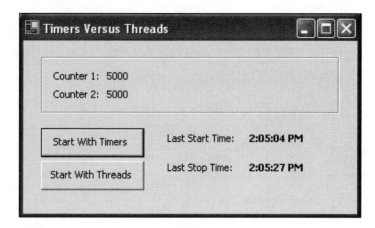

Figure 10-4: Comparing threads and timers

NOTE *You'll find you can cheat with the test by hiding the window, or dragging it around the screen while the labels are being updated. These tricks temporarily suspend the window refreshing, which is by far the slowest part of the operation. Thus, the test will complete much more quickly.*

Wrapping a Thread in a Class

There's one obvious drawback with the application the way it stands. At the beginning of this chapter, I pointed out how multithreading can help make programming more efficient because it allows you to manage multiple requests with the same piece of code, replicated on different threads. Our current example, however, relies on two nearly identical subroutines to perform almost the same task: updating the label!

You might think that this modification would work:

```
Private Sub RefreshLabel1(lbl As Label)
```

Here, the refreshing procedure is modified to accept a reference to a label control, allowing it to work for both threads. Unfortunately, the constructor for the thread object requires a subroutine with no parameters. A thread can store a reference to the appropriate procedure, but it can't retain any information, such as parameters that need to be used.

The best way to handle this limitation is to create a class that encapsulates the procedure that you want to use, and any data that it needs. In this case, the only data required is the label object to be modified. The following class works well:

```
Public Class LabelRefresher

    Private LabelToRefresh As Label

    Sub New(ByVal lbl As Label)
        LabelToRefresh = lbl
    End Sub

    Public Sub Refresh()
        Dim i As Integer
        For i = 1 To 5000
            LabelToRefresh.Text = i.ToString()
            LabelToRefresh.Refresh()
        Next
    End Sub

End Class
```

As a nice touch, every instance of this class receives the label it should process as an argument in its constructor.

You can now remove the other refresh subroutines. The code in the click event handler should be modified to look like this:

```
Private Sub cmdStart_Click(ByVal sender As System.Object, _
  ByVal e As System.EventArgs) Handles cmdStart.Click

    Dim LabelRefresher1 As New LabelRefresher(Label1)
    Dim LabelRefresher2 As New LabelRefresher(Label2)
    Dim MyThread1 As New Thread(AddressOf LabelRefresher1.Refresh)
    Dim MyThread2 As New Thread(AddressOf LabelRefresher2.Refresh)
    MyThread1.Start()
    MyThread2.Start()

End Sub
```

If you run the program now, you'll find that it works the same as before. Under the hood, however, the design is much more elegant and extensible.

One of the reasons this works so well is that each thread has its own data. There's no need to worry about exchanging or synchronizing information, as each thread is independent. If you stick to this type of multithreading, you'll have little to worry about.

In fact, unsynchronized multithreading can be very useful. For example, you might want to process a batch of data while prompting the user to enter more information. Or, you might want to create a graphical arcade game, where the background music is handled by a separate thread that queues the appropriate music files.

Basic Thread Management

The example we've used so far is simplified in a few respects. For one thing, it assumes that you can create a thread and then leave it to do its work without ever worrying about it again. In the real world, however, you often need to know when a thread is complete. You might even need to pause or kill a thread.

Thread Methods

You've already seen how to start a thread. You can also stop a thread by using the Abort method, which will finish it off by raising a ThreadAbortException.

```
MyThread.Abort()
```

Your thread class can handle this exception to try and end as gracefully as possible, and perform any necessary cleanup in the Finally block.

Using the Abort method is a relatively crude way to stop a thread. It's more typical for a long running thread to take the responsibility of polling a variable that indicates whether or not it should continue. This relies on the thread being well behaved, but it also allows processing to end at a natural stopping point, rather than be rudely interrupted. If you are wrapping your thread in a class, it makes sense for this to be a public class variable or property.

```
Private Sub ThreadFunction()
    Do ntil ThreadStop = true
        ' Do some work here.
    Loop
End Sub
```

You can also pause and resume a thread with the Suspend and Resume methods:

```
MyThread.Suspend()
' Do something in the foreground that requires a lot of CPU work.
MyThread.Resume()
```

The Suspend and Resume methods generally aren't used much in multithreaded applications, because they can easily lead to deadlocks (as you'll see later in this chapter). If the suspended thread has a lock on a resource another thread needs, the other thread will be forced to stop processing as well. A better approach is to use different thread priorities, which are introduced in the next section.

And you can pause a thread for a preset amount of time using the Sleep method:

```
MyThread.Sleep(TimeSpan.FromSeconds(1))
```

This is a common method to use in a CPU-intensive or disk-intensive process to provide a bit of time during which other threads can get their work done. The example here uses the System.TimeSpan class to send the thread to sleep for one second, which makes the resulting code very readable.

One other commonly used method is Join. It waits for a thread to complete. When you use the Join method, your code becomes *synchronous,* meaning that your application is locked until the thread is finished. The Join method can also be used with a TimeSpan that specifies the maximum amount of time that you will wait before continuing.

When you abort a thread with the Abort method, it does not necessarily terminate immediately, because the thread may be running exception-handling code. If you need to ensure that the thread is stopped before continuing, use the Join method on the thread after the Abort method.

And how do you know what a thread is up to? You can examine its Thread-State property and compare it against the possible enumerated values. Here's an example:

```
MyThread.Join(TimeSpan.FromSeconds(10))
If MyThread1.ThreadState = ThreadState.Stopped Then
    MessageBox.Show("We waited with Thread.Join, and the thread finished.")
ElseIf MyThread1.ThreadState = ThreadState.Running Then
    MessageBox.Show("We waited 10 seconds, but the Thread is still running.")
End If
```

A Thread Management Example

The online samples provide a simple program that lets you start and stop a thread. The thread has the unglamorous task of updating a label continuously in a loop, ensuring that the label always has the current time of day (see Figure 10-5). This is quite impractical, but it shows how a background thread could be put to an important, continuous task like playing music or generating a background animation.

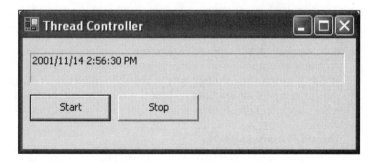

Figure 10-5: A thread controller

The interface is simple, and consists of a Start and Stop button. The Thread object is stored in a form-level variable called DateThread. Interestingly, if you click Start to assign a new thread to the DateThread variable, the current thread will continue working; you just won't have any way to access it! Clearly, this could lead to a problem in a real program if you didn't defend against it.

Thread Priorities

All threads are created equal, but they don't have to stay that way. *Priorities* allow you to make sure that some threads are always executed. Threads with low priorities, on the other hand, may not do much work if the system is heavily bogged down with other tasks.

You can set a thread's priority to various values, including AboveNormal, BelowNormal, Highest, Lowest, and Normal, which is the default. These priorities are only important in the way that they compare with other currently executing threads in your program or other programs. For example, if all your threads share the same priority, it doesn't make much difference whether that priority is Normal or Highest (assuming, for the moment, that there aren't any other programs or processes competing for the CPU's attention).

Setting a priority is a straightforward process:

```
MyThread1.Priority = ThreadPriority.Lowest
```

A thread with a high priority may need to use the Sleep method to allow other threads a chance to get their work done. Fine-tuning this sharing of the CPU is an art that requires significant trial-and-error experimentation.

Background Threads

You can also set the IsBackground property on a thread to make it into a *background* thread. A background thread only lasts as long as other *foreground* threads are running. If you abort all foreground threads and end your application, all background threads will also stop running automatically.

When Is Too Much Not Enough?

When using threads, it's a good idea to test them on the minimum computer your application will support. When you create too many threads, particularly on a slower computer, some threads may not receive enough CPU time to be able to perform their work properly. The sorry state that results when too many threads compete for too little resources is called *thread starvation*, and it can make an application perform poorly, or render some functions inoperative.

Thread Priority Example

The chapter sample code provides a thread priority tester that allows you to satisfy your urges and create as many simultaneous threads as you want (see Figure 10-6). These threads "compete" to increment their individual counter variables. The ones that receive the most CPU time will increment their counters the fastest.

A separate thread class, ThreadCounter, provides this counter functionality and incorporates a boolean "stop signal" variable named ThreadStop:

```
Public Class ThreadCounter

    Public LoopCount As Integer
    Public MaxValue As Integer
    Public Priority As String
    Public ThreadStop As Boolean

    Public Sub New(ByVal MaxValue As Integer, ByVal Priority As String)
        Me.MaxValue = MaxValue
        Me.Priority = Priority
    End Sub

    Public Sub Refresh()
        ' Increment the counter.
        For LoopCount = 0 To MaxValue - 1
            ' Check for the signal to stop abruptly.
            If ThreadStop = True Then Exit For
        Next
    End Sub

End Class
```

The interesting part is that the program uses a collection called ActiveCounters to store references to all the objects that are running on different threads (and another collection called ActiveThreads to store references to the actual Thread objects). Periodically, a timer fires, and a routine in the form code loops through the ActiveCounters collection and prints out the status of every thread in a label.

```
Private Sub tmrThreadMonitor_Tick(ByVal sender As System.Object, _
  ByVal e As System.EventArgs) Handles tmrThreadMonitor.Tick

    lblThreads.Text = ""
    Dim Counter As ThreadCounter
    Dim i As Integer

    For Each Counter In ActiveCounters
        i += 1
        lblThreads.Text &= "#" & i.ToString() & " at: "
        lblThreads.Text &= Counter.LoopCount.ToString() & " ("
        lblThreads.Text &= Counter.Priority & ")"
        lblThreads.Text &= vbNewLine
    Next

End Sub
```

The ThreadPriorities program allows you to set the priority of each thread when
you create it. This allows you to verify that a high-priority thread will increment
its counter far faster than a low-priority one. You'll also notice that when you create a thread with a high priority, your application (and your computer) will
become noticeably less responsive until the thread is finished incrementing its
counter.

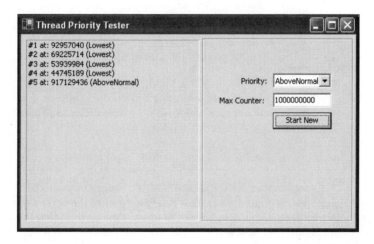

Figure 10-6: Testing threads

When you end the program, it performs some thoughtful cleanup by iterating
through the ActiveThreads collection and stopping each thread. Rather than use
the Thread.Abort method, this program does things the nice way, setting the
ThreadStop variable for each ThreadCounter object, and then waiting on each
thread with the Join method to verify that it has stopped. This is actually much
faster than aborting each thread.

```
Private Sub ThreadPriorityTester_Closing(ByVal sender As Object, _
  ByVal e As System.ComponentModel.CancelEventArgs) Handles MyBase.Closing

    ' Signal each thread to stop.
    Dim Counter As ThreadCounter
    For Each Counter In ActiveCounters
        Counter.ThreadStop = True
    Next

    ' Wait to verify that each thread has stopped.
    Dim CounterThread As Thread
    For Each CounterThread In ActiveThreads
        CounterThread.Join()
    Next

End Sub
```

Thread Debugging

One very useful technique when debugging a multithreaded project is to assign each thread a name. This allows you to distinguish one thread from another, and verify what thread is currently executing. It's not unusual when debugging a tricky problem to discover that the thread you thought was at work actually isn't responsible.

To name a thread with a descriptive string, you simply use the Thread.Name property:

```
CounterThread.Name = "Counter 1"
```

To check what thread is running a given code procedure at a specific time, you can use code like this, which uses the shared CurrentThread method of the Thread class:

```
MessageBox.Show(Thread.CurrentThread.Name)
```

Visual Studio .NET also provides some help with a special Threads debugging window (Figure 10-7). This window shows all the currently executing threads in your program, and indicates the thread that currently has the processor's attention with a yellow arrow. The Location column even tells you what code the thread is running.

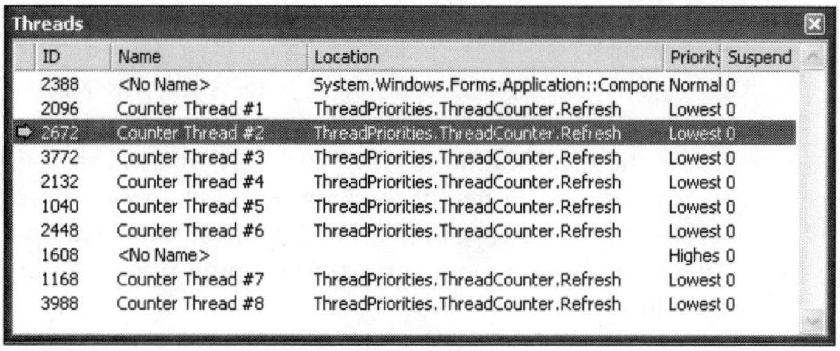

Figure 10-7: Controlling threads at run time

To access the Threads window, you need to pause your program's execution. You can then use some advanced features for controlling threads. For example, you can set the active thread by right-clicking on a Thread and selecting Switch to Thread. You can also use the Freeze command to instruct the operating system to ignore a thread, and not give it any processing time (until you select the corresponding Thaw command to restore it to life). This fine-grained control is ideal for isolating problematic threads in a misbehaving application.

Retrieving Information from a Thread

One of the reasons our examples have worked so well is that the information the threads return is sent directly to the appropriate label control in the window. There is no need for your program to determine whether a thread is finished, or to try to retrieve the result of its work. Most programs won't work this way. It is far more common (and far better program design) for an application to use a thread to perform a series of calculations, retrieve the results once they are ready, and then format and display them in the user interface, if necessary.

There are various ways to do this. Checking the thread's state is not a good one, as you will need to perform periodic checks, and your code will become more complicated because you will have to keep careful track of which thread is responsible for which task. Ideally, in a sophisticated application, threads can be reused for a number of different tasks, and your program won't know which thread is performing a specific piece of work at any given time.

Using Callbacks

A common way of retrieving information from a thread is to use a callback when the thread is complete. This works best in an application where threads are used to accomplish a single large, time-consuming task, such as processing information from a DataSet to provide report data.

In order to use callbacks, our example uses *delegates*. Events could also be used, provided the AddHandler function is also used to dynamically connect thread events to our event handler at run time.

The delegate definition looks like this:

```
Public Delegate Sub CallBackRoutine(ByVal ModifiedLabel As Label)
```

This is the specification for the procedure that will receive the notification that the thread has finished its work. In this case, we're still working with the label program, so there isn't really any important information to return. To illustrate this point, however, our threads will submit references to the labels that they have just finished updating.

Now you need to add the subroutine that will receive the notification. It has to match the delegate that we are using, and should be included in the class for your Windows form. The following subroutine works because it has the same signature (arguments and return type) as our delegate definition:

```
Public Sub ThreadFinished(ByVal ModifiedLabel As Label)
    MessageBox.Show("Finished " & ModifiedLabel.Name)
End Sub
```

Every time a thread is completed, it will call this procedure, and a message box will display a message that identifies which label has just been updated.

The LabelRefresher class has to change a little too:

```
Public Class LabelRefresher

    Private LabelToRefresh As Label
    Private CallBack As CallBackRoutine

    Public Sub New(ByVal lbl As Label, ByVal MyRoutine As CallBackRoutine)
        LabelToRefresh = lbl
        CallBack = MyRoutine
    End Sub

    Public Sub Refresh()
        Dim i As Integer
        For i = 1 To 1000
            LabelToRefresh.Text = i.ToString()
            LabelToRefresh.Refresh()
        Next
        CallBack(LabelToRefresh)
    End Sub

End Class
```

The class now has a CallBack variable to store a reference to the callback routine. This allows our code to "wire up" the ThreadFinished subroutine to the thread objects we create. The process has been made even easier with the modification of the constructor, which now requires that the appropriate event-handling routine be submitted as an argument.

The Refresh method works the same way as it did before, except that it now ends by calling the callback procedure stored in the CallBack variable. Everything is nicely interconnected.

In the button's click event, the following logic comes into play:

```
Private Sub cmdStart_Click(ByVal sender As System.Object, _
  ByVal e As System.EventArgs) Handles cmdStart.Click
    Dim LabelRefresher1 As New LabelRefresher(Label1, AddressOf ThreadFinished)
    Dim LabelRefresher2 As New LabelRefresher(Label2, AddressOf ThreadFinished)
    Dim MyThread1 As New Thread(AddressOf LabelRefresher1.Refresh)
    Dim MyThread2 As New Thread(AddressOf LabelRefresher2.Refresh)
    MyThread1.Start()
    MyThread2.Start()
End Sub
```

The only change from before is that a reference to the ThreadFinished subroutine is supplied to the constructor for the LabelRefresher class. The AddressOf keyword is required so that Visual Basic will know not to try to run the procedure immediately or try to return a value. Both LabelRefresher instances use the same callback routine, which is a safe thing to do. The subroutine will actually be executed inside the thread that calls it, so no conflicts will occur.

The end result? Our program will run as usual, and as soon as the threads have been completed, two message boxes will spring into view at once (Figure 10-8):

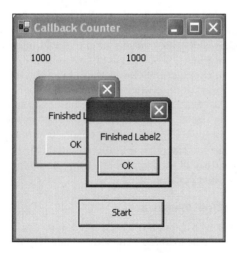

Figure 10-8: Receiving thread callbacks

This callback system can be the foundation for much more complex operations. Best of all, once the infrastructure is set up, your application doesn't need to worry about synchronization or about keeping track of executing threads.

Synchronizing

The mistake that most novice programmers make when they start creating multi-threaded applications is simple: They assume that everything they want to do is thread-safe. In other words, they assume that any action that can be performed by a synchronous piece of code can be moved into a thread. This is a dangerous mistake that ignores the effects of concurrency.

Potential Thread Problems

Remember, threads work almost simultaneously as Windows switches from one thread to another. This means that the interaction between multiple threads can vary. Sometimes Thread A might perform a given action before Thread B, and other times Thread B might take the lead. You can configure the priorities of individual threads, as you've seen, but you can never be absolutely sure when a thread will act, or what the order will be for operations on different threads.

What's more, if you have more than one thread dealing with the same class or variable, then eventually they will both try to access or update it at once. Consider a situation where you have a global counter used by multiple threads for keeping track of the number of times an operation takes place. Sooner or later, Thread A will try to increment the value from, say, 10 to 11 at the same time that Thread B is trying to increment the value from 10 to 11. The result? The count will be set to 11, even though the value should really be 12. The more threads there are (and the greater the delay between reading and updating the counter variable), the worse the problem will become.

Concurrency and synchronization problems are particularly tricky because they often don't appear when an application is being tested, but lead to bugs later in random situations, after the application has been deployed. If your application does not give adequate consideration to synchronization issues, there is no way to know when a problem could appear. Many programmers don't realize the dependencies of the objects they are using. Trying to use an object in two different ways at once when that object has not been designed to be thread-safe is likely to cause a data error in the best case, and a runtime error in the worst. Most classes in the CLR are not thread-safe, because addition of the required synchronization code would dramatically slow down their performance. One example of a class that isn't thread-safe is the base System.Windows.Forms.Form class that all windows inherit from. As the next section will explain, this has significant consequences.

Multithreading and User Interface

Though you may not realize it, I've already engaged in some extremely questionable behavior in the preceding examples. Good threading practice mandates that you should never modify the user interface of a form from a thread other than the one that created it. Unfortunately, the current LabelRefresher class does exactly that.

In order to solve this problem, and prevent strange bugs from creeping into your Windows applications, you must perform the label modification on the correct thread. An easy way to do so is to use the MethodInvoker delegate contained in the System.Windows.Forms namespace. The MethodInvoker delegate points to a subroutine that contains code for manipulating a control. You execute this code by passing the delegate to the Invoke method provided by the control you want to modify. .NET will then ensure that the code executes on the same thread that created the control. The Control.Invoke method is really the key—it has the built-in smarts to execute the submitted delegate on the right thread.

Here is a revised LabelRefresher class that takes this into consideration, and performs its label updates in a thread-safe manner (changed lines are highlighted in bold):

```vb
Public Class LabelRefresher

    Private LabelToRefresh As Label
    Private i As Integer
    Private CallBack As CallBackFunction

    Public Sub New(ByVal lbl As Label, ByVal MyFunction As CallBackFunction)
        LabelToRefresh = lbl
        CallBack = MyFunction
    End Sub

    Public Sub Refresh()
        For i = 1 To 1000
            ' Create the delegate.
            Dim Invoker As New MethodInvoker(AddressOf UpdateLabel)

            ' Ensure that it executes on the thread that owns LabelToRefresh.
            LabelToRefresh.Invoke(Invoker)
        Next
        CallBack(LabelToRefresh)
    End Sub

    Public Sub UpdateLabel()
        ' To verify this code is in the right place, name all your threads,
        ' and uncomment the following line:
        ' MessageBox.Show(Thread.CurrentThread.Name)
        LabelToRefresh.Text = i.ToString()
        LabelToRefresh.Refresh()
    End Sub

End Class
```

This tricky issue also affects the thread's callback routine. If this routine (called ThreadFinished in our example) updated any of the user interface controls, it would also need to use the MethodInvoker technique. Even though the ThreadFinished code is contained in the form class, it will still execute on the thread that calls it, not the main application thread that owns the user interface! (To verify this sticky point, assign a name to all your threads, and use the MessageBox.Show command to display the name of the current thread in the ThreadFinished procedure.) Using an event instead of a callback does not solve this problem—in fact, the exact same behavior persists.

Basic Synchronization

The best approach to avoid data synchronization problems is often to refrain from modifying variables that are accessible to multiple threads. If this isn't possible, the next best thing is to use basic synchronization. The idea behind synchronization, as mentioned earlier, is to lock a resource before you access it. Any other thread that tries to access the resource will be forced to wait. This process prevents collisions, but it also slows down performance.

In Visual Basic .NET, the handy SyncLock statement provides automatic synchronization support for you. The details are actually fairly involved, but once again, Visual Basic .NET does an excellent job of hiding the technical infrastructure from you. All you need to do is place code that uses shared objects inside a SyncLock/End SyncLock block. The first line of this block identifies the item that is being synchronized. This item must be a reference type, such as an object or an array; it can't be a simple data type.

When you use the SyncLock statement, Visual Basic .NET waits until it has exclusive access to the object you've specified. It then performs all the commands in the SyncLock block. While these commands are being executed, any other thread that tries to access the synchronized object will be temporarily paused. When the final End SyncLock statement is reached, life returns to normal. Again, however, performance can suffer, because threads trying to access a synchronized object are blocked.

A Sample Synchronization Problem

To demonstrate how synchronization works, we will use a variant of a global counter type of program. There are many different ways to observe the effects of thread synchronization problems, but this one is based on the earlier examples in this chapter.

The first basic ingredient is a GlobalCounter class:

```
Public Class GlobalCounter
    Public Counter As Integer
End Class
```

An instance of this class is provided as a public variable in the form class:

```
Public MyGlobalCounter As New GlobalCounter()
```

There is also a class that wraps our threaded operations, as before:

```
Public Class IncrementThread

    Private Counter As GlobalCounter
    Private LocalCounter As Integer
    Private ThreadLabel, GlobalLabel As Label

    Public Sub New(ByVal Counter As GlobalCounter, ByVal ThreadLabel As Label, _
      ByVal GlobalLabel As Label)
        Me.Counter = Counter
        Me.ThreadLabel = ThreadLabel
        Me.GlobalLabel = GlobalLabel
    End Sub

    Public Sub Increment()
        Dim i As Integer
        Dim GlobalCounter As Integer

        For i = 1 To 1000
            LocalCounter = LocalCounter + 1
            GlobalCounter = Counter.Counter
            Thread.Sleep(TimeSpan.FromTicks(1))
            Counter.Counter = GlobalCounter + 1
        Next i

        ' Assume that ThreadLabel and GlobalLabel are on the same window.
        Dim Invoker As New MethodInvoker(AddressOf UpdateLabel)
        ThreadLabel.Invoke(Invoker)
    End Sub

    Private Sub UpdateLabel()
        ThreadLabel.Text = LocalCounter.ToString()
        GlobalLabel.Text = Counter.Counter.ToString()
    End Sub

End Class
```

Our threading class is clearly designed to hold a reference to a Global-Counter object. It also has its own LocalCounter variable. When it has finished its operation (the Increment method), it uses the MethodInvoker to update the label with its local and global counters. Thus, the value of the global counter will be an interim value after the first thread finishes. When the second thread finishes, it will be updated with the final total.

Another interesting detail is the way that the global counter is incremented. Instead of writing it all in one line, our example uses two lines, and it pauses the thread for one tick (a small interval of time equal to 100 nanoseconds) in between the time that the value is read and the time that the counter is updated. This pause is meant to simulate thread latency, even though the code only uses two threads. The same effect can be illustrated without a forced pause, provided that several threads are competing for the CPU. (Remember, one of the most devious aspects of synchronization problems is that they often don't come out of the woodwork when you are testing under simple conditions.)

As before, the threads are created and started in a click event handler for a button on the form. The following code is used:

```
Private Sub cmdStart_Click(ByVal sender As System.Object, _
 ByVal e As System.EventArgs) Handles cmdStart.Click
    MyGlobalCounter.Counter = 0
    Dim Increment1 As New IncrementThread(MyGlobalCounter, lblThread1, lblGlobal)
    Dim Increment2 As New IncrementThread(MyGlobalCounter, lblThread2, lblGlobal)
    Dim MyThread1 As New Thread(AddressOf Increment1.Increment)
    Dim MyThread2 As New Thread(AddressOf Increment2.Increment)
    MyThread1.Start()
    MyThread2.Start()
End Sub
```

There isn't much difference here.

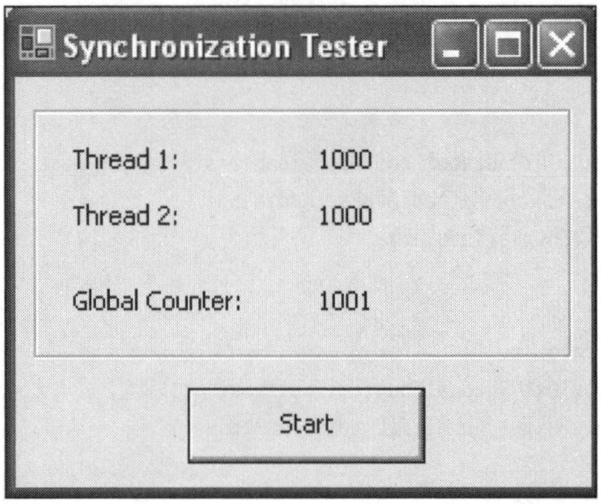

Figure 10-9: A flawed global counter

The result is shown in Figure 10-9. Each thread has kept track of its own private local counter information, so that much is accurate. However, the global counter is completely wrong. It should be 2000, to represent the fact that each thread has incremented it 1000 times. Instead, when the thread slept for a few nanoseconds, the other thread jumped into action, read the counter information, and prepared to increment the counter as well. It all unfolded like this (assuming the counter was at 12):

1. MyThread1 reads the value 12.
2. MyThread2 reads the value 12.
3. MyThread1 sets the value to 13.
4. MyThread2 sets the value to 13—which it already is.

Using SyncLock to Fix Our Problem

In this case, the fix is quite easy. We can deliberately make GlobalCounter a class, which means that we can use SyncLock to gain exclusive access to it. If GlobalCounter had been a variable, there would be no obvious solution.

However, we solve our current problem by rewriting the Increment method of the IncrementThread class:

```
Public Sub Increment()
    Dim i As Integer
    Dim GlobalCounter As Integer
    For i = 1 To 1000
        LocalCounter = LocalCounter + 1
        SyncLock objCounter
            GlobalCounter = objCounter.Counter
            Thread.Sleep(TimeSpan.FromTicks(1))
            Counter.Counter = GlobalCounter + 1
        End SyncLock
    Next i

    Dim Invoker As New MethodInvoker(AddressOf UpdateLabel)
    ThreadLabel.Invoke(Invoker)
End Sub
```

Now the result, as shown in Figure 10-10, will be correct:

Figure 10-10: A successful global counter

If you were timing the application, however, you might notice that it has slowed down. All of the automatic pausing and resuming of threads can create some overhead. But when you consider the frustrating problems that SyncLock can help you avoid, you'll be eager to put it to work in your applications.

What Comes Next?

This chapter has endeavored to give you a solid understanding of the fundamentals of threading, and a knowledge of the issues involved. Mastering all the aspects of threading could almost be a life's work, and many books and articles have been written on the subject.

If you're in search of more threading information, the best place to start is the online MSDN library. Both the help files and the MSDN website provide white papers describing the technical details of threading, along with code examples that show it in action in live applications. One interesting advanced example is Donkey .NET, a driving simulation game that can be found at http://msdn.microsoft.com/vbasic/donkey.asp.

11

SETUP AND DEPLOYMENT

If you've read through the last few chapters, you've gained the knowledge you'll need to make a professional, useful application in Visual Basic .NET. In fact, you may already have created one or more programs that you want to share with others, deploy internally, or even market to the world. But how does a .NET application make the transition from your workstation to a client's computer?

To answer that question, you need to have an understanding of assemblies, the .NET way of packaging files. You also need to understand file dependencies, or "what does my program need to be able to run?" This chapter starts by explaining these concepts, and leading you a little further into the concepts of .NET, including zero-impact installations and side-by-side execution.

Once you've learned which files you need, you can copy and set up your program on another computer. If the program is being used only internally (for example, from a company server), or if your only goal is to transfer the program to another development computer, you won't need to know much more. In some cases, you can even use a rudimentary batch file or script to copy all the required files. However, if you're developing a program to multiple users or selling it as a package, you probably need a more convenient, automated solution. Using Visual Studio .NET, you can create a full-featured setup program that selectively copies files, allows the user to configure options, and creates appropriate shortcuts and registry settings. This chapter describes these features, and shows how you can use them to create professional, off-the-shelf products.

New in .NET

Could the end of versioning headaches, deployment struggles, and multiple-application conflicts finally have arrived? In this chapter you'll see the changes in Microsoft's new deployment philosophy. Some of these changes include:

Assemblies

If you are an experienced developer, you've seen how COM can simplify code reuse by allowing programmers to create and share distinct components. You've probably also seen how much trouble can be caused when different shared components conflict, and installing one program breaks another. Assemblies are Microsoft's replacement to components and traditional application files, and they include built-in metadata designed to help you avoid DLL Hell.

No More Registration

The advent of assemblies means that you no longer have to rely on the registry to maintain important information about your component. Instead, it's all stored directly in your program files, making it easy to copy applications and components from computer to computer, and share components in your programs without worrying about versioning details.

Visual Studio .NET Setup Projects

Visual Basic 6 provided a utility called the Package and Deployment Wizard to help you create setup programs for your applications. Unfortunately, there was little room for customized deployment or advanced configuration options. Visual Basic .NET introduces a much more powerful setup project that can be added directly to your solution files, and configured extensively. You may never need to resort to a third-party installation tool again.

Introducing Assemblies

Traditionally, application components were deployed as .exe or .dll files. To run an application, the user would look for an .exe file. This program might make use of other components, such as .dll files with libraries of old-fashioned C routines. Or, the application might use COM components, which could be located in various places on the computer (but were usually found in the Windows system directory) and were stored in their own .exe or .dll files. (The only exception is ActiveX controls, which used a special file type with the extension .ocx.)

In the .NET world, the same .dll and .exe file extensions that are used for traditional programs and COM components are reused for .NET assemblies. But though these file types have similar names for backward compatibility, they don't work the same way. They also have a new name: assemblies.

An *assembly* is often referred to as a "logical DLL." Quite simply, an assembly is some grouping of program functionality, which usually corresponds to a single component or application. For the programs you've been creating so far, all the functions and features have been coded inside a single assembly, which becomes an .exe file when you compile it. If, however, you wanted to make separately distributable components, you would divide your program into several distinct units of functionality, which would then become individual assemblies.

The reason an assembly is called a "logical DLL" instead of a "physical DLL" is that you can, technically speaking, create an assembly that's made of more than one separate file. Typically, you won't need to create a multi-file assembly, and there's no easy way to do it in Visual Basic .NET—it's really a convenience for advanced deployment. (For example, it could speed up an Internet installation, because an end user might not need to download all the files in an assembly if some files correspond to little-used features, such as international character set support.)

Assemblies Versus Components That Use COM

At this point, you are probably wondering why we need assemblies when we already have a system for creating components. The reason is that .NET is once again making a clean break with COM. By introducing assemblies, it is widely believed that all the common versioning headaches and DLL problems that developers have been suffering through for years will finally end. It's not just hot air—assemblies have a few unique features that make them completely unlike anything Windows programmers have used before.

Assemblies Are Self-Describing

The most revolutionary aspect of assemblies is the fact that they are self-describing. Every assembly you create contains one or more program files and a *manifest*. The manifest includes additional information called *metadata*. (Metadata is "data about data." Essentially, your program code is the data, and the metadata is the information about your program, such as its name, version, publicly available types, and dependencies.) The manifest replaces the type library and registry information used with COM components. That brings us to our next point . . .

Assemblies Don't Need the Registry

All the information needed to use a component or run an application is contained in the assembly's manifest, which is usually built into the corresponding .dll or .exe file. It is impossible to create a program in .NET without automatically generating a manifest and a proper assembly. This means that you can copy your applications and components to any other computer using .NET, and they will work automatically. There's no need to fiddle around with regsvr32 or other awkward tools to add information to the registry.

In Visual Basic 6, you can transfer a simple application from computer to computer easily enough (provided you include MSVBVM60.dll, the Visual Basic runtime). But as soon as your application uses other COM components or ActiveX controls, you develop several new problems. In .NET, you can simply identify and copy the needed files—no registration is required. Of course, if you forget a dependent file, you'll still run into trouble.

Assemblies Are Rigorous Version Trackers

The manifest also records information about the current versions of all the included files. Whenever you compile a program in Visual Basic .NET, this version information is written into the manifest automatically, meaning that there's no possibility for it to become out-of-date, or not be synchronized with the underlying application code. The manifest also contains a short block of cryptographic hash code based on all the files in the assembly. Whenever you run an assembly, the Common Language Runtime verifies that the version information and hash code are still valid. If a change is detected that isn't reflected in the manifest (which is impossible, unless the file is corrupted or it has been modified with another low-level tool), it won't let you run the application.

This is a stark difference from the way that COM components and ActiveX controls work. With COM components, you have to trust that the information in the registry and any associated type library is up-to-date—and this trust is rarely rewarded.

Assemblies Can Be Privately Shared

A Visual Basic 6 application can use two broadly different types of components: those that have been developed in-house to share company-specific functionality, and those that have been developed (and may even be sold) by third-party component developers or by Microsoft. The latter type of components requires some kind of central repository. In traditional COM programming, that's the WINDOWS\System or WINNT\System32 directory, where all the files are piled in a somewhat disorganized mess. In .NET development, the GAC (Global Assembly Cache) serves much the same purpose, and we'll explore it later in this chapter.

In the other scenario—company-specific code modules—components don't need to be shared across the computer. They may only be used by a single set of applications, or a few applications created by the same developers. In COM development, there was no easy way to implement this approach. Private components still had to be tossed into the system directory with everything else, which meant extra registration steps, unnecessary information added to the registry (such as a GUID, or Global Unique Identifier), and a clutter of components that couldn't be reused by other programs.

If you've ever tried to explore the full list of COM components and add them to your Visual Basic projects, you've surely discovered that many of the items that appear on the list aren't thoughtful examples of shared procedures and resources provided by other application developers. Instead, they are designed for use with a specific application that you have installed on your computer, and are essentially useless outside of that program. They may even have licensing restrictions that prevent you from creating an instance of a component in your applications.

In .NET, private assemblies are private. You store these components in your application directory, or in an application subdirectory.

Assemblies Can Be Run Side by Side

How many times have you installed a new application only to discover that it overwrote a file required for another application with a newer version that broke backward compatibility? No matter how hard developers struggle, the ideal of backward compatibility will never be universally followed, and any system that uses a single component and a single version for dozens of different applications will run into trouble (or DLL Hell, as it is affectionately known).

.NET sidesteps this problem by adding a landmark new feature called *side-by-side execution*. Under this system, you can install multiple versions of a single component. When you run an application, .NET uses the version of the component that it was developed with. If you run another program at the same time that uses the same component, the Common Language Runtime will load the appropriate version for that program as well. No unexpected behavior or incompatibilities will appear, because every application uses the set of components that it was designed for.

NOTE *Technically, developers have had rudimentary ability to use side-by-side execution with COM components since Windows 98. However, it required extra effort to set up, and was rarely used.*

Why Haven't We Seen These Features Before?

It wasn't just shortsightedness that lead Microsoft to create the COM we know, love, and hate today, with its obvious versioning nightmares. Some of the features that assemblies use just weren't practical in the past. For example, side-by-side execution can multiply the amount of memory required when several applications are running, because the same component can't be reused. Today, it's fairly easy to buy a few hundred megabytes more of RAM to prevent this problem, but in the past, an operating system designed without code sharing in mind would quickly grind to a standstill. Similarly, allowing multiple versions to be tracked and stored separately on a computer just wasn't efficient with the limited disk space of the past. Today, with physical space so absurdly cheap, the effect is much less severe.

In other words, COM and the entire Windows platform were created with the vision of a single, centralized component repository. The emphasis was on saving space and memory to provide better performance, rather than on the relative luxury of making applications (and the life of a developer) easier, more convenient, and more consistently reliable. Today, more and more mission-critical applications are being designed in the Windows environment, which has shifted from a home user's toy to a professional business platform. The current emphasis is on reliability and on structured, fail-safe designs, even if a few megabytes have to be wasted in the process.

Looking at Your Program as an Assembly

As mentioned earlier, all the applications you've created to this point are genuine .NET assemblies. If they weren't, the Common Language Runtime would refuse to execute them. To see what your program looks like as an assembly, you can use an interesting program called ILDasm.exe (IL Disassembler). This file can be found in a directory like C:\Program Files\Microsoft Visual Studio.NET\FrameworkSDK\ Bin, depending on where you have installed the .NET framework.

Once you run ILDasm, you can choose to open any .NET assembly (.exe or .dll file). In the following example, you'll see the ObjectTester utility from Chapter 5.

ILDasm uses a tree to show you information about your program. All the types that are defined in your projects are automatically defined in metadata in your program's assembly. This makes it easy to browse through a specific definition of our Person object, as shown in Figure 11-1.

Figure 11-1: Dissecting the Person object

You can double-click a method or property, and see the list of related .NET instructions that was created based on your program code, as shown in Figure 11-2.

```
/ Person::GetIntroduction : string()

.method public instance string  GetIntroduction() cil managed
{
  // Code size      94 (0x5e)
  .maxstack  3
  .locals init ([0] string GetIntroduction,
           [1] string Intro,
           [2] valuetype [mscorlib]System.DateTime _Vb_t_date_0,
           [3] string[] _Vb_t_array_0)
  IL_0000:  nop
  IL_0001:  ldc.i4.5
  IL_0002:  newarr     [mscorlib]System.String
  IL_0007:  stloc.3
  IL_0008:  ldloc.3
  IL_0009:  ldc.i4.0
  IL_000a:  ldstr      "My name is "
  IL_000f:  stelem.ref
  IL_0010:  nop
  IL_0011:  ldloc.3
  IL_0012:  ldc.i4.1
  IL_0013:  ldarg.0
  IL_0014:  callvirt   instance string ObjectTester.Person::get_FirstName(
  IL_0019:  stelem.ref
  IL_001a:  nop
```

Figure 11-2: IL code for the GetIntroduction method

If you've ever used any other disassembling tools, you probably realize that .NET code is quite different. Usually, the best you can hope for when looking at a compiled program is to find a list of low-level machine instructions. .NET, on the other hand, compiles programs to a special intermediary language called IL. IL instructions don't look the same as normal VB .NET code, but they retain enough similarities that you can often get a general idea of what is happening in a section of code.

Because the IL instructions retain so much information about your program, the Common Language Runtime can perform optimizations, guard against illegal operations, and protect memory when running an application. It also makes it fairly easy for other programmers to peer into some of the internal details about how a competing program works. This is a problem that has plagued Java for a while, and in the future there will probably be special third-party tools that allow you to scramble your code so that it's difficult for humans to interpret it. (For example, one technique is to give all variables meaningless numeric identifiers in the compiled program file.) For now, though, paranoid programmers should beware.

Dependency Information

At the top of the tree is an item that represents the manifest for your assembly. If you double-click on it, you will see such information as your assembly's version and locale settings. Most importantly, you can see information about dependencies, which will appear as `.assembly extern` statements:

```
.assembly extern System.Data
{
  .publickeytoken = (B7 7A 5C 56 19 34 E0 89 )              // .z\V.4..
  .ver 1:0:2411:0
}
```

This example indicates that in order to function correctly, the current assembly requires the System.Data assembly included with .NET. There is also additional information that specifies the required version of the System.Data assembly: 1.0.2441.0. This number is in the format *major.minor.build.revision*. When you run this application, it will look for an application with the same major and minor version numbers, but it will use the latest build and revision that it finds. By default, build and revisions are considered compatible "hot fixes," and they are always used.

If the .NET framework can't find a version of the System.Data assembly that has the correct major and minor versions, along with a build and revision that are at least as recent as those specified in the manifest, the program won't be allowed to run. Remember, several different versions of a single assembly such as System.Data can be installed at once, so just because you have one doesn't mean that you have the right version.

Setting Assembly Information

The dependency information is added automatically to the manifest when you create an assembly. But what about other information, such as product name and version number? All of these details are specified in a special file that every Visual Basic .NET project contains. It's called AssemblyInfo.vb.

The AssemblyInfo file contains a number of special attributes specifying information that should be added to your program. The attributes are listed here, with some sample information added:

```
<Assembly: AssemblyTitle("FileIOTester")>
<Assembly: AssemblyDescription("Test VB .NET I/O features.")>
<Assembly: AssemblyCompany("No Starch Press, Inc.")>
<Assembly: AssemblyProduct("The No Starch VB .NET Examples")>
<Assembly: AssemblyCopyright("Copyright 2001")>
<Assembly: AssemblyTrademark("No Starch(TM)")>
<Assembly: CLSCompliant(True)>
```

These options replace the project properties used in older versions of Visual Basic for setting basic project information. You can find this information in the file properties for the compiled assembly, as shown in Figure 11-3.

Figure 11-3: The Assembly information

The most important attribute, however, is the version:

```
<Assembly: AssemblyVersion("1.0.*")>
```

By default, you specify only the major and minor numbers for the version number, and include an asterisk (*) for the remaining build and revision property. Visual Basic .NET will then automatically increment these numbers every time you compile a new .exe file (even when you do so for testing purposes by clicking on the run button in the IDE). Note that these numbers increment by more than 1. A typical version number using this system might be something like 1.0.594.21583.

Retrieving Assembly Information

Sometimes it's useful to be able to retrieve assembly information programmatically. The most obvious example is an About box, where your program displays such information as the current version. This information can't be hard-coded into the program, because it would need to be altered with every build, and would not have guaranteed accuracy. Instead, the information can be retrieved via the System.Windows.Forms.Application class, which is similar to the App object in previous versions of Visual Basic.

```
lblProductName.Text = Application.ProductName
lblProductVersion.Text = Application.ProductVersion
lblPath.Text = Application.ExecutablePath
```

In most cases, this class provides the basic features that you need. However, you can also delve into more interesting territory with the System.Reflection. Assembly class. This class uses *reflection* to retrieve information about an assembly. Using System.Reflection.Assembly, you can even drill-down to examine individual files and classes in your project—performing the slightly mind-bending trick of examining one piece of your code with another piece of your code.

To get started, you can use the GetExecutingAssembly method to return a reference to the current assembly for the project. Our next example uses the assembly and retrieves all the defined types (which includes classes and other constructs, such as enumerations). Then, the code searches each class for a list of its events. Along the way, a TreeView is constructed.

```
Dim MyAssembly As System.Reflection.Assembly
MyAssembly = System.Reflection.Assembly.GetExecutingAssembly()
lblAssemblyInfo.Text = MyAssembly.FullName

' Define some variables used to "walk" the program structure.
Dim MyTypes(), MyType As Type
Dim MyEvents(), MyEvent As System.Reflection.EventInfo
Dim node As TreeNode

' Iterate through the program's classes.
MyTypes = MyAssembly.GetTypes()
```

(continued on next page)

```
For Each MyType In MyTypes
    node = treeTypes.Nodes.Add(MyType.FullName)

    ' Iterate through the events in each class.
    MyEvents = MyType.GetEvents
    For Each MyEvent In MyEvents
        node.Nodes.Add(MyEvent.Name & " - event handler signature: " & _
        MyEvent.EventHandlerType.Name)
    Next

Next
```

The end result is a TreeView control that maps out a crude picture of the program's structure, showing every class and its events (Figure 11-4). In this case, there is only one class, which is the custom form class.

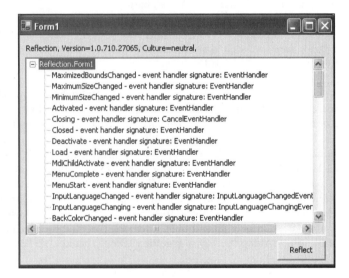

Figure 11-4: Reflection information

Reflection is useful in countless unusual scenarios, but it's usually not a part of day-to-day development. Sometimes, it's interesting to experiment with reflection just to get a better idea of how the .NET engine works, and how it classifies and organizes types and metadata.

You may find it interesting to explore reflection in more detail. Use the Assembly class as a starting point, and let it lead you to the other "info" classes in the System.Reflection namespace. Each one is customized to provide information about a special type of code construct and its metadata (for example, the preceding code uses the EventInfo class to examine events). You may also be interested in the online example for this chapter, which uses a slightly more complete "code walker" program that reflects on properties, methods, and events.

Creating a .NET Component

A good way to understand .NET assemblies is to create a simple component of your own. As in earlier versions of Visual Basic, a *component* is a collection of one or more classes that contains a set of related functions and features. These classes are provided in a .dll file, and the client can create objects based on these classes as though the class definition were part of the current project.

Creating a Class Library Project

The Person and NuclearFamily classes we created in Chapters 5 and 6 could form the basis of a logical component. Currently, these class definitions are located inside the Windows Forms project that was designed to test them. By extracting these classes into a separate component, we acquire a separately distributable, shareable component that can be used in any type of application, including ASP.NET sites and Web Services. In small-scale projects, this pattern—where a class is developed inside a project, and later made into a separate component—is a common one.

To create a component, choose File • New • Project from the Visual Studio .NET menu. Then choose the Class Library project type from the Visual Basic Projects group (Figure 11-5).

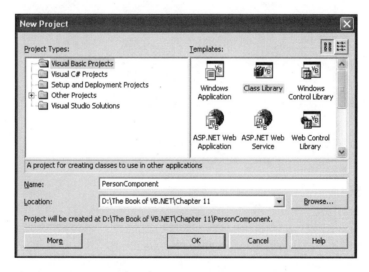

Figure 11-5: Creating a Class Library

An ordinary VB .NET project will be created, without any graphical components such as Windows Forms. You can use as many files as you want for creating classes. In our example, the class library will use code that has already been developed in another project. To transfer the code, you can import the existing .vb files into the project, or you can open another instance of Visual Studio .NET, open the source project, and cut and paste the appropriate class definitions for the NuclearFamily and Person classes.

Once the code has been copied, you only need to build the project. You can build it by clicking on the standard start button. A .dll file with the project name will be compiled in the bin directory, and you will receive a warning message informing you that the project can only be compiled, not executed. Unlike stand-alone applications, components need a client that uses them, and can't accomplish anything on their own. To skip the error message, just right-click on the project in the Solution Explorer, and click on Build whenever you want to generate the assembly.

Creating a Client

To create a client, you either open an existing project or start a new Windows Forms application. Right-click on References in the Solution Explorer, and choose Add Reference. Don't bother searching through the list provided for you; it corresponds to all the assemblies in the GAC (Global Assembly Cache), not the private assemblies designed for internal use.

To add your reference, click the Browse button at the .NET tab, and hunt for the .dll file from your class library project, as shown in Figure 11-6.

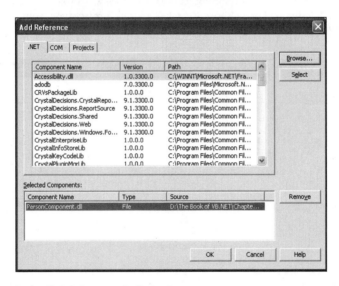

Figure 11-6: Referencing the PersonComponent

Once you have chosen the right file, click on OK to continue. Visual Studio .NET will copy the .dll file to the bin directory of the current project. This is an important fact to remember, because any new changes in your class library project will not be available in your client project until you copy the newly compiled .dll file and overwrite the previous copy in the client project.

The classes defined in your class library project will now automatically be available in your current project, just as though you had defined them in that project. The only difference is that you need to use the namespace of your project library in order to access its classes, as shown in Figure 11-7.

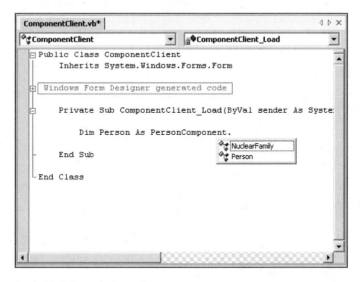

Figure 11-7: Using the PersonComponent

This is code sharing at its most efficient, and it easily crosses language barriers. You can work with C# classes in VB .NET and vice versa, without even being aware of the difference. You can even inherit from and extend a class in a .dll file, using any .NET language. The actual .dll assembly is language-neutral, and has its code stored in special IL instructions, like those you saw in the ILDasm program.

When you decide to deploy your new client project, you will once again notice how dramatic the differences are between COM and .NET. In COM development, you would need to first copy the custom component to the Windows system directory on the new computer, register it, and then use the client program. In .NET development, no registration is required. The class library .dll and client .exe files can be copied to any directory on the new computer, and they will work automatically. The .exe file has all the information that .NET needs in its manifest about dependencies. It will automatically locate the class library .dll, as long as it is present in the same directory.

Other .NET Requirements

One aspect that's been ignored in this whole discussion is that the so-called copy-and-run deployment isn't quite as easy now as it should be in a few years. The problem is that while your assemblies have all the metadata they need to identify themselves and their dependencies, they will still only work on another computer with the .NET framework. If you copy your application to a program that does not have the .NET runtime, it won't work.

Luckily, Visual Studio .NET allows you to create setup projects that include a special .NET redistributable that installs everything the client needs to run your application. Alternatively, you can ensure that a computer is .NET-ready by installing the .NET framework separately. Check Microsoft's website for the latest redistributable setup that can be downloaded for free (although it will number several megabytes). In the future, the task should become easier as Microsoft streamlines the upgrade process and probably starts sneaking the .NET files into such applications as Internet Explorer and Windows operating system upgrades.

The Global Assembly Cache

Not all assemblies are private. For example, no one would want to install a separate version of the .NET class library in the directory for each .NET application. For these situations, Microsoft still includes a central component repository. This time, instead of tossing files into a system directory shared with drivers and other system devices, Windows uses a dedicated area called the GAC (Global Assembly Cache). The GAC differs from the Windows system directory in a number of other important respects as well. For example, it allows—and, in fact, encourages—multiple versions of the same component to be installed. It doesn't lock files so that they can't be updated when in use; instead, it phases out existing users and provides the updated version for new users (or when the program is restarted). Finally, it allows you to put customized versioning policies into place that dictate exactly which component version an application will use.

Even with all these advances, you should resist the urge to start throwing components into the GAC. Many of the factors that required a global component store in the past simply don't apply in the .NET world. With COM, a component had to be part of the global registry in order to be used. In .NET, this isn't the case. If you develop your own component, there's no reason to use the GAC. In fact, even if you purchase a third-party component to use with your applications, there may still be no reason to put it in the GAC. You'll probably be better off just copying the file into your application directory. Remember, the .NET philosophy values easy, painless deployment over a few dozen extra megabytes of disk space. When in doubt, use a local, private assembly.

On the other hand, if you are developing your own components for developers to use in their applications, or some other type of assembly that you want to make globally available on an entire system, the GAC may be exactly what you need. To take a look at the GAC, browse to the directory C:\WINNT\ Assembly in Windows Explorer. A special plug-in allows you to see assemblies with their name, culture, and version information, as seen in Figure 11-8.

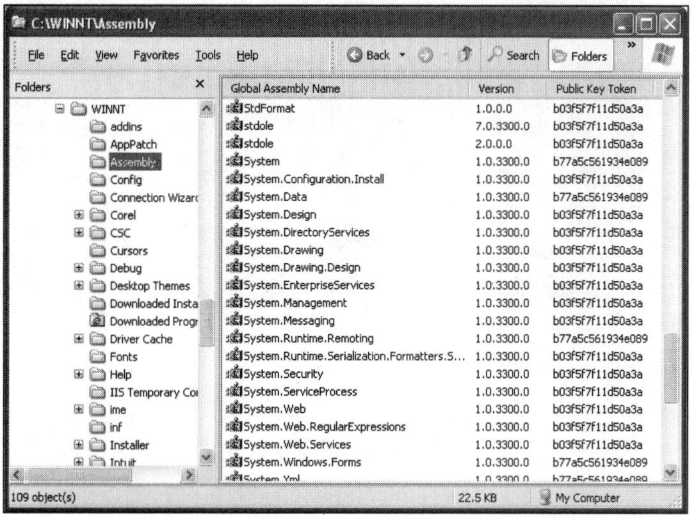

Figure 11-8: The Global Assembly Cache

The GAC is slightly less intimidating then the world of COM, because it has fewer components. More components and controls are bundled together in single assemblies. Also, the only assemblies that will be present initially are part of the .NET framework.

The GAC "Under the Hood"

The appearance of a single list of files in the GAC is slightly deceptive. This simple approach would lead to two obvious problems:

- **Name collision.** What would happen if you installed another assembly with the same filename as an existing assembly?

- **Versioning problems.** One of .NET's greatest advances is its ability to store more than one version of an assembly in the GAC, so that every program uses exactly the version for which it was designed. However, how is this possible if assemblies use the same filename?

The GAC reality is a little more surprising. What you see in Explorer is the product of a thoughtful Explorer plug-in. If you use a low-level utility to view directories, or a command prompt listing, you'll see a very different picture of the GAC (Figure 11-9).

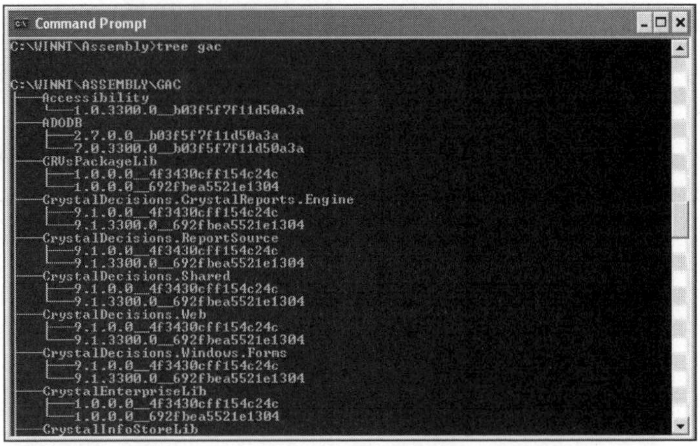

Figure 11-9: A partial listing of GAC directories

Instead of a simple list of assembly files, the GAC is really a complex directory structure. This structure allows multiple versions of any assembly, and uses special strong names to ensure that a name collision is impossible. The actual assembly file is given the name you see in the GAC plug-in, but it's stored in a special directory that uses the version number and a uniquely generated ID (such as C:\WINNT\Assembly\GAC\System.Web\1.0.2411.0__b03f5f7f11d50a3a, which contains the System.Web.dll assembly).

Creating a Shared Assembly

Now that you know the truth about the GAC, it probably won't come as a surprise to find out that you can't copy a private assembly directly into it. (In Explorer, the Paste command is disabled.) Instead, you have to create a special shared assembly.

Before you can copy a file to the GAC, you need to create a strong name for it. A strong name is a special concept introduced by .NET to help ensure that DLL Hell is never an issue. The idea is that all the assemblies you create are signed with a special key that only you possess. This system makes it impossible for anyone else to create an assembly that pretends to be a new version of your component. The strong name you use for a shared assembly also includes an ID that is guaranteed to be statistically unique (much like a GUID).

To make a long story short, you need to follow three steps:

1. Create a key.

2. Add the key to your assembly. Then compile your assembly.

3. Install the assembly into the GAC.

Acquiring a Key

For this step, you need to find and use a utility included with the .NET framework called sn.exe. You use the –*k* parameter, and specify the name for your key, like this:

```
sn -k MyKey.snk
```

You can enter this at the command line, or by using the Run command. (It's not an example of VB .NET code.)

Each key file has a combination of a private and a public key. The public key is typically made available to the world. The private key is carefully guarded, and should never be released to more than a selected few people in a specific organization. Private and public keys provide a special type of encryption. Anything encrypted with a private key can be read only with the corresponding public key. Anything encrypted with the public key can only be read with the corresponding private key. This is a time-honored encryption system used in email and other Internet applications.

In .NET use, the private key is used when the assembly is created, and the public key is stored in the assembly's manifest. When someone runs the assembly from the GAC, the Common Language Runtime uses the public key to decode information from the manifest. If a different private key is used, the operation will fail. In other words, by using a key pair, you can be sure that only a person with access to this .snk file can create an assembly with your identity. On the other hand, anyone can run a properly signed file, thanks to the included public key.

Using the Key

You reference the appropriate key file in your project by using the appropriate attribute in the AssemblyInfo.vb file. You should add a line that looks like this:

```
<Assembly: AssemblyKeyFile("c:\KeyFiles\MyKey.snk")>
```

Then, the next time you compile the project, the key information will be added to the assembly.

Installing the Assembly into the GAC

You now have a variety of options for installing the assembly into the GAC. You can use a dedicated setup program, the GACUtil.exe utility, or you can drag and drop the assembly using the Windows Explorer plug-in. In this final step, the special directory structure is created for you automatically, and your assembly will appear on the GAC list.

Advanced Policy Files

One of the most exciting features of .NET assemblies is that you can configure their versioning settings. You do this by creating a file with the same name as the corresponding .dll or .exe file, and adding the extension .config. This file will be automatically examined by the Common Language Runtime for additional information about where to search for assemblies and which versions to allow. The information in the .config file is stored in a readable XML format.

However, we're not going to discuss the format of the .config file. If you're curious, you can explore the MSDN help files. Instead, I recommend that you use a convenient management snap-in provided by Microsoft and shown in Figure 11-10. To run the .NET Framework Configuration utility, select Settings • Control Panel • Administrative Tools • Microsoft .NET Configuration from the Start menu.

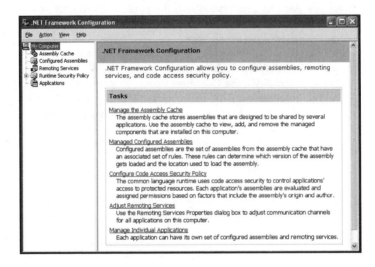

Figure 11-10: The .NET Framework Configuration utility

There are at least two cases where you might want to run this tool:

1. You have installed a newer assembly to the GAC that is still backward-compatible and improves performance. However, because it uses a new version number, it won't be used by existing applications. On an application-by-application basis, you can instruct programs to use the new version.

2. You have a private assembly in a special company-defined location. You want several of your programs to use this assembly without needing to copy it to the GAC (which is an unnecessary extra headache). However, your programs don't know where to find this assembly. Using the .NET Admin Tool, you can provide applications with a new search path for assemblies.

There are countless other useful operations that you can perform with the .NET administrative tool, including reviewing and installing assemblies, viewing dependencies, and configuring security policies, but these two tasks provide a good introduction.

Specifying a Version for a Shared Assembly

Browse to the Configure Assemblies node in the tree, and click on Configure an Assembly, which brings up the window shown in Figure 11-11.

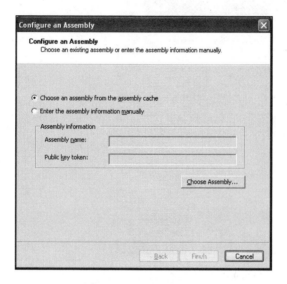

Figure 11-11: Configuring an assembly

Click the Choose Assembly button, and select the appropriate assembly from the GAC. Once you have confirmed your selection, a tabbed Properties window will appear that allows you to change assembly options:

- The General tab provides basic information about the assembly.
- The Binding Policy tab allows you to configure version policies, which is our focus in this example.
- The Codebases tab allows you to specify a path for automatic downloading and updating of assemblies.

To set a new version policy, you need to add entries to the Binding Policy tab. Each entry links a requested version (or a range of requested versions) to a new version number. The requested version is what the client application attempts to access. The new version is the assembly that the Common Language Runtime decides to use instead. Essentially, .NET forwards the request for the assembly to another version of the same assembly.

In the following sample configuration (Figure 11-12), the component will use the version 2.0.0.0 when a request is received for any version between 0.0.0.0 and 1.9.9.9. This version is known to be backward-compatible and to provide the best performance. A similar specification is made for versions between 3.0.0.0 and 3.9.9.9. However, a request for any other version (like 2.5.0.2, for example) will not be forwarded, and the request assembly version will be used, if it exists.

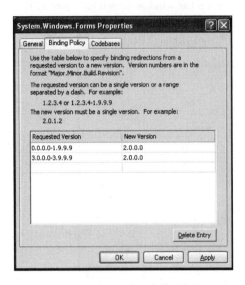

Figure 11-12: Creating a version policy

Specifying a Search Path for a Private Assembly

In the case of a private assembly, you need to configure each individual application that uses the assembly. To do so, you first have to add the appropriate application. Click on the Applications node, and then on the Add an Application to Configure link. You can choose the application from the list of previously executed .NET applications, or by browsing.

Once you make your selection, the application will be added as a node under the Applications group. Expand it, and choose Configured Assemblies. Then, click on the Configure an Assembly link. Choose the assembly from the list of dependent assemblies for this application (Figure 11-13).

Choose Assembly From Dependent Assemblies

Name	Public Key Token	Version
mscorlib	b77a5c561934e089	1.0.3300.0
Microsoft.VisualBasic	b03f5f7f11d50a3a	7.0.3300.0
System	b77a5c561934e089	1.0.3300.0
System.Data	b77a5c561934e089	1.0.3300.0
System.Drawing	b03f5f7f11d50a3a	1.0.3300.0
System.Windows.Forms	b77a5c561934e089	1.0.3300.0
System.Xml	b77a5c561934e089	1.0.3300.0
PersonComponent		1.0.710.27...
System.EnterpriseServices	b03f5f7f11d50a3a	1.0.3300.0
Accessibility	b03f5f7f11d50a3a	1.0.3300.0
System.Runtime.Serialization.Formatters.Soap	b03f5f7f11d50a3a	1.0.3300.0

Assembly name: `PersonComponent`

Public key token: ` `   **Select**

Version: `1.0.710.27494`   **Cancel**

Figure 11-13: Dependent assemblies for the PersonComponent application

A tabbed window will appear, displaying the settings. In this case, you need to modify the settings in the Codebases tab (Figure 11-14). Every entry links a version to a specific search location. This feature is customized for Internet deployment, so you will need to add the file:///prefix to specify a local assembly.

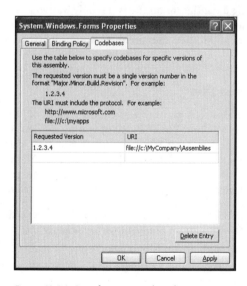

Figure 11-14: Specifying a search path

Remember, when you use the .NET Admin tool in this way, what you are actually doing is taking a shortcut to creating the XML configuration file. Rather than repeating these manual steps on another computer, you can copy the finished .config file with your application. You can also edit the .config manually or through a setup program if other fine-tuning is required (for example, if you need to indicate a different search path).

Here's what the PersonComponent.exe.config file will look like after you change the search path for the dependent PersonComponent assembly:

```
<?xml version="1.0"?>
<configuration>
  <runtime>
    <assemblyBinding xmlns="urn:schemas-microsoft-com:asm.v1">
      <dependentAssembly>
        <assemblyIdentity name="PersonComponent" />
        <codeBase version="1.2.3.4" href="file:///c:\myapps" />
      </dependentAssembly>
    </assemblyBinding>
  </runtime>
</configuration>
```

These types of configuration files usually aren't needed, but in some situations they are indispensable. You may remember that the end of Chapter 4 showed that creating a configuration file is the only way you can use the Windows XP visual styles for controls in your application. Now you should have a better idea of why configuration files are used, and how broad the scope of their settings can be.

Introducing the Windows Installer

Several quiet revolutions took place with the introduction of Microsoft's Windows 2000, Windows ME, and Windows XP operating systems. One of these was the introduction of the Microsoft Windows Installer service. This service, which is included in all new versions of the Windows operating system (and available as a separate download for Windows 98 and Windows NT 4), provides a new way to create setup programs. Some of its special features include:

- Support for a special installation database that Windows maintains and uses to uninstall software without damaging other applications.

- Support for self-repair, which allows modified or deleted files to be restored automatically from a Windows Installer setup file if a curious end user has accidentally made changes.

- Support for transactional installation, which means that if a user cancels a setup procedure, or if the setup fails halfway through, any changes that have been made up until that point are rolled back, leaving the computer in the exact same consistent state that it was in before the installation began.

You may have installed applications from Windows Installer setup files already without realizing it, since the user interface for the installation program resembles the typical Setup Wizard. One difference between ordinary setup files and Windows Installer files is that Windows Installer files have the extension .msi. Another difference is that the setup file contains the program you want to deploy, along with special setup configuration options, but it does not contain a traditional stand-alone setup program (such as an .exe file). Instead, .msi files rely on the Windows Installer service built into the Windows operating system. As with .exe setup programs, you can double-click on a Windows Installer file to automatically launch the setup.

Creating a Windows Installer setup in Visual Studio .NET is easy. It's also extremely useful. If you develop products that will be distributed to other users on CD media or over the Internet, you will almost certainly want to use the Windows Installer technology to create a full-featured program that takes care of creating shortcuts, making any important registry settings, and copying the actual files. While .NET is intelligent enough that a simple copy operation can transfer an application, it still makes sense to provide a customized, wizard-based approach for your product's end users.

Creating a Windows Installer Setup

With the Microsoft Installer features in Visual Studio .NET, we once again have a topic that could be expanded into an entire book. The setup and deployment features provided by .NET are comprehensive and configurable enough to handle almost any setup requirement. Luckily, unlike the rest of the .NET platform, the Installer requires few design decisions or best practices for you to worry about. This means that you can explore unusual Windows Installer features that aren't described in this section, and still be reasonably confident that you won't implement them in a problematic way. The same can't be said of developing Web Services or multithreaded applications, where this book should be your first point of reference.

The Windows Installer Project

A Windows Installer project is a special type of Visual Studio .NET project. Unlike the other project types this book has discussed, it is not language-specific. Instead of writing scripts, you configure setup options through special designers and property windows.

You can create a stand-alone Windows Installer project, and then import the output from another .NET project, or you can add a Windows Installer project to an existing solution that contains the project you want to deploy. This second option is usually the most convenient.

First, open an existing project. Then, right-click on the solution item in the Solution Explorer window, and choose Add • New Project. Choose Setup Project from the Setup and Deployment Projects group, as shown in Figure 11-15.

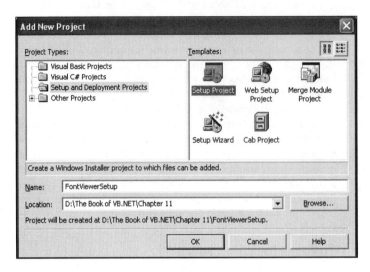

Figure 11-15: Creating a setup project

Then, enter the name, and click OK to add the project. You will now have two projects in your solution, as shown in Figure 11-16.

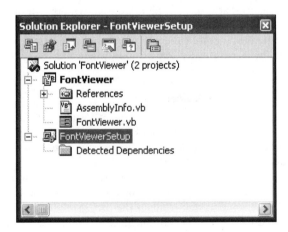

Figure 11-16: A solution with a Windows application and its setup project

Make sure you set the application to be the startup project. Compiling a setup file can take some time, and it's only required when you want to deploy the finished application, not during testing. To create the .msi setup file at any time, just right-click on the setup project and choose Build. An .msi file for your setup will be created in the bin directory, with the name of your project.

Basic Setup Project Options

The setup project is unlike any other type of .NET application. Instead of writing code, you configure options in a variety of different designers. Finding the designer you need and setting the appropriate options are the keys to creating your setup project.

To start, use the Properties Window to set some of the basic setup options, such as Author, Manufacturer, ManufacturerURL, Title, ProductName, and Version. Most of these settings are descriptive strings that are used in the Setup Wizard or in other Windows dialog windows, such as the Support Info window (which can be launched from the Add/Remove Programs window). You can also set the AddRemoveProgramsIcon (the icon that represents your program in the list of currently installed applications for the Add/Remove Programs window), and the DetectNewerInstalledVersion setting (which will abort the setup if a newer setup program has already been used to install software). Each setting is described individually in the MSDN help files. Just click on a setting in the Properties window, and press F1.

To configure more sophisticated options, you will have to use one of the setup designers. To navigate to the main designers, right-click on your setup project in the Solution Explorer, and select View. There are six different designer options, depending on the settings you want to configure (Figure 11-17).

Figure 11-17: The setup designers

Over the next few sections, we'll quickly explore each of these setup options. The first and most important is File System.

File System

Initially, your setup project is a blank template that does not install anything. You can change this by using the File System options window, which allows you to specify the files that should be installed during the setup procedure. Once you've configured this window by adding your application, along with any dependent files and shortcuts, you can create a fully functional .msi file simply by building the project. All the other windows provide additional options that you may or may not need.

By default, a short list of folders provides access to commonly needed folders on the destination computer. You can add links to additional folders by right-clicking in the directory pane and choosing Add Special Folder (Figure 11-18). There are options that map to the computer's Fonts folder, Favorites folder, Startup folder, and many more, allowing you to install files and shortcuts in a variety of places. Folders that have already been added to the list are grayed out so that you can't choose them again.

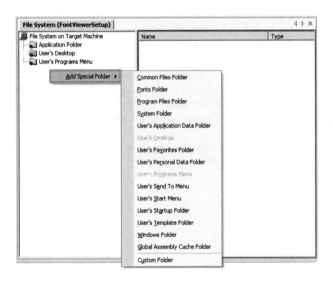

Figure 11-18: Setup folders

Adding a Project File

On their own, these links don't actually do anything. However, you can add files and shortcuts into the folders they represent. For example, to add an application file, click on the Application Folder item. Then, on the right side of the window, right-click and choose Add • Project Output.

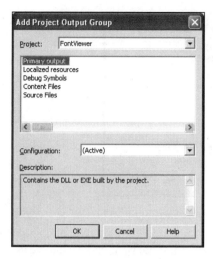

Figure 11-19: Adding a project output

The other project in your solution is automatically selected in this window (Figure 11-19). Choose Primary output and click on OK. (Primary output is the .exe or .dll file a project creates when you click on the start button.) Figure 11-20 shows a setup project with a project output added and ready to be installed to the user-selected application folder.

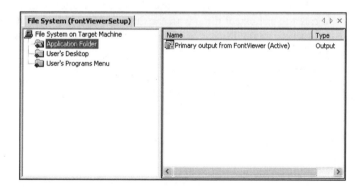

Figure 11-20: The FontViewer project output

Now, whenever you build this setup program it will create an .exe file based on the project, and add it to the setup. At the same time, any dependent assemblies will also be added, including a set of .NET redistributable files. The redistributable files (taken from the merge module dotnetfxredist_x86_enu.msm) allow your application to work on computers that haven't installed Visual Studio .NET or the .NET framework. To create a smaller and speedier setup, you can exclude these files, and manually install the .NET framework files on the destination computer. Figure 11-21 shows how to remove the redistributable files from your setup.

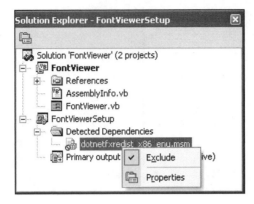

Figure 11-21: Excluding the .NET redistributable

You should also note that you can right-click in the file list and select Add to insert any other dependent files, such as pictures or XML documents. You can also create as many layers of subdirectories as you need. Lastly, you can click on any folder to display additional information about it in the Properties window. You can see, for example, that the standard format for naming directories (ProgramFiles\[Manufacturer]\[ProductName]) is used by default for the application directory.

Adding a Shortcut

You can also use the File System designer to add shortcuts for your application. You can add a shortcut directly to the desktop by including it in the User's Desktop folder, or to the Programs group in the Start menu by using the User's Programs Menu folder.

Once again, just right-click in the list space on the right. Choose Create New Shortcut. A special window will appear that allows you to choose the linked file from one of the other folders. For example, you can browse to the application folder, and choose the application's .exe file for the shortcut target. Figure 11-22 shows a setup project with a shortcut added to the Program menu for the main application executable (project output).

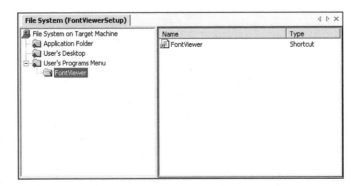

Figure 11-22: A FontViewer shortcut

You can then use the Properties window to fine-tune your shortcut, changing its name, icon, default window state (the ShowCmd property), and startup or working folder. Note that in order to assign a special icon for the shortcut, you must have added it to the setup project.

TIP *At this point, you've created a fully functioning setup that can install your application, complete with a basic wizard, shortcut, and uninstall feature. All you need to do is build the setup project and double-click on the .msi file. All the other options we'll consider in this chapter are for adding enhanced features to your setup program.*

Registry

The Registry designer (as shown in Figure 11-23) allows you to create registry entries in the destination computer as easily as you create shortcuts and copy files. The display is similar to the familiar Windows regedit program. Right-click on the list at the right to add a new registry key or value. This value will be created automatically during the setup. If you use one of the setup variables, which is enclosed in square brackets (for example, [Manufacturer]), the setup program will use the corresponding value defined in the project properties. This is a good way to design a generic setup that can keep up with frequent product updates or even company name changes.

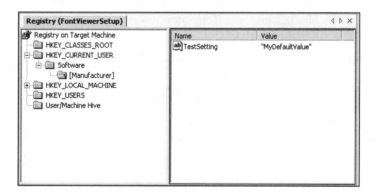

Figure 11-23: The Registry designer

It's a good idea to reduce your reliance on these registry settings. Even if your application is designed exclusively through deployment with your custom setup, there may be situations where you want the ease and convenience of a simple file copy deployment. In this case, your application should be intelligent enough to use default registry settings if none are specified, or raise a nonfatal error and query the user for more information. You should not rely on the success of this setup program. The best use of the registry features in a Windows Installer project is to preconfigure directory settings, based on the location where the application is installed. The application should *not* fail without this information.

File Types

The File Types designer allows you to associate your program with specific extensions, a trick that was awkward with the Package and Deployment Wizard in earlier versions of Visual Basic. A file association allows Windows to automatically launch the correct program when you double-click on a file (for example, .pdf files are opened in Adobe Acrobat, and .txt files are usually opened in Notepad).

If you are deploying a document-based application, you may want to use your own registered file types. Make sure, however, that your file types have reasonably unique names, to prevent them from conflicting with other programs. File types do not need to be restricted to three characters. Also, don't ever try to take over such basic file types as .bmp, .html, or .mp3. It is almost certain that the user will have a preferred program for accessing these types of files, and trying to override such preferences is certain to annoy and even anger your clients.

To add a file type association, right-click in the Window and choose Add File Type (Figure 11-24). Before the file extension is considered complete, you must specify the following details:

- The name of the type of document (Name)
- The associated extension (Extension)
- The program to launch for the extension (Command)
- Ideally, a nice icon (Icon) and a two- or three-word description of the format (Description)

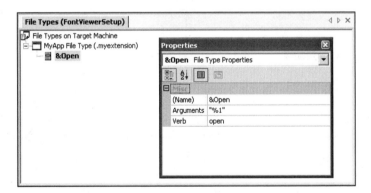

Figure 11-24: A custom file type

You can then add actions to each of your file types. The most common action is Open. When you double-click a file or right-click on it and choose Open, the owning program will launch, and should open the program automatically. By convention, the filename is passed to your program, and it is your program's responsibility to check its command-line arguments and take the appropriate action (in this case, opening the file). The "%1" symbol in the Arguments property indicates that the action passes the filename to your program as a command-line parameter.

In some cases, you might want to add other actions, such as a Print command that would automatically open your application with the selected document, and print out the corresponding file. To do this, alter the Arguments property to some other format that your program can recognize. For example, you could set it to /p "%1" and specifically check in your program for the /p parameter.

Before you use this setting, you should test it out with your program, and fine-tune it as needed. You should also look at how the icon and description appear in Windows Explorer. To test a custom file type, add it manually using Windows Explorer. (Choose Tools • Folder Options from the menu, and select the File Types tab.) If you're trying this out for the first time, it will also be helpful to see how other file types are registered.

User Interface

For a simple setup, you can let the Windows Installer generate all of the user interface for you using its default options. For a more sophisticated setup, you may want to configure some of the Setup Wizard options using the User Interface designer.

The Windows Installer user interface is *not* created using .NET, or even Visual Basic code. Instead, it is configured through a series of options that you can specify within your setup project. These limitations are designed to make setup creation easy, and to restrict setup variations so that Setup Wizards follow a highly consistent pattern.

With the User Interface designer, you can see the windows that will be displayed to the user. Windows are listed in the order they will be presented in, and are grouped by setup type, and then subgrouped by setup stage, as shown in Figure 11-25.

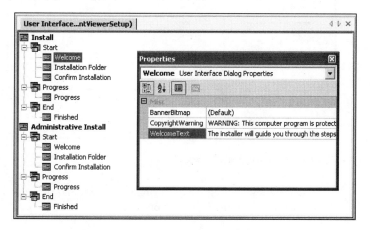

Figure 11-25: Configuring the Setup User Interface

You will see two versions of your setup listed: a normal user install, and an administrative install. To access the administrative install, you run the .msi setup file with the /a command-line parameter. Usually, the administrative install is used if you need to provide a network setup.

To customize your setup, there are four tasks you can perform:

- Modifying options for a window, using the Properties Window.
- Rearranging the order of windows by right-clicking on one and choosing Move Up or Move Down.
- Removing a window from the setup by right-clicking on it and selecting Delete.
- Adding a new window to the setup by right-clicking on a setup state and selecting Add Dialog. All windows are chosen from one of the predefined window types available to you.

Predefined Window Types

You can add one of several predefined windows to the Setup Wizard (Figure 11-26).

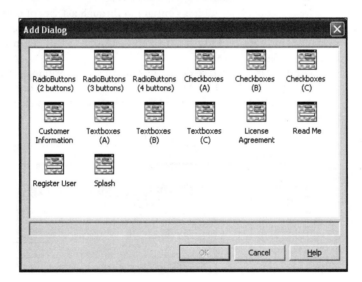

Figure 11-26: Adding Setup windows

Each window is designed for a single purpose, and provides an extremely limited set of functions. Some options include:

- A Splash window, which displays an image file for the product, and is sometimes used as the first window in a setup project.

- A License Agreement or Read Me window, which shows information from a linked .rtf file. If you add a license agreement, users must accept it, or they will not be allowed to continue.

- A Register User window, which launches a custom program if the user clicks the Register Now button. You can also add a Customer Information window which requires a Name, an Organization, and a serial number, which can be validated by comparing it with the format specified in the SerialNumberTemplate property.

- A choice window, which uses radio buttons, checkboxes, or text boxes to allow the user to enter additional information.

These windows are described in more detail in the MSDN help files. Generally, though, they only provide a few self-explanatory properties. Some aren't even configurable at all! Also, you will notice that a combination of four checkboxes or three radio buttons is the most sophisticated interface that you can use. The Setup Wizard does not provide more complex options, the idea being to force you to create a straightforward setup that is consistent with most other Windows products.

Choice Windows

Choice window is the catchall term I use to describe the setup windows that request additional selections from the user, through such basic interface controls as checkboxes. Seeing as a setup project does not allow you to write any actual code, you might be wondering how you can use the results of a user selection. The answer is quite straightforward.

First of all, you must choose a choice window to add to your project. Each choice window is based on a single type of control. The different versions of each window (A, B, and C) are identical, but each window can only be used once. Clearly the language used to create Windows Installer files is not built using .NET class-based technology! However, Microsoft is unlikely to change this system in the future. Presenting more than three configuration windows using similar controls is a nightmarish scenario that would frustrate many average users. If possible, a setup should always default to the most common value—or not provide an option at all. Remember, whenever presenting users with a choice, you are demanding that they make a decision.

To create a simple choice window, add a checkbox window. You can set values for up to four checkboxes by modifying the corresponding properties: CheckBox1Visible, CheckBox1Label (the descriptive text), and CheckBox1Value (the default setting, checked or unchecked). You match this checkbox to a global setup variable by setting the property named CheckBox1Property.

Figure 11-27: Setting a CheckBox variable

If the user checks CheckBox1 from the example in Figure 11-27, the variable MYCHECKBOX1 will be set to True. This introduces another ugly feature of setup project design—variable names are almost always typed in uppercase.

Conditions

To use the MYCHECKBOX1 variable, you need to assign it to a Condition. Conditions are provided as properties of all sorts of elements in the setup project. For example, you can find a file or a shortcut using the File System designer, or a registry setting using the Registry designer, and set its condition property to MYCHECKBOX1. If this value evaluates to True (meaning the checkbox was selected from the original window), the file will be copied or the entry will be added. Otherwise, the operation will be skipped. For example, Figure 11-28 shows a conditional file operation that will only be carried out if MYCHECKBOX1 was selected.

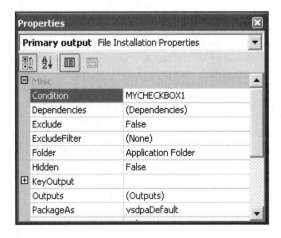

Figure 11-28: Making a file operation conditional

If you are working with a text data type, or a radio button window that assigns different numeric values to a property, you can still create a condition. For example, you might create a condition such as SELECTEDBUTTON = 1, assuming you've added a radio button choice window with the ButtonProperty of SELECTEDBUTTON, and assigned the value 1 to one of the buttons (for example, Button1Value). This condition will only evaluate to true if the user chose the SELECTEDBUTTON with the value of 1.

Conditions and choice windows provide a fairly crude way to manage user selections, but they are ideal for the simplified Setup Wizard application. Always make sure that the choice window is displayed *before* the setup action that evaluates the condition. For example, if you place a choice window at the end of your setup project, after the files have been copied, you won't be able to make the file copy operation conditional.

Built-in Conditions

The choice window isn't the only source of conditions. There are also about a dozen conditions that are always available with some basic information. These are special environment variables that provide information about the destination computer.

All of these built-in properties are described in the MSDN help files. Some of the most useful are COMPANY and USERNAME (which correspond to the information entered in the CustomerInformation window, if you are using it), LogonUser (the username of the currently logged-on user), ComputerName, PhysicalMemory (the number of megabytes of installed RAM), VersionNT (the version number of Windows NT/2000/XP operating system), and Version9X (the version number of a Windows 95/98/ME operating system).

Custom Actions

Custom actions allow you to run code at the end of an installation to perform additional configuration. As you've seen so far, the features built into the Windows Installer are extremely easy to use, but they provide a set of defined options with little extensibility. If you need to perform other tasks, such as configuring a database, adding a user account, or setting up some other type of application-specific configuration file, you can create a separate .exe file, and run it when the setup is complete by using a custom action. You can even make custom actions dependent upon other options, such as a choice window or the version of Windows installed on the current computer. Keep in mind, however, that if a custom action generates an unhandled error or fails, your entire setup will be rolled back and your program will be uninstalled.

You can add a custom action to one of several different installation phases (Figure 11-29). Right-click on the appropriate phase, and choose Add Custom Action. You must choose the program from the files included in your setup project (as there is no guarantee that any other files will be available).

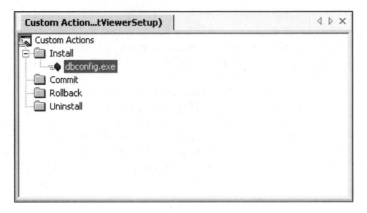

Figure 11-29: A custom action

Of course, most users like to set up a program with a minimum of fuss. Remember that in many environments, the person installing the program and the person using it are typically two different people. For these reasons, it is sometimes better to add a special configuration window to your application (perhaps one that launches the first time the program is executed) rather than add a custom action to your setup program.

Launch Conditions

Launch conditions allow you to specify the ingredients that a setup must have in order to run. If these conditions are not met, the setup will be automatically cancelled, and the error message you define will be displayed.

A launch condition has two parts. First, there is a search operation, which hunts for the registry, file, or component that you identify. You have to set a variety of properties to set the scope of the search and the type of match. A Boolean True or False is set using the corresponding Property. For example, if you add a Search For File operation and set its Property to FILEFOUND, that will be the global variable you can use in other conditions.

You can use the search result at any point in your application, but it is typically used with a corresponding item in the Launch Condition group. Just set the Condition property to the appropriate variable name (in this case FILE-FOUND), and specify a Message property which indicates the error message that the setup will display if the condition has not been met. Figure 11-30 shows a launch condition that searches for a custom file, and prevents the setup from continuing if the file cannot be found.

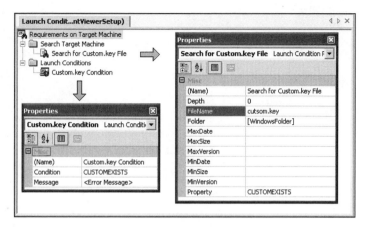

Figure 11-30: Anatomy of a launch condition that searches for a file

Launch conditions are really just an extension to the Windows Installer way of dealing with conditions. You can create a search and use the global variable for another conditional operation (a file copy, for instance), or you can create a launch condition that uses one of the built-in variables (such as Version9X or VersionNT). By default, every setup has a launch condition that verifies that the Microsoft Installer service is installed and available.

What Comes Next?

This chapter has explored the heart of .NET versioning, and how it differs radically from the COM way of life. Much of the complexity explored here won't affect you—thanks to .NET's planning, deploying an application is often just as easy as copying a directory. If you want a deeper understanding of the .NET framework, you can play with such tools as reflection, ILDasm, and the .NET Framework Configuration tool, all of which were introduced here.

This chapter also introduced setup projects. Rather than reviewing a full setup example, we took a comprehensive look at every designer. Setup projects are simple to create, and there aren't any hidden dangers. However, you need to know exactly what is possible and what isn't. Remember, setup projects aren't written in .NET code and really have little in common with true .NET projects, except for the fact that they are easy to create in Visual Studio .NET.

To see an actual setup project, refer to the online samples for this chapter, which include a simple setup program for a FontViewer utility. The FontViewer utility has relatively modest requirements—it simply provides a list of all the fonts installed on the computer, and allows the user to preview each one—but it provides a good example of a fully configured setup project. (As a side note, the FontViewer utility also shows you how to enumerate the fonts on your computer, and draw directly on a Windows form using the .NET class library.)

12

WEB FORMS AND ASP.NET

Creating web applications with earlier versions of Visual Basic was a bit of a mess. To start with, there were a dizzying number of different options. Visual Basic 6 shipped with a "kitchen sink" of competing web technologies, including templates for applications built out of Dynamic HTML, ActiveX documents, and Active Server pages (in which case you had the additional choice of Web Classes, Visual Interdev, Notepad with VBScript, or a good stiff drink and a new career).

In Visual Studio .NET, Microsoft has an ambitious new strategy for web development, and this time it's not going to cost you a few months of sleepless nights. With ASP.NET, life for the web developer is going to get a whole lot simpler. You'll be able to take care of your application's business logic (that is, what your program actually accomplishes) while using Microsoft's class infrastructure to handle all the messy Internet-specific details. The long-promised dream—being able to create software for the Web as easily as for Windows—has finally come true.

New in .NET

Most of the web technologies you had to choose from in earlier versions of Visual Basic are completely gone in Visual Basic. NET.

- Programs based on Dynamic HTML and ActiveX documents were just too restrictive in their browser requirements, and they suffered from a substantial learning curve. These technologies have been removed from Visual Basic. NET.
- Active Server Page (ASP) technology has been transformed into ASP.NET. Along the way, such tools as Web Classes and Visual Interdev have disappeared, replaced by the much more flexible and straightforward Web Form Designer.

With Visual Basic. NET, programming an Internet application automatically means creating an ASP.NET application.

A Web Development Outline

If you're like most Visual Basic programmers, you've never created a web application. This chapter will teach you the basics, and help you understand the special considerations that apply to Internet programming.

The development plan for an ASP.NET project goes something like this:

1. You design your web application's interface, using as many Web forms as you need.
2. You write the code behind your forms and add any classes you need, just as you would with an ordinary Windows application. The only difference is that you have to spend some time thinking about *state,* or how your program remembers information in between user requests. I'll spend a large portion of this chapter examining different kinds of state management.
3. You deploy your completed web application to a Windows web server.
4. The user navigates to one of your application's Web forms, using a web browser. Behind the scenes, the web server examines the user's browser, and sends him a version of the page that is tailored to make the most of the features it supports. As the user selects different options and clicks on different buttons, the web server runs different code components and navigates to different Web forms, creating the appearance of a fully integrated application.

What Was Wrong with ASP?

Quite simply, a lot. ASP made it all too easy to create disorganized, inefficient programs that mixed together HTML markup code and programming logic. It was possible to create a world-class ASP application, but the lack of structure in ASP led to—and even encouraged—poor programming.

- ASP programs emphasized an old-fashioned, script-based style of programming. ASP.NET is completely component-based, and as you know from Chapter 6, component-based programs are more elegant, efficient, and easy to maintain.

- ASP programs provided part of the infrastructure you needed in order to create a web application, but some tasks were still a chore. ASP.NET provides a host of addictive frills, including graphically rich controls, an easy way to validate user input, and painless state management.

- Well-designed ASP applications were generally built out of ASP pages and ActiveX components created in Visual Basic. This was a good system, but it imposed additional headaches when you configured, installed, and versioned your applications. We won't get into the details here, except to note that ASP.NET applications are a breeze to install and update.

- ASP applications were notoriously difficult to debug if you didn't have a spare web server in the office. With ASP.NET, you can use all of Visual Basic's debugging tools while running the application from a browser on your local computer.

- ASP pages used VBScript, a stripped-down flavor of Visual Basic with its own quirks and idiosyncrasies. ASP.NET no longer supports VBScript, and now uses Visual Basic natively.

- ASP.NET compiles your pages automatically the first time they are used and every time they are updated. It may seem like a small detail, but it's one of a series of performance improvements that makes ASP.NET the fastest version of ASP yet.

Still the Same

If you've programmed with ASP before, you'll find that not everything has changed. If you look hard enough, you'll even find familiar objects, such as Request and Response, although you won't need to use them nearly as much this time around. One detail that hasn't changed is that ASP.NET applications are hosted by IIS (Internet Information Server), a built-in service of any Windows 2000, Windows XP, or Windows NT web server. While clients using your application are free to work with any type of browser or operating system, you still need to host your application on a Windows web server.

Web Application Basics

It used to be that you needed a special computer to act as a web server. These days, any computer with a modern Windows operating system can install the necessary IIS (Internet Information Services) hosting software from the Windows setup CD.

Of course, in most cases you still won't develop an ASP.NET application directly on the web server that will host it. Doing so could hamper the performance of the server, or even lead to crashes that would make your website unavailable (not to mention the fact that the web server is often located at a different site). Instead, you will generally perfect your web application on another computer, and copy the project directory to the web server when all your work is complete.

The trick is that in order to debug your web application, your computer needs to act as a web server. When you test a local ASP.NET application, you will actually be making requests through HTTP to the local IIS service that runs ASP.NET. In other words, there is no difference between the way you interact with your web application while testing, and the way a remote client will use it over the Internet. The only distinction between your local testing and the final deployed application is that your test website is not visible or accessible to other clients on the Internet.

IIS Setup

In order for your computer to act like a web server, it needs to have the IIS software installed. Although IIS is a part of the Windows operating system, it isn't necessarily installed by default. To check if IIS is installed, try typing the following request into an Internet browser: `http://localhost/localstart.asp`. Localhost is the special "loopback" alias that always refers to the current computer. Localstart.asp is a traditional ASP file that is stored in the root directory of your computer's website home directory.

You should see the picture shown below:

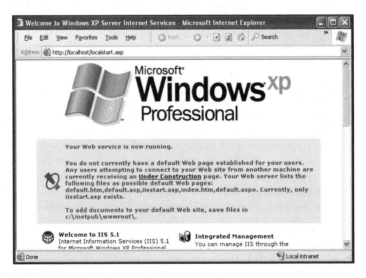

Figure 12-1: The Localstart.asp homepage

You could also request the file using the specific name of your computer (as in `http://MyComputer/localstart.asp`).

If you receive an error message, check that you have IIS installed. To do this, click the Start button, and select Settings • Control Panel. Then, choose Add or Remove Programs, and click Add/Remove Windows Components. Find

Internet Information Services in the list (see Figure 12-2), select it, and click Next to install the appropriate files.

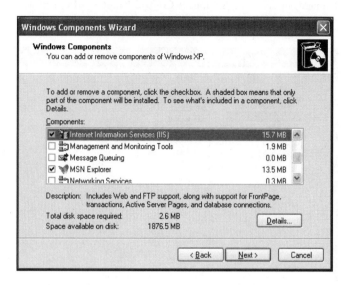

Figure 12-2: Installing IIS

Virtual Directories

By default, your website's home directory is the physical directory c:\Inetpub\wwwroot, and the localstart.asp file is contained in this directory. If you try to double-click on localstart.asp to run it directly from Windows Explorer, you will receive an error. This file can only be rendered by ASP, which must be invoked by IIS in response to a web request. ASP processes the .asp page, and returns an HTML page that can be displayed in the browser. This is essentially the same way that ASP.NET works with .aspx files.

When you are creating new web pages, you have two choices. You can place them in c:\Inetpub\wwwroot, or one of its subdirectories. For example, if you create a directory c:\Inetpub\wwwroot\MyFiles and place the file Test.html in it, you can request this page over HTTP by entering http://localhost/MyFiles/Test.html.

A more flexible approach is to create your own *virtual directory*. A virtual directory represents a physical directory on the web, but it doesn't need to use the same name as the physical directory, and it doesn't need to be a subdirectory of c:\Inetpub\wwwroot. For example, you could expose the directory c:\WebApps\01 as the virtual directory Sales. Then, you can request the Test.html file from the c:\WebApps\01 directory by entering http://localhost/Sales/Test.html.

Virtual directories are easy to create, but you don't use Visual Studio .NET to do the work. Instead, you have to use the IIS Manager utility. You can run IIS Manager by selecting Settings • Control Panel • Administrative Tools • Internet Services Manager from the taskbar (Figure 12-3).

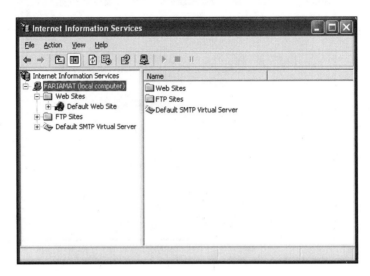

Figure 12-3: IIS Manager

NOTE *The Web Applications included with the online samples must be hosted in a virtual directory called NoStarchWeb with the physical source C:\NoStarchWeb in order for Visual Studio .NET to open the project successfully. In order to run the sample code, you either need to create this virtual directory and copy the sample files into it, or you need to import the sample files into one of your own web projects. The following list of steps will get you started creating a virtual directory.*

1. To create a virtual directory, you first create the physical directory on your hard drive.

2. Then, use the virtual directory wizard in IIS manager. Right click on the Default Web Site item (under your computer in the tree), and choose New • Virtual Directory from the context menu.

3. Click Next to get started. The first piece of information required is the Alias (Figure 12-4), which is the name that your virtual directory will have for web requests. Click Next to continue.

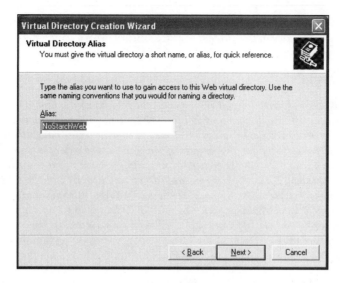

Figure 12-4: The Virtual Directory Creation Wizard

4. The second piece of information is the physical directory that will be exposed as the physical directory. This can have the same name as the virtual directory, but it doesn't need to. Click Next to continue.

5. The final wizard window gives you the chance to configure the permissions for the directory (Figure 12-5). The default settings allow clients to read the directory and run ASP.NET pages, but not make any modifications. This is the recommended configuration.

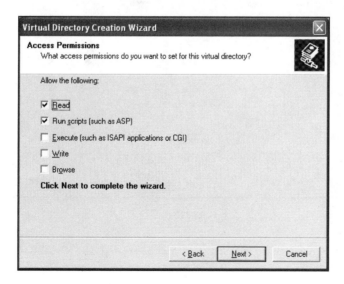

Figure 12-5: Virtual directory access permissions

6. Click Next, and then Finish to end the wizard. You will see the virtual directory in the IIS Manager tree display with a package icon next to it. Once you have created a virtual directory, you can create a web project in it using Visual Studio .NET.

When you create a virtual directory with the IIS Manager wizard, it's also marked as a web application. That means that the ASP.NET files in this directory will run in their own isolated memory space, use their own set of local session data, and have their own independent configuration settings. If you create a subdirectory in your virtual directory, this directory will also be accessible over the Internet, but it will be a part of the same application. For example, if you create the virtual directory Sales for the physical directory c:\WebApps\01, the subdirectory c:\WebApps\01\Special will be available as http://localhost/Sales/Special. Any ASP.NET files in this subdirectory will be considered a part of the Sales application, and will have the same settings and run in the same memory space.

Starting a Web Application

Before going any further, let's dive right into our first ASP.NET application. Create a new project, and select ASP.NET Web Application (Figure 12-6). For the location, you need to specify a valid virtual directory (or a subdirectory in a virtual directory).

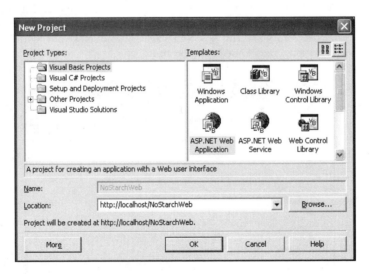

Figure 12-6: Creating an ASP.NET project

When you click OK, the project will be created, and Visual Basic will automatically add a list of different files to your project (Figure 12-7).

Figure 12-7: Web project files

Ingredients of an ASP.NET Project

Every web project is made up of the following types of files:

- **Web.config** allows you to fine-tune advanced settings, including security and state settings, that apply to your entire application. These options are outside the scope of this chapter, but you can read up on them in the MSDN help files.

- **Global.asax** is the file where you place code that responds to global events. Examples of this type of code include Application_Start (which is fired when the first user browses to a page in your web application) and Session_Start (which is fired whenever a new user browses to a page in your web application).

- **Styles.css** is a standard HTML Cascading Style Sheet that you can use to help apply consistent formatting to static content. If you want to experiment with this file, refer to one of the many excellent HTML references on the web (try http://www.ncsa.uiuc.edu/General/Internet/WWW/HTMLPrimer.html to get started, or just search Yahoo! for "HTML reference").

- **.disco** files are used for dynamic discovery of Web Services, which are discussed in Chapter 13.

- **.aspx** files are the ASP.NET pages. Each Web form you create will have an .aspx file that contains controls and formatting information. The .aspx file is sometimes called the *presentation template* of a Web form.

- **.vb** files are used to hold the code "behind" each Web form. For example, a typical Web form named HelloWorld would have its visual layout stored in the file HelloWorld.aspx, and its event-handling code in the Visual Basic file HelloWorld.aspx.vb. The Web Form Designer links these files together automatically.

Some other files are created to help Visual Basic manage your project. These include files with the extensions .sln and .suo. These files are maintained automatically, and you should never modify them directly.

NOTE *You might think that it is a serious security risk to have your source files located in a publicly accessible virtual directory. However, ASP.NET is configured to automatically reject requests for files like web.config, and any .vb file.*

Designing with Web Forms

Web forms are designed to work as much like Windows forms as possible. However, there are still some basic differences between the two. There is no direct way to display a Windows-style dialog box from a web page, so throw away any ideas about using floating tool windows, message boxes, and multi-document interfaces. A Web form's ultimate destination is an HTML page, delivered to a user working on an Internet browser. The ASP.NET engine may make use of JavaScript or Dynamic HTML to improve the appearance of your page if it detects that the client's browser supports these enhancements, but every Web form still boils down to basic HTML output.

That said, you'll find that Web forms aren't programmed like static web pages. Unlike ASP pages, which were often created with cryptic Response.Write commands, a Web form can (and usually should) be composed entirely of web controls that have properties and events, just like the controls in a Windows form.

ASP.NET provides this kind of magic by using *server-side controls*. The basic idea behind a server-side control is that the display of the control is sent to the user in HTML, but the user's interaction with the control is handled at the server. All of the Web controls in ASP.NET are server-side controls.

Adding Controls to a Web Form

The Web Form Designer provides many of the same controls as the Windows Form Designer, including labels, text boxes, and buttons. Unlike the Windows Form Designer, the Web Form Designer works is one of two modes. In *grid layout* mode, controls can be positioned in exact locations in the web page. This makes page design easier (and more like Windows application design), but it can also lead to some problems. For example, if you place two label controls next to each other, and then fill them with text in code, the first label may overlap the second one (see Figure 12-8), because the second will not be automatically moved down the page to accommodate the extra page content.

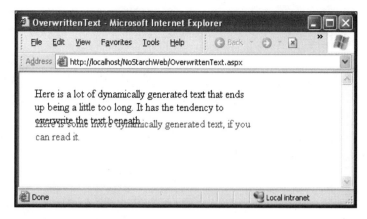

Figure 12-8: Overwritten text in grid layout

In *flow layout* mode, this problem can't occur because elements are positioned relative to one another, like they are in a word processor. However, that also means you can't place controls exactly. Instead, you need to add spaces and hard returns to position them on the page. You also need to drag and drop controls onto the page instead of drawing them on.

To set the layout mode, click on the page, and set the pageLayout property (see Figure 12-9).

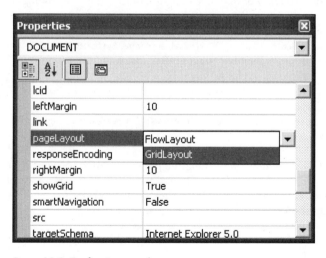

Figure 12-9: Configuring page layout

Before continuing, try creating the MetricConverter page, shown in Figure 12-10, so you can follow through the rest of the example. It's easiest to design in grid layout mode.

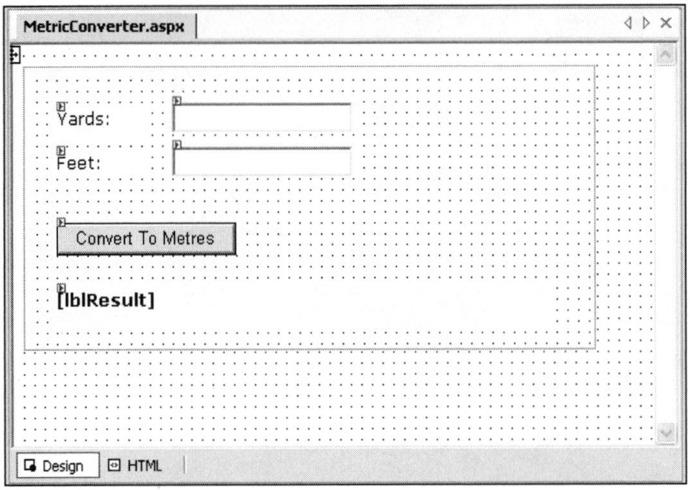

Figure 12-10: Designing a web page

Adding an Event Handler

Web Forms event handlers are created exactly as they are in the Windows Form Designer. For example, you can add a Click event handler to the button in the MetricConverter program by double-clicking on the button. Add the following code. (You may have to make slight modifications, depending on the names that you have given your controls.)

```
Private Sub cmdConvert_Click(ByVal sender As System.Object, _
  ByVal e As System.EventArgs) Handles cmdConvert.Click
    Dim Inches, Metres As Single
    Inches = 36 * Val(txtYards.Text) + 12 * Val(txtFeet.Text)
    Metres = Inches / 39.37
    lblResult.Text = "Result in metres: " & Metres.ToString()
End Sub
```

You can now try running the program. When you start it, Internet Explorer will be launched automatically, and your Web form will appear. Enter some numbers in the text boxes and click the Convert button, and the label will be refreshed with the result of the conversion.

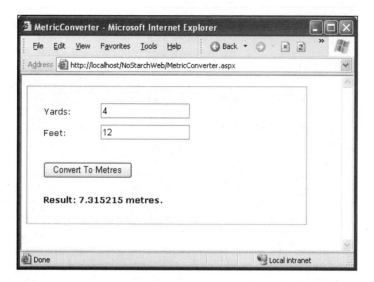

Figure 12-11: The MetricConverter page

TIP   *If you have added more than one web page to your project, the MetricConverter page may not appear when you click the start button. To configure which page is launched initially when debugging, right-click on the page in the Solution Explorer, and select Set As Startup Page.*

How Does it Work?

What happens in our MetricConverter program is relatively simple: The server creates an HTML page with a form submission button. When you click on the button, the page is transmitted back to the server, changed, and then refreshed at the client end.

Every time a user interacts with a control that fires an event, a similar "round trip" occurs from the client to the server and back. This round trip is called a *postback*.

The AutoPostback Property

The button we've created is a special type of control that will always cause a postback when clicked. Other controls are not as straightforward. For example, consider the TextChanged event of a TextBox control. In the MetricConverter program, we don't use this event. However, another program might update the display dynamically as new text is entered, or as CheckBox or RadioButton controls are selected. In this case, you would need to set the AutoPostback property for each of these controls to True.

Because a postback involves getting a new page from the server, it can slow things down a little, and the user may notice the page flicker as it is being refreshed. For that reason, the default AutoPostback setting is False. When Auto-Postback is disabled, the control's events will be delayed until another control (like a button) triggers a postback. Thus, the code in the control's event handler will not execute immediately.

Web Control Events

Events in Web form controls are slightly different than they are in Windows form controls. For example, the CheckedChanged event occurs when a RadioButton selection is changed, not necessarily every time it is clicked. Similarly, the TextBox event occurs when a user moves to a different control on the page after modifying the text box, not every time he or she presses a key. These changes are designed to minimize the number of postbacks. If a postback occurred every time the user pressed a key in a text box, the web page would be constantly reloading, the user would be quickly frustrated, and the web developer responsible would need to find a new line of employment. For similar reasons, events such as MouseMove and KeyPress aren't implemented at all.

In our MetricConverter example, we can leave AutoPostback set to False for all our controls.

A Web Form "Under the Hood"

Here's an interesting question: What's the difference between Visual Basic. NET and ASP.NET?

The answer is that ASP.NET is a kind of intermediary language for the graphical portion of a Web Form. Generally, it's HTML with some special tags. You won't usually write ASP.NET code directly; instead, you'll let the Web Form Designer create it for you. The process works like this:

1. You create a Web Form with the Visual Basic Web Form Designer.
2. Visual Basic builds a page of ASP.NET code (an .aspx file).
3. When a user requests the .aspx file, the ASP.NET engine on the web server interprets the code and replaces the ASP.NET tags with the required HTML elements.
4. The HTML version of the page is sent to the user.

We won't be examining ASP.NET code in this book because the code works transparently. However, if you fall in love with ASP.NET and decide to devote yourself to web development, you might want to take a closer look under the hood. To do so, click on the HTML button at the bottom of the Web Form display. Figure 12-12 shows the ASP.NET markup that defines the controls and layout for the MetricConverter page.

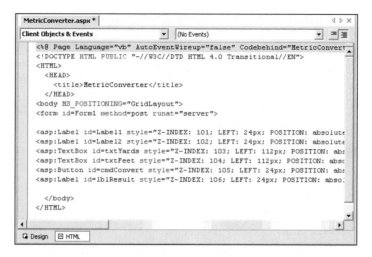

Figure 12-12: ASP.NET code for the MetricConverter

A sample ASP.NET tag is shown here:

```
<asp:label id=lblYards runat="server">Yards:</asp:label>
```

To see the HTML *output* that the web server generates from this ASP.NET code, run the program in your browser, and look at the source. To do this in Internet Explorer, you select View • Source from the menu. Figure 12-13 shows the HTML output ASP.NET sends to the client for the MetricConverter page. It's similar, but different from the original ASP.NET tags, which can only be understood by the ASP.NET engine, and not by ordinary Internet browsers.

Figure 12-13: HTML output for the MetricConverter

The best part about all of this is that you don't need to understand the quirky details of HTML, because the ASP.NET engine on the web server takes care of it for you. For example, if you create a TextBox web control, ASP.NET might use an HTML text box, password box, or text area element, depending on the properties you've set. Similarly, you can use advanced controls, such as the Calendar control, even though there are no direct equivalents in HTML code. In this case, the ASP.NET engine will use several HTML elements to create the control, and will handle all the processing and redirecting of events.

NOTE *This point is so amazing that I have to repeat it. If you know anything about HTML elements, forget it now. Not only will the ASP.NET engine translate your Web form flawlessly every time, it can also circumvent some the ugliest limitations of the HTML language.*

View State

You probably take it for granted that the values in the two text boxes in the MetricConverter program remain after you click the Convert button. This is intuitively how we expect an application to work—but it's not the way that traditional ASP pages worked.

Ordinarily, every time your page makes a round trip to the server (for instance, when an event occurs), all the information entered in the user interface controls is lost. This is because the web page is essentially recreated from scratch every time the user requests it. ASP.NET just loads the .aspx template to set up the initial page appearance, runs the appropriate event handler code to respond to the current action, and then returns the final HTML output.

Losing information can be a traumatizing experience for users, so ASP developers have traditionally toiled long and hard to make the controls store and reload data. The great news with ASP.NET is that the server can perform this chore by recording information about the current state of web page controls in a hidden field on the web page. This hidden field is then transmitted back to the server with each postback. ASP.NET automatically uses this information to fill your control objects with the appropriate data before it runs your event handling code. The end result is completely transparent, and your code can safely assume that information is retained in every control, as it would be in an ordinary Windows application.

You can see the information in this hidden field by looking at the HTML page in Notepad or another text editor. Information in view state is lightly encrypted to prevent the casual user from being able to tell what it contains.

```
<input type="hidden" name="__VIEWSTATE" value="dDwyMzc0MTY5ODU7Oz4=" />
```

In order for a control to maintain its state, its EnableViewState property must be set to True (the default). This property doesn't just apply to user input controls, but to any control that you can modify in code, including labels, buttons, and lists. If you are absolutely sure that a control doesn't need to maintain state (for example, a label that always has the same static text and never changes), you can set the EnableViewState property to False. This may speed up your web page a little, as there will be less information to be transmitted in each web request, but the effect is usually minor with simple controls.

The Page Processing Cycle

To make sure that you understand view state, it helps to consider the actual life cycle of a web page.

1. The page is posted back when the user clicks a button or modifies an AutoPostback control.

2. ASP.NET recreates the page object using the .aspx file.

3. ASP.NET retrieves state information from the hidden view state field, and fills the controls. Any control that does not maintain state will be left with its initial (default) value.

4. The Page.Load event occurs.

5. The appropriate event handling code runs (such as the Click event for a button or TextChanged event for a textbox).

6. ASP.NET creates the HTML output for the final page and sends it to the client.

7. The Page.Unload event occurs and the web page object is unloaded from memory.

Note that the Page.Load event occurs every time the page is posted back, because the page is essentially being recreated from scratch with each user request. If you use this event to do some page initialization, be sure to check the Web form's IsPostBack property first, as shown here:

```
Private Sub Page_Load(ByVal sender As System.Object, _
   ByVal e As System.EventArgs) Handles MyBase.Load
    If IsPostback Then
        ' Do nothing, this is a postback.
    Else
        ' The page is loading for the first time,
        ' so you can perform any required initialization.
        txtFeet.Text = "0"
        txtYards.Text = "0"
    End If
End Sub
```

Other Controls

As with the Windows Forms engine, Microsoft provides a full complement of controls for Web Forms. Here's a quick overview of some of the most useful:

Controls for Web Forms

Function	Control	Description
Text display (read-only)	Label	Displays text that users can't edit.
Text edit	TextBox	Displays text that users can edit.
Selection from a list	DropDownList	Allows users to either select from a list, or to enter text as in a standard combo box.
	ListBox	Displays a list of choices. Optionally, the list can allow multiple selections.
Graphics display	Image	Displays an image.
	AdRotator	Displays a sequence (predefined or random) of images, which usually correspond to separate banner advertisements.
Value setting	CheckBox	Displays a standard checkbox.
	RadioButton	Displays a standard option button.
Date setting	Calendar	Displays a calendar that allows the user to select a date and browse from month to month. Extensively configurable (much more than the Windows DateTimePicker control)—you can even add text into individual date cells or make certain dates un-selectable.
Commands	Button	Displays a button that the user can click to cause a postback and run some code.
	LinkButton	Like a button, but it has the appearance of a hyperlink.
	ImageButton	Like a button, but it incorporates an image instead of text.
Navigation control	HyperLink	Creates a web navigation link that gets your user to another page.
Table controls	Table	Creates a standard HTML table. You can configure this table in code by adding rows and columns, but these changes will not be persisted in view state and remembered across postbacks.

(continued on next page)

Controls for Web Forms (continued)

Function	Control	Description
Grouping other controls	CheckBoxList	Creates a collection of checkboxes. The HTML code doesn't know that they are related, but ASP.NET does.
	Panel	Creates a borderless box on the form that serves as a container for other controls.
	RadioButtonList	Creates a grouping of radio buttons. Inside the group, only one button can be selected.
List controls	Repeater	Displays information (usually from a database) using a set of HTML elements and controls that you specify, repeating the elements once for each record in the DataSet. A powerful tool for some custom database viewing/editing applications.
	DataList	Like the Repeater control, but with more formatting and layout options, including the ability to display information in a table. The DataList control comes with pre-built editing capabilities.
	DataGrid	Like the DataList, but even more powerful, with the ability for automatic paging, sorting, and editing. It's designed to display information from a data source (like a DataSet).

Thinking about State

There is one area where web programming is completely unlike Windows programming. HTTP, the protocol used to communicate over the Internet, is stateless, which means that it does not maintain connections.

Anatomy of a Web Request

In a typical web request, the client's browser connects to the web server and requests a page. As soon as the page is delivered, the connection is broken, and the web server immediately forgets everything it ever knew about the client. This method of communication is highly efficient. Because a client needs to be connected for only a few seconds, a typical web server can easily handle thousands of requests without a performance hit. However, life gets a little more interesting when you want your web server to be involved not only in displaying content, but also in running a web application.

In the world of ASP, every time a new web request was made, your program had to store every piece of information that it needed and reload it as required. In ASP.NET, there are some pre-built state management features that make the web request process a lot easier. You've already seen how view state manages the state of user controls for you automatically. The next step is to learn how to harness it for storing your own information, like private form variables.

Witnessing the Problem

To see what can happen when your web server needs to display content and run a web application simultaneously, we'll return to our MetricConverter program, and make the small enhancement shown in the following code. Our intention is to use the private variable Counter to keep track of how many times the user performs a conversion.

```
Private Counter As Integer

Private Sub cmdConvert_Click(ByVal sender As System.Object, _
  ByVal e As System.EventArgs) Handles cmdConvert.Click
    Dim Inches, Metres As Single
    Inches = 36 * Val(txtYards.Text) + 12 * Val(txtFeet.Text)
    Metres = Inches / 39.37
    lblResult.Text = "Result: " & Metres.ToString() & " metres. "

    Counter += 1
    lblResult.Text &= Counter.ToString() & " conversions performed."
End Sub
```

If you try this code out, you'll see that it doesn't work the way we intended. The counter never rises above a value of 1, because with each new web request, the Counter variable is discarded and recreated.

Clearly, in order to keep track of the counter in between requests, the server will need to store the Counter variable in its memory. However, in a scenario with hundreds of users and operations that require a lot more persistence than a single integer, the server might quickly run out of memory (or at least start to show reduced performance). There are several ways to solve this problem. The easiest is to use a special collection feature called the *State Bag*.

Using the State Bag

The State Bag is an extension of the view state capability that allows an ASP.NET application to automatically refresh its controls. Every time you enable the MaintainState property for a control, you're telling ASP.NET to keep track of the control's information in the State Bag. But you can also add and retrieve values to the State Bag ourselves, including arrays and even DataSets! As with our controls, this information is encoded in hidden fields and sent back from the client with each round trip.

Here's a code example:

```
Private Sub cmdConvert_Click(ByVal sender As System.Object, _
  ByVal e As System.EventArgs) Handles cmdConvert.Click
    Dim Inches, Metres As Single
    Inches = 36 * Val(txtYards.Text) + 12 * Val(txtFeet.Text)
    Metres = Inches / 39.37
    lblResult.Text = "Result: " & Metres.ToString() & " metres. "
```

```
    ' Retrieve the state information.
    Counter = CType(ViewState("Counter"), Integer)

    ' Update the counter and display the result.
    Counter += 1
    lblResult.Text &= Counter.ToString() & " conversions performed."

    ' Store the new value.
    ViewState("Counter") = Counter
End Sub
```

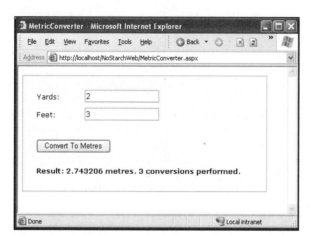

Figure 12-14: A MetricConverter with State Management

As you can see, every item in the state bag is indexed by a name. (This example uses the name Counter.) When you assign information to a state value that doesn't exist, it's created automatically. If you try to retrieve a state value that doesn't exist, you'll just end up with a null value.

If you mistype the name of an item in the State Bag, you won't receive an error; you'll just receive blank space. A good way to help safeguard yourself is to create properties for every item in the State Bag, as shown next. (To refresh your memory about properties, review Chapter 5.)

```
Private Property Counter() As Integer
    Get
        Return CType(ViewState("Counter"), Integer)
    End Get
    Set (ByVal Value As Integer)
        ViewState("Counter") = Value
    End Set
End Property
```

Are there any drawbacks to this method? The State Bag is an excellent way to store information without affecting web server performance. However, there are a few things you might want to consider:

- Even though State Bag information is scrambled in the hidden field, it's transmitted back and forth across the Internet without secure encryption. This means that you shouldn't use the State Bag for extremely sensitive or confidential information.
- The State Bag is stored in the HTML output, and can slow down transmission times, both when receiving the page and when sending it as part of postback.
- The State Bag relies on the hidden field in the current Web form. If your user navigates to a different Web form, you'll need a method of passing information from one form to another. This is the issue we'll discuss next.

Transferring Information

So far you've learned enough to create a basic, one-page web application. But what happens in a multi-page project? Unlike the Windows Forms engine, the Web Forms feature won't let you display a new page by invoking another form's Show method. In fact, you can't refer to another form at all. Instead, you must use the Web form's filename in a URL.

There are two basic ways to navigate to another page:

- Use the Hyperlink web control.
- Use the built in Redirect method of the built in Response object, as in `Response.Redirect("WebPage2.aspx")`. Because the new Web form will be in the same directory as the current Web form, you don't need to enter a full URL (such as http://www.mysite.com/myapplication/WebPage2.aspx).

The only problem is that these new pages won't have the benefit of our special hidden field, and so they won't be able to access the State Bag. And if we navigate back to the original page with another hyperlink or Response.Redirect command, we'll start over again with a blank web page and no stored information.

Passing Information in the Query String

If you've ever studied the URL bar in your web browser while exploring popular sites, you might have noticed the appearance of some extra information. For example, after you perform a search in Yahoo!, the URL looks a little like this:

```
http://search.yahoo.com/search?p=dogs
```

Clearly, the first part of this line is telling your browser where it should connect. The interesting part occurs after the question mark. The user in this case has entered a search looking for websites about dogs, and Yahoo! has stored this information in the URL, under the variable p. This type of augmentation is called a *query string*, and you can use it in ASP.NET.

Programming the Query String

The query string is similar to the State Bag in that it contains a list of name/value pairs that you can retrieve from a collection. However, the only way you can add to the query string is by supplying a new URL, with the appropriate values added at the end of the browser string. You could do this with a hyperlink, or by using the Response.Redirect command.

For example, consider a modified MetricConverter that displays the conversion results in a separate page, by passing the information in a query string. Here's the code that executes when the user clicks the Convert button:

```
Private Sub cmdConvert_Click(ByVal sender As System.Object, _
  ByVal e As System.EventArgs) Handles cmdConvert.Click
    Dim QueryString As String
    QueryString = "?Yards=" & txtYards.Text & "&Feet=" & txtFeet.Text

    ' Send the information to the QueryStringResult page
    ' and redirect the user there.
    Response.Redirect("QueryStringResult.aspx" & QueryString)
End Sub
```

Note that to pass more than one value in the query string, you need to separate it with an ampersand (&) symbol.

The QueryStringResult.aspx page processes this information in a Page.Load event handler, and displays the output shown in Figure 12-15.

```
Private Sub Page_Load(ByVal sender As System.Object, _
  ByVal e As System.EventArgs) Handles MyBase.Load

        ' Retrieve the query string information.
        Dim Feet, Yards As Single
        Feet = Val(Request.QueryString("Feet"))
        Yards = Val(Request.QueryString("Yards"))

        ' Perform the calculation
        Dim Inches, Metres As Single
        Inches = 36 * Yards + 12 * Feet
        Metres = Inches / 39.37

        ' Display the result
        lblResult.Text = Yards.ToString() & " yards + " & Feet.ToString()
        lblResult.Text &= " feet = " & Metres.ToString() & " metres. "

End Sub
```

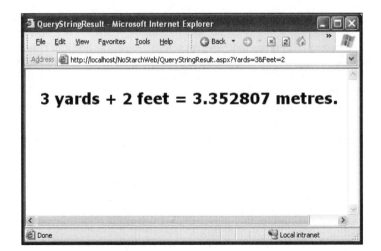

Figure 12-15: The QueryStringResult.aspx page

Best of all, the query string stores information without affecting the performance of your web server, just like the State Bag.

The query string is often used to display detailed information about a specific item. For example, you might have a page that displays a catalog of products, and allows the user to choose a product to view additional information. Upon selecting a product, the user would be redirected to another page, and a query string argument would be set to specify the selected product (as in ?ProductID=34). The Page.Load event handling code in the new page would open the file or database, retrieve the appropriate product information, and display it.

Convenient as it is, there are some drawbacks to using the query string that you might want to consider.

- The amount of information you can store is limited. To ensure compatibility with all browsers, you shouldn't make the query string more than about 1000 bytes.

- The information is extremely insecure. Not only it is transmitted in clear text over the Internet, but it's also clearly visible to the person using your application. In fact, it might be too visible . . . giving the user the opportunity to alter information by changing the query string manually, or just revealing too much about how your program works and what variables it stores.

- You can't store complex information in the query string. Everything is stored as a string, meaning arrays and objects won't work.

If you need to get around these limitations, you have another option. You can use Session state to store information in the server's memory.

Using Session State

Session state is one of the most useful tools for tracking information. It stores user-specific information that's available to every Web form in your application.

A session begins when a user navigates to a page in your web application. A session ends when you end it programmatically (Session.Abandon), or when it times out after the web server stops receiving requests from the user. The standard timeout is about twenty minutes, but you can configure this default using the web.config file, by modifying the highlighted line in the section shown below (the other lines configure advanced session state features designed for hosting web applications on multiple web servers).

```
<sessionState
        mode="InProc"
        stateConnectionString="tcpip=127.0.0.1:42424"
        sqlConnectionString="data source=127.0.0.1;user id=sa;password="
        cookieless="false"
        timeout="20"
/>
```

Finding the right timeout interval is not as easy as it seems. You don't want to erase a user's information too quickly, in case the user returns and need to start over again. However, you also don't want to waste any of the memory on your server and potentially make life difficult for other users.

How Session State Works

Session information is stored on the server. Even after the client receives a web page and breaks its connection, session information remains floating in memory on the web server. When the client reconnects by clicking a control or requesting a new page, the web server looks up the user's session information and makes it available to your code. The whole process is automatic, and generally works because the web server stores a small information file (or *cookie*) on the client's computer that uniquely identifies that user.

Programming Session State

To create a MetricConverter page that uses session state instead of view state doesn't take very much effort. We're still using a collection of name/value pairs, except that this time they are stored in the built-in Session object. Remember, session information will be accessible from any web page in your web application (typically, any other .aspx file in this virtual directory).

```
Private Sub cmdConvert_Click(ByVal sender As System.Object, _
  ByVal e As System.EventArgs) Handles cmdConvert.Click
    Dim Inches, Metres As Single
    Inches = 36 * Val(txtYards.Text) + 12 * Val(txtFeet.Text)
    Metres = Inches / 39.37
    lblResult.Text = "Result: " & Metres.ToString() & " metres. "

    ' Retrieve the state information.
    Counter = CType(Session("Counter"), Integer)

    ' Update the counter and display the result.
    Counter += 1
    lblResult.Text &= Counter.ToString() & " conversions performed."

    ' Store the new value.
    Session("Counter") = Counter
End Sub
```

Because session information is stored on the server, and never transmitted to the client, Session state is more secure than any of the other kinds of state management I've discussed. It also allows you to store just about any type of information you need, including objects. However, Session state does come with one potential drawback: It consumes server memory. Even a small amount of information can occupy extensive server resources if hundreds or thousands of users are using the web application simultaneously. To help reduce problems, you'll have to follow these guidelines:

- **Acquire late, release early**. Store information only when you need it, and release it as soon as you don't. (In the preceding example, we would use the line Session("Counter").Remove to release our state information.)

- **Consider all state possibilities**. Before you store information in Session state, consider if it would be better suited for the State Bag.

- **Reduce the amount of information you need**. Store only what you need. It sounds simple, but you would be amazed how many problems can occur when a web application decides to store multiple DataSets in server memory.

Using Application State

Application state is identical to Session state, except that it applies to the whole application, not just a single user. Once you add something to the built-in Application object, it's available to all users for the entire lifetime of your web application. (Generally, your web application's lifetime is as long as the server is running. Once it's started, it won't stop on its own.) For example, if we stored our Counter in Application state, we could track the combined number of times that every user has clicked the Calculate button.

Unfortunately Application state isn't quite as simple as it seems. For one thing, you can run into problems if multiple users try to modify a variable with Application state at the same time. To get around this, you can use the Application object's Lock and Unlock method, as shown here, but this method can cause a significant slowdown in a multi-user scenario.

```
' Store the new value.
Application.Lock()
Application("Counter") = Counter.ToString()
Application.Unlock()
```

It's probably best to avoid using Application state unless you absolutely need it. And don't try to use Application state to store important information to increase performance. It's much better to use ASP.NET's caching features. For more information, read up on the built-in Response.Cache object in the MSDN help files.

Where Are All These Built-in Objects Coming From?

It probably seems pretty convenient that I pull out a new built-in object each time you need a different kind of state management. To get the lowdown on exactly how this is possible, you need to know a little bit about the object structure of an ASP.NET application. All the built-in objects are provided through references in the System.Web.UI.Page class, which is the basis for every ASP.NET page, as shown here in Figure 12-16.

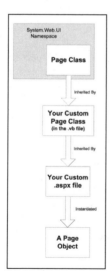

Figure 12-16: The System.Web.UI.Page class

The Page class is fully described in the .NET class reference included in the MSDN help files.

A Summary of Different Types of State Management

Type of state management	Scope	Storage Location	Lifetime	Security
State Bag (includes View State)	The current page and user.	A hidden field in the current page	Lost when you browse to another page.	Insecure, but cannot be modified by the user.
Query String	The specified page and user, although it can be passed along from page to page if your code redirects the user.	The browser's URL string	Lost when you type in a new URL or close the browser. However, can be stored between sessions in a bookmark.	Insecure, and can be modified by the user.
Session state	The entire application for the current user.	Server memory	Times out after a predefined period.	Secure
Application state	The entire application; shared with all users.	Server memory	Never times out; remains until you remove it.	Secure
Your own cookies	The entire application for the current user.	Client's computer	Set by the programmer, and can persist between visits.	Insecure, and can be modified by the user.
Database	The entire application; shared with all users.	Server hard drive	Permanent unless removed.	Secure

We haven't discussed the last two options in this table, because they require more programming work than the others. They tend to be specialty items.

- Cookies are small files that are stored on the client computer to remember items of information. They are similar in function and use to other state management methods, and, like the query string, they can only contain strings. The only difference is that every cookie includes an expiration date that you can use to store information for long periods of time (for example, in between customer visits). You use a cookie by creating an instance of the HttpCookie class, and using the Response.AppendCookie method to add it to the Response object's cookie collection.

- Server-side database storage requires custom programming logic, and isn't supported by any special built-in objects. It's an extremely flexible system, but you have to design all the logic from scratch. If you've read Chapter 9 about databases, you already know everything you need.

Data Binding

Before this chapter ends, I want to add a few words about data binding, which represents a convenient way to retrieve and display information from a database in an ASP.NET application. Data binding works quite a bit differently with ASP.NET than in does in a Windows application. When you use data binding with a web control, the information can only travel in one direction. It flows from the data source into the control, where it becomes ordinary content. Any modifications to the control do not affect the original DataSet—in fact, the original DataSet ceases to exist as soon as the operation is complete and the page is presented to the user.

Web controls work differently in this regard because they are designed for optimal web application performance. Even with this limitation, data binding still provides a very useful way for retrieving information from a database and displaying it in a web page with a minimum amount of coding. Best of all, the ADO.NET data access code is identical whether you are programming for the web or the desktop.

The online examples contain a simple ASP.NET page called DataBinding.aspx that demonstrates data binding in action (Figure 12-17). It binds a drop-down list, checkbox list, and DataGrid control.

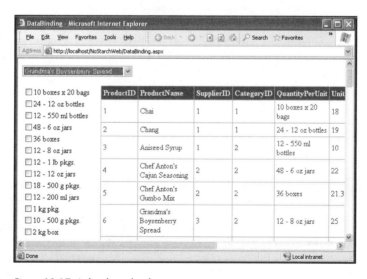

Figure 12-17: A data-bound web page

The most noticeable difference in the code is that you must explicitly trigger data binding, either by calling a control's DataBind method, or by calling the page's DataBind method to bind the entire page at once. It's at this point that the web controls are filled. If you forget to call this method, the controls will never be filled.

```
Private Sub Page_Load(ByVal sender As System.Object, _
  ByVal e As System.EventArgs) Handles MyBase.Load

    Dim Connect As String = "Data Source=localhost;Integrated Security=SSPI;" & _
      "Initial Catalog=Northwind;"
    Dim con As New SqlConnection(Connect)
    Dim SQL As String = "SELECT * FROM Products"
    Dim cmd As New SqlCommand(SQL, con)
    Dim adapter As New SqlDataAdapter(cmd)
    Dim dsNorthwind As New DataSet()

    con.Open()
    adapter.Fill(dsNorthwind, "Products")
    con.Close()

    ' Bind the grid.
    gridDB.DataSource = dsNorthwind.Tables("Products")

    ' Bind the drop-down list to the ProductName field.
    lstName.DataSource = dsNorthwind.Tables("Products")
    lstName.DataTextField = "ProductName"

    ' Bind the checkbox list to the QuantityPerUnit field.
    lstQuantity.DataSource = dsNorthwind.Tables("Products")
    lstQuantity.DataTextField = "QuantityPerUnit"

    ' Move the information from the DataSet into the controls.
    Me.DataBind()

End Sub
```

NOTE *When you bind to multiple controls at once in a Windows application, the controls are automatically synchronized. If you select a record in one control, the corresponding information appears in all the other controls. This is not the case in ASP.NET, where the controls act ordinarily (as though they had been filled manually). That is because data binding in ASP.NET only exists while the page is being processed. When the final HTML output is received by the client, only ordinary HTML content remains.*

What Comes Next?

ASP.NET almost qualifies as a programming language of its own. If you work with the concepts in this chapter, you're well on your way to creating substantial web applications. However, if you want to become an ASP.NET guru, there are a few topics you might want to start exploring:

- Performance can be critical when you're working on the Internet. Seemingly small changes can increase efficiency quite a bit. To improve performance, you might want to use the caching feautures. You can read up on the System.Web.Caching.Cache class in the help files.

- Get to know all the web controls you have to choose from, and try them out. As you become more experienced, you might even create your own. Controls like the Calendar, DataGrid, and AdRotator completely hide the underlying HTML reality.

- As indicated earlier in the chapter, once you create a form in the Web Form Designer, it's translated into an ASP.NET-enriched flavor of HTML. To get a glimpse at what's going on underneath the hood, and get a subtler understanding of ASP.NET, click the HTML button in the Web Form Designer.

- Many web applications involve databases, and there's a lot you can do with data binding to get information out of a database and into HTML format with a minimum of code. Review Chapter 9 for some hints, check the MSDN library for information about creating templates for controls like the DataGrid and DataList, and then start experimenting!

- And lastly, if you're interested in reading an entirely separate book that delves into web programming, you could do worse than my own *ASP.NET: The Complete Reference*, available from Osborne McGraw-Hill.

13

WEB SERVICES

Web Services are a new introduction to Visual Basic .NET, and are being touted by Microsoft as a new and revolutionary way to program with the Internet. All this excitement raises the inevitable question: Are Web Services really the future of programming, and a sound career investment, or are they doomed to become the "next great thing" that wasn't?

A little background on the subject should help us find the answers. First of all, the concept of Web Services hasn't been created by Microsoft. It represents an exciting new area that several companies are clamoring to gain control of, including such heavyweights as Sun Microsystems and IBM. However, Microsoft has been planning their implementation of Web Services for quite a while, and it shows. Microsoft has made Web Services incredibly easy to program in .NET, while retaining the ability to let Web Services work seamlessly across different browsers and operating systems. A great deal of thought has gone into Web Services, and there is good reason to believe that they are destined to become another powerful tool in the advanced programmer's arsenal, along with ActiveX, COM, and other revolutionary technologies from the past.

This chapter starts by asking "What is a Web Service?" and takes you through the process of creating, deploying, and interacting with one. Luckily, .NET makes Web Services so quick and convenient that you can be creating simple examples in no time at all. However, it may take many more months of experimentation before you start to realize all of the possible ways Web Services can be used. The end of this chapter includes some helpful web links to live examples of Web Services.

New in .NET

Web Services are making their debut in Visual Studio .NET—they haven't existed in any form before. Some developers may have created custom Web Service implementations using Microsoft's SOAP toolkit, but only for highly specialized applications.

In fact, Web Services are so new and so promising that they are sometimes identified synonymously with the entire .NET platform. Of course, now that you have read Chapter 1 of this book, you know what .NET is really about. How large a part Web Services will play in Microsoft's strategy of integrating languages, embracing open standards, and programming the Internet remains to be seen.

The Vision of the Interactive Web

What is a Web Service anyway? Clearly, many sites on the Internet provide useful "services." A common example is a shipping company, which allows you to look up the location and delivery date of packages using a tracking number. Is this a Web Service?

The delivery date lookup meets one of the criteria of a Web Service—it's a discrete unit of functionality that serves a single purpose: returning information about your package. But in order to get this information, you have to navigate to the correct HTML page, select an option from a menu, and then enter your tracking number. In other words, you have to use an Internet application—represented by the shipping company's website—in order to get the information you need.

Web Services: COM for the Internet?

One of the great developments in Windows programming was COM (some parts of which are also called ActiveX), a technology that allows code components to be easily shared among applications. When COM was introduced, it added flexibility. Instead of using monolithic applications, custom utilities could be created that reused a subset of all the capabilities provided in COM components.

In this respect, Web Services are like COM for the Internet. With a Web Service, you can take a unit of logic in a web application, and allow it to be seamlessly accessed and used by other Windows or Internet applications, in a variety of different ways. A Web Service is like a business object: It accepts information and returns information. Your program uses Web Services, without needing to involve the user, and takes care of providing the appropriate user interface. This is particularly important in the world of the Internet, where a user might be accessing information from a full-featured Internet Explorer browser, or from a stripped down interface on a cell phone or other wireless device. In this case, the Web Service used would be the same, but a different application would take care of the display. Like a COM object, a Web Service doesn't need to be tied to any specific interface.

In one important way, however, Web Services are *not* like COM technology. COM relies on a proprietary Windows standard, which means that it's useless for Macintosh computers, UNIX systems, or any other non-Microsoft platform.

Web Services, however, are built on open standards such as SOAP, XML, and WSDL, which will be described in this chapter. This means that any application can interact with them (though none so easily as a .NET application), and that they can transmit data painlessly over HTTP. Because data is exchanged in a text XML format, there's also no problem sending a Web Service request or receiving its response, even when the Web Service is behind a corporate firewall.

Web Services Today

You are probably already making use of "first generation" Web Services. These are examples of Internet procedures that are integrated into desktop programs, but require company-specific and site-specific standards. For example, you may use a personal finance desktop application that can automatically retrieve stock portfolio information from the Internet. This type of application retrieves information from the Internet, and doesn't bother you with the details of the process. However, it relies on having information provided in a specific way, which was been planned and set up in advance, according to the particular application. It does not use an independent, widely accepted standard, as Web Services will with .NET. As a consequence, other applications can't easily extend or work with its functions and features. They must be recreated for every application that require them.

Now imagine a world with thousands of Web Service components, where a desktop application has access to all kind of features that require up-to-the-minute information from the Web. In all likelihood, everyone will have some type of "always on" broadband Internet access, and you won't even be aware when your application is interacting with the Web. Programmers will no longer have to try and constantly redesign off-the-cuff solutions that schedule Internet downloads or parse HTML files manually, looking for specific information.

Of course, that's the future. Today, Web Services will allow you to further modularize Internet applications, and provide components that can be consumed and reused by any other application. Web Services can also use authentication and login procedures, allowing you to support various subscription models. In other words, you can sell units of application functionality to other developers, just like programmers sell ActiveX controls today.

Are Web Services Objects?

Web Services are *not* objects, at least not in the traditional sense of the word. The main distinction is that Web Services don't maintain state, unless you specifically take extra steps to store information in a database or ASP.NET's Session state collection. In fact, a Web Service that maintains state is rarely a good idea because it means the web server must allocate a portion of its precious memory for each client, which can quickly impose a noticeable performance penalty as the number of clients increases.

Web Services also don't support object-oriented basics like overloaded functions and property procedures. Constructors work, but the Web Service class is destroyed and reconstructed with each request, even if the client maintains a reference. This makes sure that Web Services perform well, but it also means that they can't be used like a local business object. It's best to think of a Web Service as a utility class made up of shared members. You can call a remote function to get a piece of information, but you shouldn't expect to keep a Web Service around and store information in it.

Creating Your First Web Service

Creating a Web Service is easier than you might think. All you have to do is create a class that incorporates some useful functions. This class should inherit from the System.Web.Services.WebService class (for maximum convenience), and all the methods that are going to be made available over the Web must be marked with <WebMethod> attributes.

To start creating this application, begin a new project and choose ASP.NET Web Service. A series of support files will be created, as with an ASP.NET application. The actual Web Service is contained in the .asmx file (named Service1.asmx by default). The design view of the .asmx file isn't used, but the code view will start off with a couple of sample lines needed to define the Web Service class.

> **NOTE** *A Web Service, like the ASP.NET applications we saw in the previous chapter, must be hosted on a web server in a virtual directory. The Web Service examples for this chapter are contained in the NoStarchWeb virtual directory. Web Service clients, on the other hand, can be located in any directory.*

Now consider a very rudimentary example of a Web Service class for providing information about a package tracked with a shipping company:

```
Imports System.Web.Services

Public Class PostalWebService
  Inherits System.Web.Services.WebService

    <WebMethod> Public Function GetDeliveryDate(ByVal TrackID As String) As Date
        Dim PackageInfo As Package
        PackageInfo = GetPackageRecordFromDB(TrackID)
        Return PackageInfo.Date
    End Function

    Private Function GetPackageRecordFromDB(ByVal TrackID As String) As Package
        ' Some database access code here.
    End Function

End Class

Public Class Package
    Public PackageID As String
    Public DeliveryDate As Date
End Class
```

The Package class encapsulates information about a package. Notice that it doesn't inherit from WebService class or use the <WebMethod> attribute because it isn't a Web Service. Instead, it is used internally in the PostalWebService class, to pass information.

The PostalWebService class has two functions. The GetDeliveryDate function is marked with a special attribute, <WebMethod>, which indicates that it will be provided in the public interface of the Web Service. No other functions are available. GetPackageRecordFromDB is used internally by your code to get information, but it is not made available to any clients.

Now, believe it or not, any application using this Web Service will have access to the features and operations of the GetDeliveryDate function. All you need is a class that inherits from the basic WebService class, and uses the <WebMethod> attribute. Could it be any easier?

Touching Up Your Web Service

To improve your Web Service, you might want to add a description to the <WebMethod()> attribute. This description may be displayed for the client developing the application that will use your Web Service, depending on the type of development tool they are using.

```
<WebMethod(Description:="Use this function to ...")>
```

You should also specify a namespace for your Web Service. Ideally, your namespace should be uniquely identified with you—your company name, for example, or best of all, your web address. If you do not specify a namespace, the default (http://tempuri.org/) will be used. Be aware that this is an XML namespace, not a .NET namespace. An XML namespace looks like an URL, but it doesn't need to correspond to a valid Internet location (although it often does). XML namespaces are just used to distinguish portions of an XML document.

To specify a namespace, change the first line of your class declaration to use the WebService attribute:

```
<WebService(Namespace:="http://mycompany.com/post")> _
Public Class PostalWebService
```

Enhancing the PostalWebService class

You can also make a more useful Web Service that returns a custom object with several pieces of information at once, as shown in the following example. Notice that the Package information has been separated into two classes; we'll assume here that you will not want to provide the entire database record to the client, in case it includes sensitive information (such as a credit card number).

```
Public Class PostalWebService
  Inherits System.Web.Services.WebService

    <WebMethod> Public Function GetPackageInfo(ByVal TrackID As String) _
      As ClientPackageInfo
        Dim PackageInfo As Package
        PackageInfo = GetPackageRecordFromDB(TrackID)
        Return PackageInfo.BasicInfo
    End Function

    Private Function GetPackageRecordFromDB(ByVal TrackID As String) As Package
        ' Some database access code here.
        Dim PackageInfo As New Package()

        ' To perform a crude test, uncomment the following two lines.
        ' PackageInfo.BasicInfo.PackageID = TrackID
        ' PackageInfo.BasicInfo.DeliveryDate = Now

        Return PackageInfo
    End Function

End Class

Public Class Package
    Public BasicInfo As New ClientPackageInfo
    Public CreditCardNumber As String
End Class

Public Class ClientPackageInfo
    Public PackageID As String
    Public DeliveryDate As Date
End Class
```

Database and OOP mavens will realize that there are many different ways to implement this type of scenario. (You may also wonder why the credit card is stored with each package.) In a real world example, security concerns will shape the whole construction of the database.

In any case, this example demonstrates that a .NET Web Service can pass many types of information to the client, including DataSets, .NET objects, arrays, and simple variables. Keep in mind, however, that if you were to pass an object with a built-in method, the method would be lost. Only the data is preserved.

Testing Your Web Service

So now that you have created a Web Service, how can you use it? Or maybe you're still wondering exactly what is provided with the Web Service we've created. Fortunately, Internet Explorer includes a handy feature that allows you to preview and perform a limited test on any Web Service.

Your Web Service in Action

To try out this useful feature, run your Web Service. Remember, Web Services are designed to be used from inside other applications, not executed directly. However, when you choose to run a Web Service in Visual Studio .NET, your browser will display the test page shown in Figure 13-1.

Figure 13-1: The Internet Explorer test page

This window lists all the available Web Service methods. (In this case, only one, GetPackageInfo, is available.) The Service Descriptions link will display the WSDL description of your Web Service. (WSDL is described in the next section of this chapter.)

Click on the GetPackageInfo link, and the following test page will appear:

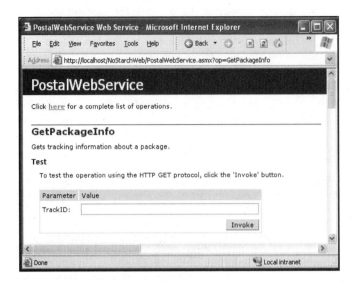

Figure 13-2: Testing a Web Service method

Ignore the puzzling XML code at the bottom of the page for now, and concentrate on the first portion of the page, which provides a prefabricated way for you to test your application. Try it by entering a package ID and clicking on Invoke. If you've entered the preceding example, and uncommented the hard-coded package values, you will receive the result shown in Figure 13-3.

Figure 13-3: A Web Service response

At this point you'll probably start to wonder if your Web Service has worked at all. However, on close examination, it turns out that the appropriate information is present; it's just been marked up in a special XML format. What you have received is a translated version of the ClientPackageInfo class. The class is marked with a beginning and an ending tag, and inside are the members, including a PackageID and a DeliveryDate field.

You don't need to understand the format of this information if you are programming in Visual Basic .NET. As you'll discover later in this chapter, .NET provides special utilities that abstract away this layer of XML. These features allow you to call a Web Service and retrieve its data as thought it were a local function inside your application. However, understanding this format can give you some additional insight into what's really going on with Web Services.

The Open Standards Plumbing

Much of the excitement over Web Services results from the fact that they are built on open standards. It's this foundation that makes them more flexible and extensible than previous attempts at allowing distributed component-based programming, including such existing standards as DCOM (Microsoft's own Distributed COM), and RMI (Java's Remote Method Invocation).

XML and WSDL

Web Services use remote function calls written in XML language. XML language is ideally suited to Web Services because it is text-based, which means that unlike binary data, for instance, it can easily flow over normal HTTP channels on the Internet without getting stopped by corporate firewalls. XML is also excellent because it is self-describing, and it provides a way to identify (or "mark up") information.

XML, however, is only the starting point. XML is just a tool for describing data, much as SQL is a tool for accessing databases. Both are generic, and both can be used in countless different ways. What is needed is an agreed-upon standard for encoding information in XML, guaranteeing that other clients will be able to decode the information by following a uniform set of rules.

The standard way of describing your .NET Web Services is WSDL, an XML-based language that has been accepted by Microsoft, IBM, and a host of other vendors. If you want to find out all the low-level details of WSDL, you can read up on it at http://msdn.microsoft.com/xml/general/wsdl.asp. However, for most developers, these details won't hold any more interest than the kinds of technology that underlie many of the other aspects of the .NET platform. What is more interesting is examining the WSDL information that Visual Basic .NET generates automatically for your particular Web Service. To display this information, click on the Service Description link on the Internet Explorer Web Service test page. You'll see a lengthy—and perhaps intimidating—document that describes the types and the functions used in your Web Service.

A portion of the WSDL document for the PostalWebService is shown in Figure 13-4.

Figure 13-4: Part of the WSDL document describing a Web Service

SOAP

WSDL describes your Web Service, but another standard is needed to communicate with it. In fact, there are three different ways to communicate with a Web Service. The first is HTTP GET, which Internet Explorer uses automatically when you click on Invoke on your test page. The second is HTTP POST, which is very similar to HTTP GET. Internet veterans will realize that a POST request sends information in the body of an HTTP request instead of in the query string. The final method is SOAP, which is what .NET will use transparently when you create a client later in this chapter.

SOAP is another XML-based standard, and it predates the .NET platform. Essentially, when you send information to and retrieve information from your Web Service in a .NET application, your requests and responses are packaged in the SOAP format. The SOAP format looks similar to the HTTP response we got before, but it is not identical. The test web page shows the actual format for SOAP and HTTP requests and responses when you click on a method.

Accessing a Web Service Directly

Now that you understand a little bit about the standards underlying Web Services, you may realize that you don't really need to go through the Internet Explorer test page, although it is very convenient.

To see the WSDL contract for a Web Service, just add ?WSDL after the filename in your Internet browser. This works for any .NET Web Service, including those that have been created by other developers. The Web Service WSDL contract for the PostalWebService can be retrieved with this line (assuming it's in a virtual directory called NoStarchWeb on the local computer):

```
http://localhost/NoStarchWeb/PostalWebService.asmx?WSDL
```

You can also interact with the Web Service through HTTP GET by typing the parameter list into the URL. In fact, if you enter the value 221 for the GetPackageInfo function and click Invoke, this is what Internet Explorer links to:

```
http://localhost/NoStarchWeb/PostalWebService.asmx/GetPackageInfo?TrackID=221
```

In other words, Internet Explorer just passes the function name and the TrackID parameter as part of an HTTP GET request. At this point, you might start to realize that if communicating with Web Services is this straightforward, it really is possible to access them on different operating systems and platforms.

When IIS receives a web request like the one shown above, it passes it to the ASP.NET worker process, which then creates the Web Service. The Web Service runs the appropriate function, returns the result as an XML page, and is destroyed. The end result appears as a page in your Internet browser.

The next section looks at how .NET applications consume Web Services by using SOAP calls, which allows you to retrieve the results of a Web Service in a .NET program instead of a browser.

Consuming a Web Service

At this point, you've seen your Web Service in action, but you haven't usefully incorporated it into another program. Clearly, if users had to rely on the Internet Explorer test page, they would be better off with a full-featured Internet application!

In this section you'll learn how to create a Web Service client in VB .NET. Best of all, you'll learn how to get Visual Basic .NET to create all the infrastructure code you need.

The Proxy Class

Web Service clients communicate with Web Services through a proxy class that you can create automatically with the .NET framework. The proxy class translates your actions into the appropriate SOAP calls, and then interacts with the Web Service. The whole process is seamless, so you might not have even realized it was happening if you hadn't seen the following diagram:

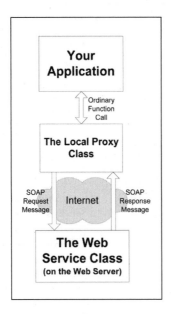

Figure 13-5: Web Service interaction

Adding a Web Reference

To create the proxy class, you need to add a web reference in Visual Basic .NET. First, add a new Windows application project to the current solution by right-clicking on the Solution Explorer and selecting Add • New Project. This project should not be created in the virtual directory where the Web Service is located because it will not be hosted on the web server.

Then, right-click on the new project and select Set As StartUpProject. Now, right-click one more time, and choose Add Web Reference. The Add Web Reference window will appear (Figure 13-6).

Figure 13-6: Adding a web reference

To add a web reference, you need to supply a discovery file. A discovery file is the first step in the interaction process; it's where an application "discovers" what Web Services are available, what methods they have, and what information they require and return.

You may have noticed that Visual Basic .NET automatically added a .vsdisco file to your Web Service project. This is the file you now need to select. Click the Web References on Local Server link. On the right, a list will appear of the discovery files residing on your current computer. If you have already created an ASP.NET application, you may find more than one discovery file. Choose the one that is in the appropriate directory.

Once you have made your selection, information will appear about the Web Services specified by the discovery document you've chosen. You can click on the View Contract button to see all the WSDL information again, or click on the Add Reference button to link to this Web Service and generate the required proxy class automatically.

Inspecting the Proxy Class

Visual Basic .NET hides the proxy class it creates from you, because you don't really need to see it or modify it directly. However, it's always a good idea to peek under the hood of an application and get a better understanding of what's really happening along the way.

To see the proxy class, select Project • Show All Files from the menu. Then, look for the folder under Web References with the .WSDL file. Double-click to expand this entry, and you'll see the Visual Basic proxy file (typically called Reference.vb), as shown in Figure 13-7.

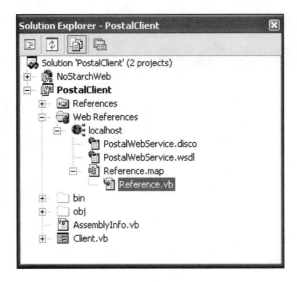

Figure 13-7: The hidden proxy class

This file includes all the methods from your WebService, in slightly modified form. It also includes the ClientPackageInfo class that you need to use to retrieve the information from the GetPackageInfo method. Interestingly, Visual Basic .NET is intelligent enough to leave out the Package class, so the client will have no idea that the Web Service uses this class internally and won't be able to snoop out its internal details.

Take a quick look at the modified version of the GetPackageInfo function contained in the proxy class. (The attributes that precede it are not included here.)

```
Public Function GetPackageInfo(ByVal TrackID As String) As ClientPackageInfo
    Dim results() As Object = Me.Invoke("GetPackageInfo", New Object() {TrackID})
    Return CType(results(0), ClientPackageInfo)
End Function
```

This function converts the TrackID input string into a generic object, and retrieves the result as a generic object, which is then converted into the appropriate ClientPackageInfo object. In between, it accesses the Web Service through the appropriate SOAP request and waits for the response, although all this is taken care of automatically in the Me.Invoke method, with the help of the .NET attributes that provide additional information to the Common Language Runtime.

Another interesting aspect of the proxy class is the constructor, which sets the URL. If you change the location of your Web Service, you can modify this method, rather than regenerating the proxy class. Notice, however, that localhost is specified, regardless of the name of your computer. Localhost is a "loopback" alias that always points to the current computer.

```
Public Sub New()
    MyBase.New
    Me.Url = "http://localhost/WebService/PostalWebService.asmx"
End Sub
```

Using the Proxy Class

The proxy class is the key to using a Web Service. Essentially, you create an instance of this class, and call the appropriate methods on it. You treat the proxy class as though it were a local class that contained the same functions and methods as the Web Service.

Add the following code to the Load event of your startup Windows Form:

```
Dim ServiceInstance As New localhost.PostalWebService()
Dim PackageInfo As New localhost.ClientPackageInfo()
PackageInfo = ServiceInstance.GetPackageInfo("221")
MessageBox.Show("Received the delivery date: " & PackageInfo.DeliveryDate)
```

Now run the application. If Visual Studio .NET loads up the Web Service web page, you have to stop the project and set the Windows application as the startup project, using the right-click menu in the Solution Explorer window.

If you have configured everything correctly, you'll see the window in Figure 13-8.

Figure 13-8: The Web Service results

Once again, the technical details are pretty sophisticated, but the actual implementation is hidden by the .NET framework. Calling a Web Service is as easy as creating one, once you have set up the web reference.

Debugging a Web Service Project

When debugging a solution that includes a Web Service project and client, you will find that any breakpoints or watches you set for the Web Service code are ignored. That is because, by default, Visual Studio .NET only loads the debug symbols for the startup project, which is the client.

To solve this problem, you need to configure Visual Studio .NET to load both projects at once. Right-click on the solution item in the Solution Explorer, and select Properties. Then, browse to the Common Properties • Startup Project tab, and specify Multiple Startup Projects, so that both your client and the Web Service will be built when you click the start button (Figure 13-9).

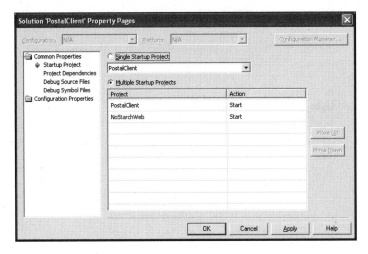

Figure 13-9: Starting multiple projects

You still need to make one more change. By default, Visual Studio .NET starts the Web Service project by displaying the Internet Explorer test page. In this case, however, you don't want any action to be taken other than loading the debug symbols so that the Web Service code is available for debugging.

Right-click on the Web Service project, and select properties. In the Configuration Properties • Debugging tab, select "Wait for an external process to connect" as your start action (Figure 13-10). You can now use the full complement of debugging tools with your Web Service and client code.

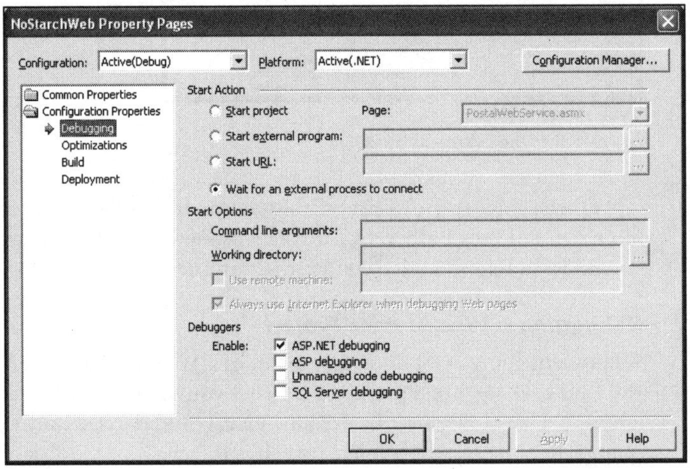

Figure 13-10: Loading the Web Service debug symbols

Asynchronous Web Service Calls

You may have noticed that the proxy class actually contains more than just the GetPackageInfo function. It also includes BeginGetPackageInfo and EndGet-PackageInfo procedures. These routines allow you to retrieve a Web Service result asynchronously. For example, your code can submit a request with Begin-GetPackageInfo, perform some additional tasks, and then retrieve the result with EndGetPackageInfo. This allows your program to remain responsive, even when waiting for a response over a slow Internet connection.

```
Dim ServiceInstance As New localhost.PostalWebService()
Dim PackageInfo As New localhost.ClientPackageInfo()

' Create a special handle that will allow us to retrieve the result.
Dim ResultHandle As IAsyncResult

' Submit the request.
ResultHandle = ServiceInstance.BeginGetPackageInfo("221", Nothing, Nothing)

' (Perform other time-consuming tasks.)

' Retrieve the final result, using the ResultHandle.
PackageInfo = ServiceInstance.EndGetPackageInfo(ResultHandle)

MessageBox.Show("Received the delivery date: " & PackageInfo.DeliveryDate)
```

In this example, ResultHandle is a special IAsyncResult object that tracks the current request. You can have multiple asynchronous web requests submitted at the same, as long as you keep track of them with different IAsyncResult objects.

When the EndGetPackageInfo method is called, the request becomes synchronous. That means that if the response has not yet been received from the Web Service, your code will wait until it is received (or until the request times out, according to the proxy class Timeout property).

Alternatively, you can call BeginGetPackageInfo with the address of a subroutine in your program. When the Web Service result is received, this routine will be called automatically. This technique is ideal if you are requesting some information that is not critical, and you want to allow your application to continue its normal behavior. By using a callback, you can respond immediately when the information arrives, but your application doesn't need to sit idle waiting for it.

Here's an example where a button click submits an asynchronous request with a callback:

```
Private ServiceInstance As New localhost.PostalWebService()

Private Sub cmdAsyncCallback_Click(ByVal sender As System.Object, _
  ByVal e As System.EventArgs) Handles cmdAsyncCallback.Click
    ' Create a special handle that will allow us to retrieve the result.
    Dim ResultHandle As IAsyncResult

    ' Submit the request, with a callback.
    ServiceInstance.BeginGetPackageInfo("221", AddressOf ResultReceived, Nothing)
End Sub
```

When the result is received, the ResultReceived subroutine will be called immediately, and a MessageBox will appear alerting the user. (A more common action might be to use the information to update a portion of the user interface.) The PostalClient included with the online samples demonstrates these different ways of retrieving information from a Web Service asynchronously.

```
Private Sub ResultReceived(ByVal ar As IAsyncResult)
    ' Retrieve the final result, using the ar event arguments..
    Dim PackageInfo As New localhost.ClientPackageInfo()
    PackageInfo = ServiceInstance.EndGetPackageInfo(ar)

    MessageBox.Show("Received the delivery date: " & PackageInfo.DeliveryDate)
End Sub
```

TIP   *You could also use the threading techniques described in Chapter 10. For example, you could create a procedure that calls a series of web methods on a separate thread and then raises an event to notify your program.*

Web Service Discovery

One aspect of this process that I've glossed over a bit is the discovery file. The *discovery file* represents Microsoft's goals for easily sharing Web Services and making them available to the appropriate clients. You don't need to worry about these sharing issues if you are creating a Web Service exclusively for use in your company website, or with a few select clients. However, if you are trying to develop and market a Web Service that provides powerful features that you want to provide as a subscription service, discovery matters quite a lot.

Discovery is the process that allows a client to find the WSDL information that describes your Web Service. Your server may have one discovery document that points to multiple Web Services, or it may have several different discovery files in various virtual directories. Alternatively, you might not use a discovery file at all.

A discovery document is yet another type of XML file. All it contains is a list of web links (URLs) to the WSDL document of various Web Services. Here is a sample discovery file for our PostalWebService:

```
<?xml version="1.0" encoding="utf-8" ?>
<disco:discovery  xmlns:disco="http://schemas.xmlsoap.org/disco"
 xmlns:wsdl="http://schemas.xmlsoap.org/disco/wsdl">
    <wsdl:contractRef ref="http://fariamat/NoStarchWeb/PostalWebService.asmx?WSDL"
</disco:discovery>
```

By default, discovery files use dynamic discovery, and look a little different. With *dynamic discovery,* every subdirectory in the current directory will be scanned for Web Services. Here is a sample dynamic discovery file:

```
<?xml version="1.0" encoding="utf-8" ?>
<dynamicDiscovery xmlns="urn:schemas-dynamicdiscovery:disco.2000-03-17">
  <exclude path="_vti_cnf" />
  <exclude path="_vti_pvt" />
  <exclude path="_vti_log" />
  <exclude path="_vti_script" />
  <exclude path="_vti_txt" />
  <exclude path="Web References" />
</dynamicDiscovery>
```

The exclude path attributes tell the discovery process not to look in those folders. This can be used to save time (for example, by restricting directories that contain only images), or to restrict a Web Service from appearing in a discovery process (although it will still be accessible unless you have specifically written authentication or security code).

TIP *How can you add a web reference if you don't have a discovery file? You can manually type the Web Service location into the address bar of the Add Reference window. You don't even need to worry about supplying the ?WSDL at the end to locate the WSDL document, because Visual Studio .NET is smart enough to add that for you automatically.*

What Comes Next?

This chapter has provided an overview of how Web Services work, and how to use them. Leading edge companies and developers have already started inventing all kinds of imaginative Web Services. Some examples include Microsoft's Passport, which allows other companies to provide authentication using the engine that powers the Hotmail email system, and CodeSwap (www.vscodeswap.net), a Microsoft-supported initiative that allows you to share code fragments with other developers as easily as you could once share MP3 files in the original Napster program.

If you want to continue learning about and working with Web Services, here are some interesting places to start:

- Microsoft provides a Web Services portal that provides such information as low-level technical information about the SOAP and WSDL standards, code samples of professional Web Services, and white papers discussing the best ways to design Web Services. Check it out at http://msdn.microsoft.com/webservices.

- UDDI (Universal Description, Discovery, and Integration) is an emerging standard that will make it easy for developers to locate discovery files and available Web Services on the Internet. You can find more information, and some interesting examples of Web Services, at http://uddi.microsoft.com/visualstudio.

- Various other Web Service search engines are appearing on the Internet. You can use them to see what other developers are up to. To get started, try out http://www.gotdotnet.com/playground/services and http://www.xmethods.com.

- Remember, you can enable Session support in a Web Service, and use some of the same techniques that you would use for authentication in an ASP.NET application. For more information, check out the MSDN help library.

14

MIGRATING TO
VISUAL BASIC .NET

A traditional computer book usually discusses migration—the question of how to work with existing data files—early on. In many programs, including office productivity software such as Microsoft Word, working with files from a previous version is just as easy as creating new documents. Unfortunately, Visual Basic .NET doesn't work this way. As you've discovered in the preceding thirteen chapters, Visual Basic .NET introduces an entirely new programming framework called .NET. To program well in .NET, you have to surrender many time-honored habits and adopt a new, object-oriented style. When it comes to migration, the question is not how you can import your existing applications, but whether you should at all.

This chapter surveys the major changes between Visual Basic 6 and VB .NET, and in doing so, provides a nice summary of the .NET philosophy. We'll take a look at the Upgrade Wizard, and see how a sample VB 6 project weathers the transition to .NET. You'll also learn about how to *integrate* legacy code, which is useful when migration is simply too painful. Specifically, we'll examine how you can access COM components and ActiveX controls—the "old world" of programming—in a .NET project. These techniques allow you to make maximum use of your existing code, while pursuing new development in Visual Basic .NET. Integration and interaction may not always be convenient, but it will be an essential ingredient of .NET programming for the next few years. It will also be the best strategy in many cases where migration is not possible and re-coding is just too time-consuming.

Introducing .NET Migration

Visual Basic .NET compromises backward compatibility in a number of trouble-some ways. Hopefully, the advances you've seen over the course of this book will make these complications worthwhile. Once you're in the .NET world, there's really no easy way back.

Visual Basic 6 in the .NET World

Visual Basic 6 is a mature, well-developed programming environment. There's no immediate need to replace a VB 6 program (and there's no shame in maintaining a program in Visual Basic 6). Think of Visual Basic 6 as a well-worn, austere language at the end of its evolution. It still has a nice autumn glow to it, but it will gradually fade into disuse. On the other hand, Visual Basic .NET is a young, dynamic upstart at the beginning of its life cycle. As with any new program, changes will abound in VB .NET over the next few years. However, it's Visual Basic .NET, not Visual Basic 6, that will power the next generation of VB applications.

A key theme in this chapter is breaking down the barriers between VB 6 and VB .NET. There may not be an easy migration solution for many of your projects. Instead, you may need to start over again in .NET, and make heavy use of the COM compatibility layer that is built into .NET, in order to use your existing VB components.

File Compatibility

There is no file compatibility between Visual Basic .NET and earlier versions. In Chapter 3, we explored the new file formats used in VB .NET projects. These files have different extensions (.vb instead of .mod or .frm, and .vbproj instead of .vbp). VB .NET files also use a block structure that allows modules, forms, and classes to be combined in a single file, while Visual Basic 6 used a special syntax for its form files (as explained in Chapter 4).

The syntax of the language of itself has been updated, and the alterations range from minor cosmetic changes to entirely new concepts such as namespaces. All these technical details have a single result: There is no way to open a Visual Basic 6 project in VB .NET. Instead, you have to *migrate* the project.

The Upgrade Wizard

Migration is a special procedure carried out by Visual Studio .NET's built-in Upgrade Wizard. Essentially, the Upgrade Wizard scans through every line of every file in your project. It examines the line, analyzes it for a variety of potential problems, and tries to assign an equivalent VB .NET statement. When dealing with simple programs (for example, utilities that have only one window, or that have the majority of their capabilities concentrated in a few core procedures), it does remarkably well. However, for complex programs that manage a sophisticated user interface and a large amount of data, it works almost embarrassingly badly. In these cases, migration usually isn't a feasible option.

Migrating a Simple Project

Here's a relatively simple VB 6 project using several concepts that are foreign to VB .NET. The full project is available with the samples for this chapter.

It starts with a simple startup procedure, contained in a module file:

```
' VB 6 code.
Public Sub Main()
    frmSplash.Show vbModal
    frmMain.Show
End Sub
```

The first line launches a window modally—a splash screen with a company logo. The window uses a timer that unloads itself automatically after a set amount of time:

```
' VB 6 code.
Private Sub tmrClose_Timer()
    Unload Me
End Sub
```

Then the code continues to the second line, launches the main program window nonmodally, and allows the Main subroutine to end. The main window consists of a simple form with an MSFlexGrid control and a single button. When the user clicks on the button, a short routine runs, retrieves information from a database table, and uses that information to fill the grid, as shown in Figure 14-1.

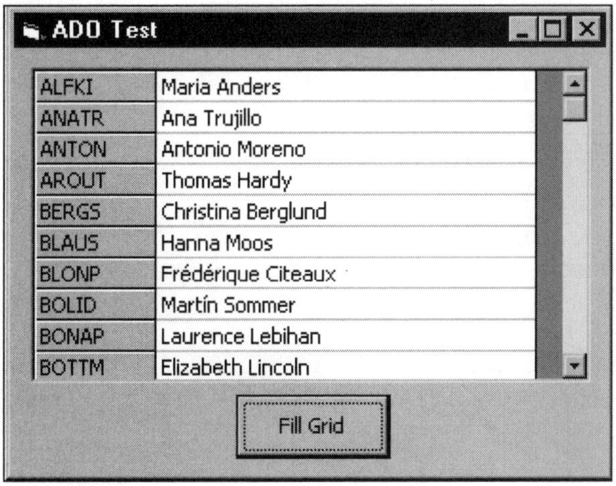

Figure 14-1: A VB 6 program

The code is quite straightforward. The Form_Load event handler configures the grid appropriately, and opens a database connection (using the form-level variable con):

```
' VB 6 code.
Private con As ADODB.Connection

Private Sub Form_Load()
    grid.Cols = 2
    grid.Rows = 0
    grid.ColWidth(1) = 3000
    grid.ColAlignment(0) = 1

    Set con = New ADODB.Connection
    con.ConnectionString = "Provider=SQLOLEDB.1;Data Source=localhost;" & _
     "Initial Catalog=Northwind;Integrated Security=SSPI"
    con.Open
End Sub
```

Of course, opening a database connection in the Form_Load event and closing it in the Form_Unload event is an extremely bad design practice, because it ties up a limited database connection for an undetermined amount of time. The individual using the computer could easily forget, leave the computer running, and go on holiday, tying up the connection indefinitely. However, there's nothing invalid in this code (and probably nothing unusual either).

The button event handler contains the following code:

```
' VB 6 code.
Private Sub cmdFill_Click()

    Me.MousePointer = vbHourglass
    grid.Rows = 0


    Dim rs As ADODB.Recordset
    Set rs = con.Execute("SELECT * From Customers")

    Dim i As Integer
    Do While rs.EOF <> True
        grid.AddItem (rs("CustomerID") & vbTab & rs("ContactName"))
        rs.MoveNext
    Loop

    Me.MousePointer = vbDefault

End Sub
```

Don't spend too much time analyzing this code; it uses the ADO library, which is the connection-based predecessor to ADO.NET. ADO works quite a bit differently, using a live connection and a MoveNext method to access all the information in a Recordset (instead of a Rows collection in a DataSet). This technique is similar to the way you use ADO.NET's special DataReader object.

You might also notice that this code uses the MousePointer property to thoughtfully turn the user's mouse pointer into an hourglass, indicating that a database operation is underway and that no other user action can be taken until the operation is finished.

One additional frill is the form's automatic resizing code:

```
' VB 6 code.
Private Sub Form_Resize()
    grid.Width = Me.Width - 350
    grid.Height = Me.Height - 1200
    cmdFill.Top = Me.Height - 1000
    cmdFill.Left = (Me.Width - cmdFill.Width - 60) \ 2
End Sub
```

While this code can't stop the form from being made too small, like our VB .NET code can, it still manages to ensure that the button and grid use the appropriate amount of space. The drawback is the introduction of hard-coded values, and generally ugly code, into the Form_Resize event handler. Interestingly, this code is the manual equivalent of two different VB .NET concepts we take for granted. The grid's size changes, but its position does not; this is an example of manual docking. The command button's position changes, but its size is constant, which is an example of anchoring.

Clearly, this is an extremely simple program. However, it does have some aspects that can pose difficulty in the .NET world. They are:

- The use of ADO, which is a database technology built on COM. (Remember, COM isn't native to .NET.)

- The use of the MSFlexGrid control, which is an ActiveX control. Like all ActiveX controls, it's also based on COM, and so there is no direct equivalent in the .NET class library.

- The treatment of forms. In Visual Basic .NET, forms are classes, and you have to create an instance of a form before using it. Clearly, the startup routine in our example doesn't follow these rules. If you'd known that this program was destined for VB .NET migration, you could have programmed accordingly by dynamically creating forms, even in your VB 6 code. However, if you haven't specifically planned for this step, or if you are dealing with an older application, this technique probably hasn't been used.

Design-wise, there are a couple of other potential problems in this example, such as the way the database connection is held open. However, you can create a poorly designed program in VB .NET with the same ease that you could in Visual Basic 6. This example of poor programming should not affect the migration process.

Importing the Project

To import this project into Visual Basic .NET, all you need to do is open the .vbp file. The Upgrade Wizard will automatically appear, as seen in Figure 14-2.

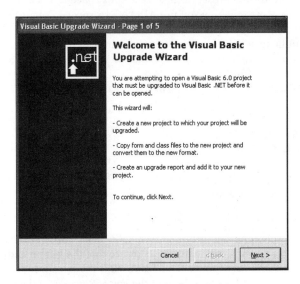

Figure 14-2: The Upgrade Wizard

At this point, it's just a matter of clicking on Next several times, and the conversion will begin. Along the way, you will be prompted to choose a new directory where the .NET version of our project will be stored (see Figure 14-3).

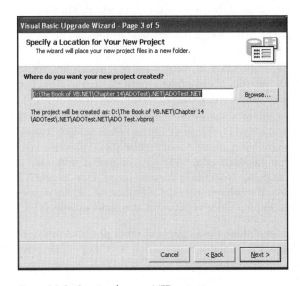

Figure 14-3: Creating the new .NET project

Remember, this a complex migration, not a simple File Open operation. The whole process is surprisingly slow, as you'll notice with any real-life application. Even with this simple program, Visual Studio .NET may still take a couple of minutes to complete the migration.

Once the process is completed, the first thing you should do is read the migration report that has been created for you. You can find this as an HTML file (_UpdateReport.htm) in the Solution Explorer. If you double-click on it, you'll see an impressive file-by-file analysis of the project (Figure 14-4). Each section lists migration problems and warnings, and can be expanded or collapsed individually.

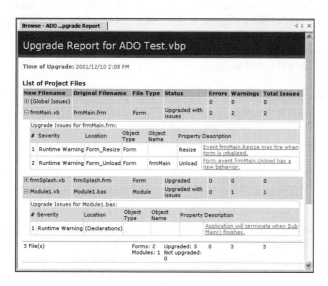

Figure 14-4: The upgrade report

In the case of the simple ADOTest project, no errors are reported, but three warnings are flagged. You can read a full description of these issues by clicking the provided hyperlink, which takes you to a help topic. Usually, though, you'll want to investigate the code yourself. The appropriate area will be marked with a comment and another hyperlink to the help topic:

```
' UPGRADE_WARNING: Form event frmMain.Unload has a new behavior.
' Click for more: ms-help://MS.MSDNVS/vbcon/html/vbup2065.htm
Private Sub frmMain_Closed(ByVal eventSender As System.Object, _
  ByVal eventArgs As System.EventArgs) Handles MyBase.Closed
    con.Close()
End Sub
```

In this case, the Wizard has changed the event handler for the Unload event to the corresponding Close event. (The Wizard has also taken care of additional details, such as adding the Handles clause and changing the event handler signature to the .NET standard.)

The second warning is a similar false alarm that alerts us that the Resize event may occur when the form is first initialized. The third warning in the migration report informs us, rather cryptically, that the application will end when the Main subroutine ends. This warning highlights another difference between VB .NET and VB 6: In Visual Basic 6, a program wouldn't end until every window was closed. If you used a startup routine to begin your program, the startup routine could end and leave the other windows running to take care of the rest of the program. In VB .NET, applications work a little differently.

If you use a startup subroutine in Visual Basic .NET, the program will close as soon as the subroutine ends, even if other windows are still open (somewhat like using the End statement).

```
Module StartupModule
    Public Sub Main()
        frmSplash.DefInstance.ShowDialog()

        ' Program will end immediately after executing the next line.
        frmMain.DefInstance.Show()
    End Sub
End Module
```

This migration problem could have been avoided if the original program had displayed both windows modally from the Main subroutine. In that case, the subroutine would pause until the frmMain window had closed, rather than ending early. To fix this minor problem, all you need to do is make this modification:

```
Module StartupModule
    Public Sub Main()
        frmSplash.DefInstance.ShowDialog()
        frmMain.DefInstance.ShowDialog()
    End Sub
End Module
```

Forms and the Default Instance

You may notice another unusual feature in this portion of the code: the reference to DefInstance. A logical .NET startup routine would look more like this:

```
Public Sub Main()
    ' Create and show first window.
    Dim Splash As New frmSplash
    Splash.ShowDialog()

    ' Create and show second window.
    Dim Main As New frmMain
    Main.ShowDialog()
End Sub
```

The .NET Upgrade Wizard doesn't have enough intelligence to make this change. In fact, the problem is potentially a lot more complicated. In traditional VB code, the Wizard really has no way of knowing when you are referring to a form, and when you are trying to create it. In VB 6, a form is loaded automatically the first time it is referred to in code, even if it isn't displayed. This system allows the following kind of logic to work:

```
' This is VB6 code.
frmMain.TextBox1.Text = "Hi"    ' The form is created and loaded automatically.
frmMain.Show                    ' Now the form is displayed.
```

To emulate this logic, the Upgrade Wizard adds a special block of code to every form under the collapsed Upgrade Support region that works like this:

```
Private Shared m_vb6FormDefInstance As frmMain
Private Shared m_InitializingDefInstance As Boolean

Public Shared Property DefInstance() As frmMain
    Get
        If m_vb6FormDefInstance Is Nothing _
          OrElse m_vb6FormDefInstance.IsDisposed Then
            m_InitializingDefInstance = True
            m_vb6FormDefInstance = New frmMain()
            m_InitializingDefInstance = False
        End If
        DefInstance = m_vb6FormDefInstance
    End Get

    Set
        m_vb6FormDefInstance = Value
    End Set
End Property
```

The logic here is quite interesting. It works like this:

- Every form has a shared property called DefInstance. Because it is shared, it can be accessed even without creating a form instance. (Also, because it is shared, every class uses the same code for this property, and returns the same result.)

- When you retrieve the DefInstance property in your code, the Property Get procedure checks the form's private m_vb6FormDefInstance shared variable. This variable is designed to hold a reference to the current form (in our example, frmMain). If this variable hasn't yet been initialized, the Property Get procedure creates the form automatically, effectively mimicking the VB 6 form behavior.

- The end result is that whenever a part of your program uses the DefInstance property, it gets the instance of the form stored in the m_vb6FormDefInstance variable. If necessary, the form is loaded on the spot automatically.

This special block of "upgrade support" code is a trick that allows you to use forms in the VB 6 way, as long as you call the form's default instance instead of just the form's class name. If you have the time, it may make sense to go through your code, remove the default instance logic, and recreate your form properly. However, this isn't strictly necessary.

TIP *Incidentally, this code violates an important recommendation of object-oriented programming: namely, that retrieving information from a property procedure should never change the state of the object. In this case, retrieving the property of an uninitialized form causes it to be created.*

Other Changes

The Wizard makes some other modifications. For example, it converts the form's MousePointer property using the equivalent .NET code, shown here:

```
Me.Cursor = System.Windows.Forms.Cursors.WaitCursor
```

This trick is also fairly impressive. Clearly, the Wizard needs to draw on a comprehensive database of some sort that stores VB 6 properties, and their .NET equivalents, because the .NET class library really has little in common with the traditional Forms engine.

Another change appears in the Resize event handler, which now uses slightly more cumbersome code to convert the hard-coded values to pixels, the measurement used in VB .NET. A sample line is shown here:

```
grid.Width = VB6.TwipsToPixelsX(VB6.PixelsToTwipsX(Me.Width) - 350)
```

So far, the Upgrade Wizard has done a great job. If you try running the program, you'll be surprised to find that it works perfectly. The old-fashioned resizing code and database code works without a hitch. Some better options are available for improving your program to take advantage of VB .NET, particularly with the resizing code, but the original code still works as designed.

COM Components in .NET

Perhaps the most impressive aspect of this conversion is the fact that the ADO components work exactly as they did in Visual Basic 6, even though they are COM-based. If you look at the references for this project, you'll find that an ADO reference has been added (as shown in Figure 14-5). This reference uses the ADODB.dll wrapper distributed with .NET.

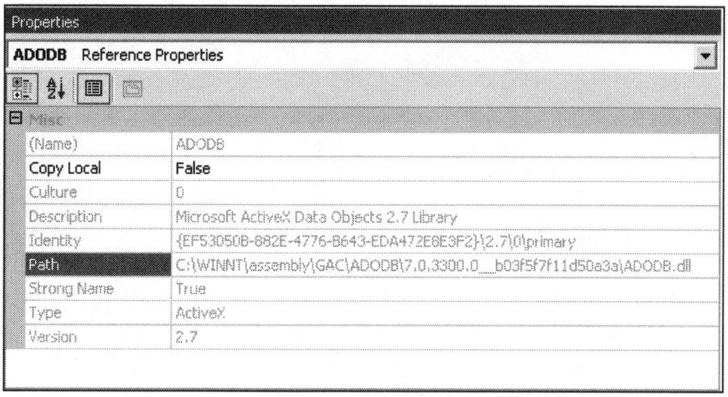

Properties	
ADODB Reference Properties	▾

⊟ Misc	
(Name)	ADODB
Copy Local	False
Culture	0
Description	Microsoft ActiveX Data Objects 2.7 Library
Identity	{EF53050B-882E-4776-B643-EDA472E6E3F2}\2.7\0\primary
Path	C:\WINNT\assembly\GAC\ADODB\7.0.3300.0__b03f5f7f11d50a3a\ADODB.dll
Strong Name	True
Type	ActiveX
Version	2.7

Figure 14-5: The ADODB reference

This file isn't a part of the original project—in fact, it's part of the .NET framework. When you use an ADO object in your .NET code, you are really using an object from the ADODB.dll file. This file is a normal, managed .NET assembly. Behind the scenes, it uses .NET's COM Interop features to create the corresponding COM object and pass along instructions according to your program's actions. In other words, ADODB.dll provides a thin translation layer between your program and traditional ADO, bridging the gap between COM and .NET. In most cases, this trick works perfectly well, causing only a slight performance degradation. The translation layer ensures that you can continue using COM components for the foreseeable future.

Of course, you don't need to migrate a project in order to use this built-in compatibility layer. Visual Studio .NET makes it just as easy as adding a reference. First, right-click on References in the Solution Explorer, and then choose Add Reference. Next, select the COM tab (as shown in Figure 14-6). (There will probably be a slight delay while Visual Studio .NET loads all the system information.)

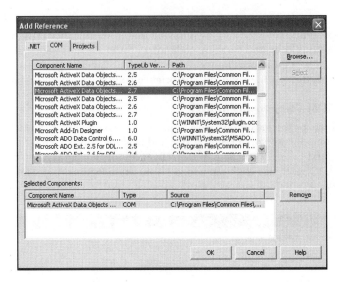

Figure 14-6: Adding a COM reference

Double-click on an item to add it to the selected list. When you click on OK, .NET will search for a primary Interop assembly, which is a .NET translation assembly created by the appropriate vendor. If it can't find one, you will receive an ominous warning message and be given the option to create your own wrapper automatically. The DLL wrapper file will then be added to your project's support files in the obj subdirectory.

Believe it or not, this COM interoperability is almost seamless, and it will save you a lot of headaches. Just remember that when you want to install your program on another computer, you will need to copy these Interop files. (You will also need to install and registered the appropriate COM files; .NET setup projects won't detect these components or set them up automatically.)

TIP *It's perfectly reasonable to create your own Interop assemblies for third-party components when developing and testing an application. However, when you deploy the application, you should use the Interop assembly provided by the appropriate vendor (like the ADODB.dll assembly provided by Microsoft, and included in the .NET framework). This way, you are guaranteed that the .NET layer works properly with all aspects of the component.*

ActiveX Components in .NET

ActiveX components work in essentially the same way as COM objects, since every ActiveX component is really just a special type of COM object. You'll recall that our original VB 6 test program uses an MSFlexGrid control, which is an ActiveX control with no obvious .NET equivalent. The .NET framework does not include a primary Interop assembly for the MSFlexGrid control, so the Upgrade Wizard creates one automatically.

To witness what's really happening, select Project • Show All Files from the main menu. Now if you expand the bin or obj directory, you'll find a file with a name like AxInterop.MSFlexGridLib_1_0.dll. The "Ax" at the beginning of the name identifies the fact that this Interop assembly derives from the System.Windows.Forms.AxHost class, as do all the Interop files for ActiveX controls. It's an ordinary .NET managed assembly that has the built-in smarts to talk to the original ActiveX component through COM (Figure 14-7).

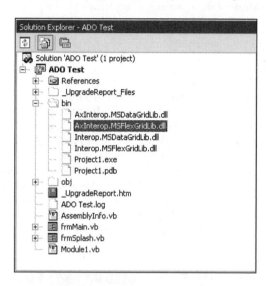

Figure 14-7: The .NET wrapper for MSFlexGrid

TIP *You can find more information about the generated wrapper assembly by double-clicking on it. Expand the tree until you reach the last (version) element, and double-click on that for information about the current version of the file:*

This wrapper is slightly different from the ADO wrapper, because it represents the actual .NET control that is placed on your Windows form. You can verify this fact by examining the automatically generated designer code:

```
Public WithEvents grid As AxMSFlexGridLib.AxMSFlexGrid
Me.grid = New AxMSFlexGridLib.AxMSFlexGrid
```

This control quietly communicates with the original ActiveX control, and mimics its behavior on the form. You can see this in action by examining the following designer code, in which the wrapper class retrieves state information from the ActiveX control instance that it contains:

```
grid.OcxState = CType(resources.GetObject("grid.OcxState"), _
  System.Windows.Forms.AxHost.State)
```

Interestingly, this control is a blend of the old and the new. Because AxHost inherits from the base Control class, it supports all the properties that a typical control does. For example, the designer code sets the size and location like this:

```
Me.grid.Size = New System.Drawing.Size(297, 137)
Me.grid.Location = New System.Drawing.Point(8, 8)
```

The dual nature of the control also explains why the properties and methods in some portions of code now have slightly modified names:

```
grid.set_ColWidth(1, 3000)        ' This was grid.ColWidth(1) = 3000
grid.set_ColAlignment(0, 1)       ' This was grid.ColAlightment(0) = 1
```

This syntax would obviously not be valid in Visual Basic 6. However, the AxMSFlexGrid control *is* a real .NET control. It just requires the use of an ActiveX control behind the scenes. This also means that you can use .NET event-handling procedures, including the Handles keyword and the AddHandler statement, without any difficulty. Of course, you might have trouble determining the correct parameter list, because there won't be any information on the newly created control in the .NET MSDN help library. To track down this information, select View • Other Windows • Object Browser. You can then take a look inside the corresponding AxInterop.MSFlexGridLib_1_0.dll assembly, and find out exactly what .NET members Visual Studio .NET has created for you, as shown in Figure 14-8.

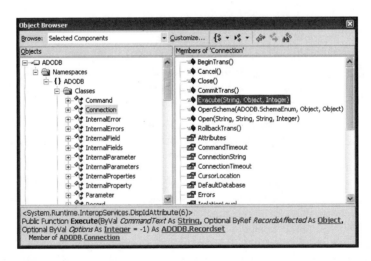

Figure 14-8: The Object Browser

The end result of our migration example is an MSFlexGrid control that works perfectly well. Keep in mind that in many cases, it might be better to use a true .NET control instead, to ensure best performance and easiest deployment. However, in this case the ActiveX control does not cause any obvious problems.

In the future, there will certainly be a flood of .NET controls. Until then, you may need to rely on these built-in Interop features in order to reuse your existing ActiveX controls. For example, there are currently no equivalents to the old Microsoft Charting and Internet Explorer Browser components. In some cases, it might be easy to build better versions of these controls using the functions and features available in the .NET class library, or even to substitute similar .NET controls. But having the Interop features is a huge advantage, especially when using unusual or one-of-a-kind controls.

To add an ActiveX control to one of your projects, right-click on the toolbox and select Customize Toolbox (Figure 14-9). Then select the COM Components tab, find the appropriate control on the list, and put a checkmark next to it.

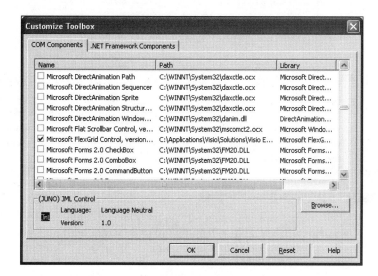

Figure 14-9: Adding a wrapped ActiveX control

The Interop assembly won't actually be created until you place the control on a form. Then you can work with the control as though you were using Visual Basic 6. For example, when you resize the ActiveX control or change its properties, its appearance will be automatically updated. Similarly, you can configure properties through a custom tabbed property window, if such a window is provided with the control (Figure 14-10).

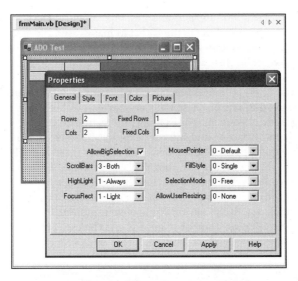

Figure 14-10: Design-time support for ActiveX controls remains

It's important to remember that the COM and ActiveX Interop features can be used even when you're not migrating a project. In fact, it often makes most sense for you to use these features in order to continue using as many elements as you can from your existing programs without rewriting them. Creating a .NET program that makes heavy use of existing COM components will often work much better than trying to migrate the code for all these components into the .NET world.

Migrating a Sophisticated Project

The scenario we've worked with so far is ideal in many respects. While Visual Studio .NET's migration features are impressive, they rarely work as well as described with a real application. In fact, for many programs they will be essentially unworkable.

The next sample project is a typical midsize Visual Basic 6 program. It consists of about three-dozen forms, most of which are used to provide different product listings. The user selects any combination of products to create a priced order, and then either emails the order to the appropriate company (by means of a built-in COM component for MAPI email), or creates a professional looking printout that can be faxed or kept for reference. Other options are available, such as the ability to preview the report with a RichText control, and the ability to switch between different price sets (US dollars and UK pounds, for example). We'll call this program VB6OrderMaker.

Figure 14-11 shows it in action:

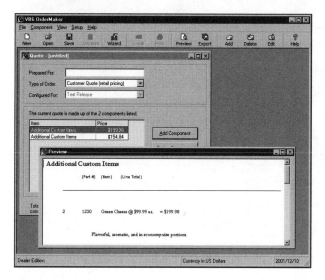

Figure 14-11: The VB6OrderMaker

This program is far too long to be reproduced in its entirety, and you wouldn't gain much from seeing the details. Overall, it's an intricate program (as it has a lot of details), but it is fairly straightforward. Best practices are not always followed, but the design is not overly haphazard. It doesn't make use of classes or interfaces. Ultimately, it's a good example of a typical, slightly old-fashioned Visual Basic 6 program.

Unfortunately, it's difficult to tell exactly how much of the program's functionality has made the jump to the .NET world. There are so many .NET incompatibilities woven into the fabric of the program that the migrated project would never compile, even if hours were spent reworking it. It's safe to say that re-creating this program from scratch would be far more successful than migrating the existing program.

The migration report contains 360 errors, 2889 warnings, and 3249 total issues, making for an average of about 80 issues per module (Figure 14-12 shows a partial list). Even more amusing, the Upgrade Wizard has spent several hours struggling to make the changes needed for .NET. The only file that has survived without any problems is the module used to run functions from the Windows API.

Rather than trying to step through this mess, it makes sense to consider the major issues that have derailed this migration attempt, and examine how they can be solved or avoided. (You'll find that similar issues will occur with many complex migration projects.)

Browse - confi... Upgrade Report ◁ ▷ ✕

Upgrade Report for VB6OrderMaker.vbp

Time of Upgrade: 2001/08/04 3:58 PM

List of Project Files

New Filename	Original Filename	File Type	Status	Errors	Warnings	Total Issues
⊞ (Global Issues)				0	0	0
⊞ about.vb	about.frm	Form	Upgraded with issues	1	0	1
⊞ Admin.vb	admin.frm	Form	Upgraded with issues	4	36	40
⊞ Author.vb	author.frm	Form	Upgraded with issues	10	45	55
⊞ CFPlayer.vb	cfplayer.frm	Form	Upgraded with issues	5	49	54
⊞ convert.vb	convert.frm	Form	Upgraded with issues	17	16	33
⊞ CourtFLOW.vb	CourtFLOW.frm	Form	Upgraded with issues	1	51	52
⊞ Dealer.vb	Dealer.frm	Form	Upgraded with issues	10	9	19
⊞ Declarations.vb	Declarations.bas	Module	Upgraded with issues	0	7	7
⊞ EditCustom.vb	EditCustom.frm	Form	Upgraded with issues	12	142	154
⊞ Functions.vb	Functions.bas	Module	Upgraded with issues	2	82	84
⊞ GenericTab1.vb	GenericTab1.frm	Form	Upgraded with issues	25	136	161
⊞ Hubcalc.vb	Hubcalc.frm	Form	Upgraded with issues	3	10	13
⊞ liccalc.vb	liccalc.frm	Form	Upgraded with issues	5	59	64
⊞ main.vb	main.frm	Form	Upgraded with issues	6	10	16
⊞ MDIMain.vb	MDIMain.frm	MDI Form	Upgraded with issues	2	534	536
⊞ Menu.vb	Menu.frm	Form	Upgraded with issues	3	15	18
⊞ Order.vb	Order.frm	Form	Upgraded with issues	10	85	95
⊞ Parts.vb	parts.frm	Form	Upgraded with issues	11	12	23
⊞ passcheck.vb	passcheck.frm	Form	Upgraded with issues	1	6	7
⊞ password.vb	password.frm	Form	Upgraded with issues	2	18	20

Figure 14-12: Partial list of VB6OrderMaker errors

Showstoppers

Before we get into the details of this troublesome project, let's review some types of programs that really are not fit for any type of migration to .NET. Generally, you shouldn't (or can't) even try to migrate a project if it falls under one of these categories:

- A complex distributed application with several different layers of objects communicating through COM. Despite Microsoft's optimism, this type of program will rarely survive the transition. However, on the good side, you can probably start by creating a .NET client that interacts with some or all of the other COM components, allowing you to ease into the migration process slowly, and continue conversions one component at a time.

- A Visual Basic 5 program that hasn't made the transition to Visual Basic 6. For all its differences, VB 6 is still one step closer to VB .NET than any earlier release of Visual Basic. Make the change to Visual Basic 6 before getting more ambitious.

- An Internet project using Web Classes, ActiveX Documents, or DHTML. None of these development technologies is supported in .NET. Projects based on Web Classes can be upgraded to ASP .NET Internet projects, but are likely to provide many additional headaches.

- A database project based on the Data Environment, which is also no longer supported.

- A database project that uses significant data binding to other controls. These features can be upgraded under some circumstances, but will definitely fail with the DAO and RDO data access technologies.

- An ActiveX control or ActiveX DLL project. While you can create the .NET equivalents of these COM-based types of programs, you will lose all of their existing COM features. If you have controls or components that are still being shared among numerous applications, it will probably be easier to use them in .NET or to make additional .NET versions, rather than trying to migrate them and replace the originals.

Common Migration Problems

In this section, we'll examine some of the problems that can derail .NET migration. If you can find these problems in your own Visual Basic 6 applications, it may be a good idea to fix them within that environment before migrating the project—or call off the migration process altogether.

TIP *If you're still developing projects in Visual Basic 6, the information in this section will help you make choices that will facilitate migration in the future.*

Arrays

Arrays can thwart any attempt at migration. Visual Basic .NET's new insistence that every array have a lower boundary of zero can cause all sorts of trouble. In our original VB6OrderMaker project, array indexes are chosen with specific meanings. For example, the elements 1 and greater are used to contain the items in an order. Element 0 contains a combined line with price totals, and negative array indexes are used to contain licensing information for the ordered items. Even though these specific array indexes are stored in variables instead of being hard-coded, updating them to comply with the zero-boundary requirement would not be easy, and would requires hours of modification and retesting. Some early Microsoft documents promised that the Upgrade Wizard would create special array classes that will mimic normal arrays and allow any lower boundary that you need. This flexibility never materialized in the beta or release versions, and it's uncertain whether or not the new array classes would help at all, or just complicate life even more.

However, it's fairly easy to create a Visual Basic 6 program that won't suffer from this array problem. The best choice is not to use zero-bounded arrays at all, but to move straight to collections or other custom classes. In our VB6OrderMaker application, the Visual Basic 6 code would be clearer and more elegant if orders were stored in an Order class that contained a collection of ordered items as a property (for example, Order.Items), and any other required license-specific properties. This class could also contain built-in methods for retrieving the total cost of all ordered items, and for converting prices to different currencies. The Order class approach would improve encapsulation, and would result in a data structure that doesn't depend on miscellaneous conversion and helper functions in other modules of the program.

Variants

Variants are a special Visual Basic 6 data type that can store different types of information, including strings or numbers. A variant converts itself automatically according to how you try to use it. Historically, this automatic conversion led to a variety of annoyances, although it was useful in some situations.

In Visual Basic .NET, variants aren't supported, but the System.Object type provides the same flexibility. If Option Strict is disabled for your application (as it is by default when you are migrating a project), you can use the generic object type in almost the exact same way as you would variants, with the same automatic conversion feature. If Option Strict is enabled, you need to convert object types manually when performing operations with them. This is explained in Chapter 7, but a quick review is helpful:

```
Dim x As Object, y As Object, z As Object
x = 1
y = 2
z = x + y      ' Will only work in Option Strict is off.
z = CType(x, Integer) + CType(y, Integer)    ' Always works without a hitch.
```

The Upgrade Wizard will convert all variants into generic objects. After a typical migration, you may find yourself with many more generic objects than you expected. The problem is that even though variants are rarely used deliberately in VB 6 code, variables could be inadvertently defined without data types, as shown here:

```
' VB 6 code.
Dim intA, intB As Integer    ' intB is an Interger, but intA will be a variant.
```

This oversight, which occurs most often when simple counters and other unimportant temporary variables are defined, causes Visual Basic 6 to use its default data type, which is the variant. During the migration of the VB6Order-Maker program into .NET format, many unspecified counter variables ended up as objects. The Upgrade Wizard flagged every subsequent line of code that performs any operations with these variables, indicating that it can't determine the default properties for those objects:

```
Dim intA As Integer, intB As Object
intA = 0

' UPGRADE_WARNING: Couldn't resolve default property of object intB.
' Click for more: ms-help://MS.MSDNVS/vbcon/html/vbup1037.htm
intB = 0
```

This minor issue isn't a problem—in fact, this portion of the code will still work perfectly. However, this idiosyncrasy led to a large number of additional warnings in the VB6OrderMaker upgrade report.

Default Properties

Why is the Upgrade Wizard so aggressive in flagging the unstructured use of an object? In VB6OrderMaker, these objects really represent simple value types, and the default value is automatically available as long as Option Strict is Off. However, this type of operation could create a problem in other circumstances.

In .NET, standard default properties aren't supported, and attempts to use an object's default property will fail. Usually, the Upgrade Wizard will add the necessary information to qualify a default property (for example, change `txtBox = "Text"` to `txtBox.Text = "Text"`). However, when you have a mysterious late-bound type that's defined only as an object, this trick fails. For example, if *x*, *y*, and *z* were real objects with numerous properties (such as x.Value), the statement `z = x + y` wouldn't work. Visual Basic .NET would have no way of knowing what properties to use for this calculation.

The solution to this problem is simple. When programming in Visual Basic 6, be careful to always define data types. Also, don't use late-bound objects. Not only are they slower, because VB has to inspect them before they are used, but they may lead to migration headaches.

Load Statement

In Visual Basic 6, you could use the Load statement to create a form without displaying it:

```
' VB 6 code.
Load frmMain
```

In Visual Basic .NET you can accomplish the same sort of thing by creating an instance of your form class, but not displaying it.

```
Dim frm As New frmMain()
```

Both of these techniques allow you to pre-configure the form and its controls before displaying the form. In VB6OrderMaker, Load statements are used extensively to provide Wizards that automatically load other forms, use their objects and procedures to calculate totals and create order items, and then unload them. This approach is well organized, but not nearly as efficient or easy to use as a real class-based design. It also leads to migration errors, because the Load statement is not automatically upgraded.

There is at least one easy way to replace the Load statement in a migrated project:

```
frmMain.DefInstance
```

This code initializes the form and makes it available through the shared DefInstance property.

Printing

The Upgrade Wizard is not able to update printing code. During the migration of VB6OrderMaker, the code used to select the printer, configure device settings, and output an order was flagged with error messages. The only way to resolve such problems is to rewrite the code for the new PrintDocument object in the .NET class library. If you've spent hours generating custom formatted output in your original application, you will not enjoy the migration process.

The Clipboard

Code that interacts with the Windows clipboard will also fail to work after a migration. Once again, the Upgrade Wizard leaves the hard work to you, and you need to rewrite the code with the .NET equivalent. In VB6OrderMaker, the clipboard was used to transfer information into the RichText control for a preview. Clearly, a better approach is to use .NET's new PrintPreview control. Unfortunately, there's no migration path between the two. If you are still working on a VB 6 project, you have no easy way to use print preview features similar to those available in VB .NET, and you will have to resort to third-party components or nontraditional approaches, such as those found in VB6OrderMaker. In .NET, however, there's really no reason *not* to use the bundled PrintPreview control.

Context-Sensitive Help

The HelpContextID property is not supported in Visual Basic .NET. If you want to create context-sensitive help, you'll need to use the HelpProvider control, which was discussed in Chapter 4. This control provides a number of minor enhancements, but once again, the Upgrade Wizard won't help you make the coding changes. Any program—VB6OrderMaker, for instance—that makes significant use of context-sensitive help will need at least some rewriting.

Menu Controls

In Visual Basic .NET, you can't use the same menu component for an application (pull-down) menu and a context menu. In Visual Basic 6, you had to create a pull-down menu before you could use it in a context menu. Microsoft schizophrenia once again?

The VB 6 code used to display a context menu looked like this:

```
' VB 6 code.
Private Sub Form_MouseDown(Button As Integer, Shift As Integer, X As Single, _
  Y As Single)
    If Button = 2 Then
        PopupMenu mnuOrderOptions
    End If
End Sub
```

When importing a project that uses context menus, the Upgrade Wizard leaves the PopUpMenu command in its original state, and flags it as an error.

Before you can make it work, you have to create a new ContextMenu object. Then, you have to copy the ordinary menu information into the ContextMenu:

```
Dim mnuPopUp As New ContextMenu()
Dim mnuItem As MenuItem

For Each mnuItem In mnuOrderOptions.MenuItems
    ' The CloneMenu method ensures that the context menu and main menu items
    ' have the same event handlers.
    mnuPopUp.MenuItems.Add(mnuItem.CloneMenu())
Next


Me.ContextMenu = mnuPopUp
```

The last line here assigns the new context menu to the form's ContextMenu property. The only reason you should do this is to make sure that a reference to the context menu is conveniently available when you need it—for example, in the form's event handler for a MouseDown event. Because the current form is always available through the Me keyword, it provides a convenient place to attach the ContextMenu reference.

The code for displaying a context menu in VB .NET is similar to that used in VB 6, but not exactly the same:

```
Private Sub Form1_MouseDown(ByVal sender As System.Object, _
  ByVal e As System.Windows.Forms.MouseEventArgs) Handles MyBase.MouseDown
    If e.Button = MouseButtons.Right Then
        Me.ContextMenu.Show(Me, New Point(e.X, e.Y))
    End If
End Sub
```

The best way to manage your context menus, and the best time to create them, are up to you. Once again, the Upgrade Wizard won't offer any help beyond identifying the problem.

Control Arrays

Control arrays present a particularly unpleasant example of what can go wrong with migration. In Visual Basic 6, control arrays were often the best way to solve problems. With a control array, numerous similar controls are placed into an array. In VB6OrderMaker, control arrays allow the program to loop through a series of controls and update them based on array information. For example, you can copy pricing information into a series of text boxes using this syntax:

```
' VB 6 code.
For i = 0 to UBound(PriceArray)
    txtPrice(i).Text = Val(PriceArray(i)
Next i
```

In .NET, this approach can be replaced in various different incompatible ways, including data binding, new list controls, or collection classes. Control arrays, however, aren't supported.

Control arrays also allowed a program to use a single event handler for numerous similar controls, which was an extremely useful convenience. For example, you could implement a set of dynamically highlighting labels, like this:

```
' VB 6 code.
Private Sub Description_MouseMove(Index As Integer, Button As Integer, _
   Shift As Integer, X As Single, Y As Single)
     Description(Index).ForeColor = &H800000
End Sub
```

In .NET, control arrays aren't needed to handle multiple events. Instead, you can use the Handles clause or the AddHandler statement to link up as many controls as you want to a single event handler. You can then use the *sender* parameter to interact with the control that fires the event, as discussed in Chapter 4.

```
Private Sub Highlight(ByVal sender As Object, ByVal e As MouseEventArgs) _
   Handles lblLine1.MouseMove, lblLine2.MouseMove
     ' You can add more events to the Handles list,
     ' or use the AddHandler statement instead.
     Dim lbl As Label = CType(sender, Label)
     lbl.ForeColor = Color.RoyalBlue
End Sub
```

To summarize: Control arrays were a quirky if useful tool in VB 6, but they have been replaced with a more modern system in VB .NET. However, if you import a program such as VB6OrderMaker that uses control arrays, the Upgrade Wizard doesn't convert them. Instead, it uses a special compatibility class, depending on your control. For example, if you have a control array of label controls, you'll end up using Microsoft.VisualBasic.Compatibility.VB6.LabelArray. This control allows VB .NET to "fake" a control array, with predictably inelegant results.

This is an example of the Upgrade Wizard at its worst: importing legacy problems from VB 6 into the .NET world. There's no easy way to design around it in VB 6, since control arrays are often a good design approach in that environment. Unfortunately, this is one of the Upgrade Wizard's fundamental limitations.

Automatic Re-initialization

In Visual Basic 6, if you defined an object with the New keyword, it had the strange ability to automatically recreate itself:

```
' VB 6 code.
Dim objPerson As New Person
Person.Name = "John"
Person = Nothing        ' The Person object is destroyed.
Person.Name = "John"     ' At this point, an empty Person object is reinitialized.
```

This was generally not what programmers expected, and it led to quirky errors and memory waste. In Visual Basic .NET, the New keyword simply allocates space for the object; it does not cause any unusual re-initializing behavior.

If you've made use of this trick, either deliberately or unwittingly in VB 6, the code won't work in .NET. When you try to use the destroyed object, you will receive a null reference error. You'll have to rewrite the preceding example like this:

```
Dim objPerson As New Person()
Person.Name = "John"
Person = Nothing        ' The Person object is destroyed.

Person = New Person()
Person.Name = "John"
```

Re-initialization may be a minor detail, but it's also one more potential migration headache, particularly if the project you want to import has not been created using best practices.

GDI

Visual Basic 6 had built in methods for drawing circles and other shapes directly onto a form. In Visual Basic .NET, these graphical routines have been enhanced and replaced by the GDI+ library, which you can access through the System.Drawing namespaces. Once again, any original code you may have written will need to be scrapped. This includes palette management, which VB6OrderMaker used to ensure that the splash screen is displayed properly on older 256-color monitors.

Class_Terminate Code

In Visual Basic 6, you might have used the Terminate event to perform automatic cleanup tasks, such as closing a database connection or deleting a temporary file. In Visual Basic .NET, this technique is a guaranteed to cause problems, because the .NET framework uses non-deterministic garbage collection.

Garbage collection in VB .NET works in much the same way that garbage collection works in many actual communities. In most neighborhoods, residents can pinpoint the time that garbage is placed into the appropriate receptacle, but they really have no idea when someone will be motivated to take it out. Similarly, in .NET garbage collection may be put off until the system is idle, and can't be relied upon to release limited resources. You might find other surprises if you use the Terminate event to try and interact with other forms in your application. Generally, these techniques won't work in VB .NET.

As with control arrays, a substantial difference in programming philosophies underlies this problem. In Visual Basic 6, using the Terminate method was a useful approach to making sure that cleanup was always performed the moment the class was released. In Visual Basic .NET, you are better off adding a Dispose method, and relying on the programmer to call this method after using an object and just before destroying it. The Upgrade Wizard tries to encourage this change: It places code from the Terminate event into a new, separate method so that you can easily call it when needed. It also overrides the Finalize method and adds a call to the new method to ensure that cleanup is performed:

```
Public Sub Class_Terminate_Renamed()
    ' Code goes here.
End Sub

Protected Overrides Sub Finalize()
    Class_Terminate_Renamed()
    MyBase.Finalize()
End Sub
```

This a good start, but you would be better off putting the code in a method called Dispose (rather than Class_Terminate_Renamed, as the Upgrade Wizard uses in our example). You'll also still need to modify the code that uses the class, because you'll want to make sure that it calls the Dispose method before destroying the object.

VarPtr, StrPtr, ObjPtr

These undocumented functions have traditionally been used by Visual Basic experts to find the memory addresses where variables or objects were stored. These functions allowed addresses to be passed to a DLL routine or to the Windows API, which sometimes required this information. In Visual Basic .NET, you hopefully won't need to have this kind of low-level access to memory information, as it complicates programs and can introduce obscure bugs. If, however, you need to interact with a DLL or code component that needs an address, you can still retrieve it—but you need to "pin down" the memory first. Pinning down the memory ensures that the Common Language Runtime won't try to move a value between the time when you find its address and the time when the DLL tries to use it. (This automatic movement feature is one of the ways by which the .NET runtime attempts to improve performance.)

The following example creates and pins down a handle for an object called MyObj. It uses a special type called GCHandle in the System.Runtime. InteropServices namespace:

```
' You will need to import the namespace shown below to use this code as written.
' Imports System.Runtime.InteropServices

Dim MyGCHandle As GCHandle = GCHandle.Alloc(MyObj, GCHandleType.Pinned)
Dim Address As IntPtr = MyGCHandle.AddrOfPinnedObject()
' (Invoke the DLL or do something with the Address variable here.)

' Allow the object to be moved again.
MyGCHandle.Free()
```

Of course, the coding you use is up to you, but be aware that the Upgrade Wizard will simply place an error flag if it finds the unsupported VarPtr, StrPtr, or ObjPtr function.

Memory Storage for User-Defined Types

In Visual Basic 6, you could assume that user-defined types represented a contiguous block of memory. This is not true for the .NET equivalent, structures, which use a more efficient allocation of space. This change only has an effect if you are using low-level DLLs or COM components (for instance, a legacy database that expects data to be passed as a block of memory). To resolve this issues, you'll have to delve into some of .NET's advanced data type marshalling features, which are beyond the scope of this book, but detailed in the MSDN class library reference under the System.Runtime.InteropServices namespace.

Optional Parameters

Optional parameters in VB .NET require default values, as explained in Chapter 3. This is a relatively painless change. However, one consequence is that you can't rely on IsMissing to tell if a value has been submitted (although you can check for your default value or use IsNothing, which is the Upgrade Wizard's automatic change). Keep in mind that overloaded functions often yield better .NET options than do optional values.

Goto and Gosub

Support for these statements was scaled down in early beta versions of VB .NET, but has been added back for the final release. But even though you can doesn't mean you should! Goto and Gosub are archaic programming concepts, and using them is a direct road to programming nightmares. It's a surprise that they remained all the way through Visual Basic 6, let alone made the jump to the .NET world.

Other New Behaviors

"New behavior" is the term that the Upgrade Wizard uses in its upgrade report when it makes a change from one property or method to another that is similar, but not identical. In many cases, this warning just represents an improvement to a control. In other situations, it may represent a deeper problem that requires significant reworking.

Most experienced Visual Basic developers have spent significant time learning their favorite controls, and know how to exploit all the associated quirks and idiosyncrasies. This poses a problem for migration, where optimized code might not work at all (or worse, might appear to work, but will then cause problems under unusual future circumstances).

NOTE *This issue raises a larger question. Namely, when is it safe to migrate a project? Even if the process appears to succeed, you will need hours of testing to verify its success before you can trust the updated application enough to release it into a production environment.*

Preparing for VB .NET

Are the migration features in Visual Basic .NET impressive or depressing? It really depends on how you look at it. Certainly, they represent a minor technological feat. At the same time, many developers argue that they are useless for using real VB 6 applications in the .NET environment. Even if you can import a project, the result may be a rather ugly mess of old concepts, dressed up with workarounds added by the Upgrade Wizard. This kind of application can be difficult to work with and enhance, thus defeating the purpose of migration.

In you're working on a Visual Basic 6 project today, your best choice is to make rigorous use of class-based designs. If you take this protective step, then even if you can't import an entire project into .NET, you will at least be able to import or recreate all of your business objects and data classes. Generally, data classes are much easier to import than other components, because they don't use such VB 6-specific features as file or printer access, and they don't directly create user interface or require forms support. You can then import your business objects, add a new .NET user interface tier (taking advantage of the latest features in Windows Forms), and add lower-level data access components, if necessary, to support ADO.NET or .NET file access through streams. The ability to upgrade is one of the remarkable benefits of a structured three-tier design. The more you can break your application down into functional units, the better chance you'll have to reuse at least some of its elements in the .NET environment.

What Comes Next?

This chapter has shown both the beauty and the ugliness of backward compatibility. Visual Basic .NET is at its most elegant when dealing with COM interoperability, allowing you to work with most components and even drop ActiveX controls into your application without a second thought. However, the picture sours if you need to import an average, midsized Visual Basic project, which is almost guaranteed to crumble in the face of numerous incompatibilities.

As always, remember that just because a program is created in an older version of Visual Basic it does not mean it needs to be brought to .NET. These "legacy" programs will be supported on the Windows platform for years to come. Conversely, just because an ActiveX control can be inserted into your project doesn't mean that you can't reap more benefits by trying to achieve the same effect using the class library. However, you're likely to have at least some third-party ActiveX controls that you don't want to abandon in certain situations. Remember to consider the tradeoff—if converting to .NET requires that you import dozens of COM components, then you may be better off maintaining your program in unmanaged Visual Basic 6.

If you are a COM guru (or are planning to become one), you will probably want to explore .NET's advanced COM support features. These include tools for handling COM interoperability on your own, such as the System.Windows.Forms.AxHost class and the types in the System.Runtime.InteropServices. Be forewarned: Unless you are a war-hardened COM veteran, you won't be able to do much with these namespaces that you can't do even better with the automatic wrapper class generation features in Visual Studio .NET.

INDEX

E

e event argument, 106
encapsulation
with database stored procedures,
284–285
with protected members, 168
with SQL statements, 279–280
violations with user interface, 134,
166
enumeration, with arrays, 68
enumerations
bitwise combination, 235
described, 153–156
with file attributes, 235–236
recommended organization,
158–159
using specific numbers with,
156–157
environment settings, Visual Studio
.NET, 44–45
errors
in IDE, 197
preventing, 195–6
in the task list, 198
types of, 194–5
event handlers, 106. *See also* events
EventArgs
creating your own, 145–146
described, 106
EventInfo class, 341–342
events
advisory about thread change, 328
connecting handlers dynamically,
110
handling, for controls, 105–106
handling multiple, 107
raising your own, 142, 145–146
standard arguments, 106
tracking mouse movement, 106
in web applications, 382–384
Exception class, 211–213
exception handling, 209–218
versus On Error Goto, 211
exceptions
debugging settings, 215
deriving your own, 217–218
filtering by condition, 215–216
filtering by type, 214
hierarchy, 215
inner, 213–214
StackTrace property, 212
types of, 215
EXE files. *See* assemblies
ExecuteReader, DataReader method,
274
extern statements, in manifest, 339

F

fast-forward database access, 271
file
attributes, 235–236
copying/deleting/moving, 234
and directory relationships,
236–237
making setup conditional on,
368–369
monitoring for change events,
238–240
properties, for assemblies, 340
retrieving information about,
233–236
file access. *See also* serialization; XML
converting variables in binary files,
230
reading/writing binary files,
229–231
reading/writing text files, 228
storing DataSets, 300–302
Visual Basic 6 style, 231–232
File class, 233–234
file system designer, in setup,
358–359
file types, registering in setup,
362–363
FileGet statement, 231
FileInfo class, 234–235
FileOpen statement, 231
FilePut statement, 231
FileStream class, 227
FileSystemWatcher class, 218–239
FillSchema, DataAdapter method,
289–290
filtering exceptions, 215–216
flow layout, in Web forms, 381
FontViewer setup, 369
For Each, with arrays, 67
form interaction, 111–112
forms
AcceptButton and CancelButton,
89
anchoring, 89–90
binary information in, 104–105
as classes, 98
creating, 98
default instance in migrated code,
431–432
dialog, 112–114, 122
dock padding, 92–93
docking, 91–92
events, 105
generated code, 102–104
inheritance, 99, 173
interaction between, 111–112
limiting size, 88
MDI, 114–116
modal, 99–100
opacity, 94
owned, 114
resizing, 89–93

migration *(continued)*
  default properties, 443
  fatal problems with, 440–441
  GDI, 447
  Load statement, 443
  menus, 444–445
  mouse cursor changes, 432
  optional parameters, 449
  pointers, 448–449
  preparing for .NET, 450
  printing, 444
  resize changes, 432
  upgrade report, 429
  upgrade warnings, 429
  Upgrade Wizard, 424, 489–429
  user-defined types, 449
  variants, 442
modal forms, 99–100
module blocks, 64
modules, versus shared members, 162–163
monitoring file system events
  change events, 239–240
  described, 238–239
MSDE, 268–269
MSDN
  assembly information, 57
  search online, 23
MSFlexGrid control, 425
MSIL, 13
MTS, 192
Multi-Document Interface, 114–116
multiple inheritance, 173
multiple projects, with Web Services, 418
multithreading. *See also* threads
  with callback, 323–325
  debugging, 322–323
  described, 309
  design scalability, 311
  interaction with user interface, 326–327
  versus single-threading, 310–311
  synchronization, 328–332
  thread management, 317–318
  thread priorities, 319
  thread starvation, 320
MustInherit keyword, 172
MustOverride keyword, 172

N

name collision, prevention in GAC, 347
Namespace keyword, 65
namespaces
  aliases, 60
  contrasted with assemblies, 57
  described, 55
  importing, 59–60
  project-wide imports, 60–61
  setting for your projects, 65–66
  useful ones in .NET, 61–63

XML namespaces in Web Services, 407
.NET class library. *See* class library
.NET Framework Configuration tool, 350
.NET framework overview, 9–15
.NET redistributable, 346, 360
New keyword
  with automatic re-initialization, 446–447
  with classes, 130–131
nodes
  TreeView. *See* TreeView
  XML. *See* XML
nondeterministic finalization, 141
NonSerialized attribute, 244
Northwind database, 268
Nothing keyword, releasing an object with, 131
NotifyIcon control, 120–121
Now, DateTime property, 71
null reference error, 132

O

object assignment, 131
Object Browser
  described, 147
  with imported ActiveX controls, 436
object cleanup, 141–142
object comparison, 185
object equality, 132
object death, 140–141
object-oriented programming. *See* OOP
object serialization, 240–244
objects. *See* classes
objects, versus Web Services, 405–406
ObjPtr, 448
ODBC provider, 269
OLE DB providers, 269. *See also* ADO.NET
On Error Goto, versus exception handling, 211
one-to-many relationship, with DataSets, 290–293
OOP
  described, 127
  principles of, 150–152
  versus tradition structured programming, 127–128
opacity, of forms, 94–95
OpenFileDialog, 122
operations
  changes from Visual Basic 6, 72–75
  conversion, 69–70, 74
  declaration, multiple, 73
  initializers, 72
  math, 74
  math with dates and times, 71
  random numbers, 75

registry *(continued)*
    lack of use with assemblies, 335
    storing form size, 255–256
    working with, 255–256
relational data, 267–268
Relations, DataSet property, 290–291
release mode compilation, 51
repair, in setup programs, 354
Replace, String method, 70
Request.QueryString property, 393
resizable forms, 89–90
resizable split windows, 93–94
Response.Redirect method, 392
.resx file, 104–105
Return keyword, 75–76
rollback, in setup, 367
Rows, DataTable property, 288
RowUpdated event, 296–297
Run To Cursor, debugging command, 203
runtimes, 10

S

scope changes from Visual Basic 6, 75
scrolling in forms and panels, 96–97
search path, for an assembly, 352–353
searching arrays, 71
security
    with CLR, 10
    with SQL Server, 272
Seek method for binary files, 231
self-repair, in setup programs, 354
Serializable attribute, 240
serialization
    with binary storage, 241–242
    for cloning, 244–245
    described, 240
    partial, 243–244
    with XML/SOAP storage, 242–243
session object, 396
session state, 395–396
Session.Abandon method, 395
Set Next Statement, debugging command, 203
setup designers
    custom actions, 367–368
    described, 357
    file system, 358–359
    file type, 362–363
    launch conditions, 368–369
    registry, 361
    user interface, 363–367
setup projects. *See also* GAC; setup designers
    adding files, 360
    adding project outputs, 358–359
    adding shortcuts, 360
    basic options, 357
    choice windows, 365–366
    conditions, 366–367
    configuring registry, 361
    custom actions, 367–368

described, 355–357
    launch conditions, 368–369
    .NET redistributable, 346
    predefined windows, 364–365
    registering file types, 362–363
    user interface, 363
shared assemblies. *See also* assemblies; GAC
    binding to new versions, 351–352
    binding to other paths, 352–353
    creating, 348
    creating policy files for, 350–354
    installing, 349
    signing, 349
shared members
    described, 160
    versus modules, 162–163
    shared methods, 160–161
    shared properties, 162
shortcut, adding to setup, 360
Show, Form method, 111–112
Show Next Statement, debugging command, 203
side-by-side execution, 336–337
signing assemblies, 349
single-step execution, 202–203
single threading, versus multithreading, 310–311
Sleep, Thread method, 318
.sln file, 48, 63
sn.exe utility, 349
SOAP
    proxy class, 414
    serialization, 242–243
    in Web Services, 412
SoapFormatter class, 242–243
solution files, 48
Solution Explorer window, 32
sorting arrays
    with basic data types, 71
    with objects, 185
source event argument, 106
splitting windows
    in a form, 93–94
    in IDE, 30–31
SQL
    dynamically generated, 279
    encapsulating in a helper class, 279–280
    Select statements, 273
    Update statements, 278
    Where clause, 273
SQL Server. *See also* ADO.NET
    authentication, 272
    connecting to ADO.NET with, 269
    Enterprise Manager, 290
    versus MSDE, 268–269
SqlClient, 270
StackTrace, Exception property, 212
start page, 21–26
startup class, using, 112
state bag, 390–392

W

X

THE BOOK OF VISUAL STUDIO .NET

by ROBERT B. DUNAWAY

This comprehensive guide surveys each .NET server and related technologies, with a focus on Visual Studio 7 (VS7). Hands-on examples cover building forms, data retrieval, moving to COM+, and implementing web services. Other key issues and solutions include upgrading from Visual Basic, source control services, and remoting.

JUNE 2002, 456 PP., $49.95 ($74.95 CDN)
ISBN 1-886411-69-7

THE BOOK OF VMWARE
The Complete Guide to the VMware Workstation

by BRIAN WARD

This comprehensive guide to installing and running VMware includes sections on device emulation; configuring the guest operating system; networking and file transfers; and troubleshooting common questions and answers.

FEBRUARY 2002, 352 PP., $39.95 ($55.95 CDN)
ISBN 1-886411-72-7

THE BOOK OF SCSI
2ND EDITION
I/O for the New Millennium

by GARY FIELD, PETER M. RIDGE, ET AL.

This thoroughly updated second edition offers down-to-earth instructions for installing, implementing, utilizing, and maintaining SCSI on a PC.

2000, 428 PP. W/CD-ROM, $49.95 ($77.50 CDN)
ISBN 1-886411-10-7

JOE NAGATA'S LEGO® MINDSTORMS™ IDEA BOOK

by JOE NAGATA

Over 250 step-by-step illustrations show how to build 10 cool robots using LEGO MINDSTORMS, with ideas for building many more.

2001, 194 PP., FOUR-COLOR INSERT, $21.95 ($32.95 CDN)
ISBN 1-886411-40-9

STEAL THIS COMPUTER BOOK 2
What They Won't Tell You About The Internet

by WALLACE WANG

An offbeat, non-technical book that tells readers what hackers do, how they do it, and how to protect themselves. This new edition covers viruses, cracking, and password theft, Trojan Horse programs, illegal copying of MP3 files, computer forensics, and encryption. The CD-ROM contains over 200 anti-hacker and security tools for Windows, Macintosh, and Linux.

"An engaging look at the darker side of the information superhighway."
—*Amazon.com*

2000, 462 PP. W/CD-ROM, $24.95 ($38.95 CDN)
ISBN 1-886411-42-5

Phone:

1 (800) 420-7240 OR
(415) 863-9900
MONDAY THROUGH FRIDAY,
9 A.M. TO 5 P.M. (PST)

Fax:

(415) 863-9950
24 HOURS A DAY,
7 DAYS A WEEK

Email:

SALES@NOSTARCH.COM

Web:

HTTP://WWW.NOSTARCH.COM

Mail:

NO STARCH PRESS
555 DE HARO STREET, SUITE 250
SAN FRANCISCO, CA 94107
USA

Distributed in the U.S. by Publishers Group West

UPDATES

This book was carefully reviewed for technical accuracy, but it's inevitable that some things will change after the book goes to press. Visit **http://www.nostarch.com/ vbdotnet_updates.htm** for updates, errata, and other information.